MRS
MAN

We talk of you
and Mrs you. —*Henry James*

GERMAINBOOKS

Colophon	Irene Burns
Calligraphy	Thomas Ingmire
Gravestone photographs	Naomi Weissman

Library of Congress Cataloging in Publication Data

Stannard, Una, 1927-
  Mrs Man.

  Bibliography: p.
  Includes index.
    1. Women--Social conditions. 2. Women--Legal
status, laws, etc. 3. Feminism. 4. Names, Personal.
  I. Title.
  HQ1121.S78   301.41'2   76-58834
  ISBN 0-914142-02-X

MRS MAN

1   WIFE OF   1

2   MRS GEORGE WASHINGTON JONES   3

Elizabeth, Not Mrs Henry   3
Mrs Elizabeth Elstob, Spinster   4
From Subordination to Merger   7
A Man Wife   10
Mr and Mrs John Jones   12
The Name of Power   15

3   MRS ASTOR'S PROFESSION   19

A Name and Fame   19
Leechery   21
The Flukes   27

4   THE SECOND OLDEST PROFESSION   34

5   THE VEILED LADIES   40

6   GETTING A HEAD   47

I Hate Learned Women   47
The Seed Is a Drop of the Brain   49
Silent, as a Lady Ought to Be   53
Ergo, She Is Not a Woman   55
Hear Me as the Mouthpiece of Mrs Child   57
The Same Intellectual Constitution as Man   59

7   THE QUIET NAME OF WIFE   63

    Married and Faded into the Mists   63
    Mr Woman   67

8   NOMINAL POLYANDRY   72

9   DOUBLE IDENTITIES   80

    A Professional Name   80
    Mrs Mary Jones Smith   82
    Mrs Mary Jones-Smith   84
    Mrsnomerism   89

10 LUCY STONE (ONLY)   93

    Miss Lucy Stone   93
    Mrs Lucy Stone   95
    Lucy Stone, Wife of Henry Blackwell   101
    *1879—A Married Woman Must Vote Bearing Her Husband's
       Surname*   106

11 LUCY STONE v. THE STATUS QUO   111

    Lucy Stone v. The Commonwealth of Massachusetts   111
    Her Maiden Surname Is Absolutely Lost   123

12 A NAME OF THEIR OWN   132

13 THE MINOR POINT OF A NAME   151

    Nominal History   151
    A Sort of Half-Established Individuality   153
    A Plea for Mrs John Smith   158
    The Disgraceful Custom   160

14 TWO NAMES ON A GREENWICH VILLAGE DOOR   163

    The Changing Feminine Ideal—1901-1910   163
    This Miss Wife—1911   168
    Married but Not Renamed—1912-1920   175
    Secretly Proud of Being Mrs Riggs   181

15 THE LUCY STONE LEAGUE   188

    Origins   188
    The First Three Years   192
    Comptroller General McCarl   202
    Passports   204
    Chaos in Women's Names—1926   210
    1927-1934   214

16 DWINDLING INTO A WIFE   219

    Are the Twain No Longer One Flesh?   219
    Swallowed Up by a Man   225
    In and Out of Names   228
    This Nominal Obstacle Race   232

17 FIAT LEX   239

    Correct Name of Married Woman   239
    Redefining Legal Name   245
    Redefining Common Law   248
    The Great Weight of Legal and Judicial Precedent   251

18 MANNERS MAKE LAWS   262

    The New Lucy Stone League   262
    A Creampuff Cause   265
    A Grass-Roots Movement   268
    The Legal Stone Wall   272
    Common Law Revived   277
    What's in a Married Name?   284

19 THE MOTHER OF US ALL   289

    Male Mothers   289
    Sole Progenitor   298
    Absolute Sovereignty   305
    The Conjugal Centaur   313
    The Male Maternal Instinct   319

20 BEYOND WIFEHOOD   331

    No Less Perfect than Man   331

Liberation Names   *334*
No Longer Destined for the Home   *337*
A Dying Breed   *346*

SOURCES   353

CASE INDEX   367

INDEX   369

ILLUSTRATIONS, *following page 268*

"Wife Who Retains Her Maiden Name and Won't Obey"
    St Louis Post—Dispatch May 14, 1899

"No Mrs Badge of Slavery Worn by This Miss Wife"
    The World November 29, 1911

"Married in All but Name"
    Oakland Tribune October 1, 1922

"Married, She'll Not Be Mrs"
    The Minneapolis Star December 17, 1971

There is a great deal in a name. It often signifies much, and may involve a great principle.

Elizabeth Cady Stanton, May 1, 1847

1

WIFE OF

Of your charitie pray for the soull of Alys late the wyf of Thomas
Baldry merchant somtyme the wyfe of Master Robert Wymbyll
Notari . . .

from a brass in St Mary at the Tower, Ipswich 1506

On this English memorial tablet is condensed the history of woman. Thomas
Baldry had been a merchant, Robert Wymbyll had been a notary, and Alys
What-ever-name-she-was-born-with Wymbyll Baldry had been a wife. During
most of history men had had a variety of occupations by which they could be
identified, but women had been wives and in some form or another had
always borne the label "wife of."

When women married in the Luo tribe of Kenya, they wore for the rest of
their lives a tail on their backside called a *cieno*. Women in other tribes fastened iron ankle rings on their legs, just as women in western societies put a
ring on their finger. Whether a woman shaved off her eyebrows or her hair or
blackened her teeth or put on a special cap, she assumed a prominent badge of
office, one that told the world she had become a wife. Henceforth she was
spoken of as "Haoua, wife of Idda," to use a Tuareg name, or "Urbilia, wife of
Primus," to use a Roman name, or "Johanna Jackwyf" or "Syssat, wife of
Thomas the Cook," to use medieval English names, or after people acquired
surnames, "Agnes de Sibbeford, wife of Ralph Clement." When, starting
about the thirteenth century, women informed the world they were married by
changing their surname to their husband's, an Agnes de Sibbeford would
become Agnes Clement. But she would appear in parish registers under "Ralph
Clement and Agnes his wife" or just as likely, "Ralph Clement and wife."

For married women really needed no names. Wife of Idda, wife of Primus
or Mrs Clement was enough to identify her, just as Lot's wife was enough to
identify the wife of Lot, whose name was not recorded in the Bible, nor need it
have been. For accurate identification a woman needed only the name of the

man for whom she was performing the job of wife. As Henry James expressed it in an 1884 letter to William Dean Howells, "We talk of you and Mrs you," which form of address poignantly testifies to woman's wifely nonentity, her total absorption into the role of wife, into the life of her husband.

The history of married women's names is as much the history of men as of women, of men's desire to make and keep women wives and of women's inability for thousands of years to have any other role. "To make a good husband is but one branch of a man's duty, but it is the chief duty of a woman to make a good wife," pronounced Henry Home, Lord Kames in his *Loose Hints upon Education* (1781), a piece of advice men had been giving women for hundreds of years. But Lord Kames' platitude did not seem so self-evident to a few women even in his own time, women who were daring to assert that women were not a subspecies solely created to be wives but were also capable of being doctors, professors, mathematicians, even government officials. The history of the feminist movement from the late eighteenth century to the late twentieth century has essentially been a history of women's attempt to have another occupation besides that of wife. The difficulties of that struggle—women's desire for new roles and their fear of abandoning the old one—are recorded in the names women used or refused to use and in the harassment suffered by the few women who defied convention and discarded the label "wife of."

2

MRS GEORGE WASHINGTON JONES

Elizabeth, Not Mrs Henry

In September 1852 at the National Woman's Rights Convention in Syracuse, New York, after a Mrs Smith spoke on woman's right to preach and even command armies, the Reverend Samuel J. May, an ardent feminist, "moved that Mrs Stephen Smith be placed on a Committee in his stead." Lucretia Mott, president of the Convention, "quickly replied: Woman's Rights' women do not like to be called by their husbands' names, but by their own.

"Mr May corrected himself and said—*Rosa Smith.*"

The early feminists had adopted the policy of using their own first name at the very first Woman's Rights Convention in Seneca Falls, New York in July 1848 where the sixty-eight women who signed the Declaration of Sentiments proclaiming "all men *and women* are created equal" used their own female names and with no Miss or Mrs to indicate marital status.

That policy had undoubtedly been adopted because of the strong convictions of Elizabeth Cady Stanton, who for many years had had unorthodox views on women's names. In 1840, not long after she married, she informed her friends they were never to address her as Mrs Henry B. Stanton but as Elizabeth Cady [her maiden surname] Stanton. Women's names was a subject she had thought much about and discussed with her friends. In 1847 she wrote to Rebecca Eyster:

> Last evening we spoke of the propriety of women being called by the names which are used to designate their sex, and not by those assigned to males. You differed with me on the ground that custom had established the rule that a woman must take the whole of her husband's name, particularly when public mention is made

of her . . . . I have very serious objections, dear Rebecca, to being called Henry. There is a great deal in a name. It often signifies much, and may involve a great principle. Ask our colored brethren if there is nothing in a name. Why are the slaves nameless unless they take that of their master? Simply because they have no independent existence. They are mere chattels, with no civil or social rights. Our colored friends in this country who have education and family ties take to themselves names. Even so with women. The custom of calling women Mrs John This and Mrs Tom That, and colored men Sambo and Zip Coon, is founded on the principle that white men are lords of all. I cannot acknowledge this principle as just; therefore, I cannot bear the name of another.

Elizabeth Cady Stanton never allowed anyone to address her as Mrs Henry. In 1860 when Wendell Phillips sent a letter to Susan B. Anthony in "Care of Mrs H. B. Stanton," by return mail he received a lecture on "the new gospel of individual sovereignty." "Only think of it—one of the champions of freedom denying to woman, at this late date, her own name . . . women and negroes are beginning to repudiate the name of their masters and claiming a right to a life-long name of their own."

Stanton also objected to and occasionally spoke against a wife's loss of her surname, but in general the early feminists took a stand only against the custom of calling wives, to quote Stanton again, "Mrs John or James, Peter or Paul, just as she changes masters." From the late forties through the late sixties a feminist could be distinguished from a non-feminist by her use of her own not her husband's first name. It was a conscious revolutionary gesture, symbolic of her belief that a wife's individuality and rights must not be sacrificed to her husband, that marriage must be a partnership of equals, of Elizabeth and Henry Stanton, not a total identification of the wife with the husband's interests implicit in the form "Mrs Henry Stanton."

Mrs Elizabeth Elstob, Spinster

The early feminists seem not to have realized that the use of their own first name was more reactionary than revolutionary. It is true that in the forties the Mrs John Jones style was an established custom, but it had only recently become so. Indeed, as late as 1860 a judge in the Texas Supreme Court felt the custom of calling a married woman "Mrs John Smith, and Mrs George Washington Jones" was merely a fashion "in polite society," a fashion he thought did "not extend to the great mass of people throughout the country," and he hoped never would. Many later judges were to regard the new style with such disfavor they ruled that in legal proceedings a wife could not use the "Mrs George Washington Jones" form.

It was perhaps to be expected that tradition-minded judges should dislike the new-fangled nomenclature of wives, but at least as late as 1832 the majority of American wives also disliked the custom. In that year Eliza Leslie wrote her story, "Mrs Washington Potts," in which the woman who so denominated herself was satirized as a snob with social pretensions, and that story, published in *Godey's Lady's Book* (a nineteenth-century *Ladies' Home Journal),* won the annual prize for 1832. Leslie continued to write what the public wanted; in her later stories only women who think themselves better than their neighbors call themselves "Mrs Washington Potts" or "Mrs Blake Bentley."

Mrs Washington Potts was imitating the English among whom the Mrs John Jones style came into use earlier. Jane Austen, for example, used the form frequently in her letters, but in America during the early decades of the nineteenth century the form was not used much. In Elisabeth Dexter's *Career Women of America 1776-1840,* the new mode of address does not occur until after 1800, and then its use was occasional. For example, a "Mrs Edmund Burke Hamilton" announced in an 1806 Philadelphia newspaper that she would be performing a series of readings, and a "Mrs Laurence Nichols" announced in a Boston newspaper in 1835 that she was opening an ice-cream shop. But the average businesswoman during this period would have called herself "Mrs Ann Nichols." In the letters of Margaret Bayard Smith, which deal with Washington society from 1800 to 1842, the new style was used only to distinguish one wife with a common surname from another. Thus, "Mrs Robert Smith" was differentiated from "Mrs Andrew Smith" and "Mrs Cashier Smith (cashier for the Bank)." Another wife was called "Mrs Lawyer Jones" to distinguish her from other Mrs Joneses.

Margaret Smith was using the new style the way it had formerly been used. In George Washington's letters he sometimes differentiated one Mrs Washington from another in the large Washington clan by calling her "Mrs W. Washington." Or, in a 1779 article in the *United States Magazine* two female patriots with the same surname were distinguished by calling them "Mrs John and Samuel Adams." But even that particular usage was rare, and the Mrs John Jones style as a general mode of address for wives was even rarer. In Elisabeth Dexter's study of American businesswomen from the 1670s to 1776, the new style occurs only once. Almost universally, Colonial wives called themselves plain Anne Jones or Mrs Abigail Jarvice or Mrs Benedicta Netmaker. When Hannah Chapman's husband died and she remarried, she advertised her "smelling Nectar that will cure the Itch" as Hannah Kitchin; she changed only her last name. When Widow Copley married the painter Peter Pelham, she became Mrs Mary Pelham, not Mrs Peter Pelham. In 1756 there was published *A Narrative of the Sufferings . . . of William and Elizabeth Fleming,* not Mr and Mrs William Fleming. Betsy Ross was known and addressed as such, not as Mrs John Ross. When Benjamin Franklin wrote to the wife of William Greene, he addressed her as Mrs Catharine Greene. George Washington in his diary referred to Abigail Adams as "Mrs Adams (lady to the Vice-President)," not as Mrs John Adams. Abigail Adams did not sign her letters Mrs John Adams and never used the Mrs John Jones form in her letters.

She did not because her correspondents would have been puzzled, as puzzled as we would now be by "Miss John Jones." "John, a female name?" we would ask, and until at least the mid eighteenth century "Mrs John Jones" would have provoked the same question, for the title Mrs then meant adult female; it did not as yet mean wife.

Mistress, from which Mrs derived, had originally been a general title of courtesy and high rank. Henry VIII addressed Anne Boleyn as "Mistress" to show his respect for her rank. By the mid seventeenth century the title had been abbreviated to Mrs and was also used by females of the middle class regardless of marital status or age. One of Milton's daughters, who died in 1657 when she was not yet six months old, was called on her tombstone "Mrs Kathern Milton." Gradually Mrs became the title used for all classes of women; there was no special title for unmarried women.

The title Miss began to be used in the seventeenth century, but it did not mean a woman was single; it was an insult: a "Miss" was a woman of loose morals, married or unmarried. By the 1660s, however, female children began to be called Miss, but it was a title girls stopped using as soon as they decided they were grown up, which at that period could be thirteen or earlier. Actresses, as might be expected, kept on calling themselves Miss much longer than other women. On November 8, 1740 when Peg Woffington had her title on the playbills changed from Miss to Mrs, she was in her twenties; her change of title meant she had stopped playing ingénues. All women past a certain age called themselves Mrs. Elizabeth Elstob (1683-1756), an Anglo-Saxon scholar, though she never married, was always addressed as Mrs Elstob.

Starting about the third decade of the eighteenth century, Miss began to mean a woman, no matter how old, was unmarried. In her letters Lady Mary Wortley Montagu used Mrs as a general title for adult women until about 1720 when she started using Miss for all unmarried women. That usage seems to have originated in the upper classes and for several decades only unmarried upper class women were called Miss. For example, in Richardson's 1740 novel, the unmarried maidservant is Mrs Pamela, but the unmarried daughters of gentry are Miss. However, in 1745 Horace Walpole noted as an accomplished fact that "a woman is not called Mrs till she is married," and in 1754 *The Connoisseur* asserted that "Every unmarried woman is now called 'Miss'." Nevertheless, the new way of differentiating married and single women took a long time to become universal. In 1798 the *Monthly Magazine* noted that there had died at Windsor Castle "Mrs Hannah Corbett, a maiden lady," and well into the nineteenth century many women continued to be called Mrs although they were single. The author Hannah More (1745-1833), a spinster, was always called Mrs More. (The American country custom, still in use, of calling all adult females "Miz" derives from this older usage.)

It was not until Mrs meant, and unambiguously meant "wife of," that a married woman could be called Mrs John.

From Subordination to Merger

The development of the Mrs John Jones style did not solely depend upon the establishment of a special title for married women. To a seventeenth-century mind "Mrs John Jones" would have been not only incomprehensible, but once understood, sacrilegious. For hadn't God created man in His Own Image and woman out of man's rib? and wasn't it woman who first disobeyed God's commandments? Woman was innately the inferior sex. For which reason, to call a woman by the names designated for the superior sex would be to mock the divine order. A female name, like a negro's dark complexion, was a sign of low caste. A woman's use of a man's name would have been regarded as an outrageous presumption, almost as wicked as wearing men's clothing.

Moreover, the Mrs John Jones form, which makes a wife almost indistinguishable from her husband, would have been shocking to people who believed God had made wives subordinate to husbands. The Bible said the husband was the head of the wife and husbands continued to rule over wives as unquestioningly as God ruled over mankind. Ministers and those who wrote on THE WHOLE DUTY OF WOMAN were still reminding eighteenth-century wives to let their every action reveal their "consciousness of *inferiority,* which, for the sake of *order,* the all-wise Author of nature *manifestly* intended." A husband would as soon have allowed his wife to call herself by his full name as he would have allowed his servant to do so.

Before a wife could presume to call herself Mrs John Jones, the old concept of the unity of husband and wife would have to take on a new meaning. We tend to think that concept as old as Adam, who cleaves to Woman and they become one flesh—Adam. But although for centuries clergymen discoursed on the unity of husband and wife, what they generally meant by it was sexual union, the act "wherein one man and one woman are coupled and knit together in one flesh and body," to use the words of a sixteenth-century tract on "the duty of married folkes." Sexual union was the "the great mystery" that according to St Paul in Ephesians 5:28, made a woman her husband's body, Scripture that was interpreted as meaning that the woman became, as it were, the womb of the marriage while the husband acted as the head. Husband and wife were also a unit in the sense that the husband, like a king, commanded, and the wife, like a subject, served and obeyed. The husband commanded because he had the divine right of his superiority, and the wife obeyed because she was *non compis mentis,* like a child or an idiot, innately incapable of acting without supervision. The old concept of the unity of husband and wife depended upon there being two persons—one who commanded and one who obeyed.

The new concept depended upon there being one person, the husband, in whom the wife was totally merged and who therefore obeyed not because her husband was her ruler but because she was one with him and could not do otherwise. Of course, the idea of the merger of the wife with the husband was always inherent in the old concept of the unity of husband and wife, but it was rarely developed because it had implications that might lead to female insubordination. One can see the danger in a legal treatise compiled in 1632, *The Lawes Resolutions of Womens Rights.* The author, known only as T. E., illustrated how "man and woman are one person" by comparing woman with "a small brooke or little river," which when it "incorporateth with Rhodanus, or the Thames, the poor rivulet looseth her name" and is carried along into her "new associate," who becomes her "new self," "her superior; her companion her master." Because the wife is "the poor rivulet" and the husband the mighty Thames, T. E. probably thought he had maintained the proper unequal status relationship of husband and wife. It may not have occurred to him that the rivulet, after merger, might think of herself, as she now calls herself, the Thames. To be sure, she lost her identity, but she has been resurrected into the superior sex. To avoid such presumptuous implications, clergymen did not discourse much on the essential oneness of husband and wife but rather on the wife's inferiority to her husband.

It was not until mid eighteenth century, at the same time as the title Mrs was being appropriated by married women, that the idea of the wife's merger into her husband began to be fully developed. Blackstone's *Commentaries on The Laws of England* (1765-1769), was a product of its time and shows the old concept of subordination fighting with the new one of merger. Observe the tensions in Blackstone's famous statement of the doctrine of the unity of husband and wife:

> By marriage, the husband and wife are one person in law; that is, the very being or legal existence of the woman is suspended during the marriage, or at least is incorporated and consolidated into that of the husband: under whose wing, protection, and *cover,* she performs everything.

Notice that the phrases "husband and wife are one person" and "the very being" of the wife are immediately qualified by "in law" and "or legal existence," converting the wife's literal merger into her husband into a legal fiction. Again the verb "suspended," which suggests the wife has temporarily ceased to be, is followed by the legal terms "incorporated and consolidated," but because these terms have strong metaphoric connotations of the wife's bodily fusion into her husband, they are at once qualified by an image of the wife as a chick nestling under the "wing, protection, and *cover"* of her husband. Every time Blackstone merged the wife into the husband, he felt compelled to show her as separate and/or subordinate.

Blackstone, a conservative jurist, was struggling with a new way of thinking about wives he somewhat distrusted. But philosophers during the same period loved to dwell on the idea of the wife's literal merger into her husband. Swedenborg, in *Conjugial Love* (1768), said that woman has an innate desire to become one with her husband, and wives long to be "bound more and more closely with their husbands" because without such a union a woman has "no true self." Similarly, Fichte, in *The Science of Right* (1796), said that a woman's "dignity requires that she should give herself up entirely [to her husband] . . . and should utterly lose herself in him. The least consequence is, that she should renounce to him all her property and all her rights. Henceforth she has life and activity only under his eyes and in his business. She has ceased to lead the life of an individual; her life has become a part of the life of her lover. (This is aptly characterized by her assuming his name.)"

She has ceased to lead the life of an individual; her life has become a part of the life of her lover. Husbands used to assert mastery over wives by teaching women they were inferior beings. Now husbands assert mastery by teaching women they are not women until their life has been merged into that of a husband. Male mastery used to be forthright, a crack of the whip. Now mastery became devious, brainwashing. In the past an insubordinate wife felt she was disobeying GodMan; now an insubordinate wife suffers an identity crisis; she feels she is not a true woman because she is at odds with her husband. In 1836 when Jane Grey Cannon married James Swisshelm and discovered she was his intellectual superior, for several years she gave up reading (except the Bible): "I must be the mate of the man I had chosen; and if he would not come to my level, I must go to his."

In the nineteenth century, woman's love was almost always seen as a sacrifice of self, or rather as the gaining of a true self when she merged her life with her lover's. That was why Byron wrote in 1819 that "Man's love is of man's life a thing apart, / 'Tis woman's whole existence," and why John Stuart Mill wrote in 1832 that when a woman loves "her natural impulse will be to associate her existence with him she loves and to share his occupations," or as a writer in *The Bridal Ring,* an 1868 annual, more crudely put it: woman is the "living satellite of man, [who] follows through life in the orbit to which her husband draws her."

One can now see one reason why the period developed the Mrs John Jones form—it was an expression of the new belief that a wife was almost literally one with her husband.

A Man Wife

On the night of April 14, 1874 a young girl stared at herself in the mirror and thought that on the next day, her wedding day, "Miss Jennie Jerome will be gone forever." And on the next day Jennie Jerome was gone forever; she had been transformed into Lady Randolph Churchill. As her new name indicated, she had left the life of Jennie and become—dare one say it?—a man.

We are so used to a married woman calling herself Mrs John Jones that we do not attach significance to her having acquired a male name. But to a primitive mind, her change of name would have meant she had in fact become a man. For among early peoples, a name was believed to be identical with a person's self. "As his name is, so is he," says the Old Testament of Nabal, who because his name meant churlish was churlish. The name of the Furies was changed to the Eumenides (the kindly ones) to change their character. A weak or stupid child would have his name changed to Lion or Fox to give him strength or cunning. A newborn child was given the name of a dead person to continue that person's life. A change of name was believed to transform a person to a new self. After his initiation ceremony a boy was given a new name because he had been transformed into a man. After her wedding ceremony a woman was given a new name because she had been transformed into a particular man—her husband. That at least would have been the conclusion of a primitive mind.

It may be that our minds no longer work primitively and that a woman's change of name from Mary Smith to Mrs George Washington Jones tells us nothing about her essential identification. But in the nineteenth century, at any rate, there is a good deal of evidence to suggest that marriage was the means by which a woman took on a male identity.

When Isabel Arundell (b. 1831) was a young girl, she wrote in her diary: "If I were a man I should like to be a great general or statesman, to have traveled everywhere, to have seen and learnt everything, done everything; in fine, to be the Man of the Day!" She spent hours envisioning her ideal male self, who was strong, handsome, adventurous, masterful: "As God took a rib out of Adam and made a woman of it, so do I, out of a wild chaos of thought, form a man unto myself." But since she was not a man, all she could do was hope to marry her fantasy male self: "This is the creation of my fancy, and my ideal of happiness is to be such a man wife." She vowed that unless she could discover "my other half, to fill the void" and make herself "complete," she would never marry.

When she met the adventurer Richard Burton, she knew immediately she had found her self. "I worship ambition," she wrote in her diary after meeting him. "Fancy . . . making your name a national name! . . . I wish I were a man: if I were, I would be Richard Burton. But as I am a woman, I would be Richard Burton's wife." She prayed to God "to give me that man's body and soul." When they first embraced, she felt as if her soul had left her body, and when she married him "a peace came over me that I had never known." It was the peace of at last becoming what she had always wanted to be—a man.

Isabel Burton was no lesbian. She was a well-adjusted nineteenth-century woman who went about achieving her identity the way all true women were supposed to—not by developing herself but by becoming, as she called it, "a man wife," marrying her ideal male self and sharing his life of adventure in exotic countries. Mrs Burton did not believe new fields should be opened to women. "A female doctor," she once said, "is as unnatural as a married priest." Her advice to a girl who wanted to be a doctor would have been to marry the doctor she would have liked to be. It was the advice routinely given ambitious nineteenth-century girls. In 1856 Jessie Meriton White was denied permission to enter the school of medicine at the University of London; instead of becoming a doctor, she married one of Garibaldi's officers and nursed his wounded soldiers in the field. In 1878 when Alma Bridewell of Kentucky was sixteen she was converted to Methodism and felt strongly the Lord was calling her to preach the gospel, but she was advised by her pastor to marry a minister and make her contribution through him, which is what she at first did.

Ambition, however, was not supposed to enter a nineteenth-century girl's head. Ideally, she had none until she married and identified with her husband's ambitions. Harriet Martineau said of the wife of the geologist Sir Charles Lyell that "she evidently considered herself only a part of him. Having no children, she could devote her life to helping him. She traveled over half the world with him, entered fully into his pursuits, and furthered them as no one else could have done." After Mary Leiter married George Curzon, Viceroy to India, she totally subordinated her life to his. "My thoughts never, never leave you," she once wrote to him, "my whole interest in people is what they may tell me that may interest you." Such self-abnegation was regarded as natural womanliness, and yet by that same abnegation, women, as it were, slipped into their husbands' skin. Having been taught they were not women until, as Fichte said, they had "utterly lost" themselves in their husbands, women became male identified. Of course, the average bride had no such conscious awareness, and if she thought of it at all, regarded her transformation from Mary Smith to Mrs George Washington Jones as evidence of her feminine modesty, of her desire to subordinate her life to her husband's. And yet by giving up her identity in favor of her husband's, a woman was able presumptuously to identify with a male. Marriage was the means by which the despised sex could enter the world of manhood, as the form Mrs John Jones reveals.

Mr and Mrs John Jones

The new psychology that a woman did not become a woman until she had utterly lost herself in a husband also meant that marriage was the means by which a male could make a female part of himself. Of course, in a male-dominant culture only the woman's psychology will be talked of, thus allowing the man to conceal his desire to merge with the inferior sex. But the new names of wives revealed the merger was mutual: Mrs John is not only a woman masculinized, it is a man feminized; Mrs John Jones is not only Mary Smith transformed into a man, it is John Jones, woman incorporated. And when the Mrs John Jones form was developing in the late eighteenth and early nineteenth centuries, the sexes were discovering they were far more like each other, or rather, that women were far more like men than had ever been realized.

The new realization is seen most nakedly in women's clothing which, starting in the 1790s, completely broke with tradition. For the first time in centuries women's dresses revealed what they had previously concealed—that women had those masculine appendages, legs. It has almost been forgotten that legs used to be a male secondary sexual characteristic, that for centuries it had been men only who displayed their legs, priding themselves on muscular calves, for which reason calf-padding was extremely popular. But at the end of the eighteenth century women began to wear semi-transparent sheaths, often with a slit up one side, that clearly revealed (in flesh-colored tights) that women as well as men had legs.

It must have been upsetting to men's sense of sexual identity to see "male" legs on females, which may explain why men began wearing tight breeches of a jersey-like material that clearly outlined their primary sexual part, for which reason these garments acquired many euphemisms, like "inexpressibles" and "unmentionables." Some men wet their unmentionables to make them reveal even more, and some women oiled their bodies so their thin dresses would outline every curve. For women were revealing not only that they, like men, had legs, but that they, like men, were sexual beings, and women during this period were beginning to demand equal sexual freedom with men.

It was the first modern era of open experimentation with free love, when Mary Wollstonecraft lived with Gilbert Imlay and William Godwin and when her daughter Mary lived with Shelley. In 1804 Amelia Opie, a popular novelist, published *Adeline Mowbray,* a sympathetic account of a free love relationship that failed only because a hypocritical society ostracized the woman. As an inevitable corollary of attempts by women to be as sexually free as men, there was a renewed interest in birth control methods; in 1820 in England a pamphlet was published addressed "To the Married of Both Sexes" that gave detailed contraceptive instruction.

Women were also boldly declaring they were no different from men in brain power. In a 1790 article on "The Equality of the Sexes" in the *Massachusetts Magazine,* "Constantia" [Judith Sargent Murray] asked if it were "reasonable that a candidate for immortality . . . should at present be so degraded, as to be allowed no other ideas" than those concerned with cooking and sewing? Mary Wollstonecraft, in her *Vindication of the Rights of Women* (1792), asserted that women must be as highly educated as men because they were, like men, primarily rational creatures and only secondarily wives and mothers. In 1814 Emma Willard opened a seminary for girls that taught them such "male" subjects as mathematics and science. In 1818 in Boston Hannah Mather Crocker announced in her *Observations on the Real Rights of Women* that "the sentiment must predominate that the powers of mind are equal in the sexes." In 1826 public high schools for girls were opened in Boston and

New York; in 1832 Genesee Seminary (later Syracuse University) admitted a woman to its first class; in 1833 Oberlin College was founded in order to extend the benefits of education "to both sexes."

Women further asserted that they, like men, should participate in government. Abigail Adams suggested to her husband that the new code of laws being drawn up in America in 1776 should not "put such unlimited power into the hands of husbands," and that American women were determined not to "hold ourselves bound by any laws in which we have no voice or representation." Olympe des Gouges in the first year of the French revolution more boldly demanded that "All official appointments . . . be open equally to men and to women" because "women are born with equal rights with men." In England in 1825 William Thompson and Anna Wheeler wrote an *Appeal of One Half the Human Race, Women, Against the Pretensions of the Other Half, Men, to Retain Them in Political and Thence in Civil and Domestic Slavery.* They demanded votes for women, seats in parliament for women and condemned men for "priding themselves in a sexual superiority entirely independent of any merit."

A few women, moreover, began acting as if they were the superior sex by invading professions that had previously been exclusively male. Frances Wright during 1828-29 got up on a public platform and lectured, sometimes in Turkish trousers. Angelina and Sara Grimké during 1837-38 lectured against slavery throughout New England, Angelina becoming the first woman to speak before a state (Massachusetts) legislature. During the 1840s Margaret Fuller was working as a journalist, Elizabeth Blackwell was studying to be a doctor and Antoinette Brown to be a minister. In France George Sand was successfully publishing novel after novel and acting like a man among men in the French literary world—wearing men's clothes, smoking cigars and taking lovers as casually as men did.

It was also during this period that a few men realized that men themselves could not achieve full equality until women did. "Can man be free if woman is a slave?" asked Shelley in 1817 in *The Revolt of Islam,* a poem in which the revolt of a woman against male tyranny is seen as fundamental to a successful revolt against governmental tyranny.

Just as important a recognition of the similarity of the sexes, though hardly noticed except by scientists, was the discovery by von Baer in 1827 of the female ovum. For centuries men had believed semen was the sole life force, that woman's role in generation was merely that of brooder, and this despite the fact the ovum is visible to the naked eye. Yet it had not been seen, and its possible existence had been vehemently denied. When the ovum finally was seen, the first step was taken in at last proving that women contributed equally with men in the genetic structure of new life.

The truth that women were not a race apart—that they had legs and brains like men and equal sexual, political and professional rights and capacities, that the ovum was as much a life force as semen—that truth began to impinge on man's consciousness during the late eighteenth and early nineteenth centuries, a new truth that was reflected in a new mode of address in which a man and woman are differentiated by a single letter—Mr and Mrs John Jones.

The Name of Power

"The establishing of woman on her rightful throne is the greatest revolution the world has ever known or ever will know," said Elizabeth Cady Stanton in 1869. She was right, and because she was, because the truth that men and women are in most ways alike was potentially more destructive of the foundations of society than the Darwinian truth that man traced his descent from an ape, society recoiled in fear. It was not ready for so great a revolution.

The egalitarian dress of the sexes was abandoned. No longer could men and women reveal their natural bodies, which are more similar than dissimilar. Instead the natural body was so distorted by clothes that the sexes seem to be of different species. In no previous period in the history of mankind did clothing become so sexually differentiated. Man concealed his genitals and legs in tunnel trousers, had his jackets cut straighter, his collars stiffer and put on a top hat, converting his body into a ramrod of upright propriety. Woman, similarly, converted her natural sexuality into a gross sexual symbol. Her skirts expanded into a wider and wider circle, underneath which her legs were again hidden, and mention of that feature she had in common with men now made her blush. To look as unlike man as possible, she constricted her waist as much as nature could endure and exposed her bosom almost to full view. Victorian men and women, like children playing statues, held rigid poses of masculinity and femininity.

It was as if they were afraid if they relaxed, they would lose their sexual identity, which is unconsciously what they were afraid of. For however loudly Victorian men and women insisted that women were radically different from men, the culture had not forgotten what the late eighteenth and early nineteenth centuries had taught it about the similarity of men and women. Indeed, it was that fearful knowledge that compelled the Victorians to exaggerate sexual differences. But the old unquestioned assumption of female inferiority no longer existed. Men of course continued to claim women did not have the intellectual powers of men, but now they feel they must measure skulls to prove it. Moreover, women were now told they must keep their customary lowly place not because it was a natural consequence of their inferiority but because if they stepped out of their place society would collapse.

The Boston public high school for girls that was opened in 1826 was closed two years later because it was so successful. Too many girls enrolled who proved as capable of learning as boys and the citizens of Boston panicked, fearing that a generation of educated women would, like men, enter the professions and refuse to become wives and mothers, and how then would the human race increase and multiply? In 1837 the Reverend Jonathan F. Stearns of Boston preached a sermon on "Female Influence; and the True Christian Mode of its Exercise" in which he told women they must stop being ambitious, must stop striving to see their "name blazoned on the rolls of fame." And not because they were incapable of great achievements. Stearns conceded women had "talents and abilities," but he argued that God had meant them to use their abilities differently from men, for God had given women another talent, her "almost magic power over men," which meant that women were supposed to influence the world by influencing a man. Only by such indirect use of her powers, Stearns contended, did a woman fulfill "the design of her being," for which reason, a woman who was a true woman did not "desire to abate one jot or tittle from the seeming restrictions imposed upon her conduct."

An even cruder awareness that the differences between the sexes resulted from the restrictions society imposed on women, not from the natural superiority of men, was revealed in an editorial in *The New York Times* on August 2, 1852 in which the *Times* frankly admitted it had refused to print the notice of a woman's rights convention as a matter of pure self-defense. Does it make sense, the *Times* asked, to help those who "desire to evict us"? For if we help women, they "will enter per force the walks of fame, and honor, and wealth, we now occupy, to compete with us, and strip us of our present monopoly . . . Therefore . . . to furnish the slightest amount of aid or comfort to them in such an undertaking would be treason to our sex." Posterity, the *Times* predicted, will "brand the stamp of infamy" on any man who helps women "rob manhood of all its grand prerogatives," ones that have descended in the male line since Adam. The *Times* then described the horrors that would ensue if women should succeed in evicting men. Woman would descend from "the pedestal she now occupies" "into the crowded ways, among human cares and brow-furrowing anxieties, and social responsibilities," and man would "do domestic duties; rule in the nursery; appal [*sic*] the kitchen; appetize the dining-room; and spread sunshine through the parlor."

The *Times* could have been describing the thousands of transvestite cartoons produced by the Victorian era in which emancipated women in trousers smoke cigars in saloons while men in skirts sit at home feeding the baby, as if the differences between the sexes were a mere matter of clothes and social conventions. But a few Victorian men actually expressed that irrational fear; in a speech against woman suffrage in 1890, the Hon. E. W. Miller of South Dakota said that "when women voted men would have to suckle the babies." Less hysterical men did not relish the prospect of having to tend the baby while their wives perchance lectured at a university. And women did not relish that prospect either. The average woman was as appalled as the average man by the feminists' demand for male rights, and she insisted just as vehemently as men that women were meant to be wives and mothers and had neither the intellectual nor the physical strength to compete in the male arenas of power. And yet Victorian women were not as resigned as women had once been to their inferior position in the world, nor were men so guiltlessly able to regard that inferior position as God-ordained or natural.

For both men and women the Mrs John Jones form was a neat solution to a painful dilemma, for it was a way of giving and yet not giving women a higher position in society and thus maintaining traditional male-female roles. When a woman married and became Mrs George Washington Jones she achieved full nominal equality with a man—the prestige and power of a man's name, though no direct power herself; that power, however, she pretended not to want. Without striving to be ambitious herself, without endangering the male power monopoly, a conventional woman could by marrying participate in male glory, and nineteenth-century women were greedy to have a share in that glory, for it was in that century that wives began to be seen next to their husbands in places they had not been seen before. When in 1888 Cleveland ran for a second term his wife's pictures were used in the campaign posters; in no campaign before had a wife been similarly displayed. In 1909 the wife of William Howard Taft succeeded in doing, to use her own words, what "no woman had ever done before"—after the inauguration she sat beside her husband in the triumphal carriage that drove them back to the White House. It was in the nineteenth century that the tradition began of allowing wives to participate publicly in the fame their husbands had earned, and not only did they share their husbands' honors, wives appropriated the titles their husbands had earned. In the second half of the eighteenth century one occasionally finds a woman referred to as Mrs Mayoress or Mrs Judge, but she does not use the title herself. However, the wife of John Tyler delighted in the appellation "Mrs Presidentess" and after the expiration of her husband's term and his death, she insisted on being called Mrs Ex-President Tyler. Nineteenth-century women flaunted their husbands' titles as if they were feathers in their own cap; they called themselves, to use real names, Mrs Governor Robinson, Mrs Judge Humphrey, Mrs Senator Ingalls, Mrs Professor Crosby, Mrs General Banks, the Reverend Mrs Ames, Mrs Dr

Jenkins. But Mrs General and Mrs Dr thought of themselves as modest retiring wives. The Mrs John Jones form flourished because, like a neurosis, it satisfied contradictory impulses and preserved old patterns of behavior.

By granting women full nominal and titular equality with husbands, the nineteenth century set back the time bomb of women's rights that was threatening to destroy the status quo. It was a shrewd and successful device for keeping women in their place because most women were (and are) content with merely the name of power, which should not be surprising. For how many men would choose to achieve wealth or status by proving themselves in the harsh competitive world if society allowed them, nay encouraged them, to become Mrs Cornelius Vanderbilt or Mrs President Tyler by the simple ceremony of marriage?

Of course there was a price to pay. Women were given equal nominal rank with men on one condition. The woman herself must become anonymous; when she gave up her female name and acquired a male one, she was agreeing not to seek power herself. As Isabel Burton said in the preface to *The Highlands of Brazil* (1869), one of the many books she proofread for her husband: "I am humbly standing unknown in the shadow of his glory." Total self-abnegation was the price a woman was supposed to pay for the male name she acquired, but her own namelessness allowed her to reflect the glory her alter ego had made for himself.

By becoming Mrs John or Mrs Peter, the nineteenth-century lady indicated she was willing to achieve power indirectly, by assimilating with a man, just as by her tight corsets, the cage of her crinolines and the vise of her ignorance she signaled to the world she had no intention of stalking the male preserves of physical freedom and intellectual power. That was why the nineteenth-century lady thought it was feminine to be addressed as Mrs John and accused the woman who called herself Mrs Elizabeth of being unsexed. In nineteenth-century terms Mrs Elizabeth was unsexed; she wanted real power, directly and as a female; she was not satisfied with the nominal power of male merger that was the perquisite of Mrs George Washington Jones.

3

MRS ASTOR'S PROFESSION

A Name and Fame

I am humbly standing unknown in the shadow of his glory. That lament of Isabel Burton reveals that despite having achieved her heart's desire by becoming "a man wife," she was not satisfied; she chafed at her nonentity. Feminists were not the only women discontented with the old purdah. Women in general had begun to desire "that Fame which Men have engross'd to themselves and will not suffer us to share," to quote Lady Mary Wortley Montagu's eighteenth-century complaint.

Throughout history woman's lot had been to disappear from the earth as if she had never lived, the only testimony of her existence a tombstone that told passers-by she had been "wife of" a man. Only a rare woman had been able to make a name for herself. Woman had been consigned to oblivion, had, indeed, been taught it was unwomanly to come into public notice at all. "It is great glory in a woman . . . not to be talked of, either for good or evil by men," said Thucydides in the fifth century BC, and almost twenty-five centuries later Rousseau told woman that "her dignity consists in being unknown to the world; her glory is in the esteem of her husband."

Women were well and thoroughly conditioned. Straight through the nineteenth century many women felt the female sex ought to remain unknown to the world. From "extreme dread of seeing her name in a newspaper," Jane Grey Cannon in 1836 actually hesitated about getting married. In 1871 when James Anderson was about to marry Dr Elizabeth Garrett (the first female physician in England), his old nurse had doubts about Garrett's moral character because her name had so frequently been printed in the papers. There were even women who would not let their names appear in the membership list of clubs, they clung so to the belief that a lady's name should be seen in print only when she was born, when she married and when she died.

Women who had themselves achieved prominence nevertheless preached to their sisters on the evils of fame for women. In 1850 the popular writer Grace Greenwood exhorted women not to "unsex" themselves for "greatness"—"The worship of one true heart is better than the wonder of the world." A Southern author, Louisa McCord, in an article protesting a woman's rights convention, sternly told her sex: "Woman was made for *duty,* not for *fame.*"

Yet despite the continued belief that women ought not to be famous, the nineteenth century became the first century in history when women in large numbers did become famous. "Let us now praise famous men," says Ecclesiasticus, and in the Bible "famous men" means males, there being 3037 men who left names behind them and only 181 women. In the nineteenth century that unequal ratio began to be evened out, and the women who in the greatest numbers broke the fame barrier were not the feminists, like Susan B. Anthony, not the first female physicians and lawyers, and not even the actresses and authors. The most famous women in the nineteenth century were the ladies of high society—Mrs William B. Astor Jr, Mrs Cornelius Vanderbilt Jr, Mrs August Belmont, Mrs Stuyvesant Fish and their sister peeresses.

With the full approval of the culture the Mrs Astors were allowed to take center stage and break the centuries old tradition that women should stay unnoticed in the background. Whereas as late as 1899 a newspaper accused Susan B. Anthony of really being a man because of her "well-developed desire to see her name in print," and whereas feminists and women who invaded the male professions were repeatedly accused of having unsexed themselves for fame, society ladies were rarely similarly accused although their names appeared in print a thousand times more often.

It has been forgotten how famous society ladies were. At first gossip sheets, like *Town Topics,* published descriptions of society ladies' gowns and dinner parties and balls, then every newspaper did, and at great length. The ball that Mrs William K. Vanderbilt gave in March 1883 was regarded as front page news by *The New York Times.* The ups and downs in the romance of Grace Wilson and Cornelius Vanderbilt Jr were detailed in the newspapers, and their marriage made the front page. In 1902 a New York newspaper devoted four and one-half columns to the latest party of Mrs Vanderbilt but only one column to President Theodore Roosevelt's political tour. The comings and goings of the "Four Hundred" were recorded in the Society Pages, a creation of the nineteenth century. Society ladies were as famous as Hollywood starlets were to be in the 1930s.

Why were society ladies allowed to bask in the limelight whereas feminists were told to get out of the newspapers and go home where they belonged? The answer is psychological conditioning. The culture gave the Mrs Astors fame, that is, a great deal of space in the newspapers and magazines, because it wanted *their* way of life to become the way of life for all women; it wanted Mrs Astor to be the model for the new woman, not the suffragists and female doctors. If women wanted a larger place in the sun, society was now willing to give it to them provided they pursued Mrs Astor's profession.

Leechery

The nineteenth century allowed the Mrs Astors of the world to become famous because they were pillars of the status quo, upholders of the male power structure that depends for its survival on the continued dependence of women. And the Mrs Astors, supported by wealth earned by their merchant princes, achieved new excesses of female parasitism, abandoning themselves to a life of Oriental luxury. Rarely has the leecherous life been lived so fully and so guiltlessly.

When Cornelius Vanderbilt Jr was a child in Newport, he once saw a maid hanging up laundry and asked his mother, "Whatever is that lady doing?" "That's not a lady, darling," answered his mother, "that's a woman." A lady, Mrs Cornelius Vanderbilt explained, never did menial tasks but wore silk stockings and silk gloves and had perfect manners. She might have added that ladies had room-long wardrobes filled with gowns from Worth and Pacquin, shoes and hats by the dozens, dazzling displays of diamonds, yard-long strands of pearls, drank champagne and ate terrapin, gave fancy dress parties that could each cost $250,000, vacationed on yachts, and traveled to Newport, London, Paris, Rome and Berlin in time for each city's social season.

That leechery flourished in the nineteenth century was perhaps inevitable, for it was the most obvious way society could protect itself against the increasing menace of females demanding equality. Just as the equal sexuality of early nineteenth-century clothing was abandoned in favor of clothing that grossly exaggerated sexual differences, so under the same fear of equality, the dependence of women upon men was converted from a necessity of life into a highly desirable luxury. The newspapers spread the sweets of leechery before the public like a daily Turkish delight, and the vast majority of the female population read about and envied Mrs Astor & Co. and, as much as possible, imitated them, just as women were later to envy and imitate Jean Harlow. Leechery became the cultural ideal for women, who dreamed of entering a Paradise of Opulence and Glory by marrying a Millionaire.

Leechery was able to be the answer of the status quo to demands for equality because the nineteenth century was the age of the millionaire, the word invented by the century to denominate the new breed of men who were making vast fortunes and who advertised their financial success by means of a conspicuously consuming woman. "What else have I toiled and struggled for all these years?" asks Henry James's American millionaire. "I have succeeded, and now what am I to do with my success? To make it perfect . . . there must be a beautiful woman perched on the pile, like a statue on a monument."

There were few women averse to being perched on the pile as the show-piece of a man's money. Just as a man achieved the ultimate success by acquiring a fortune, so a woman achieved the ultimate success by acquiring a man's fortune and leading the life of a lady, dissipating her energies on shopping, visiting, fancy needlework, opera-going, party-giving, traveling, and the beautification of her person and home. Except for childbearing and whatever child rearing could not be left to nurses, the ideal nineteenth-century woman was a lady of leisure, a kept woman. Shaw's Mrs Warren, a successful madam, felt she was no different from "a respectable girl [who is] brought up . . . to catch some rich man's fancy and get the benefit of his money by marrying him." But the respectable girl was different from the bad one—she kept sex under lock and key. The century produced so many pure women who prided themselves on their frigidity because that was the chief way a good woman could differentiate herself from a bad one. The bejeweled Mrs Astor in Newport scorned the bejeweled demimonde in Saratoga (America's city of sin), but the proverbial man from Mars would have found it difficult to distinguish the rich man's wife from the rich man's mistress, except in bed.

In France courtesans used to be called "les grandes horizontales," perhaps to slyly link them with "les grandes dames," the upright ladies of high society who did not have to assume the horizontal to enjoy a man's money. Certainly, so far as appearances went, courtesans looked like ladies, or rather, ladies looked like courtesans. For "les grandes horizontales," who achieved their fame about a generation before "les grandes dames," had taught the ladies how to dress—fashionably, lavishly jeweled, sexily—and eventually instructed their virtuous sisters in the arts of cosmetics and perfume so that by the end of the century it became impossible to tell the one from the other. The custom therefore arose in Paris when a gentleman went out for a drive for him to seat his wife on his right, his mistress on his left, thus signaling to his friends which woman they should bow to and which one they should pretend not to see.

Whether or not courtesans also taught ladies how to decorate their homes, the homes of both were equally and similarly plush, and both courtesans and ladies had the same concept of the good life. As Shaw's Mrs Warren detailed it—"a new dress every day . . . theatres and balls every night . . . a lovely house and plenty of servants. . . [and] the choicest of eating and drinking." Of necessity, then, both courtesans and ladies worshiped money. The courtesan Léonide Leblanc frankly confessed she wanted "money, and more money, always money." Ladies, who could afford to spend thousands of dollars on one party, could pretend money did not make their world go round. But fundamentally, it was money that set ladies and courtesans apart from the mass of humanity, each living in a charmed circle, each consorting with the richest men and the noblest names.

For courtesans and ladies had a fatal attraction to nobility. With courtesans to have a noble name was an open sesame. Blanche d'Antigny systematically solicited all the noble names; La Barucci made it a point to sleep with every man in the Jockey Club; Cora Pearl boasted of her intimacies with the Prince of Orange and other members of royalty. The goal of every courtesan was to marry into the nobility and a fair number did. Marie Duplessis (the original of *La Dame aux Camélias*) married Comte Edouard de Perregaux in 1846 and became a Comtesse. Elisabeth-Céleste Vénard became Mme la Comtesse de Chabrillan in 1854; when her husband died five years later his family tried to persuade her to stop using his name, but, as she said, she clung to the "noble name which had exorcised her past." Thérèse Lachmann, who in 1851 succeeded in marrying a Portuguese marquis, is alleged to have said the morning after the wedding: "You wanted to sleep with me, and you've done so, by making me your wife. You have given me your name, I acquited myself last night. I have behaved like an honest woman, I wanted a position and I've got it." The now Mme la Marquise de Païva, although she soon separated from her husband, retained her title until she was able to get another one—in 1871 she married again and became Countess von Donnersmark.

If courtesans used to boast whenever Prince Napoleon or Prince Edward slept in their beds, the Mrs Astors used to boast whenever Prince Edward or Prince Napoleon dined at their homes. And society ladies contrived as much as courtesans to marry themselves or their daughters into the nobility. The nineteenth century was the age of title mania, the age when "American belles" were "willing to exchange all the glorious privileges of American citizenship for the glitter of a coronet, or the empty name—in many instances—of a title." Thus in 1879 wrote the Washington correspondent of the Cincinnati *Gazette,* whose long article, "Beauties Won by Titles," was reprinted in *The New York Times.* The writer, though ostensibly lamenting title mania, was really boasting that American belles had succeeded in capturing titles "in almost every civilized nation under the sun." Among his list of titled beauties were a May Parsons of Ohio and a Florence Kate Smith of Nebraska who married, respectively,

Prince Lynar of Darmstadt and Lord Clifford of Lea, England. But most of the belles were from the east coast, one of the first being Jennie Jerome of New York who had married Lord Randolph Churchill in 1874. During the last quarter of the century, title mania increased and multiplied, the eagerness of rich girls for titles being equaled by the eagerness of impoverished nobility for their money. Thus Belle Wilson became Lady Michael Herbert, Mattie Mitchell the Duchesse de la Rochefoucauld, Adele Sampson the Duchess of Dino, Florence Davis Marchioness of Dufferin and Ava, Consuelo Vanderbilt the Duchess of Marlborough, Daisy Martin Princess Henry of Pless, and so on and so on at great length. The lust of American belles for men with titles was a manifestation of woman's new lust for her own self-aggrandizement, but like courtesans and properly conditioned girls everywhere, ladies satisfied their longing to be important by attaching themselves to the most important men they could find.

By imitating the life style of courtesans, ladies succeeded in creating a new role for wives. Courtesans were women conspicuously at leisure, housekeeping and any accidental children being relegated to servants. Similarly, the ideal nineteenth-century wife was no longer seen as an efficient housekeeper and good mother; such duties, at any rate, were now carried on behind the scenes. Instead, a wife presented herself to the world as a lady of leisure, elegantly dressed, standing in a drawing room graciously welcoming other ladies and gentlemen. The ideal wife now practiced Mrs Astor's profession—she was a hostess.

The Mrs Astors had created the new role to further their own social ambitions, that is, by wearing the most expensive jewels and the latest fashions and giving the biggest parties and dances and the most elaborate dinners, they strove to become top lady in the Four Hundred pecking order. It was necessary for the Mrs Astors to have a husband, but he tends to fade into the background and the Mrs Astors emerge as leading ladies, virtually independent figures, like actresses. Not so with wives of lesser rank. They too strove to become the Mrs Bigfish in their particular social pond, but for them a husband by their side was essential because they functioned as hostesses, ostensibly at any rate, not to further their own social ambitions but their husbands' professional ambitions. In 1881 when President Rutherford B. Hayes' term of office was nearing its end, Mrs Hayes was praised for having lent "additional strength to her husband's administration" by means of her "successful career as the first lady of the land," a career that consisted in keeping the White House and herself well decorated and in giving parties, teas and dinners and in other ways being a good hostess, like Mrs Astor.

It will be noted that Mrs Hayes' career was given the title "first lady," a title that had probably been invented in 1877 by Mary Clemmer Ames to describe Mrs Hayes. Its creation was another manifestation of female title mania. Just as the wife of an English Lord became a Lady, so the wife of America's chief lord now became a "first lady." But the adjective "first" had democratic implications, for if the wife of the president was the "first" lady of the land, then other wives were also ladies in their secondary spheres. And Mrs Hayes' "successful career as the first lady of the land" was in fact seen as offering a model for "her sex in all other positions and conditions." For every wife was now supposed to function as the *maîtresse d'* of her husband's career, to be, as it were, her husband's first lady.

In America's new female aristocracy Mrs Astor was pleased to be dubbed the "Queen of the Four Hundred," Mrs Vanderbilt "Her Grace," the wife of the president acquired the title "first lady" and marriage conferred on women married to men sufficiently rich the honors, status and ceremonial roles of ladydom. America had been founded by men who were discontented with an artificial aristocracy, one based on the accident of birth and wealth, not talent. But nineteenth-century America encouraged the growth of an artificial aristocracy among women based on the accident of marriage, not on the development of women's innate abilities. But that of course was the point. American women were raised to ladydom and Mrs Astordom was honored precisely because ladies, like aristocrats, did not work. Mrs Astor and her sister peeresses did not try to develop whatever abilities they might have been born with; they did not try, like the feminists, to invade the male professions; instead they created a new playground for women.

But a word must be said in praise of the new playground. It did enlarge woman's sphere of action. A woman married to a rich man had new outlets for her energy because hostessing on a large scale is a full time job. "I know of no art, profession, or work more taxing on the mental resources than being a leader of society," said one of the female Vanderbilts. Indeed, it is hard work to run a house as large as an hotel, arrange twenty course dinners for one hundred or more people, settle the protocol of who sits next to whom at what position at the table, and maneuver to entertain Princes and Dukes. Moreover, ladies whose energy was not used up by hostessing could do more; they could organize Easter egg-rolling for children on the White House lawn, start the custom of having a White House Christmas tree, plant cherry trees in Washington, as did some of the wives of presidents.

So long as a lady's work related to beautification, children or hostessing, she could make use of her brains, her aggression, her need for power and her political skill without incurring society's displeasure. She could also achieve fame, and not only if she were a Mrs Astor; the wife of a small town bank president could achieve local fame in the society pages of her Country Gazette. And neither Mrs Astor nor Mrs Smalltown Banker were accused of having unsexed themselves for fame, as the feminists were. Similarly, whereas an Elizabeth Cady Stanton was accused of being a man because of her aggressive political skill in manipulating suffrage meetings, the Mrs Astors were not accused of being men although their successful careers as hostesses depended upon their being efficient hotel managers, aggressive businessmen and consummate politicians. After Mrs Cornelius Vanderbilt Jr gave her first major parties, *Munsey's* magazine complimented her on being "essentially talented as a woman." Ward McAllister did not regard Mrs Astor as an unsexed woman ruthlessly striving for power but as a lady manifesting "the power that all women should strive to obtain, the power of attaching men to her . . . calling forth a loyalty of devotion such as one yields to a sovereign." So long as a woman used the traditionally male abilities to arrange dinner parties and balls, her abilities were seen as feminine. So long as a woman strove to be a leader of society not a member of Congress, so long as a woman used her head to learn the minutiae of the British peerage not the nerves of the body, society did not brand her with the scarlet M, meaning MAN.

Under the threat of the loss of sexual identity, almost all women who could afford to stayed in women's playground. Indeed, they usually succeeded in hiding their own abilities from themselves, insisting, for example, that the female sex was innately limited mentally. That was why ladies regarded higher education for girls as indecent and labeled a woman who did learn medicine or law a freak of nature, or to use the nineteenth-century slur—an hermaphrodite. The abilities of a real woman directed her to decorate her person, and having thus achieved a husband, she then devoted herself to giving parties or in other ways dissipating her time. No wonder nineteenth-century America honored the ladies. Why shouldn't a male culture, its power threatened, have given fame to these legal fancy women? They were not rocking the boat. Their leechery was the ballast of the male ship of state.

And as the figureheads on their husbands' merchant ships, as women whose male names signify their assimilation with a male culture, Mrs William B. Astor Jr, Mrs William Waldorf Astor, Mrs Cornelius Vanderbilt, Mrs Stuyvesant Fish, Mrs August Belmont sail through time, their names evoking not the lives of particular individuals so much as a way of life, a way of life they created and that most women still aspire to—the life of Mrs Richman Millionaire.

The Flukes

Just as there are sons of rich men who instead of becoming playboys in the jet set use their father's name, money and power as a catapult for their own careers, so there were ladies who used their husband's name, money and established position to launch themselves into the male world of power. These ladies were not content, like Mrs Astor, to strive for leadership in women's playground; they wanted power in the male world and they got it.

On the surface, however, Mrs Jack Gardner, Mrs Potter Palmer and Mrs Frank Leslie seemed to be merely ladies, that is, supported by their husbands' wealth, they lived the rich life to the hilt—lavish homes, European trips, salons, balls, the opera. As a matter of course, they all spent enormous amounts of money on clothes and each was known for her jewelry. Mrs Gardner not only had her famous ropes of pearls but two huge diamonds that sparkled in her hair. Mrs Palmer had a necklace made of 2268 pearls and seven diamonds, and she often wore at the same time a tiara, necklace, earrings, brooch, stomacher, rings and bracelets. When Mrs Frank Leslie was presented to the Governor of New York in 1875 she was wearing $70,000 worth of diamonds. These ladies, needless to say, took society seriously. Mrs Gardner, though somewhat erratically, wooed Boston society; Mrs Palmer became the leader of Chicago society and even managed to be accepted by Newport and London society and to get her niece married to a prince; Mrs Leslie, though Mrs Astor would not have deigned to notice her, imitated the life of high society in New York, having a salon, going to the opera only on the fashionable nights, riding in the parade of carriages in Central Park at the fashionable hour, and at one point in her life trying to marry a prince.

But Mrs Gardner, Mrs Palmer and Mrs Leslie were not authentic ladies; they were not merely hostesses in women's playground; they worked in areas outside the limits set for females and developed their extraordinary abilities as far as the conditions of their life and times permitted. Mrs Gardner's work was regarded as the least unfeminine since she collected art, and art was then classified with "the finer things of life" that were the special province of women. But Mrs Gardner's art collecting was not comparable to fancy needlework. She used her excellent taste, perfectionism, persistence and shrewdness to collect great works of art and build one of the world's finest small museums. Since art collecting and perhaps even museum building are still regarded as not fully masculine activities, Mrs Gardner will probably be judged as a dilettante in the male world, but Mrs Palmer and Mrs Leslie were by any standards businessmen, entrepreneurs, tycoons.

Mrs Potter Palmer started her extra-lady career by helping her husband develop his real estate and hotel business, and she was largely responsible for the recouping of his losses after the 1871 Chicago fire. It was not until 1891 that Mrs Palmer came out from behind her husband and used her business and executive abilities on her own. In that year she got herself appointed Chairman of the Board of Lady Managers of the World's Columbian Exposition (the world's fair held in Chicago in 1893) and so outstanding was her management she was awarded the Legion of Honor. In 1892 she was made a trustee of Northwestern University; in 1900 she was appointed by President McKinley to serve on the National Commission representing the United States at the Paris exposition, Mrs Palmer being the only female member. Mrs Palmer would have liked to be in politics; being female she had to use a male front. In 1896 she tried to get her husband appointed Ambassador to Berlin. But although President Cleveland was told the appointment of Mr Potter Palmer would be a double benefit because Mrs Potter Palmer was "in every way admirably capacitated and adapted to aid her husband," Mr Palmer was not appointed, perhaps because the President realized Mrs Palmer would be the ambassador. Her own contemporaries recognized it was only her sex that barred Mrs Palmer from politics: "If Mrs Potter Palmer were a man she would make an ideal ambassador," said a magazine late in her life. In 1901 she convinced her son Honoré to run for Alderman of the Twenty-first Ward in Chicago, successfully managed his campaign, and he (or she) served for two terms. Her son's political ambitions were limited, so Mrs Palmer could go no further in politics. After her husband's death in 1902, she immersed herself in the pleasures of European society, but in 1910 when she was sixty-one, she retired from society and gave full rein to her business and executive abilities. She developed her own huge ranch in Florida, cultivating citrus fruit and breeding cattle, and became a pioneer in Florida real estate; when she died in 1918 she had doubled the eight million dollars her husband had left her.

If Mrs Potter Palmer in old age became a Napoleon in the real estate world, Mrs Frank Leslie in middle age became a Napoleon in the publishing world. Mr Frank Leslie had been a highly successful publisher of various periodicals, among them, *Frank Leslie's Illustrated Newspaper* and *Frank Leslie's Popular Monthly*. When Mrs Leslie had been Mrs Ephraim George Squier, she and her husband had been Leslie's top editors. Having divorced Squier and married Leslie, she for a while devoted herself more to society life than to editorship, but in 1880 when Frank Leslie died, his publishing business bankrupt, Mrs Leslie took over the business and within one year paid off his debts and so increased circulation she could pay herself a salary of $100,000 a year. She ran the business successfully for twenty years, besides writing books and lecturing throughout the country. When she died in 1914, she left an estate worth two million dollars.

Whatever else they were, Mrs Jack Gardner, Mrs Potter Palmer and Mrs Frank Leslie were businessmen of the first order—great organizers, shrewd, daring, persistent, capable of managing people and conducting complex negotiations. But because they were making use of abilities that were thought to belong only to men, Mrs Gardner, Mrs Palmer and Mrs Leslie made it a point to appear in public with their sexuality well displayed. Mrs Gardner wore her dresses so tight she was once surrounded by a mob in Boston Common. Mrs Palmer was never seen except fashionably dressed and excessively jeweled. Mrs Leslie wore low cut dresses, corseted her waist until it was sixteen inches and was fond of revealing her ankles. Mrs Leslie once reminded the new women who were beginning to compete in a man's world that they should "never cease, however manly they may become, to clothe themselves in the gracious garments of womanliness."

Mrs Leslie never ceased to clothe herself in excessively feminine garments because she was, much more so than Mrs Palmer and Mrs Gardner, essentially male identified. Indeed, after Mr Leslie died, she had her first name legally changed to Frank. In his will Frank Leslie had requested that his wife "continue the business of publishing under the name . . . of Frank Leslie." He undoubtedly wanted his name to continue to live in his magazines, that *Frank Leslie's Popular Monthly* not be changed to *Miriam Leslie's Popular Monthly*. It was most unlikely that he was asking his wife to change her first name to his. But in June 1881 at a special term of the New York Court of Common Pleas, Mrs Leslie had her first name legally changed to Frank. And Frank delighted in being a transvestite—an apparently ultra-feminine woman with male identity papers. Before her lectures she used to stand behind the curtain that was raised slightly so the audience could see her ankles in their bright pink stockings, a sight as exciting as the first miniskirts were to be in the 1960s. After a few minutes of titillation, the curtain was raised and a beauty with her bosom half exposed walked slowly forward, laid a bejeweled hand on the lectern and announced, "Ladies and gentlemen, if you please, I am Frank Leslie." A thrill must have rushed through the hall, Frank generously allowing her audience to participate in the excitements of female impersonation.

She kept the name of Frank Leslie as long as she played the role of her former husband and notwithstanding another husband. On October 4, 1891 she married William C. Kingsbury Wilde (the brother of Oscar Wilde), but on October 30, Mrs Wilde received permission from the New York legislature to again change her name to Frank Leslie. When a reporter once addressed her as

Mrs Wilde, she corrected him: "I have agreed to be called by my husband's name when by dint of industry and perseverance he makes a name in the world of journalism as I have." She had a well-known man's name, so why change it to the name of an unknown man? She would have changed her name if she had succeeded, as she several times tried to do, in marrying into the nobility. If, as she once wished, she had married Prince George Eristoff de Gourie, she would happily have stopped being Frank and become Princess George. Like other ladies, her own sense of importance depended upon having a distinguished man's name to confront the world with.

It was not until her old age that Frank Leslie stopped using a male name and, having traced her pedigree, proceeded to call herself Baroness de Bazus. Similarly, Mrs Jack Gardner was sixty-two when she opened the museum she called the Isabella Stewart Gardner Museum. Mrs Potter Palmer clung to her male name, rarely using her female one in public except when she contributed to the suffrage movement, then signing her name the way the feminists did— Bertha Honoré Palmer. But she is not remembered as Bertha Palmer; a white petunia named in her honor is "The Mrs Potter Palmer" and a room in the Sarasota [Florida] Memorial Hospital is called the Mrs Potter Palmer Memorial Room. It is also fitting that Isabella Stewart Gardner has come down in history as Mrs Jack and that it is not as Baroness de Bazus that Frank Leslie is remembered. For their husbands' full names became associated with their own accomplishments and characters. These women essentially preempted their husbands' names, converting a male name into a female one.

The bisexuality of their names is symbolic of their cultural not their personal bisexuality. For even Frank Leslie was not a latent lesbian. Rather, these women lived in a culture with rigid male-female roles, both of which the conditions of their lives and character allowed them to act out. They had the best of the two sexual roles—the traditional luxuries and narcissism of a kept woman and the executive powers of a man. And Frank, Mrs Jack and Mrs Potter Palmer liked playing both roles, or to put it in conventional terms, they enjoyed being extraordinary women in a male world. They flourished in the status quo.

They were therefore not revolutionaries and had only a minimal interest in changing male-female roles. Mrs Gardner was not at all interested in women's rights, although the women she preferred were those with successful careers, like the actress Ellen Terry and the writer Edith Wharton. Mrs Palmer was interested in women's rights. She believed women should have equal educational and professional opportunities, for which reason she saw to it that the Woman's Pavilion at the World's Columbian Exposition was designed by a female architect, Sophia G. Hayden, and that the theme of women's work was stressed at the fair. Mrs Palmer also contributed money to the cause of woman suffrage, but she spent far more money and energy on clothes and in hiring Chaliapin or Pavlova to entertain at her parties, where she served champagne in priceless Venetian glasses. Mrs Palmer probably felt, especially when she was building her real estate empire in Florida, that she was *living* women's rights.

Certainly, Frank Leslie regarded herself as a living embodiment of the woman of the future. Although she was a lifetime member of the National American Woman Suffrage Association and willed her money to the cause, during her life she did not come out boldly in favor of women's rights. On the contrary, her actions revealed she was like the adventuress Lola Montez, who scorned the feminists. "Women who get together in conventions for the berating of men," said Montez, never "accomplish anything." Women, she believed, participate in government by controlling the legislators "and the experience of the world has pretty well proved that a man's judgment is pretty easily controlled when his heart is once persuaded." Lola Montez had used sex to gain almost complete control over King Ludwig I of Bavaria, who conferred upon her the titles Baroness Rosenthal and Countess of Landsfeld. Frank Leslie had also used men as stepping stones to her own success. Her second husband, Ephraim George A. Squier, an archaeologist and writer fifteen years her senior, enabled her to leave the ranks of the poor and enjoy the luxuries of life until Mr Frank Leslie came along, who had far more money and power that she by sexuality proceeded to appropriate; she divorced Squier and married Leslie, through whom she was able to launch her own career as an editor. Frank used what she called "womanliness" and what we call sex appeal to get money and power. She was a nineteenth-century Helen Gurley Brown who instructed women in the art of being a *femme fatale;* she wrote mostly on such topics as "Kissing as a Fine Art," "Blondes or Brunettes" and "The Art of Beauty." She believed women had such extraordinary sexual power over men that they could manipulate them easily to get whatever they wanted. She was therefore not interested in creating a world in which the sexes would have equal rights and equal power; she thought the world as it was favored women.

She would have regarded the young Carrie Lane Chapman as a naive babe in the male woods. For in 1886 when Mrs Chapman was working in San Francisco, a business man, finding himself alone with her in an office, passionately embraced her, whereupon Mrs Chapman became so enraged that her would-be seducer, terrified, hastily opened the door for her to leave. As she was walking home, Mrs Chapman wept, not for herself, but for the abominable position of women and vowed that from that hour she would dedicate herself to securing a world in which women would not be treated as sexual objects. She soon became a leading feminist. If Frank Leslie had been in Mrs Chapman's position, the incident would not have been a revelation of the humiliating position of women nor a turning point in her life. Frank would have felt flattered and would have used the man for at least a free meal. The incident would have been further proof to her of woman's sexual power over men, of woman's ability to use men for her own purposes. Frank believed in couch casting as much as men did. She saw the world with male eyes.

Frank Leslie, Mrs Jack and Mrs Potter Palmer were female impersonators, afraid to shock society by presenting themselves as they really were—the equals of men in their desire for power and their ability to use it. However, in a fundamental way they were not men's equals. Without their husbands' established positions in the world, they themselves would not have been able to gain power. Without her husband's and father's money, Mrs Jack could not have collected art. If Mr Leslie had not been a publisher, Mrs Leslie could not have become a publishing tycoon. Without Potter Palmer's wealth and business connections, Mrs Potter Palmer would not have been appointed Chairman of the Board of Lady Managers of the World's Columbian Exposition nor would she have been able to build her real estate empire. These women were fundamentally dependent upon men; they used the established male-dominant social structure as a means of gaining power for themselves; they did not try to change the structure so that a woman would not need a wealthy and influential man in order to get ahead in the world. They were willing to work within the male power structure; they did not try to subvert it.

Their lives illustrate what was still to be true one hundred years later—that the easiest way for a woman to invade the male halls of power was to have a rich and powerful husband, that the easiest way for a woman to make a name for herself was to appropriate an important man's name.

Mrs Dwight D. Eisenhower, according to a 1969 Gallup Poll, was the most admired woman in the world. Since 1953 when her husband became president, Mrs Eisenhower was listed among the ten most admired women, a large percentage of which were also wives of prominent men, women who "have been chiefly remarkable because they bore their husbands' names," to use the words of Mary Clemmer Ames, a nineteenth-century journalist who regretted that "the women we have lauded the loudest have been essentially humdrum," women like Martha Washington who "knitted stockings well and loved her husband." "Well enough," said Mrs Ames, but why should Mrs Washington be famous and not the thousands of other women who have done the same? Mrs Ames deplored the fact that we have no women heroes, that women who might "have made their names immortal by virtue of high endowment" have through "lack of the mere chance of personal development . . . died and made no sign."

The Mrs Astors of the world, the nineteenth-century women who most frequently made the front pages, did not make their names famous "by virtue of high endowment." Mrs Jack Gardner, Mrs Potter Palmer and Frank Leslie did, but they would not have been able to use their abilities if chance had not given them wealthy and powerful husbands. They could not have made their names famous the way men did—by starting at the bottom and working their way to the top. Frank Leslie, for example, could not have got a job as a copy girl, earned herself an editorship, then become the owner of a publishing house. The jobs normally open to women were dead-end ones—shop assistant, barmaid, laundress, dressmaker, governess. Occupations by which one could achieve fame and fortune by one's own efforts were at the beginning of the nineteenth century almost all closed to women.

Two notable exceptions were the professions of acting and writing, and it was women in these professions who first began to make their own names "immortal by virtue of high endowment."

4

THE SECOND OLDEST PROFESSION

Make four women, naked, or clothed in flesh-colored cloth, rise waist-high from the sea, with tresses to the wind . . .

These stage directions from a sixteenth-century Italian interlude mark the beginning of women's entrance into the acting profession, a profession that had been a male closed shop for some twenty-five hundred years, female roles being played by boys. Of course to call the women who thus nakedly displayed themselves actors is to stretch the meaning of the word; as an English visitor in 1592 succinctly concluded: the Italians "have whores to play the women's parts." The profession of actress had not yet outgrown its original association with prostitution. In early Rome the females who were allowed on stage as dancers and mimes were legally classified as prostitutes and were treated as such—on certain days of the week the audience had the right to demand they strip.

Female actors in England, like their Italian sisters, also entered the stage through the wings of prostitution. Charles II in 1662 issued a royal patent officially permitting women to act and ordered his Lord Chamberlain to start hiring women for the female parts because during his exile in France he had been used to seeing the "pretty and diverting vision" of women on stage, and used to sleeping with them. The Lord Chamberlain was virtually the royal pimp, for the women actors (as they were then called) were chosen not for their acting ability but for their beauty and their willingness to sleep with the King and other high ranking gentlemen. Most of the early actresses regarded themselves primarily as whores and thought more of keeping an assignation than keeping a part; it was not uncommon for an actress to miss a performance when a rich lover was seized with a sudden lust. The average actress regarded herself not as a professional actor but as a professional beauty. Actresses used to fight to get the parts that allowed them to wear the prettiest costumes and refused to play old women, which for some time continued to be played by men.

"My face is my fortune," says the milkmaid in an old nursery rhyme, by which she meant that her pretty face could get her a rich husband. A pretty face could now get a girl more than that; it could procure her an independent livelihood and, if she were lucky, wealth and fame. Moreover, if a girl had more than a pretty face, if she had acting ability, she had the chance to develop her talent to the fullest and make herself, as Mary Clemmer Ames put it, "immortal by virtue of high endowment." The actress best remembered before 1800 was the pretty and voluptuous Nell Gwyn, King Charles II's mistress, but that period also produced women whose acting ability earned them a place in Westminster Abbey. Anne Bracegirdle, the most popular actress of her time, was buried in the North Cloister; Susannah Marie Cibber, a great tragedian, was buried in the East Cloister; after the death of Hannah Pritchard, famous for her portrayal of Lady Macbeth, a monument to her memory was placed in the Poets' Corner.

But although women were at last allowed to make their names famous, they were not yet allowed to keep them, that is, they were still not allowed to have a professional name that was unaffected by matrimony. Anne Bracegirdle, Susannah Cibber and Hannah Pritchard either did not marry or married only once early in life; otherwise marriage would have changed their famous names. Actresses, like ordinary wives, still took the names of their husbands, which could mean a change in professional identity in mid career, and often two or three changes. Mrs Percival, a late seventeenth-century comedienne, had a short career (she died when she was thirty-two) that managed to survive two changes of name, from Mrs Percival to Mrs Mountfort, then from Mrs Mountfort to Mrs Verbruggen. A certain Mrs Gregory, who was a well-known actress from 1754 to 1757, then transformed herself into Mrs Fitzhenry. The popular actress Priscilla Hopkins in 1778 became Mrs Brereton, the playbills informing the public that Mrs Brereton was the "late Miss P. Hopkins," but in 1787 Mrs Brereton married again and finished her career as Mrs Kemble. In the 1789-90 season, we read on a playbill of a "Mrs Powell, late Mrs Farrer," but after almost a quarter of a century of being known as Mrs Powell, in 1814 she became "Mrs Renaud, late Mrs Powell." The Anglo-American actress known from 1785 to 1791 as Ann Brunton became Mrs Merry from 1791 to 1803, after which she became Mrs Wignell, and although her husband died seven weeks after the marriage, she remained Mrs Wignell until 1806 when she married a third time and changed her name to Mrs Warren. Similarly, the woman who began her acting career as Louisa Lane became in turn Mrs Hunt, Mrs Mossop and finally in 1850 Mrs John Drew. In 1861 the actress known as Agnes Land married and became Agnes Perry; in 1867, having married a second time, she became Agnes Booth. Even very famous actresses abandoned their famous names. The celebrated Ellen Tree married in 1842 and renounced her name, from then on acting as Mrs Charles Kean, a well-known name but not so renowned as her own had been.

For a couple of hundred years, despite the theatrical tradition of stage names, actresses changed their professional identity every time they married. When a woman was merely a wife, it made sense to let the world know whose wife she was, no matter how often a new husband required her to change her name. But when a woman had a profession in which her name had become well-known, it would seem foolish and bad business to change that name. Perhaps actresses were reluctant to give up the female pleasure of letting the world know they had succeeded in getting a husband. Perhaps actresses, since their profession had for so long been linked with prostitution, wanted to prove they were not loose women by bearing the name of a legitimate spouse. Whatever their reasons, it is not at all surprising that the women whose lives contained other glories besides the glory of wifehood eventually began to distinguish themselves from ordinary wives by not allowing marriage to change their famous name. Actresses, the women whom society first allowed to achieve fame and fortune in their own right, became the first women to keep the name they had made famous.

Lucia Elizabetta Bartolozzi married Armand Vestris in 1813 and under the name of Madame Vestris became famous in England as an actress and then as a director, stage designer and lessee of theaters. In 1838 she married the actor Charles James Mathews and immediately afterwards, most confusingly, began to be referred to either as Madame Vestris or Mrs Mathews. Newspaper accounts of her activities refer to her sometimes by the one name and sometimes by the other, and with no explanation, so that the uninformed would think two persons were being discussed. In the diary of Charles Macready, under April 9, 1842, he also used the two names interchangeably: "I agreed to give Mr and Mrs C. Mathews the terms for which they stood out . . . Called at Beasley's and found there Mr Charles Mathews and Madame Vestris." Although Madame Vestris was apparently content to use the name Mathews in private life, she definitely did not want to use it in public life. She continued to be listed in the playbills as Madame Vestris, and although her husband in his speeches calls her Mrs Mathews, in her own speeches she calls herself Madame Vestris. In 1839, in her address upon retiring from the management of the Olympic Theater, she said, "in Mr Mathews' name and my own," by which she meant Vestris, for at the end of the speech she refers to "the house of Mathews, Vestris, and Company." In that speech she also said they intended to face their new difficulties "manfully and womanfully"; Madame Vestris, if not her husband, believed in the equality of the sexes and had no intention of submerging her hard won and more famous identity by using her husband's name. As time passed, the newspapers more and more often refer to her only as Madame Vestris, and it is as Madame Vestris that she is known to posterity.

In 1858, two years after Madame Vestris died, Charles Mathews married a Mrs Davenport, a minor actress, who promptly changed her stage name to her famous husband's, a form of poaching that was not to continue much longer. Custom was changing, and not only for actresses. All female theatrical performers were being required by the public to maintain a constant stage identity, whatever name changes occurred in their private life and at times in spite of their own wishes to the contrary. In 1852, after the internationally famous singer Jenny Lind married, her concert billings read: "Madame Otto Goldschmidt (late Mlle Jenny Lind)," and Jenny Lind in her pride in being a wife, signed her letters "Jenny Goldschmidt, late Jenny Lind," or "née Lind," and after a time, simply Jenny Goldschmidt. But the public refused to accept her as Jenny Goldschmidt, so in her concert billings she compromised and called herself Jenny Lind-Goldschmidt, and eventually she herself used the hyphenated surname in her own private correspondence. But though the concert billings and the critics respected her wishes to be known at least in part by her husband's name, the public did not. Jenny Lind she was and continued to be. "Why do people persist in saying 'Jenny Lind was there with her husband'?" she once asked a friend. "They ought to say, 'Herr Goldschmidt was there with his wife'." The identity of famous women in the theater had begun to be secure even from their own desires for wifely self-abnegation.

The famous actress Julia Marlowe in 1894 married the relatively unknown actor Robert Taber and at first wanted to have her name expunged entirely and have the billings read: "Mr and Mrs Taber." But business realities had to compromise with wifely self-effacement and they proceeded to bill themselves as "Julia Marlowe Taber and Robert Taber." Even so, Taber was accused of wanting to cash in on Marlowe's popularity and many managers were unwilling to book Marlowe under her new name. One manager of a Philadelphia theater felt the change in Marlowe's stage name had so injured her drawing power he refused to pay her part of her percentage; Mrs Taber had to sue in order to collect the money that was due her. In spite of such difficulties, she persisted in using the name Julia Marlowe Taber until 1897 when she and Taber separated. She then resumed the name Julia Marlowe and did not again change her stage name despite a second marriage in 1911 to Edward Sothern.

Julia Marlowe's willingness in 1894 to change her stage name to Taber was then pretty much of an anachronism. By the last quarter of the nineteenth century it had become a firmly established theatrical custom for women to maintain a constant stage name. Actresses who had previously changed their stage name did not do so when they married again. The actress known first as Agnes Land, then Agnes Perry, then Agnes Booth, married for a third time in 1885 but did not again change her name; she continued to be known as Agnes Booth, though in private life she was Mrs Schoeffel. The occasional actress who did change her stage name did so for exceptional reasons. In 1890 the popular actress Minnie Maddern married Harrison Grey Fiske and retired from the stage because she disliked the frivolous parts and inane plays she had been forced to act in. She returned to the stage in 1893, her name changed to Fiske, because she wished to assume a new identity, that of a serious actor in plays of significance. Even so, she at first billed herself as Minnie Maddern-Fiske and it was not until 1897 that she became simply Mrs Fiske. But changes of stage name, though they continued to occur, became rare; it had become the rule for actresses to have a permanent stage name whatever nominal concessions to wifehood they made in their private life. Ellen Terry, in spite of three legal and one illicit marriage, remained Ellen Terry when she acted, albeit in private life she was Mrs Watts or Mrs Godwin or Mrs Wardell or Mrs Carew.

There is little evidence to suggest that actresses wanted to retain their own identity in private life also. On the contrary, they insisted on being Mrs Whateverhisname no matter how often Whateverhisname changed. The great Sarah Bernhardt, after her marriage in 1882 to Jacques Damala, signed all legal and financial documents "Sarah Bernhardt Damala," and even after his death she signed documents "Sarah Bernhardt Damala, widow." Bernhardt did not use the name Damala because she held her husband in fond regard; he was flagrantly unfaithful, a dope addict and the marriage lasted only two years. It was that, in spite of the glory of being Sarah Bernhardt, a part of her took satisfaction in playing the role of the bourgeois wife, Mme Damala.

The famous Bernhardt took pride in being Mme Damala because the acting profession had not lost its aura of immorality. To be an actress was in the public's eye to be morally suspect. Actresses therefore liked to imitate respectable housewives and call themselves off stage Mrs Properlywed. On stage, however, they presented themselves to the public as if they were single, as Miss, a title English and American actresses (regardless of marital status) began to use in the second half of the nineteenth century, perhaps because English and American men at that time had a sexual predilection for virgins. Europeans, on the other hand, having a more mature taste in women and being accustomed to having affairs with married women, continued to call actresses above a young age Madame. But although English and American actresses presented themselves to the public as Miss, they were rarely, no more than their European sisters, Miss Innocents. For the first requisite of an aspiring actress was good looks, and she had to have extraordinary acting ability (or a protective mamma) not to submit to couch casting. In France throughout most of the nineteenth century apprentice actresses were paid only a token salary, it being assumed by the management they were being kept by a gentleman. But whether sexually loose or strict (and it *was* possible for an actress to be virtuous), actresses were as a class public beauties, women of superior looks set up on stage for everyman to ogle and everywoman to envy. Just as the Mrs Astors were featured in the newspapers to teach wives how to dissipate their time and energy, so the Miss Beauties were put on stage and given fame not only so males might be titillated but for a higher social purpose—to teach women that their role in society was to be looked at, to illustrate that the female sex achieved success in life by being good to look at.

It would seem necessary for such public beauties, like public houses, to have public names, ones that did not change, that informed the public that a particular product was still on the market and could be seen at a particular time and place. It also seems fitting that a public beauty should not have a name that meant she belonged to a husband. Moreover, on a deeper level, a name that meant "wife of" was inaccurate since an actress when she was acting was not performing the social role of wife. But actresses may have been permitted to have names that were not husbands' names simply because of the long theatrical tradition of stage names, a tradition that allowed the public to regard the name an actress used on stage as a pseudonym and her "real" name as her husband's name.

Whatever the reasons, actresses became the first women society permitted to make their own names famous. They were permitted to do what only men had previously had the right to do—work at a job that gave them the chance to achieve wealth and fame. As a consequence, actresses were freed from many of the restrictions imposed on women. Actresses, unlike ordinary women, did not have to stay modestly in the background; they could, like men, shine in the limelight. Actresses, unlike ordinary women, could dispense with an "honest" name, for their famous name permitted them, like men, to have a sex life and even illegitimate children without damaging their careers. Actresses, unlike ordinary women, could hope for more than the reflected glory of a husband's name; they could, like men, hope to get the name so long denied women—a famous one. And the noble few, the actresses who had talent not mere physical charms, got a satisfaction that had also long been denied women; like men, they had the opportunity to develop fully the talent they had been born with and to leave a name behind them that was justly famous.

5

THE VEILED LADIES

"Frank has brought me glorious news! my book is definitely accepted, and will be out in a fortnight. I have now fully decided to avow its authorship at once, by putting my name, Lillie Devereux Umsted, on the title page. This may be daring, but the audacity suits my present mood. How strange it will be to see my name placarded on Broadway! Even sitting quietly at home here, I tremble when I think of it." Thus on January 20, 1859 Mrs Umsted reacted to the acceptance for publication of her novel *Southwold*. She would be one of the daring ones and put her name on the title page.

Actresses as a matter of course had had their names on playbills, programs and placards, but it was not a matter of course for an author to put her name before the public. Early in the century Charles Lamb remarked that a woman who lets herself be known as an author invites disrespect. He himself, whenever he chose to, published under his own name, but his sister Mary, who wrote books for children, did not allow her name to appear on a title page.

It had long been customary for women to hide behind the veil of anonymity. In the seventeenth century the religious principles of Mrs Elizabeth Burnet compelled her to write *A Method of Devotions, or Rules for Holy and Devout Living,* but it was not until after her death in 1709 that her name appeared under the title; when she was alive her modesty would not permit her to be so bold. Many a female author continued to be modestly anonymous. Mary Astell's *Christian Religion* (1705) and her *Some Reflections upon Marriage* (1730) were offered to the world without allowing herself, as she put it, the vanity of "the celebrated name of *Author.*" *The Medium, or Virtue Triumphant* (1795) and *The Traveller Returned* (1796) by the American playwright Judith Sargent Murray were published anonymously and were therefore assumed to be by her husband. Fanny Burney's first novel *Evelina* (1778), Maria Edgeworth's first novel *Castle Rackrent* (1808), Jane Taylor's *Original Poems, for Infant Minds* (1808) and many other of the few books then written by women were published anonymously. Even when it became common for women to be authors, the tradition of anonymity persisted. Elizabeth Barrett's first two volumes of poetry, published in 1820 and 1826, had no name on the title page. When the first book of the Connecticut writer Louisa Tuthill was published in 1827 she refused to have her name on it; she despised literary women and had started to write only at her husband's insistence; it was not until 1839 that she allowed her name to appear in one of her books. In 1855 the English philosopher Frances Power Cobbe was too modest to put her name on her *Essay on Intuitive Morals,* and in 1856 the Southern novelist Margaret Junkin Preston refused to allow the publisher of her *Silverwood* to use her name although he offered to pay her extra.

When female authors were not Anonymous they liked to wear the genteel mask of "A Lady." From 1713, when Anne Finch, Countess of Winchilsea, published her *Miscellany Poems,* to 1811 when Jane Austen published *Sense and Sensibility* and beyond "A Lady" was the favorite disguise of a large band of female authors, some of whom distinguished themselves from other ladies by such tags as "A Lady of Massachusetts," which was the incognito of Hannah Webster Foster (1759-1840), or "A Lady of New-Hampshire," which was how Sarah Josepha Hale (later famous as the editor of *Godey's Lady's Book*) sent forth her first volume of poems in 1823, its title appropriately, *The Genius of Oblivion.*

After an author had been a successful Anonymous or Lady, she often published her later work as, for example, "By the Author of *Sense and Sensibility,*" which was how Jane Austen published *Pride and Prejudice.* Dinah Mulock, after having been Anonymous, then "The Author of *The Head of the Family,*" wrote a bestseller and was henceforth known to the world as "The Author of *John Halifax, Gentleman.*" Similarly, Mary Elizabeth Braddon, after having been Anonymous, became "The Author of *Lady Audley's Secret,*" the title of her highly popular novel. The minor novelist Anne Manning, after a bestseller, published almost fifty works as "The Author of *Mary Powell.*"

Other ladies chose to be "alphabetical phantoms," to use Lewis Carroll's phrase for them. "L.E.L." was the nameless name of Letitia Elizabeth Landon (1802-1838), and "A.L.O.E." stood for A Lady of England, namely Charlotte Maria Tucker (1825-1893), who thus published about 150 works in the second half of the nineteenth century. Another group of lady authors were partial to a single feminine name, like Philenia, Shirley, Tenella, Pansy or Estelle. Other ladies chose double alliterative or poetic names, like Fanny Fern, Jennie June, Grace Greenwood, Pearl Rivers, Annie Laurie and Nelly Bly. The identity of these ladies is known, for their flower-like names were the mere conventional blush of modesty. But many Southern poetesses who were bold enough to send their verses to local newspapers under such names as Amelia or Miss L'Connue concealed their identities so carefully it has taken exhaustive modern scholarship to ferret out who a few of them were.

Ultra-feminine names lost some of their vogue in the second half of the nineteenth century when lady authors tended to transform themselves into gentlemen, into Currer Bell, George Eliot, Cotton Mather Mills, Ennis Graham, Lucas Malet, Saxe Holm, Sherwood Bonner, Christian Reid, Octave Thanet, Charles Egbert Craddock, F. G. Trafford, John Oliver Hobbes and many many more. Female authors have never since been so partial to male pseudonyms.

Rarely has a man used a female pseudonym, but it was not at all rare for a male author to use anonyms and pseudonyms. On the contrary, in the eighteenth and early nineteenth centuries it was common for a man to omit his name from a title page, or to present himself, as Sir Walter Scott did, as "The Author of *Waverly*," or to use pseudonyms, like Elia or Cervantes Hogg. But far more female than male authors used anonyms and pseudonyms, they persisted in doing so much longer than men did, and they used them for different reasons. A man might conceal his identity because he wanted greater freedom to write about controversial religious or political matters, or because his vanity required a shield in case his book was a failure. He also might not have his name on the title page merely because anonymity used to be a publishing fashion. That fashion perhaps accounts for the sudden increase in female authors. At any rate, it was a fashion early female authors must have been thankful for because it allowed them to seem, in spite of the book they had written, modest and retiring women, not bold, aggressive, unsexed seekers of fame; far more women than men made a serious effort to keep their identity secret. When anonymous publication became unfashionable, many female authors adopted male pen names, for that device, like anonymity, gave them a chance to be judged on their merits not their sex. The culture did not require male authors to outwit social prejudice by disguising their sex, nor did the culture expect men to be modest. There was, in addition, another reason for the great popularity of anonyms and pseudonyms among female authors: it enabled them to have a constant identity (or non-identity) above the vicissitudes of the name changes to which society subjected women.

If Dinah Mulock had not been known to the world as "The Author of *John Halifax, Gentleman*," what would she have done in 1865 when she became Mrs Craik? Or if Mary Elizabeth Braddon had not published as "The Author of *Lady Audley's Secret*," what would she have done in 1874 when she married and changed her name to Mary Elizabeth Maxwell? If Charlotte Brontë had published under her own name and not as Currer Bell, what would she have done (if she had lived) after she married? published as Charlotte Nicholls?

George Eliot remained George Eliot to her public whether the name she used in private life was Marian Evans, Marian Lewis or Marian Cross. Fanny Fern could remain Fanny Fern to her readership although marriage had changed her name to Mrs Eldredge, then Mrs Farrington, and finally to Mrs Parton. The pen name Pearl Rivers protected a Southern poet from the nominal vicissitudes of her private life in which she was respectively, Eliza Poitevent, Mrs Col. A. M. Holbrook and Mrs George Nicholson. To publish as "By the Author of Bestseller," or as Grace Greenwood or Lucas Malet allowed a female writer to marry (and a second or third time) without damaging a valuable trade name, for women who did not use an anonym or pseudonym lost their professional identity every time they married.

Just as custom had required actresses to change their name with every marriage, so whenever an author who did not use a pen name married, the name on her title page changed. Sydney Owenson's name had become almost synonymous with the title of her novel *The Wild Irish Girl*; nevertheless, when she married in 1812 she changed the name she published under. The first novel she published after her marriage bore the signature—"By Lady Morgan, (late Miss Owenson)." Owenson of course enjoyed letting the world know she had become a Lady, but she would have changed the name she published under even if she had married a commoner. Convention dictated that a woman's name must reflect her marital status even when the woman was acting in the capacity of author, not wife, and even though the change of name meant a loss of professional identity. In 1829 Almira Hart Lincoln published her *Familiar Lectures on Botany*, which soon became the standard textbook in colleges throughout America; by 1842 it had gone through seventeen editions and was popularly known as *Lincoln's Botany*. But the author, who had remarried in 1831, now called herself Mrs Phelps. In 1833 her *Botany for Beginners: An Introduction to Mrs Lincoln's Lectures on Botany* appeared under the signature Mrs Almira H. L. Phelps, as if a Mrs Phelps had written an introduction to Mrs Lincoln's lectures. Perhaps to let readers know she might be the well-known Mrs Lincoln, she sometimes published as Mrs Lincoln Phelps, but most often she used the name Almira H. L. Phelps or simply Mrs Phelps.

Long after actresses had begun to maintain a constant professional name, authors were giving up their own names, no matter how famous, and signing their husbands' names to their books. It is now generally forgotten that in 1846 when Elizabeth Barrett married Robert Browning she was famous and he was almost unknown; nevertheless, she was the one who gave up her name, publishing henceforth as Elizabeth Barrett Browning. It was as if Dylan Thomas had married a minor poet and changed his name to Dylan Thomas Teasdale. One wonders what Mrs Browning would have done if Robert had died and she had remarried. Would she, although as Elizabeth Barrett Browning her fame had so increased she had been suggested for the Poet Laureateship, would she have changed her name again and published, let us say, as Elizabeth Barrett Kilmer? or as Elizabeth Browning Kilmer? or as Elizabeth Barrett Browning Kilmer? Whatever name she adopted, it is most likely she would have changed her name again. A much less sentimental woman, Anna Cora Mowatt, felt she ought to change the name she wrote under to that of her new husband. Mrs Mowatt, internationally famous both as an actress and as the author of *Fashion* (1845), the first play to satirize American social snobbery, married William F. Ritchie in 1854 and the next year, when a new edition of the play was projected, asked her publisher if it would "not be well to change the name on the title to Anna Cora *Ritchie?*" Her publisher disagreed and that edition of *Fashion* came out under her famous name, but a novel she published the next year appeared under the name Anna Cora Ritchie (formerly Mrs Mowatt). From then on she published as Anna Cora Ritchie, sometimes with Mrs Mowatt in parentheses and sometimes not.

It took an unusual husband to save a woman's publishing name. When the popular hymn writer, the blind Fanny Crosby, married in 1858, it was her husband not she herself who insisted she continue publishing under her own name; she obeyed, honoring her husband only in parentheses, that is, she published as Fanny Crosby (Mrs Alexander Van Alstyne). Other women did likewise and were thus able to have both a constant publishing name and a married name (or two). Florence Marryat signed her novels Florence Marryat (Mrs Ross Church), and when she married again, Florence Marryat (Mrs Francis Lean). But the vanity of most husbands demanded a nominal sacrifice. When Anne M. Crane married in 1869 she was known as the author of two sensational and highly popular novels about married women passionately attracted to men not their husbands; nevertheless, her next book appeared under the name Anne Seemüller. It was as if Jacqueline Susann, in mid bestsellerdom, had married again and changed her publishing name to Jacqueline Netherman.

It is only because the tradition for women to have a constant publishing name was not yet fully established that the author of *Science and Health* is known to us as Mary Baker Eddy. When the founder of the Christian Science Church published the book in 1875 it was under the name Mary Baker Glover, the surname of her first husband. But in 1877 Mrs Glover married Mr Eddy, so in 1878 the new edition of *Science and Health* appeared under the name Mary Baker Glover Eddy, the new Mrs Eddy retaining the name Glover so her followers would continue to know who she was. But three surnames are clumsy, so she tried shortening her signature in various ways, trying Mary B. Glover Eddy, Mrs Glover Eddy and Mary Baker G. Eddy.

Mary Baker Glover Eddy was obviously seriously inconvenienced by having to change her name, but when a woman has published under the name of one husband and then marries another she tends to feel it a slight to her present husband to continue to use the name of a former spouse. That, at any rate, was the reason why another famous woman changed her publishing name. In 1900 Charlotte Perkins Stetson, internationally known as the author of *Women and Economics*, married a second time and informed her publishers she would henceforth use the name Charlotte Perkins Gilman. Her publishers were horrified. "You will lose money by it," they protested. But Mrs Gilman was adamant; the loss of money was not a sufficient reason for continuing to use the name of Stetson when she was married to Gilman. She then wished she had remained simply Charlotte Perkins from the beginning of her writing career. The trouble was she had started writing after her first marriage and, like most women, she had not foreseen a divorce and remarriage and the name difficulties that would ensue.

However, Mrs Gilman's decision to change her publishing name was by 1900 unusual. For during the last two decades of the nineteenth century female authors seldom felt obliged to change the name they published under even when it was the name of a previous husband. The prolific writer of travel and art books, Clara Clement, began to write after her marriage to James Clement, but unlike Charlotte Perkins Gilman she continued to use her first husband's surname for publishing after her second marriage in 1882 to Edwin Waters. The Southern journalist known to the world as Mrs E. Burke Collins, the full name of her first husband, continued to publish under that name despite her marriage in 1884 to Robert Sharkey. The author of *Rebecca of Sunnybrook Farm* kept on publishing as Kate Douglas Wiggin despite a second marriage in 1894.

Women who began to write before their first marriage generally did not change their publishing name after marriage. The author of the internationally famous novel *The Leavenworth Case* (1878), Anna Katharine Greene, did not give up that publishing name after her marriage to Charles Rohlfs in 1884. Elizabeth Stuart Phelps, author of the bestseller *The Gates Ajar* (1868), continued to publish under her own name after her marriage in 1888 to Herbert D. Ward (except that in one of the three books she wrote with him she used the name Elizabeth Stuart Phelps Ward). The journalist Margherita Hamm continued to use that name professionally throughout her two marriages, the first in 1893 to William E. S. Fales and the second in 1902 to John R. McMahon. The children's writer Edith Nesbit started to publish as E. Nesbit when she was single and kept on signing that name to her books despite two marriages.

A fair number of female authors did continue to change their publishing name after marriage, but public opinion no longer demanded they do so. And as the names of more and more female authors ceased to be affected by marriage, authors, like actresses, began to be addressed as Miss, whether married or single. Female authors, like female actors, had finally won the right to have a constant professional name.

But why did it take authors longer than actresses to win that right? Why, when the names of actresses were on playbills were authors still hiding behind the veils of Anonymous, A Lady and Charles Egbert Craddock? Why in 1859 did Lillie Devereux Umsted feel daring, nay audacious, when she decided to put her own name on a title page? And why, late in the century, when female authors had won the right to have a constant publishing name did so many of them prefer pseudonyms, and male ones?

To answer that writing was considered incompatible with feminine modesty or that a male name was the only way a female author could get a fair hearing is not sufficient. For why did female authors have to be more modest about displaying their talent than female actors? Why didn't a female actor have to disguise her sex in order to get her talent appreciated? We laugh at such a question, just as we laugh at the thought of a female playing Hamlet. But for centuries men acted women's roles and no one laughed. The fact is we think of actresses not primarily as people endowed with acting ability but as well-endowed female bodies.

Acting was the first profession opened to women because actresses were no threat to a male-dominant society; they were conventional women set up on stage repeating the stereotypical female roles with their secondary sexual characteristics emphasized, which sexual display was by no means shockingly unconventional since a respectable Victorian woman could reveal most of her bosom. What no decent Victorian woman could reveal, what no actress did reveal, was that she had a head on her shoulders. For a woman to have a head—a thinking head not a pretty face—had been taboo for centuries. Hence the veiled ladies.

6

GETTING A HEAD

I Hate Learned Women

"A female poet, or female author of any kind, ranks below an actress," said Charles Lamb to a friend on December 5, 1826. Lamb once asked an actress to marry him, but although his own sister wrote books, he had a deep-seated prejudice against female authors. He felt that Letitia Elizabeth Landon should be locked up and fed on bread and water "till she left off writing poetry." Landon was a mediocre poet, but there were hundreds of mediocre male poets and Lamb did not devise drastic cures for them. It was as difficult for Lamb to judge a female author on her individual merits as it was for Americans to judge a black man on his merits. Let an "authoress" be mentioned and Lamb was inclined to indulge in generalized vilification. The playwright Elizabeth Inchbald happening to be spoken of, Lamb proceeded to call all clever women "impudent, forward, unfeminine and unhealthy in their minds."

Lamb's was no idiosyncratic aversion; it was an ancient prejudice. "I hate learned women," ranted Hippolytus in the fifth century BC play of Euripides, and his cry of rage has echoed down through the centuries, becoming louder and louder in the late eighteenth and nineteenth centuries when the mere thought of a learned woman made men as anxious as women are alleged to be in the presence of a mouse. "I am always seized with a kind of shivering, when I am placed near a woman who pretends to learning," said Baron von Knigge near the end of the eighteenth century in his *Practical Philosophy of Social Life*. "I have an utter aversion to bluestockings. I do not care a fig for any woman that knows even what an author means," remarked William Hazlitt in 1824. When Ruskin was reading the letters of Carlyle in 1889 and learned that Mrs Carlyle used to read Tacitus, he wrote in the margin: "A woman able to read Tacitus! How fearful!"

A man was likely to lose his temper when he discovered a book he admired had been written by a woman. Hannah More in 1788 decided to publish anonymously her *Thoughts on the Importance of the Manners of the Great* because she hoped "it might be attributed to a better person." It was attributed to the famous men of her time, like Wilberforce. When the poet William Cowper learned the book he had highly praised was by a woman, he could hardly contain his incredulous anger: "How comes it to pass, that she, being a woman, writes with a force and energy and a correctness hitherto arrogated by the man?" How comes it indeed! Seventy-one years later Henry Crabb Robinson felt a similar indignation when he learned the author of *Adam Bede* was a woman: "I would rather so excellent a book was written by any man than a woman," he confided to his diary on July 16, 1859.

A man's indignation could explode into tyrannical fury when he discovered the female perpetrator was kin. When Mary Shelley published *The Last Man* in 1826 she used the anonym "The Author of *Frankenstein,*" but her identity was known and a reviewer mentioned her name, which made her father-in-law Sir Timothy Shelley so angry he suspended her allowance. When the publisher Nathaniel P. Willis discovered the essays by Fanny Fern appearing in his own *Home Journal* were written by his sister, he stormed into his editor's office and commanded him never again to print his sister's work. Fanny Fern's other brother was also gravely shocked, as was her whole family, who felt almost as disgraced as if she had presented them with an illegitimate child.

Male horror at women who committed acts of creativity was of course shared by conventional womankind. The ladies of Boston used to ridicule the scholar Hannah Adams, author of such learned works as an *Alphabetical Compendium of the Various Sects* (1784) and a *History of the Jews* (1812). Apparently Adams was careless of her clothes and had holes in her stockings, for which reason she was pointed out to young girls as an awful warning of what happened to a woman who pursued learning. The monstrous Hannah Adams was pointed out to Lydia Maria Francis when she was a young girl, but she nevertheless took to authorship, being careful, however, to conceal herself behind the anonym "An American." When her identity was discovered, she was warned by her female friends that "no woman could be expected to be regarded as a lady after she had written a book." Miss Francis continued to write books and became a feminist, but other female authors, though highly successful themselves, were capable of advocating non-learning for other women. Anna Aikin Barbauld, a contemporary of Francis and Adams and the author of tracts on the Test Act and the sins of the government, nevertheless was of the opinion that young girls should have only "a general tincture of knowledge," enough to make them "agreeable companions to men of sense," which tincture was to be gained not at school but at home from conversations with their fathers and brothers.

In such a hostile climate it is not surprising that some women wrote their books surreptitiously. Jane Austen always kept a large piece of muslin embroidery on her desk to cover her manuscript whenever people came to call. Harriet Martineau, later famous for her work on political economy, recalled that in 1820 when she was eighteen and began to have ambitions to write, she did not even dare, like Austen, to use the family parlor; she wrote in her own room in the very early morning and late at night so that at first no one in her family knew what she was up to.

Austen and Martineau dared to write and publish what they wrote, but one cannot help wondering how many women did not dare to write at all, or having written, were too timid to publish their efforts. We do know that Fanny Mendelssohn, the sister of Felix, was a talented composer in her own right, but in deference to her parents and probably her own desire for conformity, she did not publish her compositions; Felix published them under his own name. It was not that Felix wanted to steal from her. On the contrary. In 1842 when he was received by Queen Victoria in Buckingham Palace and the Queen sang what she thought was one of his songs, he was proud to reveal his sister Fanny had written it. But both Felix and Fanny agreed with the convention that it was improper for a woman to make a public display of her talent.

So unseemly was it for women to display mental capacity of any kind that when they took pen in hand to write a letter they practically obliterated what they wrote. According to Ida Husted Harper, a nineteenth-century journalist, women cultivated "infinitesimal characters, it being considered unladylike to write a large hand." The publisher of Charles Egbert Craddock never doubted his author was a man because of the bold, heavy and clear handwriting of Craddock's manuscripts.

The Seed Is a Drop of the Brain

When learned women are laughed at, when female authors write in secret and when women's handwriting becomes almost a mode of non-communication, we are in the presence of people frightened because a taboo is being violated.

But when Charles Lamb railed at female authors, he did not realize he was like a savage horror-struck at seeing a woman enter the male secret house, that is, he did not realize he was upset merely because women were doing what the culture forbade them to do; he thought learned women were violations of nature, freaks. The nineteenth century was the era of mankind's sexual Copernican revolution. Just as sixteenth-century theologians cried "Sacrilege!" when they were told the earth was not the center of the universe, so nineteenth-century men and women cried "Impossible!" when they were presented with evidence that the male sex was not the center of the mental universe. For most of man's history it had been believed that the capacity for learning and mental creativity was unique to men. The contemporary writer Norman Mailer once said he wrote with his penis; in the past the exclusively male instrument was the head; what was perched on woman's neck was merely a dummy. Therefore, when a woman demonstrated she had a head, it was as disconcerting as a female impersonator exposing his penis. People felt sexually stunned; they were confused by the phenomenon of learned women, for hadn't God and physiology always taught that women did not have heads?

Woman officially lost her head in Judeo-Christian cultures in Genesis 3, interestingly enough for trying to acquire knowledge, for which sin God decided a woman's head was good for nothing since it only got man into trouble. God consequently decreed that Adam should rule over Woman, that Man should be the head in the body politic of marriage, or as St Paul later put it: "the husband is the head of the wife," "the head of every man is Christ; and the head of the woman is the man." Paul also said that man did not have to cover his head in church because "he is the image and glory of God," but that woman did have to and also had to cover her head at all times by wearing her hair long because she was not created in the image of God.

Paul's belief that God had given women defective heads was reinforced by the physiological theories of his time. In *The Origins of European Thought* (1951) Richard Onians amassed considerable evidence that in early civilizations men's heads were believed to contain the source of life, a belief that is seen in the etymology of words that describe the head or its functions. Dura mater and pia mater (membranes covering the brain) literally mean hard and soft mother and derive from the ancient physiological belief that men's brains had the capacity to give life. Genius, according to Onians, originally meant "the spirit in the head," the power of the head to generate. Similarly, cerebrum probably derived from ceres, meaning grain, seed. What we call brains was regarded as congealed seed (semen) that traveled down the body inside the spinal column and collected in the testicles where it waited to be discharged by the penis. As a later Pythagorean taught: "the seed is a drop of the brain." Since women had neither the casks nor the spiggot for drawing off the head's life matter, it was logical to conclude that women had no seed = life in their heads, which was why Aristotle held that a child's soul derived only from the father.

The life matter in men's heads was not only the source of the life or soul of the new being, it was also the source of all other forms of creative life, like thinking. Plato could not decide whether women should be classified among rational creatures or brute beasts because he doubted that women had the physical matter in their heads that made one capable of reason or creative thought. Because men's heads contained the stuff of life, men were able to conceive their ideas, poems, books, paintings and other creative productions, to have, as it were, mental babies, an analogy men have been fond of. Socrates, for one, compared himself to a midwife who helped men's brains give birth to their ideas. Francis Bacon equated the "images" created by men's minds with the images (copies of themselves) created by men's bodies. When Robert Schumann finished composing *The Spring Symphony,* he said he felt "like a young wife just delivered of a child—so light, so happy, and yet so ill and weak." Many twentieth-century writers still call their books their babies and sometimes complain, after having delivered one into the world, they are suffering from postpartum depression.

So far as was understood, the head was the organ men had for mental creation, whereas the womb was the organ women had for physical creation. It was a matter of either/or. A person had either a head or a womb, and heads were male and wombs were female. As schoolmaster Bartle said in George Eliot's *Adam Bede* (1859), women have "no head-pieces to nourish, and so their food all runs either to fat or to brats." Or as George Moore more elegantly put it in *Confessions of a Young Man* (1888), "A male figure rises to the head, and is a symbol of the intelligence; a woman's figure sinks to the inferior parts of the body, and is expressive of generation." The two ways of creation—mental and physical, head and womb—were believed to differentiate man from woman as much as penis and vagina.

If that were the case, wouldn't it be as much against the laws of nature for a woman to have a mental creation as it would be for a man to have a baby? Just as a man who had a baby could no longer be regarded as a man, so a woman with brains could no longer be regarded as a woman. In the last quarter of the nineteenth century it was fashionable to call women who went to college "hermaphrodites in mind." Margaret Fuller noted in 1845 that whenever a woman gave evidence of "creative genius," it was said of her, "She has a masculine mind." But not only was a learned woman's mind unsexed, so was her body; again it was either/or. Because she had a man's head, it seemed impossible for her to have a womanly procreative body. In 1873 a Dr Edward Clarke of Boston explained in *Sex and Education* that when women studied, the blood needed for menstruation went to their heads and they therefore suffered from "aborted ovarian development." Or as Nietzsche diagnosed in *Beyond Good and Evil* (1886), "When a woman inclines to learning, there is usually something wrong with her sex apparatus."

A learned woman was a sexual anomaly, for the learned sex, physiologically, was supposed to be male. Why then did women have heads at all? For beauty. That beauty in women was the opposite of or a compensation for their having nothing inside their heads was a belief that went at least as far back as Anacreon who, about 500 BC, explained that nature, having given speed to hares, flying to birds and understanding to men, had nothing left to give to women except beauty. In 1837 Alexander Walker in his discourse on *Beauty; Illustrated Chiefly by an Analysis and Classification of Beauty in Woman* explained that the beautiful woman's head was small because ideally women did not have much brains; "the mental system in the female," he asserted, "ought to be subordinate to the vital . . . sensibility should exceed reasoning power." In 1859 George Eliot's husband described their pug dog as "stupid as a beauty," a phrase comparable to our "dumb blonde," both of which continue the old belief that beauty and brains are opposites, like soft and hard. "No woman is a genius; women are a decorative sex," declared Oscar Wilde. Women's heads, like Keats' Grecian urn, were hollow *objets d'art.*

Prehistoric statues used to depict women with huge wombs and button heads. Civilized man was no different. "Woman has the form of an angel . . . and the mind of an ass," was an old German proverb. That women had the mental capacity of animals was taken for granted. "A very little wit is valued in a woman, as we are pleased with a few words spoken plain by a parrot," said Jonathan Swift in 1706. Samuel Johnson's comparison of a learned woman to an animal is famous: "A woman preaching is like a dog walking on his hind legs. It is not done well; but you are surprised to find it done at all." When women were not compared to animals they were compared to children and the mentally retarded. "Children, women and the stupid," said Maimonides in the twelfth century, "possess no wisdom, no philosophical principles, and no theoretical morality." Lord Chesterfield advised his son: "Women are only children of a larger growth. They have an entertaining tattle" but "no solid reasoning." Women "cannot reason wrong," maintained Hazlitt, "for they do not reason at all." A Mr T. Cooke in his *The Science of Physiognomy* (1870) was convinced that whereas a straight forehead indicated profundity in men, in women "it cannot indicate a quality which they neither have nor need." In 1864 at the time of the Schools Enquiry Commission in England, James Bryce felt that "The notion that women have minds as cultivable, and as well worth cultivating, as men's minds, is still regarded by the ordinary British parent as an offensive, not to say revolutionary, paradox."

Silent, as a Lady Ought to Be

In order not to be confounded by any evidence of mind in woman, men had for centuries enjoined women to be silent. St Paul had commanded women "to keep silence in the churches: for it is not permitted unto them to speak." Paul had also commanded women "to be in silence" when they disagreed with a man, for woman must not "usurp authority over the man." When Paul was not cited to keep women quiet, men tried flattery, telling women they looked more beautiful mute. "Silence gives the proper grace to women," said Euripides and "Silence is the best ornament of a woman" was a seventeenth-century proverb. Silence used to be listed as a wifely virtue in Elizabethan marriage manuals, and in Ben Jonson's 1609 comedy *Epicoene* the hero searched for an ideal wife, a "silent woman." "In large and mixed companies she is unusually silent, as a lady ought to be," said John Adams in 1775 in praise of Dorothy Hancock.

Not only was the silent woman praised, the unsilent woman was reviled. Fishwife, shrew, termagant, virago were words of censure invented by men for the woman who talked up, talked back or talked too loudly. And bad names were not a woman's only punishment. Instruments of torture were devised that literally shut her mouth. One was the ducking stool, a punishment for "common scolds," who were always women; "brawling wives" and "furious wenches" were tied to a stool at the end of a long board and ducked in a pool until they shut up. Gags were also used. In New England a cleft stick was slipped over an unquiet tongue, and in England a brank or scold's bridle was locked on the head. The brank, which was still in use in the seventeenth century, was an iron head cage with a sharpened or spiked bit that was inserted into a talkative woman's mouth so that she had to hold her tongue on pain of cutting it.

Such silencers were of course for lower class women. For women in higher classes the prime silencer was their non-existent or rudimentary education. Man having concluded that women's heads were strictly ornamental, and God having decreed that "the head of the woman is the man," it was unnecessary besides being sacrilegious to educate them. It was, moreover, dangerous for women. In the seventeenth century, when Ann Hopkins, wife of the Governor of Connecticut, went mad, John Winthrop had no doubt that her madness resulted from her "giving herself wholly to reading and writing." She should have attended to what belongs to women—"household affairs"—and not meddled "in such things as are proper for men whose minds are stronger." In the late eighteenth century when the mathematician Mary Somerville was a girl, she was discovered studying geometry and her mother was warned to put a stop to it "or we shall have Mary in a strait jacket one of these days." Learning could not only destroy a woman's mind, it could destroy the state. Sylvain Maréchal, convinced that the French Revolution had in part been caused by educated women demanding equal rights, in 1801 drew up for Napoleon a *Plan for a Law prohibiting the Alphabet to Women,* and in Maréchal's plan for an ideal society women were illiterate. A few days after an 1850 Woman's Rights Convention, *The Orthodox Puritan Recorder* quoted with approval an old Arabian proverb: "When a hen crows like a cock, it is time to cut her head off."

There were not many hens who tried to crow like cocks, that is, there were not many women who pursued learning because to do so called one's sex into doubt. Stupidity, like a hairless face, early became a female secondary sexual characteristic. To be a woman one had to be or appear to be dumb. "No dress or garment is less becoming to a woman than a show of intelligence," said Martin Luther, with which Mary Wortley Montagu in 1753 in part agreed; she hoped her granddaughter would get a good education but that she would "conceal whatever Learning she attains, with as much solicitude as she would hide crookedness or lameness." For a learned woman was thought to be a defective woman. The father of Emilie du Châtelet (the interpreter of Newton) despaired of her marrying because he believed "no great lord will marry a woman who is seen reading every day." When John Adams discovered his wife was teaching their daughter classical languages, he was deeply upset. "It is scarcely reputable," he counseled his daughter "for young ladies to understand Latin and Greek." Scarcely reputable in the same sense it was scarcely reputable in the 1950s for men to have long hair. A woman who was a woman was not long on learning. There were women who deliberately kept themselves ignorant in order to preserve their femininity. In 1803 Sydney Owenson wrote to a friend that she had dropped the study of chemistry "lest I should be less the *woman.* Seduced by taste . . . to Greek and Latin, I resisted, lest I should not by a *very woman.*" Owenson also studied music and drawing only as amusements lest she should become "a musical *pedant* or a masculine *artist.*" Sydney Owenson was not being sarcastic; she was serious. A true woman kept herself ignorant because then it was easier to be "silent, as a lady ought to be."

Ergo, She Is Not a Woman

What Sydney Owenson was afraid of learning was not chemistry or music; she was afraid she would learn she was really a man. At any rate, women who seriously pursued the arts or learning tended to regard themselves as male. In 1687 the dramatist Aphra Behn, in her preface to *The Luckey Chance*, asked for an unbiased hearing for "my masculine Part, the Poet in me." The reason for the great popularity of the anonym "A Lady" was not that women wanted to prove their gentility but their femininity, in spite of the book they had produced. In 1810 when Caroline Howard was sixteen, she ventured to write religious verses that, unbeknownst to her, were printed in a newspaper. "I wept bitterly," she recalled, "and was as alarmed as if I had been detected in man's apparel." The writer Eliza Lynn Linton's autobiography is *The Autobiography of Christopher Kirkland* (1885), that is, she wrote about herself as if she were a man. Female authors used male pseudonyms not only to get an unprejudiced hearing; their male names were a sign they thought of themselves, at least in part, as male. When Aurore Dupin Dudevant adopted the name George Sand, she used the masculine endings of adjectives when she wrote about herself. She wore men's clothes and smoked cigars and had affairs not only because she wanted these male freedoms but because the culture made her feel her creativity had unsexed her; her contemporaries were constantly coming to the conclusion she was not a woman. As Balzac said, "She has all the finer characteristics of a man; *ergo* she is not a woman."

Confronted by a talented woman, it was almost routine for a man to come to the same profound conclusion. Voltaire, who had been introduced to the thought of Newton by his lover, Emilie du Châtelet, said of her: "A woman who has translated and illuminated Newton is, in short, a very great man." In 1859 when Schopenhauer was having his bust done by the sculptor Elisabet Ney, he told her he kept trying "to discover the slightest trace of a moustache. For it becomes daily more impossible for me to believe that you are really a woman." One of the patients of Dr Mary Sherwood once asked her, "Are you a doctor or a lady?" In 1885 when Charles Egbert Craddock traveled to Boston to reveal to her editor she was really Mary Murfree, her editor pointed her out to Edwin Booth by saying, "Mr Craddock is the fellow in the front of the box, with the red rose in his bonnet." Before George Eliot's sex was known, almost everyone was certain she was a man because of the intellectuality of her writing and her easy ability to quote from Latin and Greek. After her sex was known, critics liked to discern in her every line the influence of Herbert Spencer or George Henry Lewes, that is, they wanted to believe that the *fons et origo*, the genius of her books, derived from a man. Moreover, her contemporaries often discussed her as if she were a male in disguise. In 1880 when Bret Harte met her he wrote: "She reminds you continually of a man—a bright, gentle, lovable, philosophical man."

George Eliot reminded people of a man not only because she was intelligent but because she lacked what the culture felt was as essential to femininity as stupidity—beauty. We do not know if Eliot was afflicted with the either/or complex, that is, if she believed she was not beautiful because she was intelligent, but other women had the complex. The popular writer Eliza Lynn Linton once told a friend that "she would gladly renounce any intellectual gifts to which she might lay claim, for the compelling power of great physical beauty." And Charlotte Brontë also confessed to her editor that she would have given "all her genius and all her fame to have been beautiful." If Brontë had not believed that creativity was masculine and beauty feminine and that she was not beautiful (= a woman) because she was a genius, she might not have tried to prove she was a woman by marrying a dull clergyman. The poet Lydia Huntley Sigourney, the novelist Lucas Malet and many other authors and career women wore make up before women generally did, and favored low décolletage and bright colors because these insignia of beauty assured them, and they hoped the public, that in spite of the competent head on their shoulders, they were female. The run-of-the-mill "authoress" may have maintained so thoroughly sentimental a point of view in her writing in order to prove she wrote from the heart, not from the head women were not supposed to have. The financier Hetty Green, known as the richest woman in America, encouraged young girls to pursue careers in business by telling them that "A woman need not lose her femininity because she has a good business head on her shoulders."

But Hetty Green to the contrary notwithstanding, a woman did lose her cultural femininity when she revealed she had a head. She was labeled a "strong-minded woman." Strong-minded, which had formerly been used to praise men who had vigorous and determined minds, began to be used in the 1850s to describe women who, because of their vigorous and determined minds, were not really women. In *Barchester Towers* (1857) Trollope classified Mrs Proudie with English*men* not Englishwomen "on the score of her great strength of mind." A strong-minded woman was the opposite of a true woman, who was weak-minded. A strong-minded woman was a sexual freak who wanted to prove she was the mental equal of men by writing books, becoming a doctor and even voting. "Strong-minded woman" was the nineteenth-century equivalent of "castrating bitch" and illustrates that man's quintessential maleness used to be located in his head not his penis. Male power used to be mental power not penis power.

Hear Me as the Mouthpiece of Mrs Child

How "beheaded," or as we would now say, how castrated men used to feel in the presence of a strong-minded woman is seen by their sense of outraged decency when a woman got up on a platform to speak her mind. And it was mind and mind only in woman that was indecent. For in the 1820s a ballerina could dance in a skimpy costume, an actress could play a man's role in breeches, showing off her legs, an elocutionist could get up on a stage and recite from Shakespeare and not offend men (or for that matter women). But when Fanny Wright, fully clothed, got up on a platform to deliver a lecture, the audience cried, "Shame! Shame!"

So unthinkable was it for a woman to speak her own words on a public platform that in the early 1830s at Abolitionist meetings the female members spoke only by proxy. "Repeatedly," recalled the Reverend Samuel May, "did I spring to the platform crying, 'Hear me as the mouthpiece of Mrs Child, or Mrs Chapman, or Mrs Follen.' " Mrs Child in 1833 had written a book against slavery, but she could not *speak in public* against it. Oberlin College, which had been founded in 1833 to offer "all the instructive privileges" to women as well as men, nevertheless did not instruct women in elocution, then an important subject in the male college curriculum. Women were required to attend the rhetoric classes but only to listen to the men debate. At Commencement, although both men and women were chosen to write essays, only the men were allowed to read theirs; the women's essays were read by a professor. In the 1840s when Catharine Beecher toured New England to set forth her plan for a new and enlarged concept of female education, her brother Thomas had to travel with her, for he read her speech while she sat beside him on the platform.

When Angelina and Sarah Grimké began lecturing against slavery in 1836, they at first lectured only to private gatherings of women. When they did begin to speak to mixed audiences, they so offended propriety that a minister who had agreed to open the meeting with a prayer left immediately thereafter, saying he would "sooner rob a hen-roost than hear women speak in public," by which analogy he revealed he thought women who spoke in public were thieves, stealing a male privilege. Of course, the ministry professed to be offended because women were violating Holy Writ, namely Paul's commandment that women be silent in the churches. In 1837 when the Grimkés were lecturing in Massachusetts, a Pastoral Letter, like a papal bull, was issued against females "who so forgot themselves as to itinerate in the character of public lecturers and teachers." The Reverend Jonathan F. Stearns also published a sermon against the new abomination of women orators, against the immodest, unchristian woman who longs to "hear the shouts of delighted assemblies, applauding her eloquence." Public displays of eloquence, of the head's ability to speak out forcefully, were for men only.

It continued to be indecent for a woman to speak her mind in public. Although most of the members of Temperance societies were women, they were not allowed to speak at meetings, and although two-thirds of school teachers were women, only men spoke at Teachers' Conventions. On August 3, 1853 at the New York State Teachers' Convention when Susan B. Anthony rose and asked to speak, she was the first woman who had dared to do so. The men presiding debated half an hour before deciding to let her speak, a decision that shocked most of the women, many of whom after the meeting whispered loudly near Anthony, "Did you ever see such a disgraceful performance?" "I was never so ashamed of my sex."

The next month at the World's Temperance meeting in New York when the Reverend Antoinette Brown went up to the platform to speak, there were hisses and shouts and then, as she recounted in the November *Una*, "Rev. John Chambers comes forward, stamps with impressive dignity, points the significant finger, and shouts with stentorian emphasis, 'Shame on the woman! Shame on the woman!'" It was as if she were a drunk swilling a pint of whiskey. She had to stand on the platform in the midst of a hullabaloo for an hour and a half and finally was *not* allowed to speak.

As late as 1868 George Francis Train could remark in *The Revolution* (May 28): "Man sits for hours in the concert room to hear a low-necked, bosom-exposed opera singer, but has a holy horror to see on the same stage a high-necked dressed lady lecturer." However, as more and more women dared to defy convention, the public got used to them, and eventually many women took to the lecture circuit and made substantial amounts of money. Yet as late as 1899 the Memphis *Scimitar* described Susan B. Anthony, then almost eighty and lecturing again after an illness, as returning "to the old warpath with a pair of sound lungs and a healthy and well-developed desire to see her name in print, and re-engages in the crusade against her hideous former foe, the bifurcated beast, the braggart brute . . . Man. Madly she snatches the veil from the face of her maidenly reserve." Examined closely, these words reveal the old male taunt, that Susan B. Anthony was a man, or to be exact, half a man, because the newspaper did concede that Anthony was not a "bifurcated beast." But aside from her not having legs to speak of, wasn't she, like men, engaged in war? wasn't she, like men, a "braggart" who loved to see her name in print? for which fame and glory was she not willing to appear boldly before the public and madly snatch the veil from her face, thereby revealing she had that male organ—a head?

The Same Intellectual Constitution as Man

In the nineteenth century mankind began to discover that, unfair as it might seem, women not only could have babies, they could also create with their minds, that women's heads were not hollow *objets d'art* but as filled with brains as men's. Of course men tried to deny that. One of their most effective methods was to continue to deny women access to higher education and entrance to medical and other professional schools. For whenever a woman proved she had enough brains to get a First in Greek or to be a doctor or a lawyer, the men in these professions felt sexually threatened. In 1853 when Susan B. Anthony asked to speak at the New York Teachers' Convention, the question under discussion was: "Why the profession of teacher is not respected as that of lawyer, doctor, or minister?" When Anthony was finally allowed to speak, her answer was "that so long as society says woman has not brains enough to be a doctor, lawyer, or minister, but has plenty to be a teacher, every man of you who condescends to teach tacitly admits before all Israel and the sun that he has no more brains than a woman."

To preserve their sense of sexual superiority, not only did men try to prevent women from entering the professions, the Dr Clarkes of the world continued to maintain that menstruation drained women's brains. As late as 1912 Sir Almwroth Wright MD in a letter to the London *Times* asserted that "No doctor can ever lose sight of the fact that the mind of a woman is always threatened with danger from the reverberations of her physiological emergencies." But such danger occurred only once a month; a stronger argument was needed. In 1887 Dr William A. Hammond in *Popular Science Monthly* argued that because women's brains were smaller than men's the sexes could never be equal. He was answered the following year by Helen Hamilton Gardener who in "Sex in Brain" pointed out, among other things, that the relationship between brain size and intellectual capacity in human beings had not yet been established. What was eventually established was that the key relationship was between size of body and size of brain and that women's brains were larger than men's relative to their body size. Whereupon scientists hurriedly concluded that in human beings there was indeed no relationship between size of brain and intellectual capacity and proceeded to study other sex differences in brain in order to prove that *qualitatively* men's brains were better. And Freud, living at a time when women were proving their heads were no different from men's, substituted the penis for the head as the organ of male superiority, an organ women could never prove they had.

Not all men tried to disparage women's brains or relocate the source of male supremacy. The practitioners of phrenology, the theory that a person's mental and moral qualities were revealed by the shape of his head, were important in establishing that women did indeed have heads. Although phrenologists almost always found the traditional female traits in women's heads—large amounts of Veneration, Selflessness and Affection, and small amounts of Sexual Passion, Combativeness and Reasoning Power—phrenologists never doubted women had heads whose bumps warranted careful examination. More important, some of them, like Orson Fowler, believed that in the future women's heads would be the equals of men's because "the [mental] organs can be enlarged" by use. A woman could therefore increase her bump of Reasoning Power by mental gymnastics. The advice was sound whether or not one believed that the bumps on a person's head changed as his mental organs developed. Although phrenology is now considered quackery, for several decades it was as popular and as respected as Freudianism is today and it may have been responsible for women regarding their heads not as predetermined and unchangeable entities but as capable of growth. When Johann Spurzheim, a popularizer of phrenology, visited America in 1832, he told Sarah Josepha Hale that "Excepting Christianity, Phrenology will do more to elevate woman than any other system has ever done. It gives her a participation in the labors of the mind."

But long before phrenology became popular, individual women were discovering their heads were, even as God had given them, the equals of men's. In 1800 twelve-year-old Emma Hart taught herself geometry, mastering proposition after proposition, amazed to discover a female brain could learn mathematics; later as Emma Willard she founded a school whose purpose was to teach girls subjects they had been thought incapable of learning. In the late 1850s when Jane Ellen Harrison was a little girl, she "secretly possessed herself of a Greek grammar" and although an aunt admonished her that Greek would never help her keep house, she did not desist and eventually became a Greek scholar and lecturer at Cambridge. In 1859 when Lucy Hobbs was twenty-six, although she was told she had "forgotten her womanhood," she went from dentist to dentist in Cleveland, Ohio trying to be accepted as an apprentice, for, as she later recalled, she wanted to "enter a profession where she could earn her bread, not alone by the sweat of her brow, but by the use of her brain also." She persisted and in 1866 became the first woman to be awarded a degree in dentistry. It was women like these, women who proved their heads were as capable as men's, who slowly brought about a change in mankind's thinking. Vassar Female College opened its doors in 1865, according to Matthew Vassar, because "It occurred to me that woman, having received from her Creator the same intellectual constitution as man, has the same right as man to intellectual culture and development." But the Creator had rarely before been accused of giving women the same intellectual constitution as men; Vassar's radical idea did not come to him from God or the Bible or from out of the blue; it came to him from women, the women who, in spite of ridicule, name-calling and the stubborn opposition of medical boards, judges and school administrators, were then demonstrating that women did indeed have heads.

Getting ahead for a nineteenth-century woman meant getting a head. It was when women began to understand that heads were not a male secondary sexual characteristic, that it was not unfeminine to have a head, that women began to go to college, enter the professions and speak in public. And once women became unashamed of having heads, as might have been expected, their voices became louder. In 1899 Frances A. Griffin of Alabama, speaking at the National American Suffrage Convention in Michigan, recalled: "Thirty-five years ago I read a graduating essay. I knew I was doing an unwomanly thing, and in order to preserve it I whispered the whole essay. I've quit that. Since I made up my mind to be heard, I have been heard."

Actresses had had no such psychological difficulty in making themselves heard. From the 1660s an actress could walk on stage and let her voice carry from pit to balcony and the public was upset only if she could not be heard. But actresses were, after all, merely the beautiful mouthpieces of male writers; they were not speaking their own mind. The more a woman spoke her own mind and the more publicly she did so, the greater was her difficulty in gaining social acceptance. It took longer for authors than actresses to be accepted by the public because they used the head women were not supposed to have. But because the act of writing is done in private, because authors for long hid behind the screen of an anonym or pseudonym, because the majority focused their talents on so-called women's topics—family life, love and children—the profession of author eventually came to be thought of as not unwomanly. It was the Susan B. Anthonys lecturing, the Myra Bradwells practicing law, the Elizabeth Blackwells practicing medicine who were the Medusa heads of the nineteenth century, monsters whom the public taunted with the cry, "Unsexed! Strong-minded! Hermaphrodite!" These women were reviled because their professions required them to integrate themselves into the male workaday world, to go to school with men, to practice with men. It was the women who demonstrated their intelligence in the flesh and blood presence of men who had the greatest difficulty winning a place in a society that wanted to go on believing only men had heads, that still wanted women, as Emma Goldman was to say, to "keep their mouths shut and their wombs open."

An ad that appeared frequently in *The New Yorker* in the 1970s. (Reproduced by permission of The Silent Woman Restaurant)

7

THE QUIET NAME OF WIFE

Married and Faded into the Mists

On December 23, 1842 in London Adelaide Kemble was singing *Norma* and a member of the audience wrote of that performance: "When I saw that grace and beauty and rare union of gifts, when I heard the applause break out simultaneously from all those human beings whose emotions she was swaying at will, my heart sank; this beautiful piece of art (for such it is now, and very near perfection) would be seen no more! If she does not find happiness what will atone to her for all this that she has left? It is a fearful risk. God help us all!"

Adelaide Kemble was singing *Norma* for the last time; after a brilliantly successful career she was, at the age of twenty-eight, retiring from the stage to marry. The person in the audience feeling the tragedy of her wasted talent was her sister Fanny Kemble Butler, who had herself been a famous actress and who had also given up her career when she married. There is also a record of one of her last performances. In 1834 the New York socialite Philip Hone saw Fanny Kemble play a part "with the most affecting pathos," and he then noted in his diary: "Probably her last engagement, if the report be true that she is married, or about to be married, to Mr Pierce Butler of Philadelphia." Fanny was already married and had returned to New York to finish an engagement before bidding farewell to the stage. Four years later Philip Hone refers to her in his diary as "Mrs Butler, the late Fanny Kemble," as if Fanny Kemble were dead, and in a sense she was.

The vast majority of women who started careers "married and faded into the mists," as Ishbel Ross said of Sally Joy, one of the early female reporters discussed in her *Ladies of the Press*. When Adelaide Kemble became Mrs Edward Sartoris, when Fanny Kemble became Mrs Pierce Butler, when Sally Joy became Mrs Whoeverhewas (her husband's name is unknown), they disappeared, or were supposed to disappear, into wifehood. Marriage meant the end of a woman's career and had meant the end of it as far back as she was allowed to have a career in which she could become famous. In 521 AD Byzantine singers, dancers and mimes, by an edict of Justinian, were permitted to become the legal wives of Roman citizens *if* they renounced their professions. Straight through the nineteenth century actresses and other theatrical performers as a general rule left the stage when they married. They continued their careers only if their husbands were actors or were in some other way connected with the theater. Thus Ellen Tree continued acting after her marriage to the actor Charles Kean, but when Harriet Mellon married the rich banker Thomas Coutts she gave up her career. Eliza Vestris combined a career with marriages to two actors, and when Mary Ann Dyke married the actor John Duff she continued acting, but in 1836 when she married a lawyer she renounced the stage (except for an occasional charity performance). In 1849 Abigail Hutchinson, who with her brothers had a highly popular singing ensemble, married a stockbroker, Ludlow Patton, and in obedience to her husband's wishes, ended her public career. In 1854 when the famous actress and playwright Anna Cora Mowatt married William F. Ritchie, who was the editor of a newspaper, it was taken for granted she would stop acting. As late as 1889 an actress's stage career could be cut short by marriage; in that year Emma Sheridan, the leading lady at the Boston Museum theater, married Alfred Brooks Fry, an engineer, and took up the more retiring career of writer.

But there were many husbands who objected to this less exhibitionistic career and bade their wives lay down their pens. When Lydia Huntley married Charles Sigourney in 1819 she continued writing for a while, publishing a serial, *The Square Table,* needless to say, anonymously. But when her identity was in danger of being discovered, in obedience to Mr Sigourney's wishes, she not only gave up that project but forsook her career as a writer. "Can it be, That I must bid adieu to thee?" she asked her Muse. "Oh! dearer far than words can tell, My wild, my mountain-harp—*farewell*!" Having bade farewell to her Muse, she prepared to "fill the station" her husband's "generosity" had elevated her to: she was a poor schoolteacher and he a well-to-do businessman. Cornelia Walter, for five years the editor of the *Boston Transcript*, married William Richards in 1847 and as a matter of course gave up her editorship, devoting herself to her husband and children. Harriet Farley, a former worker in a textile mill in Lowell, Massachusetts and later editor of the *Lowell Offering* (the mill girls' magazine), married John Donlevy in 1854 and since her husband disapproved of wives working, she gave up writing and faded into obscurity.

Actresses, writers, sculptors, dentists, professors, deans gave up their careers when they married. Vinnie Ream, the first woman to receive a commission for sculpture from the United States government and whose statue of Lincoln is in the Capitol Rotunda, married Richard Hoxie in 1878 and in deference to his wishes, gave up her career; she was only thirty-one. She did not return to sculpture for almost thirty years although, as she confessed in 1893, sculpturing "has never lost any of its charms, and I can not see a block of marble or the modeling clay without a quicker throb of the heart." She devoted herself to charities, especially in aid to the blind, undoubtedly the unconscious empathy of one whose artistic eyes had been virtually blinded by social custom. In 1883 when Helen Hiscock, a professor at Vassar College, married a fellow professor, Truman Jay Backus, it was of course Helen who retired from the faculty. Olga Neyman in 1886 received her DDS from the Pennsylvania College of Dental Surgery, but she practiced only seven years; in 1893 when she became Mrs Carl Glucksmann she gave up her practice, occupying her time with one daughter and women's clubs. Even the president of Wellesley College, Alice Freeman, when in 1887 she married Professor George Herbert Palmer, retired. As she later wrote:

> At a crisis hour
> Of strength and struggle on the heights of life
> He came, and bidding me abandon power,
> Called me to take the quiet name of wife.

The first dean of Barnard College, Emily Smith, did succeed in getting the trustees to allow her to continue as dean when she married George Putnam in 1899, but as soon as she became pregnant she retired, for many years devoting her energies to furthering her husband's publishing career.

"I would not object to marriage, if it were not that women throw away every plan and purpose of their own life, to conform to the plans and purposes of the man's life," wrote Susan B. Anthony in 1888 when she learned that her chief assistant in suffrage work was engaged to be married. Anthony's assistant, Rachel Foster, worked even harder for suffrage after she became Mrs Avery, but she was unusual. Most women, as Adah Isaacs Menken once observed, "sink into nonentities after this epoch in their existences." Whether a woman was a grade-school teacher or a professor, she gave up her job when she married and conformed to the plans and purposes of her husband's life. It ought in fairness to be said that most women did not have a job even as prestigious as grade-school teacher to give up. The average working woman had a low-paying routine job with no prospect of advancement and was therefore sensibly happy to leave it and become Mrs Herhusband. Indeed, even most actresses, singers and dancers, who worked hard for a small living and modest fame, were probably wise to retire into the supported role of housewife and mother and abandon the identity of Miss Rosebud Aspiranti to become Mrs Junior Accountant.

There were, nevertheless, women who wanted to continue working after marriage. But society disapproved and therefore it began to be unofficial and then official policy to fire a woman when she married. Most of the school board regulations requiring women teachers to resign upon marriage originated in the nineteenth century. In the early 1860s women employed as clerks in the Treasury Department were routinely discharged when they married, under the express order of the then Secretary of the Treasury Salmon P. Chase. Chase strongly believed in women's right to vote, but he just as strongly believed no woman should work who had a man to support her. A subordinate, F. E. Spinner, felt otherwise and when a female clerk was discharged because she married, he became furious: "Dammit, if Chase wants my resignation he can have it but he shant discharge one of my clerks. A 1400 dollar man couldnt do the work she does for 900." The girl was not discharged, but she was an exception to what became an almost universal rule in most government agencies in America and England. Thus when May Abraham, one of the first Women Inspectors of Factories under the Home Office, married in the mid 1890s, she had to resign. Even if she had not been forced to, pregnancy would have made her do so voluntarily. A woman visibly pregnant was supposed for decency's sake to stay in seclusion, and the care of young children was still assumed to be the sole responsibility of the mother.

And yet it was not pregnancy nor the practical difficulties of combining a job with marriage that made most wives give up their work. Indeed, in the nineteenth century when servants were cheap and plentiful and when a mother was not considered derelict who consigned the care of her children to a nursemaid or nanny, it was easier than it was to be in the mid twentieth century for a woman to combine a career with marriage. The fundamental difficulties were not practical; they were psychological and affected the president of Wellesley as much as the local milliner.

Is it "woman's real, true nature always to abnegate herself?" Susan B. Anthony asked when she lamented woman's propensity to throw away her own plans and conform to those of her husband. The nineteenth century certainly believed that was woman's true nature; contemporary diaries, letters and literature honored the wife who was self-effacing, who had no ambitions for herself but only for her husband and children. "Woman's power comes through a self-sacrificing spirit ready to offer up all her hopes upon the shrine of her husband's wishes," asserted an Indiana legislator in 1836 when he was speaking against a married woman's property bill. Dr Elizabeth Blackwell did not of course think woman's "self-sacrificing spirit" was the source of her power, but she knew it was an unhappy fact of life. "In all human relations," Dr Blackwell wrote to a friend in 1860, "the woman has to yield, to modify her individuality—the strong personality of even the best husbands and children compels some daily sacrifice of self." Whether or not women had an innate tendency to abnegate themselves made no difference, for as John Stuart Mill observed in *The Subjection of Women* (1869), they were "universally taught that they are born and created for self-sacrifice."

Becoming educated and pursuing a career are fundamentally self-interested because they require the development of self; therefore women with careers must have felt radically unfeminine since they were developing themselves not sacrificing their lives for others. Moreover, as we have seen, any woman who got an education felt she had also acquired the head true women were not supposed to have. No wonder so many women salvaged their sexual identity by giving up their careers when they married, sacrificing their own interests to their husband's, making him the one head in the household.

A female psychology of self-abnegation implies a male psychology of self-assertion. Women gave up their careers not only to satisfy their own culturally developed desire for self-abnegation but their husband's culturally developed desire for mastery. "The generality of the male sex cannot yet tolerate the idea of living with an equal," said John Stuart Mill. Nor could the generality of the female sex tolerate the idea of living with an equal. In Trollope's *The Duke's Children* (1880) Lady Mabel Grex is reluctant to marry Lord Silverbridge because "I could never feel him to be my superior. That is what a wife ought in truth to feel." The nineteenth-century women who gave up their careers were trying to feel what a wife ought to feel, that her husband was her superior. When an actress left the stage and quietly stayed at home tending her husband, she was re-establishing the proper male-female imbalance. The idea of marriage between equals was as disturbing to nineteenth-century men and women as marriage between homosexuals is to us.

Mr Woman

The times were changing. Although ninety-five percent and more of the women who started careers gave them up when they married, a tiny minority did not and as the century passed it became increasingly possible for a man to find himself married to a woman who was known to the world as his equal if not his superior. And how such husbands suffered! For could any man who was a man bear to have his wife bask in the limelight while he waited in the wings?

Robert Schumann certainly could not. He was relatively unknown when he married Clara Wieck, whereas she was a famous pianist. She could put a K.k. after her name, which meant she had been made a Kammervirtuosin, an imperial court pianist. She had also been elected an honorary member of the Gesellschaft der Musikfreunde and in 1838 had been ranked third among the four greatest piano virtuosos of her time. Shortly before their marriage Schumann was grateful to be awarded an honorary doctorate to balance Clara's K.k. But after marriage Schumann was soon able to feel properly superior; eight pregnancies in fourteen years prevented Clara from giving many concerts. Moreover, in the Schumann household Robert's career came first, and since the sound of Clara practicing disturbed Robert's composing, Clara practiced little. Nevertheless, in between pregnancies she did give concerts and Robert acutely resented the acclaim she received. After a concert in 1842 only Clara received an invitation to court and Robert was filled with anger and jealousy: "The thought of my undignified position in such cases, prevented me from feeling any pleasure." When Robert went with her on concert tours he was constantly in the mortifying position of being thought of as merely the husband of a famous woman; in Vienna a gentleman, after learning he was the husband of the brilliant Clara Schumann, asked him if he happened to be musical too. Even when they both performed, Clara tended to steal the show. In 1851 Robert was appointed conductor of the Düsseldorf Orchestra, and after his debut, at which Clara played a piano concerto from memory, the host toasted only Clara; Robert's whole evening was of course ruined. Robert also fiercely resented anyone suggesting that Clara's performances of his compositions at her concerts in any way helped his career. Clara's biographer, Berthold Litzmann, felt Robert would have preferred Clara to have given up her career entirely.

When Pierce Butler married Fanny Kemble he thought she had given up her career, and she had in fact given up acting. But to his great horror he discovered she intended to embark on another career. Fanny had always thought writing a higher art than acting and she wanted to begin her new career by publishing the journal of her theatrical tour in America. Butler objected; he did not wish to have a wife who was a professional writer; had she ceased being the famous Fanny Kemble only to become the famous Fanny Butler? Despite his disapproval Fanny persisted and even had the temerity to be angry when he corrected her unladylike style and cut out sections he felt would offend the public. The journal was published, after which the famous Fanny Kemble tried to be plain Mrs Butler. But her superiority to her husband, even when she was not acting or writing, was too apparent to both of them. They separated, yet even then Butler tried to keep her in retirement by permitting her to see their two children only so long as she did not return to the stage or publish anything he had not approved. When they finally divorced, it was Butler who did not want her to continue using his name. She therefore became Mrs Fanny Kemble and spared Butler the indignity of being known as the ex-husband of a famous woman because Fanny Kemble again became famous for her dramatic readings from Shakespeare.

The husband of Lydia Huntley Sigourney was finally not spared the humiliation of being known as the husband of a famous wife. For despite Mr Sigourney's disapproval, despite her vow to give up writing, despite three stepchildren and two of her own, Lydia Sigourney's poetical self rebelled against the constraints of wifely nothingness. She continued to print poems in the Hartford papers under the initial "H," the first letter of her own surname, and she eventually began to write books that were sent into the world it goes without saying anonymously but also so secretly that Mr Sigourney did not know she was continuing to write; proofs were sent to her friends. When in 1830 her editor urged her to put her name to her work because it would increase sales, she explained that since it was her "duty to conciliate her husband" and since he had a "decided aversion" to having a wife who wrote books, her publishing under the name Lydia Huntley Sigourney would "create violent displeasure." But in 1833, when the "Lady" who had just published *Letters to Young Ladies* was discovered to be Mrs Sigourney, she, after the proper protestations of modesty, allowed her name to be put on later editions, and her husband was forced to submit to the humiliation of having his wife well-known because he was in financial difficulties and his wife's writing had become their chief source of income. Instead of having a wife who "followed through life in the orbit to which her husband draws her," as all the marriage manuals said was proper and natural, Mr Sigourney had been drawn into his wife's orbit and become the satellite of her star. And a star she was; she became "the most famous of the female bards of her country," whereas her husband became, as it were, Mr Lydia Huntley Sigourney.

The insult of being known as Mr Woman could infuriate a man even after his wife's death. Charlotte Brontë died in 1855, but five years later her husband, the Reverend Arthur Nicholls, was still resentful of her fame. Elizabeth Gaskell visited Charlotte's father in 1860 and noted that Nicholls "seems to have even a greater aversion than formerly to any strangers visiting his wife's grave; or, indeed, to any reverence paid to her memory, even by those who knew and loved her for her own sake. He refused to christen Mr Greenwood's last child when he heard that it was to be named 'Brontë' after her." The child remained unchristened for six months until Charlotte's father, who was a clergyman, secretly christened it. "When Mr Nicholls came upon its name upon the register book . . . he stormed and stamped."

The Reverend Mr Nicholl's raging jealousy was extreme, but every famous wife had to be mindful of the volcano of hurt pride smoldering in her husband. Lydia Huntley Sigourney once wrote to Almira Hart Lincoln Phelps about the problem of female fame versus husbands, and Mrs Phelps replied: "There is great danger that injustice may be done in the public mind to a gentleman when his wife makes herself conspicuous. We must do all we can to prevent this." But how could a famous wife make herself less conspicuous? She could school herself in humility, as Clara Schumann did, who again and again in her diary reminded herself that Robert's career was more important than her own, that she did not have the qualities necessary for "great success in the world" but that Robert did and that she must live for him alone. A wife could also make public protestations of her inferiority to her husband. When in 1841 Lydia Maria Child was appointed editor of the *National Anti-Slavery Standard*, in her first editorial she performed the wifely ritual of making herself small: "Had Mr Child's business made it possible for him to remove to New York, his experience in editing, his close observations of public affairs, and the general character of his mind, would have made it better for the cause to have him for a resident, and myself for an assistant editor."

Famous women married to ordinary men felt compelled to aggrandize their husbands and belittle themselves. After Jenny Lind married her accompanist Otto Goldschmidt, she was furious when he was dubbed "The Prince Consort of Song" and wanted to give up her famous name and be called Madame Goldschmidt. She tried to equalize their careers; in 1853 she agreed to sing at the Düsseldorf Festival only if her husband was given the job of conductor. At home she ostentatiously treated him as lord and master. The great Sarah Bernhardt tried to have her husband Jacques Damala, notwithstanding his lack of ability, cast as her leading man; failing that she took over a theater for him. After a play in which they both had roles, when she was once being congratulated for an outstanding performance, she noticed her husband's jealous face and enthusiastically began praising his great talent. When Julia Marlowe married the second-rate actor Robert Taber, she not only changed her name to Taber, she chose to be in plays in which he could have important parts and she minor ones. The greatest actresses of their time tried to dwindle into wives, and they tried to because their fame caused them as much suffering as it caused their husbands.

There were, however, a few husbands of famous women who managed to be unresentful of their wives' superiority. The husband of Sarah Siddons, a minor actor, seems to have been more pleased by his wife's great success than she was. George Henry Lewes, the husband-in-all-but-law of George Eliot, was not jealous of Eliot's great fame, and her second husband, John Walter Cross, was prepared to devote himself proudly and unselfishly to her career. Although Robert Browning, like Robert Schumann, was undeservedly neglected by the public and had a wife more famous than he was, Browning was not blackly envious. On the contrary, he could sincerely say to his publisher, "I say nothing of my wife's poems and their sale. She is there, as in all else, as high above me as I would have her." What is remarkable is not that Browning was deceived as to the merits of his wife's poetry, his whole century was; what is remarkable is his ability to be genuinely pleased by his wife's superior fame.

There were not many husbands like Robert Browning and George Henry Lewes. Most "Women's Husbands," as Thomas Wentworth Higginson called them in an essay in the September 27, 1873 *Woman's Journal,* believed that although "Any woman is respectable who is commonly mentioned as Mr Such-a-one's wife," "Nothing can make a man respectable who is commonly mentioned as Mrs Such-a-one's husband." Higginson disagreed with that popular prejudice, believing that when "a husband's whole dignity is held to lie in overshadowing his wife, it is only petty despotism in disguise." Higginson understood, however, "that in the existing state of prejudice" it required "moral courage in a man to recognize frankly the greater ability or fame of his wife," but he hoped it would soon "become as easy for a man to recognize with enthusiasm the superior genius of his wife, as for a woman to do the same for her husband."

Higginson had the optimism of the idealist, but his essay is important because it could not have been written one hundred years before. In 1773, or even fifty years later, there were so few women's husbands that that particular sexist prejudice could not have been diagnosed. But by the 1870s, in spite of the prevalent psychology of female self-abnegation, a substantial number of women had got themselves educated and embarked upon careers. In the nineteenth century women succeeded in entering almost every profession they had previously been barred from, becoming doctors, dentists, lawyers, ministers, archaeologists, printers, painters, engineers, mathematicians, astronomers, architects, biologists and so on and so on. And a fair number of these women got married and did *not* disappear into wifehood, thus producing that new phenomenon—the man who stood in danger of being known as Mrs Such-a-one's husband.

8

NOMINAL POLYANDRY

In Shaw's *Mrs Warren's Profession* Mrs Warren's daughter Vivie repudiates her mother. Not because Mrs Warren pulled herself out of poverty by prostitution but because after making a fortune she continued in the business as a procurer and madam, inducing other girls to become prostitutes by glamorizing the life of leechery. Mrs Warren represents the old life style of woman. Her daughter is the new woman who despises the life of female luxury: "I dont want to be worthless," says Vivie. "I shouldnt enjoy trotting about the park to advertize my dressmaker and carriage builder, or being bored at the opera to shew off a shopwindowful of diamonds." Vivie vows she will not be a kept woman, legally or otherwise. She will support herself, and since she has an honors degree in mathematics from Cambridge University, she sets up chambers in London and becomes an actuary.

Shaw's play ends with Vivie eagerly attacking a pile of papers on her desk after having told a young man she will not marry him. But imagine her a few years later, a successful actuary, VIVIEN WARREN in gold letters on her office door, VIVIEN WARREN LTD at the top of her stationery. Having proved her abilities, secure financially, she relaxes a bit and falls in love with an actuary in the office next door. If this likely possibility occurred and Vivie married, it is almost inconceivable that she would have given up her career, but it is almost a certainty that she would have had new stationery made and that the gold letters on her office door would have been scraped off and replaced by, let us say, Vivien Numberman, or perhaps Vivien Warren Numberman. And if Vivie's husband died or if she got divorced and remarried, the gold letters on her office door would again have been scraped off to be replaced by her new surname.

Vivie Warren was a new woman in her attitude toward work, but she undoubtedly would have been an old-fashioned woman in regard to her name, little different from the woman memorialized on a tombstone in Mill River, Massachusetts:

POLLY RHOADES

Died Sept. 7, 1855:
Aged 86 Yr's 5 Mo's
& 3 d's.

Being the widow of 5 husbands.
1st David Rockwell,
2nd Capt. Alpheus Underwood,
3rd Dea. Amos Langdon,
4th Hezekiah G. Butler,
5th James T. Rhoades.

Polly Rockwell Underwood Langdon Butler Rhoades was somewhat unusual in having five husbands, but she was not that unusual. The memorial on the gravestone of another much married woman reads: "Elizabeth Griscom Ross Ashbourn Claypoole," for Betsy Ross, as she is now known, had three husbands. For a woman to have more than one husband, to have two or three, was fairly common. The seventeenth-century woman born as Frances Culpeper was the wife of three Colonial governors: for seventeen years she was Madam Stephens, for eleven years Lady Berkeley, and during the last fifteen years of her life Madam Ludwell. Dorothy Quincy, now best known as the wife of John Hancock, married a second time and died as Madam Scott. The woman born as Betsy Bowen, after having changed her surname to De La Croix and Brown, the names of the men she had liaisons with, succeeded in 1804 in getting a lover to marry her and became Madame Jumel, crowning her nominal life in 1833 by becoming Mrs Aaron Burr.

One could go on and on listing the women who bore at least two different husbands' names in their lifetime. The women had of course not divorced their husbands, for until the second half of the nineteenth century divorce was almost impossible. Polly Rhoades' five husbands died; before the advent of modern medicine, death at a relatively young age was far more common than it is today. Straight through the nineteenth century a woman had two or three husbands chiefly because her husbands died. During the second half of the nineteenth century, when divorce became easier, a woman might bear two or three husbands' names because of a divorce, but that was most unusual. Among nineteenth-century professional women a slightly higher percentage got divorced, but the vast majority, like plain housewives, bore several husbands' names because their husbands died. The chief difference between them and housewives was that every marriage and remarriage meant the loss of their professional identity.

Because we remember these women by the surname of their last husband, it is easy to forget the many name changes to which their careers were subjected. In 1837, under the surname of her first husband, Mary S. Gove (1810-1884) began to lecture to women on anatomy and physiology and in 1842 published her lectures under that name. In 1844 she had established herself as a water-cure physician, was a frequent contributor to the *New York Water-Cure Journal,* and was widely known as a champion of a variety of unpopular causes. She was so well-known she was included in Edgar Allan Poe's review of the *Literati of New York City.* But in 1848 Mary Gove married Thomas Nichols and the well-known Mrs Gove changed her professional identity, continuing her career as Mrs Nichols. Abigail Kelley (1810-1887), one of the first and best known abolitionist lecturers, married at the height of her fame and became Mrs Foster. After having been known as Paulina Wright (1813-1876) for sixteen years, during which she lectured to women on physiology and published many articles, Mrs Wright in 1849 remarried and her surname became Davis. Under the surname of her first husband, Hannah Tracy (1815-1896) became known as a writer, was matron of the (Columbus) Ohio Deaf and Dumb Asylum and was also principal of the female division of the Columbus High School, but in 1852 she remarried and her professional identity was changed to Mrs Cutler. Under the surname of her first husband, Belva Ann McNall (1830-1917) taught for twenty years, was principal of a seminary and later began to study law; in 1868 she remarried and it was as Belva Ann Lockwood, the name of her dentist husband, that she became the first woman admitted to practice before the United States Supreme Court. After having been Lillie Devereux Umsted (1833-1913) for eleven years and publishing two novels under that name, Mrs Umsted remarried and became Mrs Blake, the name under which she established another career as a woman's rights leader. Fanny Jackson (1837-1913), a teacher of Greek, Latin and higher mathematics, and principal of the Institute for Colored Youth in Philadelphia, married in 1881 and changed the name under which she had become well-known to Coppin. May Wright (1844-1920) was a teacher at various schools for six years; in 1872 she married and as Mrs Thompson she taught for eight more years; in 1880 she married again and her surname again changed, this time to Sewall, under which name she at first continued her career as an educator and then became active in the woman's movement. Mary Curran (1844-1920) received her MD in 1878 and then became a botanist distinguished enough to be appointed Curator of the Herbarium of the California Academy of Sciences; in 1889 she married and the surname with which her achievements were associated was changed to Brandegee. Mary Cutler (1855-1921), chief administrator of the New York State Library School, in mid career changed her name to that of the man she happened to marry—

Fairchild. The nurse Isabel Hampton (1860-1910) became superintendent and principal of the Johns Hopkins school of nursing and was largely responsible for establishing uniform nursing standards in the United States, but in 1894 she married and therefore her own accomplishments go under the name of her husband—Robb. Anne Sullivan (1866-1936), the famous teacher of Helen Keller, married in 1905 and therefore goes down in history under her husband's name of Macy. Minnie Rutherford (1868-1946), when she was using the surname of her second husband, became an important Arkansas social reformer and worked nationally for juvenile courts and against child labor; in 1915 she remarried and the celebrated Mrs Rutherford became Mrs Fuller. The general secretary of the Associated Charities of Boston and a member of the Massachusetts Child Labor Committee, Alice Higgins (1870-1920), married in 1913 and became Alice Lothrop. The portrait painter Ellen Emmet (1875-1941), after having major exhibits of her paintings, married in 1911 and changed the established name Emmet to Rand. Helen Sumner (1876-1933), after a long and distinguished career in labor reform and after writing many articles and books on American labor problems, married and at the age of forty-two changed her surname to Woodbury.

Of the women discussed above, only the name changes associated with their careers were noted, but some of them underwent additional changes of name. Minnie Rutherford, for example, was born Minnie Oliver and had changed her name to Scott before she became Rutherford. Belva Ann Lockwood was first Belva Ann Bennett, Hannah Tracy was first Hannah Conant and Mary Curran was originally Mary Layne. To record their names in full such women have to be listed as Minnie Oliver Scott Rutherford Fuller or Belva Ann Bennett McNall Lockwood. The famous revivalist Aimee Semple McPherson's full name was Aimee Kennedy (birth name), Semple (husband number one), McPherson (husband number two), Hutton (husband number three). The famous Carry Nation was originally Carry Moore and then Carry Gloyd. Two minor American poets had respectively the following names: Mary Mathews Smith Barnes Adams and Elizabeth Chase Taylor Akers Allen. Isabel Hayes Chapin Barrows were the various names of an ophthalmologist and reformer. Katherine Westcott Cook Parent Tingley were the four surnames a theosophist successively bore. The several names of a Colorado reformer were Sarah Chase (for twenty-two years), Harris (for nine years), Platt (for fifteen years), Decker (for thirteen years). The multiple names of a Quaker minister were Elizabeth Rous (for thirty-three years), Wright (for ten years), Comstock (for thirty-three years). The different names of an Illinois legislator were Anna Wilmarth (for twenty-four years), Thompson (for fourteen years), Ickes (for twenty-four years).

These women were not exceptional cases. One could go on and on citing the name changes of women who were well-known in their time, and there were thousands of women who are not now remembered or who are hardly remembered who had to change their names in mid career. For example, we know of a Delia Murphy who in 1860 opened a printing office in San Francisco that proved to be very successful, but her established business name was changed to Dearing when Miss Murphy married. If the facts of more nineteenth-century women's lives were known, one could compile a telephone book full of women whose jobs or careers had to withstand one, two or more name changes.

Such changes of name not only meant the inconvenience of losing a professional trademark, it often meant giving up the name with which a remarkable achievement was associated. Prudence Crandall, who in 1833 had the courage to open a school for negroes in Connecticut, a school she was forced to close because of the bigotry of the local citizens, married and the surname which she should have borne proudly the rest of her life was discarded and she became Mrs Philleo. The nerve pathologist Augusta Klumpke, for whom Klumpke's paralysis was named, married Joseph Déjerine and therefore could not keep the name by which her discovery is known. Rebecca Pennell, the first American Professoress, as she was called, married when she was forty-three and lost her name, becoming Mrs Dean. Lucy Hobbs, the first accredited female dentist, married and therefore her accomplishment goes under the surname of James Taylor, a painter in a railway car shop. The naturalist and mountain climber for whom Mount Mary Vaux in British Columbia is named married and the famous Mary Vaux became Mrs Walcott. A. F. of L.'s first woman organizer was Mary Kenney, but because she married her accomplishments go under the name of O'Sullivan. The first archaeologist to discover and completely excavate a Minoan town site, Harriet Boyd, married in 1906, for which reason the name under which she made her discovery was abandoned and her name changed to Hawes. The first American woman to earn a PhD was Helen Magill, but when she married in 1890 the name she made distinguished was blotted out and she became Mrs White. The first woman to graduate from Oberlin College, Zerviah Porter, became Mrs Weed, and Antoinette Brown, the first American woman minister, became Mrs Blackwell. Most of the women who achieved "firsts" in the nineteenth century are recorded in the Hall of Fame not under the name they used when they achieved their "first" but under the name of the man they later married.

The first woman to found a major religion goes down in history under the name of her third husband. The nominal history of Mary Morse Baker Glover Patterson Eddy is a moving case in point of the frequent name changes to which professional women were subjected. Born Mary Morse Baker in 1821, she published a few poems in local newspapers when she was a young girl under the name of Mary M. Baker and, according to her, under various pseudonyms. After her marriage to George Glover in 1843 she published fairly frequently in magazines as Mary M. Glover. Mr Glover died six months after the marriage, and Mary continued to use the name Mary M. Glover until 1853 when she married a dentist, Dr Daniel Patterson, and began to use the name Mary M. Patterson as the name under which she wrote a column, "Way-side Thoughts," for a Portland (Maine) newspaper. Dr Patterson proved to be an adulterer and they separated in 1866. Two years later, probably because of her husband's bad reputation, she stopped using his name and reassumed the name Glover, although she and Patterson were not divorced until 1873. At first she called herself Mary M. Glover as of old, but she soon substituted as a middle name her original surname Baker or the initial B. In 1868 she advertised a course in healing the sick "on a principle of science" as Mrs Mary B. Glover, and in 1869 in another ad she called herself "Mrs Glover, the well-known Scientist." In 1875 she bought a house in Lynn, Massachusetts on which she hung a large sign that read:

Mary B. Glover's
Christian Scientists' Home

The first edition of *Science and Health,* published in 1875, appeared under the name Mary Baker Glover, and one of its early devotees called the book "Mrs Glover's Bible." A couple who boarded with her and admired her healing powers named their baby Flora Glover Nash in her honor.

The name Glover was thoroughly established as the name of the new healing religion when on January 1, 1877 Mrs Glover married Asa Gilbert Eddy. Although she must have been called Mrs Eddy socially, she was apparently continuing to use the name Glover for professional purposes. For on March 18, 1877 a suit was filed against her in the name Glover, and a year later, on March 5, 1878, another suit was filed against her under the name Glover. It was not until May of that year that the name Eddy was used in a third suit against her. But she continued to cling to the name Glover, the name under which she had first developed Christian Science. *The Science of Man*, first published in 1876, was reprinted in 1879 under the name Mary Baker Glover. For a while she used a double surname, signing her letters "M. B. Glover Eddy" and in 1880 publishing her lecture *Christian Healing* under the name Mrs Glover Eddy. Volume II of *Science and Health* (1878) was published under the name

Mary Baker Glover Eddy, the printing order for the third edition of *Science and Health* was signed the same way, but that edition and another in 1882 came out under the name Mary B. Glover Eddy. Mrs Eddy was obviously finding a triple surname clumsy and had reduced the Baker to a B. But she soon changed her mind, reinstated Baker and reduced Glover to a G. The 1883 edition of *Science and Health* appeared and continued to appear under the name Mary Baker G. Eddy.

She may have resumed the use of the name Baker because in 1882, shortly before Mr Eddy's death, she had begun to be interested in her lineage. A relative convinced her they were both descended from Sir John McNeil of Scotland and Mrs Eddy began using the McNeil coat of arms. She later learned she was not related to the noble McNeil but to a commoner with the same name. Apparently wanting to feel she was at least descended from an old American family, she studied the genealogy of the Baker family and applied for membership in the Daughters of the American Revolution, receiving her certificate in 1894 in the name Mary Baker Eddy. In the Preface to her *Miscellaneous Writings* she said that thereafter she adopted the signature Mary Baker Eddy, except in her books where she retained the initial G. because the first edition of *Science and Health* had been copyrighted in the name Glover. Although she frequently did sign herself Mary Baker Eddy, she by no means gave up using "G.," the symbol of the name in which her new religion had originated. Many of her letters and messages to the Mother Church and finally her will were signed Mary Baker G. Eddy.

Mrs Eddy had been Mary Baker for twenty-two years, Mrs Glover for ten years, Mrs Patterson for fifteen years, Mrs Glover again for nine years, not becoming Mrs Eddy until she was fifty-five. She once received an angry letter in which she was addressed as "Mrs Glover Patterson Eddy," and her sister Abigail, who hated her, wrote her a letter that began with the salutation, "My Dear Rev. &c. &c. &c." Unlike men, who would have had one name despite as many marriages, Mrs Eddy's marital names rattled after her, like the tin cans tied to the car of a bride and groom. And more unjustly, because custom demanded she assume the names of the husbands in her life, her religion does not bear her own name nor the name under which she founded the religion but the name of the traveling sewing machine salesman who happened to be her last husband and to whom she was married for only five years.

It was as if William O. Douglas, when he was almost twenty-five and studying law, had married and changed his name to that of his first wife and become William O. Riddle, which would have been the name under which he was appointed to the Supreme Court in 1939 when he was almost forty. But because Associate Justice Riddle married three more times, he would in 1954 have become Justice Hester, in 1963 Justice Martin and in 1966 Justice Heffernan. In order to maintain some connection with his past names, Justice Riddle in 1954 might have decided to call himself Justice Riddle Hester, and in 1963 Justice Hester Martin, or perhaps Justice Riddle Hester Martin. Or he might then have felt a longing for a name that belonged permanently to him and begun to use his own surname as a middle name, so that when he married a fourth time he might have called himself Justice William Douglas R. Heffernan, retaining the initial R. because under the name Riddle he had been appointed to the Supreme Court. Whatever name or names he chose to use, he would go down in history, be listed in *Who's Who*s, encyclopedias and card catalogues under the name Heffernan, the name of the young girl who happened to be his last wife.

It used to be said that love is the history of a woman's life, and that history and only that history is recorded in the husbands' names nineteenth-century professional women successively assumed. For the name Mary Baker Glover Patterson Eddy means that Mary Baker had connubial relations with a Mr Glover, a Mr Patterson and a Mr Eddy, as if her life had been the mere history of her affections.

9

DOUBLE IDENTITIES

A Professional Name

The French painter Rosa Bonheur, reminiscing late in her life with the American painter Anna Klumpke, spoke of why she had not married. It was not, she said, because she had a "cold and indifferent nature . . . but I preferred to keep my own name. I believe I have been able to give it some renown." Bonheur was right. If she had married, she would have felt compelled, like the American miniaturist Anna Peale, to sign her work with her husband's name, which in Peale's case, since she had two husbands, led to some confusion in classifying her work. Women in fields other than acting and writing continued to change their professional name with every husband.

There were some exceptions, but they were very few. A compatriot of Rosa Bonheur continued to exhibit her paintings as Berthe Morisot after her marriage, but her husband was the brother of the famous Edouard Manet with whom she often exhibited, so that to have used the name Manet might have made people think she wanted to capitalize on his much greater fame. She was of course known as Mme Manet socially, and it is virtually certain that if she had not married a man with the same name as a fellow painter she would have signed her work with her husband's name. Almost all women (not in the theater and not authors) who did maintain a professional name had, like Berthe Morisot, a special problem or were so well-known before marriage the public found it hard to call them by a new name. The Rebel spy Belle Boyd was in her time as famous as Molly Pitcher, so that despite her three marriages the newspapers and the public almost always called her Belle Boyd, not Mrs Hardinge or Mrs Hammond or Mrs High, as her current husband might be. In her various post-marital careers she generally was Belle Boyd because she had to use her famous name when she lectured on her exploits as a Rebel spy, and when she acted or wrote she was following professions in which there was a tradition for a woman to use her own name. The sculptor Vinnie Ream had also been so well-known before her marriage that the press as often as not called her Vinnie Ream rather than Mrs Hoxie. Occasionally when a woman returned to public life after marriage, she wisely used the name the public knew. When Mme D'Arusmont returned to America in late 1835, she lectured under her old name of Frances Wright, but she was then more often than not separated from her husband and when she returned to France she was again Mme D'Arusmont.

Once in a great while a woman tried to establish her own name as a professional name. In 1880 an artist exhibited her work at the New York Etching Club under the name "M. Nimmo," but Mary Nimmo soon succumbed to convention and added Moran, her husband's name, to her signature. A rare woman did persevere. During the 1870s in New York E. Miriam Coryière ran a highly successful school furniture business and a teacher's agency. In 1884 she married for a second time and although she called herself Mrs Professor Carlos Pardo socially, she maintained the name Coryière in business. When she was asked to supply a biographical sketch of her life for Frances Willard and Mary Livermore's *A Woman of the Century* (an 1893 women's *Who's Who*), she listed herself under Coryière, mentioning her present husband's name incidentally, as if she were an actress. Among the 1470 women in the 1893 *A Woman of the Century,* Mrs Coryière was the only one (not an author or in the theater) who listed herself under her professional name not that of her current husband. Of course, there must have been other women like her, women who were not national celebrities but who nevertheless refused to lose an established professional name and changed only the name they used in private life. But they were rarities.

Considering the inconveniences endured by the Mary Baker Glover Patterson Eddys and the Minnie Scott Oliver Rutherford Fullers, it is difficult to understand why more women did not follow the lead of actresses and authors and have a double identity, a professional name and one that adapted to marital vicissitudes. It ought to be said in defense of their conservatism that actresses had not dared have a name unaffected by marriage until their profession had been established some two hundred years and that until the last two or three decades of the nineteenth century most female authors were changing their professional name with every marriage or were using pseudonyms, often masculine ones. A female doctor could not use a male pseudonym, nor could she appear in public only on a title page. She had to deal directly with the public, a hostile public that suspected her of being a freak. A woman who wanted to enter a profession that had been traditionally male was believed to want "to make herself a man," as Orestes Brownson put it. Therefore, career women who could not prove their femininity by displaying their female charms on stage or who could not disguise their sex on a title page were eager to identify themselves by the men in their lives and thus prove they were women. By wearing the camouflage Mrs Currenthusband, a biologist, architect or dentist seemed to be just a wife.

To prove their femininity despite their masculine profession, most female doctors and dentists were willing to dispense with the title they had earned or did not object to its being feminized. The first accredited female dentist was called "Miss Dr Lucy Hobbs" before her marriage and "Mrs Dr Taylor" afterwards. When Dr Cloe Buckel was serving as an administrator of nurses during the Civil War, she was called Miss Buckel. Dr Clemence Lozier was always called Madame Lozier by her patients. When Elizabeth Garrett received her MD, she chose not to use the title, feeling that since she had defied the world on the main point, she would forgo the titular sign of her defiance. (Besides, in her upper middle class circles, the profession of medicine still excited repugnance.) Dr Garrett continued to be Miss, and after her marriage Mrs; she was rarely called Dr even by the newspapers until late in her life.

It was not only to establish their female credentials that career women were willing to forgo their titles and change their names again and again. They were, after all, isolated pariahs, often the only female doctor or lawyer in their city. Why should they further isolate themselves by being unconventional in regard to their names? Since most people can not even wear their hair longer or shorter than custom decrees, it is not at all surprising that almost all professional women conformed to nominal custom when they married, especially since they lived at a time when sexual mores were strict and a Dr Cutter living in the same residence with a Mr Jones might well be accused of living in sin. To run the risk of being thought a loose woman was beyond the courage of most women and, moreover, would have been professionally harmful.

The new career women were, however, by no means totally submissive to convention; they did try to keep their professional identity afloat, safe from disappearing utterly every time they embarked on the sea of matrimony.

Mrs Mary Jones Smith

The sudden proliferation of women with triple names, names like Elizabeth Cady Stanton, Harriet Beecher Stowe and Frances Hodgson Burnett, was a nineteenth-century phenomenon, an effect of women entering public life and making names for themselves they wanted to retain after marriage.

It had long been common, particularly in America, for men as well as women to have a surname as a middle name. Among families that took pride in a mother's ancestry, children were often given the mother's family name as a middle name. It was also fairly common for the daughters of famous men to retain their famous patronymic as a middle name after marriage. Thus in 1752 when the granddaughter of the great Cotton Mather married, she was henceforth known as Hannah Mather Crocker. Or when Thomas Jefferson's daughter married in 1790, she called herself Martha Jefferson Randolph. But in the early 1840s when Elizabeth Cady married and informed her friends they were to address her as Elizabeth Cady Stanton, she did not do so because she was proud of being the daughter of Judge Cady. She was adapting the custom of retaining a distinguished patronymic to feminist purposes, as a way of protesting both against the new custom of calling wives by their husband's full name and the old custom of a wife losing the surname she was born with. What Elizabeth Cady Stanton called "the new gospel of individual sovereignty" was practiced by the early feminists and later by many of the suffragists, who thus expressed woman's new sense of herself as an individual and not merely a wife. When the suffragists Rachel Foster, Carrie Lane, Elizabeth Boynton and Sarah Knox married, they adopted the names Rachel Foster Avery, Carrie Lane Chapman, Elizabeth Boynton Harbert and Sarah Knox Goodrich. The feminist practice of retaining one's own first and last name as a preface to one's husband's surname was found immensely useful by women in the professions, who could thus manage to retain the name with which they had gained a reputation. When the Reverend Antoinette Brown married, she called herself Antoinette Brown Blackwell; when the president of Wellesley married, she signed her name Alice Freeman Palmer.

But as a way of retaining her identity, a woman's use of her own surname as a middle name worked best on paper. For though a woman signed her name as she wished it to be, in an era when people who were not intimate addressed each other by a title and a surname, professional women were commonly known as Mrs Stowe or Mrs Palmer, not as Mrs Beecher Stowe or Mrs Freeman Palmer. Moreover, in correspondence convention almost always supervened so that they received letters addressed to Mrs Calvin Stowe and Mrs George Palmer. And should a woman marry more than once, and many did, retaining one's original name could become a liability. For example, when May Wright married she used the name May Wright Thompson. She was then a high school teacher and as Mrs Thompson taught for eight years. Mr Thompson having died, she remarried and not wanting to lose her own family surname she dropped Thompson and called herself May Wright Sewall. But she thereby lost the name by which she and her work had become known. Other women, wanting to maintain some continuity with their previous identity, gave up their own surname and made their first husband's surname their middle name. Thus when Paulina Kellogg Wright remarried, she dropped Kellogg, her own name, for which she substituted her first husband's surname and became Paulina Wright Davis. Occasionally a woman tried to resolve the dilemma of whether to give up her original name or lose the surname by which she was best known by using three surnames. As we have seen, after her marriage to Mr Eddy, the woman who had been known as Mary Baker Glover used for a while the name Mary Baker Glover Eddy and for sometime could not decide whether to drop Baker or Glover. Mrs Eddy finally decided to retain Baker, but most women who married more than once gave up their original name in order to hold on to the name they had been professionally known by, so that like Paulina Wright Davis they ended by canonizing both their husbands, their original identity gone.

Mrs Mary Jones-Smith

A surer way for a woman to preserve her identity was to retain her own or former surname not as a middle name but as part of a double surname, and a surprisingly large number of nineteenth-century women were bold enough to use a double surname, generally hyphenated though occasionally not.

Fairly early in the century singers and musicians too conservative to adopt the more liberal custom of actresses and keep their own name professionally found the use of a hyphenated surname a comfortable compromise between professionalism and conformity. When Clara Wieck and Robert Schumann became engaged in 1838, Robert asked her, "What will you call yourself? Wieck-Schumann, or the other way round, or just Clara Schumann?" Clara, who once wrote to Robert, "How dreadful it would be to die without bearing your name," dropped her famous name entirely, but many other musicians and singers refused to let womanly self-effacement wholly deprive them of their famous name and hyphenated their husband's name to their own. When the singer Teresa Carreño married Emile Sauret in 1873, she listed herself on programs as Mme Teresa Carreño-Sauret. When the pianist Julie Rivé married Frank King in 1876, she became Rivé-King both on stage and in private life. After Ernestine Roessler married in 1882 she changed her name to Heink, but when she married a second time in 1893 she retained her then well-known identity by adopting the hyphenated name Schumann-Heink.

Hyphenated surnames had a slight vogue among German feminist writers.

Following the lead of Countess Ida von Hahn who, after her marriage in 1826 to her cousin Count F. W. Adolph von Hahn, adopted the name Hahn-Hahn, other German writers did likewise. For example, when Fanny Lewald finally legalized her union with Adolph Stahr in 1854, she took the name Lewald-Stahr. Occasionally an English or American author, like Gene Stratton-Porter, chose to use a hyphenated surname, but in general they were not favored, except by journalists. Needless to say, most journalists who continued working after marriage did change their name to their husband's, but a significant handful were bold enough to keep their own name and attach their husband's to it. A Mrs Jackson-Houk, wife of William Houk, wrote for Cincinnati and Chicago newspapers, and when the black journalist Ida Wells, famous for writing against lynching, married Ferdinand Barnett in 1895, she became Ida Wells-Barnett.

Double surnames were also not uncommon among physicians. As early as 1857 Dr Anna M. Longshore, after her marriage to Lambert Potts, adopted the name Dr Longshore-Potts. The first female physician in England, Dr Elizabeth Garrett, married James Anderson in 1871 and henceforth used the double surname Garrett Anderson, in this case not hyphenated. It is certain she insisted both surnames be used because her daughter, in writing her mother's biography, took the trouble always to use the double surname, as did the *Dictionary of National Biography*. It is less clear what were the wishes of the American doctor Mary Putnam after she married Dr Abraham Jacobi in 1873. She always signed her name in full—Dr Mary Putnam Jacobi—but sometimes she hyphenated the surnames and sometimes she did not. Similarly, about half her published work appeared with the surnames hyphenated and about half did not. In Boston in 1895 she spoke at the New England Suffrage Festival as Dr Putnam-Jacobi, but on other occasions she spoke as Dr Jacobi. Unlike Dr Garrett Anderson, she seems not to have insisted on the two surnames being used and was most commonly addressed as Dr Jacobi. Too little is known of the lives of other female physicians to determine how consistently they used their hyphenated surnames, but many did adopt them, and not just physicians in large cities. In Kirksville, Missouri on December 31, 1886 the osteopath Dr Alice Heath married the Reverend Charles Willis Proctor and took the name Dr Heath-Proctor.

Women in a variety of other professions, businesses and public activities also used double surnames. The kindergarten educator Marie Boelté married John Kraus in 1873 and became Kraus-Boelté, she, atypically, putting her husband's name first. The first woman to scale the second highest of the Nun Kun peaks was the former Fanny Bullock, who when she married Dr William Workman in 1881 expressed a strong preference for being called Mrs Bullock Workman. Mrs Bullock Workman's father had been a governor of Massachusetts and she herself became well-known, but women who did not have the name of a prominent father they wanted to preserve or who did not become well-known also adopted double surnames. The schoolteacher Fannie Reese, after her marriage to Dr Pugh, called herself Reese-Pugh, despite living in the small town of Hearne, Texas and being the mother of six children.

Hyphenated surnames also found favor among suffragists. Prominent in their local suffrage organizations were, for example, May Belleville-Brown of Kansas and Louisa Durham-Wilson of New Mexico. A pioneer advocate of woman suffrage in Alabama was Virginia Clay-Clopton, her double surname consisting of her first and second husbands' names. When Elizabeth Cady Stanton's daughter Harriot visited America in 1894 she was using the name Mrs Stanton-Blatch. Since her marriage she had been living in England where other feminists also used hyphenated names, among them Elizabeth Wolstenholme-Elmy and Hypatia Bradlaugh-Bonner.

When one scans the few feminist magazines and women's histories and biographical dictionaries produced in the nineteenth century, one finds many, many instances of women using double surnames, which means the phenomenon must have been fairly widespread,* and in fact a correspondent to the English periodical *Notes and Queries* recorded in the October 8, 1887 issue that "It is all the rage for Connecticut women to retain their maiden names after marriage, as 'Mrs Scott-White'." How widespread the rage was can only

---

* Because the popularity of double surnames will surprise most readers, here is a more extensive sampling.
Journalists: M. French-Sheldon of the Michigan Women's Press Association; Grace Duffie-Boylan, vice-president of the Illinois Women's Press Association; Rose Hartwick-Thorpe and Carrie Ashton-Johnson of the Southern California Press Association; Frances Gibson-Richard, an Ohio journalist.
Physicians: Dr Bethenia Owens-Adair of Oregon; Dr Salini Armstrong-Hopkins of Syracuse, New York; Dr Cora Smith-Eaton of Grand Forks, South Dakota; Dr E. M. Roys-Gavitt, editor in chief of *Woman's Medical Journal*; Dr Augusta Stowe-Gullen, first woman to get a medical degree in Canada; Dr Edith Pechey-Phipson, an English physician; Dr Henriette Tiburtius-Hirschfelt, a German dentist.
Suffragists: Bessie J. Isaacs-Savage of Washington; Anna Widman-Wallace of Kansas; Claudia Howard-Maxwell of Georgia; Susannah Clark-Shea of New Mexico; Mrs Cobden Unwin of England; Anna Hierta-Retzius of Sweden; Nanna Kristensen-Randers of Denmark; Hanna Bieber-Bohm of Germany.
Others: the mathematician Christine Ladd-Franklin; the Kansas painter Henrietta Briggs-Wall, who had a painting hung at the 1893 Chicago World's Fair; the Missouri painter Helen Woljeska-Tindolph; the French painter Virginie Demont-Breton; the Ohio piano teacher Blanche Kahler-Evans; Superintendent of Schools in Wyandotte County, Kansas Fannie Reid-Slusser; Dean of the woman's college of Northwestern University Jane Bancroft-Robinson; Rosa Bonheur's sister Juliette used the name Peyrol-Bonheur after her marriage.

be guessed, but the rage was sufficiently popular so that the temperance leader Frances Willard in her *How to Win* (1886), a feminist handbook for young girls, predicted that wives in the future would not "insist on having letters addressed to Mrs John Smith, or Mrs General Smith . . . but if her maiden name were Jones, she will fling her banner to the breeze as 'Mrs Mary Jones-Smith'."

That hyphenated surnames achieved a mild popularity may surprise us, but they had decided advantages for the new woman of the nineteenth century. Not only did they allow her to announce her respectable married state and at the same time retain an established identity, hyphenated surnames had the additional advantage of allowing a woman to hold on to part of her name in case of remarriage or divorce. When Teresa Carreño-Sauret married a second time, she merely replaced Sauret with d'Albert. Sometimes a woman chose to put her husband's name first; at one point during her second marriage Teresa Carreño-d'Albert decided to invert the order of her surnames, feeling that d'Albert-Carreño "better accented her individuality." Whether a woman put her husband's name first or last, her insistence on the double surname established the two names in the public's mind so that, however her name changed, the public did not have to learn a wholly new name. Upon divorce, she could drop her husband's name without losing her identity. After the singer Selma Koert-Kronold divorced Jan Koert, she became Selma Kronold. When the labor leader Florence Kelley-Wischnewetzky divorced her husband, she became Mrs Kelley. The woman who used a double surname was thus able to maintain some continuity despite the marital vicissitudes that were becoming more and more common in the nineteenth century.

And yet hyphenated surnames were not the perfect solution to a married woman's identity problems. In Europe and England, where such names are frequently family names, a woman's hyphenated surname tended to be respected because people thought it was her husband's name. But in America, where double surnames are rare, people seemed to find them too long to say. Despite her wish to be known as Mrs Clay-Clopton, many a sister suffragist addressed Virginia Clay-Clopton as Mrs Clopton. Before Leonora Barry married a second time, she was a labor leader of national stature; after her second marriage she tried to preserve her well-known identity by using the name Mrs Barry-Lake, but she soon became Mrs Lake. The women themselves often did not use their double names consistently. Dr Mary Putnam-Jacobi's vacillations have already been mentioned. Florence Kelley-Wischnewetzky understandably sometimes shortened her name. Her books were always signed with the two names, but her letters were often signed with only her husband's name and her friend Friedrich Engels called her Mrs or Mother Wischnewetzky, men especially disliking a woman who did not wholly merge herself with her husband. Freud refused to acknowledge the hyphenated surname of Lou Andreas-Salomé. In his letters to her after her marriage to Professor Andreas in 1887, he made it a point to address her as Frau Andreas and eventually she obeyed the master and stopped using the double surname when she wrote to him.

Official catalogues and dictionaries, like Freud, arrogantly disregarded the hyphenated surname a woman might choose to use and routinely dropped her own name in favor of her husband's. The Library of Congress catalog almost uniformly did so, even though that policy made hundreds of cross-references necessary. For example, the woman who published all her books as M. French-Sheldon was catalogued under S and listed as Mrs Mary (French) Sheldon. Although the *Dictionary of National Biography* was careful to call Elizabeth Garrett Anderson Dr Garrett Anderson, she was listed with the A's. A man with the double surname Garrett Anderson would have been listed under G.

Women who used hyphenated surnames were likely to have their own surname treated as a middle name and their husband's surname regarded as their "real" name, except, as one might have predicted, when the women were in the theater. Mme Schumann-Heink's name was apparently not too long to say, but somehow Mrs Bullock Workman became Mrs Workman. Moreover, when the double surname of a woman on the stage was disregarded, it was in favor of her own name, but when the woman was a doctor or a suffragist, it was in favor of her husband's name. Thus, although Jenny Lind wished to be called Lind-Goldschmidt, she was called Lind, but Dr Kate Hurd-Mead was called Mead, her husband's name. Society was hostile towards the women who had entered professions that had so recently been for men only, and it expressed its hostility by omitting the name that stood for a woman's professional identity and addressing her only by her husband's name. Society, like a hostess at a party, was pretending something unpleasant had not happened, that a woman like Dr Kate Hurd-Mead was just Mrs Mead, a wife, as women were supposed to be. Freud's refusal to use Lou Andreas-Salomé's hyphenated surname and the Library of Congress's refusal to acknowledge the hyphenated surnames of married women were also expressions of society's disapproval of assertions of separate individuality by wives, who were supposed to be one with their husbands not distinct entities. Most women who used hyphenated surnames soon discovered they were little better off than women who used their own surname as a middle name. Hyphenated surnames too often proved to be a mere gesture of nominal independence.

Mrsnomerism

The public ought not to have been so hostile towards the women who tried to salvage their individuality by hyphenating their surname to their husband's. At least men ought not to have been. What men failed to realize was that the professional woman who used a hyphenated surname was being considerate of her husband; by having a name distinct from his she protected his separate individuality. Many a nineteenth-century husband discovered to his sorrow the great disadvantages of having a wife in public life with the same name as his. One husband who suffered was Isaac Menken. In 1856 he had married Adah Theodore, who adopted the name Adah Isaacs Menken, adding an s [meaning son of] to Isaac as if Isaacs had been her own Jewish patronymic. She and her husband separated in 1859 and subsequently Adah Isaacs Menken became internationally famous as a semi-nude bare back rider. For the rest of his life Isaac Menken smarted under the reflected notoriety of their similar names, and Adah herself felt she had done him an injury. In 1864 she wrote to her former father-in-law (with whom she had remained friendly): "Would that it were possible for me to spare you embarrassment . . . The price of fame is great. The world knows me as Adah Isaacs Menken and it is too late for me to adopt another [name]."

There was one husband who was so distressed by his wife's use of his name for her different purposes that he had it suppressed. The Reverend Frank Besant in 1878 persuaded the publisher of his wife's lecture to omit her name from under the title; he did not want the name Besant to appear because the lecture advocated atheism. Annie Besant, in turn, legally charged her husband with interfering with the practice of her profession, which he in fact was doing because Annie had left him and was supporting herself by lecturing. Both were justifiably angry. Perhaps, out of consideration for her husband's clerical career, Annie Besant should have resumed her own name—Wood. But she had been using Besant for over ten years and was generally known by it.

And yet Annie Besant did take pleasure in embarrassing her husband, and other women, particularly when they used their husband's full name, were guilty of malice aforethought. The newspaper editor Horace Greeley was deliberately humiliated by his wife at the 1867 Constitutional Convention in Albany, New York. The question of woman suffrage was to come up for discussion and it had been rumored that Greeley was to present a report opposed to suffrage. His wife, however, believed women ought to vote and therefore allowed Elizabeth Cady Stanton, among others, to engineer it so that a petition in favor of woman suffrage headed by the name "Mrs Horace Greeley" was read at the convention just before Mr Horace Greeley read his report against woman suffrage, a family difference that made the gallery and then the newspapers laugh. Greeley was furious, so furious he confronted Stanton at a reception and accused her of being one of the most "maneuvering politicians in the State of New York." Why, he asked, "since you are always so desirous in public to appear under your own name rather than your husband's name, why did you in this case substitute 'Mrs Horace Greeley' for 'Mary Cheney Greeley', which was really on the petition?" Because, said Stanton, "I wanted all the world to know that it was the wife of Horace Greeley who protested against her husband's report." In revenge, Greeley ordered his newspaper always to print Stanton's name as Mrs Henry Stanton, a style he knew she detested. Leslie Carter, a wealthy Chicago socialite, could take no such revenge, he could only suffer when in 1889 his ex-wife, whom he had divorced for adultery, went on stage as "Mrs Leslie Carter." She had chosen to use that name not only because it was well-known and would help her career but for vengeance sake. Her husband had publicly humiliated her in the divorce court, so she publicly humiliated him by linking his upper class name with what he regarded as the immoral theatrical profession.

Other career women who used their husband's full name were ostensibly only obeying the dictates of correct female etiquette. But the wives who published as Mrs Henry Wood and Mrs Humphrey Ward must have realized the hardship they were inflicting on their husbands. Mr Henry Wood was in the consular service and a prominent member of a banking and shipping firm, and Mr Humphrey Ward was a lead writer on politics and art for the London *Times*. But the names that were theirs originally and by which they were well-known became indelibly associated in the public's mind with the names of the authors of the bestsellers *East Lynne* and *Robert Elsmere*. One even feels for Mr Stuyvesant Fish, who as Mrs Stuyvesant Fish, constantly appeared in the papers identified with the parties he loathed; he spent most of his time in the country. And the acquisitive, ungenerous Russell Sage would have risen in wrath from his grave if he could have known that his wife had used his $63,000,000 estate to establish a philanthropic foundation; on the other hand, it is unjust that the Russell Sage Foundation goes under his name and not under the name of the actual philanthropist, Margaret Slocum Sage.

When both husband and wife were in public life, it was at the very least semantically confusing for the public name of one to be the public name of the other. Why should the name Lockwood mean both the well-known lawyer Lockwood and the well-known dentist and teacher Lockwood, both working in the same city? Why should the name Fuller be identified both with a celebrated Arkansas lobbyist and a distinguished Arkansas physician? And the double identity problem became doubly confounding when husband and wife were in the same profession, as an increasing number were. For when women had careers they were likely to marry men in the same profession. Consequently, the name and title Dr Jacobi could signify the career of either husband or wife; the name Bethune could mean the architect Mr Bethune or the architect Mrs Bethune; the Reverend Eastman could identify either Annis Eastman or Samuel Eastman. In an article on "Women in the Universalist Ministry" in the April 22, 1899 *Woman's Journal* about fifteen husband and wife ministers were listed.

In a world in which wives had careers, a husband who had conferred his name on a woman as a token of wifehood could find his name coming to mean his wife's career not his own. Was it not unfair to Mr Sigourney when Mrs Sigourney made his name mean the poet Sigourney not the merchant Sigourney? Hadn't Mr Sigourney been robbed of his trademark, his soul-mark, one of his most valuable possessions? In a primitive sense the name that had used to mean him, that *was* him, had come to mean another. Was it not unfair to Mr Bloomer when his name was laughed at all over the world because of the "Bloomers" his wife urged women to wear? That may explain why on her tombstone he deprived her of her famous name, memorializing her as "Amelia Jenks, Wife of D. C. Bloomer."

Many women in public life understood they were violating their husbands' nominal rights. Adah Isaacs Menken has already been mentioned. Another was the former Mrs Seba Smith, who changed her writing name to Elizabeth Oakes Smith in part to avoid confusion between her work and her husband's. Mary Goldring-Bright wrote under the name George Egerton because she felt the name she used as a writer ought to be "independent of that which belongs to her only by right of a husband."

When husband and wife were supposed to be one—the husband—the wife's taking the husband's name signified she had merged with his interests. But when wives began to be more than wives, when a wife had a career or was active outside the home, she was representing her own interests. Since she was representing herself, not her husband, it was only fair that she should have a name different from her husband's.

In a world in which wives had careers the custom of women taking their husband's name was clearly outmoded. It no longer worked well. Not only could a husband find his name had come to stand for his wife's career not his own, the old custom created a labyrinth of identities for women, as anyone knows who has studied nineteenth-century women and looked up Clara Clement and found "see Waters," or Helen Sumner and found "see Woodbury," or Celia Logan and found "see Connelly," or found Victoria Woodhull under W only to discover later she is also listed under Martin, the name of her last husband. Needless to say, such name changes were more vexing to the women themselves, who could not call an established name their own unless they did not marry or marry a second time. Those who tried to hold onto an established name by using it as a middle name often found their names shifting like a game of musical chairs, their own name displaced by that of husband number one, then husband number one's name displaced by that of husband number two. Besides, whatever fuss a woman made about her middle name, she was nevertheless called Mrs Currenthusband. Hyphenated surnames did work better, but often they too were ignored, and when a woman remarried or divorced, her hyphenated surname was also subject to change. Moreover, a double surname is in itself a double identity, a way of telling the world I am I and a wife too, just as actresses and authors, though they had a professional name, had to have another name, a wife name, in private life. Women were still required to inform the world that whatever else they might do, they were performing the role of wife. Men no longer had role names; they were not Smith or Carpenter according to their profession, but every woman who married, no matter how great the scope of her activities, was required to be Mrs Herhusband. In a world in which wives were more than wives, for a woman with a career to go by the name of wife was mislabeling, or to coin a word, *Mrsnomerism*.

Instead of subjecting women to varieties of nominal polyandry and men to the risk of having their names appropriated, the obvious, the simplest, the fairest course would be for a woman, like a man, to continue using her own name despite marriage. Many a professional woman must have dreamed of a world in which she did not have to change her name, a world in which she could, like a man, have one identity throughout life, and in the mid 1850s a woman's rights lecturer, Lucy Stone of Massachusetts, married and decided to go on being Lucy Stone.

10

LUCY STONE (ONLY)

Miss Lucy Stone

Lucy Stone became interested in married women's names in 1847 when she was in her senior year at Oberlin College. According to her friend and fellow student Antoinette Brown, their class in a text book came upon the quotation, "Women are more sunk by marriage than men," whereupon Lucy, in a voice "vibrant with suppressed indignation" asked, "What does that mean, Professor? Why are women more sunk by marriage than men?" Professor Morgan "fidgeted, physically and mentally, offering several minor reasons; then he said emphatically: 'women lose their names, and become identified with the husband's family; the wife's family is not as readily traceable in history as her husband's; the law gives her property into her husband's keeping, and she is little known to the business world.'"

"Then and there," recalled Antoinette Brown, "began Lucy Stone's first protest against the wife's surrendering her own name. The matter dropped. But again and again she spoke to me about it."

Brown's anecdote does not ring quite true, for it presents Lucy Stone as asking Professor Morgan why women are more sunk by marriage than men as if she needed enlightenment, and Lucy Stone was not ignorant. She knew from bitter personal experience, having observed her father's ruthless domination of her mother. Moreover, when she was a child and first read such Biblical injunctions as "Thy desire shall be to thy husband, and he shall rule over thee," she ran to her mother in anguish, asking, "Is there no way to put an end to me?" She later decided God could not have so degraded women, that the Bible must have been mistranslated and that if she knew Greek and Latin and could read the original text, she would discover God had not ordered women to submit to their husbands. She determined to go to college to learn what God actually had said. By the time she was twenty she felt so keenly woman's inferior position in marriage she told her brother she had resolved to "call no man master." Instead of marrying, she would make a career for herself. At first she taught school in order to earn money for college. In 1843, when she was twenty-five, she entered Oberlin and at once became notorious for talking about women's rights, so much so that Antoinette Brown, who entered two years later, had been warned to have nothing to do with her. When Lucy Stone asked Professor Morgan why women were more sunk by marriage than men, she was being the devil's advocate, which was perhaps why the Professor fidgeted.

However, Professor Morgan probably was the first person to make her think about the significance of women losing their names when they married. Morgan, in turn, may have mentioned women's loss of their names because he had read the *Introduction to American Law* written by Timothy Walker, a lawyer then living in Cincinnati, Ohio. Walker's book, first published in 1837, was widely read and went through many editions and was for the times almost a feminist tract. In his chapter "Husband and Wife" Walker did not hesitate to say that the law as it existed in the 1830s was "a disgrace to any civilized nation," and he used the wife's loss of her name as a symbol of the "slavish subjection of the wife to the husband." Said Walker: "The merging of her name in that of her husband, is but an emblem of the fate of all her legal rights. The torch of Hymen lights up the funeral pile on which those rights are sacrificed." These words of Walker were a favorite of the early feminists. They were, for example, quoted by Lucretia Mott in a speech she gave in Philadelphia in 1849 illustrating the deplorable legal condition of married women, and by Mariana Johnson in 1850 at an Ohio woman's rights convention.

For at the same time as Lucy Stone was realizing that a wife's loss of her name was no small matter, so were other feminists. In August 1848 at the second Woman's Rights Convention in Rochester, New York, the subject was debated during a discussion of equality in marriage. The men present, although they readily conceded women should receive "equal wages for equal work," felt equality in marriage sacrilegious and impossible in practice. Sacrilegious because it was a defiance of St Paul's injunction to wives to submit to their husbands, impracticable because if the husband were not the head of the family constant wrangling would ensue. "An umpire" would be needed at all times, said a Mr Pickard, for who "should hold the property, and whose name should be retained?"

Elizabeth Cady Stanton, who for some time had felt woman's loss of her name at marriage involved "a great principle," proceeded to answer Mr Pickard. She first pointed out that "the custom of taking the husband's name is not universal." She then humorously suggested that if the custom were reversed and the man took the woman's name, a man with an ugly name or a name of ill-repute could be the gainer "by burying himself under the good name of his wife." But then Stanton became serious, and perhaps for the first time the significance of a woman taking her husband's name was discussed at a public meeting. "When a slave escapes from a Southern plantation," said Stanton, "he at once takes a name as the first step in liberty—the first assertion of individual identity. A woman's dignity is equally involved in a life-long name, to mark her individuality. We cannot overestimate the demoralizing effect on woman herself, to say nothing of society at large, for her to consent thus to merge her existence so wholly in that of another."

Lucy Stone would have loved to hear Stanton's words, but in 1847 and 1848 when she first began lecturing on women's rights, she thought she was working alone. "When I undertook my solitary battle for women's rights," she recalled, "I knew nobody who sympathized with my ideas." She went from town to town, lecturing on women's "Social and Industrial, Legal and Political, Moral and Religious Disabilities." Whether or not she discussed a wife's loss of her name is not known, but she most likely did mention it as evidence of woman's subordination in marriage. But for herself, since she did not want to marry, a wife's loss of her name was academic. She had soon become financially independent. In three years of lecturing she was able to save $7000, then a very respectable sum. She was also no longer working alone; she had discovered and joined forces with other women who were working for women's rights, or against women's wrongs, as she preferred to say. She was determined to remain single, not to be, as she put it in an 1850 speech given at the First National Woman's Rights Convention, one of "the appendages of society" on whose tombstone is written that she was merely "the 'relict' of somebody." She did nothing to make herself attractive to men. A newspaper account describes her as being eccentric in dress as well as in thought: under her "skirt of silk, reaching to the knees . . . 'she wears the breeches' of black silk with neat-fitting gaiters. Her hair is cut short and combed straight back."

Mrs Lucy Stone

The Boston Post once printed a satiric poem about Lucy Stone, the last stanza of which read:

> A name like Curtius' shall be his,
> On fame's loud trumpet blown,
> Who with a wedding kiss shuts up
> The mouth of Lucy Stone!

Curtius was a legendary Roman hero who saved the forum by leaping into a chasm that had opened in it. *The Boston Post* was therefore saying that the man who married Lucy Stone would be leaping into a deadly chasm, but if such a self-sacrificing hero could be found American manhood would be saved. For the press of course assumed that if Lucy Stone married, she would stop speaking for women's rights, not only because her husband would forbid it but because once an old maid gets a husband, so goes popular belief, she stops ranting about women's rights.

What neither the press nor Lucy Stone expected was that she would marry a man who did not shut her up, who wanted her to go on lecturing, who believed in her cause as much as she did. Henry B. Blackwell, the brother of the first American woman doctor, was an ardent advocate of women's rights, not only for the sake of women but for men too: "The interests of the sexes are inseparably connected, and in the elevation of one lies the salvation of the other," he wrote in answer to Horace Greeley, who had contended that "woman alone" should work for the cause of women. In 1853 at the Fourth National Woman's Rights Convention, Blackwell said, "If I were a woman" and believed that "she who is a wife and mother . . . must cramp her thoughts into the narrow circle of her own home . . . I would forswear marriage." And when he was trying to persuade Lucy Stone to marry him, he assured her marriage would not narrow her life but make her freer. When Lucy asked him if he would marry if the law placed a husband in the same position it did the wife, he said he would: "Give me a free man, he can never be made a slave. Give me a free woman, she can never be made one either."

When Lucy finally agreed to marry him, Henry insisted they make a public protest against the marriage laws. It was not the first such protest. In 1832 when the socialist reformer Robert Dale Owen married Mary Robinson, Owen wrote out a statement repudiating the "unjust rights" the law gave him "over the person and property of another" and divesting himself of those rights, "the barbarous relics of a feudal and despotic system." In 1838 when the abolitionists Angelina Grimké and Theodore Weld married, Weld also renounced the rights the law gave him over his wife, as did John Stuart Mill when he married Harriet Taylor in 1851. But although these advanced couples repudiated the marriage laws because they denied wives a separate legal existence, the wives did not exemplify their separateness by keeping their own names. Nor in the Stone-Blackwell protest, which is the longest of these protests, was there any specific objection to the custom of the wife taking the husband's name, and immediately after her marriage on May 1, 1855, Lucy Stone became Lucy Stone Blackwell, for her wedding cards read: "Henry B. and Lucy Stone Blackwell."

According to Elinor Rice Hays, her most recent biographer, Lucy Stone

Blackwell did not change her name back to Lucy Stone until July 1856, fourteen months after she married. However, the evidence is contradictory. A month or two after Lucy Stone married, Susan B. Anthony wrote her asking if she would be attending the Second National Woman's Rights Convention that was to be held in Saratoga, New York on August 15 and 16, 1855. In her reply, Lucy said: "When, after reading your letter, I asked my husband if I might go to Saratoga, only think of it! He did not give me permission, but told me to ask Lucy Stone . . . . With the old love and good will I am now and ever,
Lucy Stone (only)."

But at that convention she apparently allowed Antoinette Brown to introduce her as Lucy Stone Blackwell. However, the next month (September 1855), Susan B. Anthony wrote to her family that she "went into Boston on Tuesday, with Lucy Stone, to attend the Convention." On the other hand, her husband, in a letter written to her a few months after their marriage, said: "Lucy Stone Blackwell is more independent in her pecuniary position than was Lucy Stone," and on February 1, 1856 when announcing the marriage of Antoinette Brown to Samuel Blackwell, *The Liberator,* an abolitionist weekly, said that Miss Brown's husband was "a brother of the husband of Lucy Stone Blackwell." Earlier, when *The Liberator* published the Stone-Blackwell marriage protest, the editors had noted: "We are very sorry . . . to lose Lucy Stone, and certainly no less glad to gain Lucy Blackwell." Lucy was an old friend of *The Liberator* and undoubtedly would have told them not to call her Blackwell if she had definitely decided not to use Henry's surname.

We should not be surprised that Lucy Stone at first took her husband's surname and then vacillated for some months. It would have been strange if there had not been a part of her that took pleasure in letting the world know she was married. For in spite of her determination not to marry, she knew the world regarded her as one of those comical old maids whom no man wanted, a failure as a woman. At thirty-seven, when she finally married, she could not resist the psychological comfort of announcing to the world her success as a woman, that she was a Mrs not a Miss. It should also be understood that she knew if she did not take her husband's name, people would think she was one of those sinful free lovers who were then shocking the public by advocating the abolition of marriage. It may be that Lucy Stone shrewdly and deliberately took Henry's name for a while so that her marriage would be widely known, after which she intended to reassume her own name.

It may also be that her wedding cards read Lucy Stone Blackwell because she had not then learned what the law was in regard to married women's names and feared if she did not take her husband's name her marriage would be invalid. We know that she instituted an investigation into the law, but whether she did so before or after her marriage is unclear. Two of the lawyers she consulted, Ellis G. Loring and Samuel E. Sewell, were from Massachusetts, her home state. Another lawyer she consulted was Salmon P. Chase, who was from Ohio where Lucy and Henry lived during the first year of their marriage, during which year Henry helped Chase win the nomination for governor. It may be it was only after she arrived in Ohio and consulted Chase that she learned her name might be, as she signed herself in her letter to Susan B. Anthony, "Lucy Stone (only)." For Chase, who was later to become Chief Justice of the United States Supreme Court, informed her "that there was no law requiring a wife to take her husband's name; it was only a custom."

Whatever the chronology and psychological hesitation, Lucy Stone finally divested herself of her husband's surname. In July 1856 she instructed Susan B. Anthony that in the convention call for that year's woman's rights convention to "Sign . . . Lucy Stone *only* as secretary. Leave off the Blackwell." She wrote to her friends, telling them she was keeping her own name not because she was well-known but because "a wife should no more take her husband's name than he should take hers."

Elizabeth Cady Stanton, as might be expected, was delighted:

> Nothing has been done in the woman's rights movement for some time that so rejoiced my heart as the announcement by you of a woman's right to her name . . . . It may do for the slave to be Cuffee Brooks or Cuffee Douglass, just whose Cuffee he may chance to be; but for us, who have grown up into the full stature of womanhood, demanding all our social, civil, and religious rights . . . it does seem to me a proper self-respect demands that every woman may have some name by which she may be known from the cradle to the grave . . .
>
> Again, under our new property rights, married women may make contracts—buy and sell, and give deeds and mortgages. It becomes very important, therefore, that a woman should not change her name two or three times in one short life.
>
> But, if the mother retains her name, what should the children be called? It matters but little what, so that the girls have a name; for heretofore a woman, like other mere chattels, has been known but by the name of her owner.

Susan B. Anthony, at first hesitated, but then approved. She later wrote to Stone: "I am more and more rejoiced that you have declared by actual doing that a woman has a name and may retain it all through her life." Thomas Wentworth Higginson, the minister who had married her and Henry, was another friend who approved: "As to your scruple about your name, dear Lucy, it would be strange indeed if I did not respect it, when I have always wondered that women did not feel as indignant about the merging of their own individuality as I felt for them. I have always reproached my wife with not caring about it, and I rejoice that you do . . . I hope others will follow your example. My wife sends her love, though she doesn't agree about the name."

Most of Lucy Stone's friends were like Mrs Higginson: they did not approve. According to Susan B. Anthony, the only two women who "stood by Lucy Stone in keeping her own name were Mrs Stanton and myself." In a speech given in 1896 when Anthony was trying to prevent the members of the Woman Suffrage Association from passing a resolution repudiating Elizabeth Cady Stanton's *The Woman's Bible* (an exposé of sexism in the Bible), she said, "Suppose . . . when Lucy Stone did not take the name of her husband . . . we had passed resolutions against a woman not taking her husband's name. Thank God! we had the strength not to do it."

That remark suggests that in 1856 there had been a movement to pass such a resolution. At any rate, pressure was put on Anthony and Thomas Wentworth Higginson (who were organizing the convention that year), for in spite of Stone's instruction to list her as Lucy Stone only, "leave off the Blackwell," her name was printed on the Convention Call as Lucy Stone Blackwell. When she received a copy of the Call and saw her name, Lucy felt Anthony and Higginson had betrayed her. How, she asked, could two of her dearest friends violate her deepest wish. "Oh! Susan," she wrote, "it seems to me that it has wrought a wrong in me that it will take many years to wear out. I had faith in human beings and in human possibilities . . . I have lost something which has darkened all my heavens."

She told Anthony that on seeing her name listed as Lucy Stone Blackwell, she was so upset she felt "faint and sick until a flood of tears relieved me." Why so profound a reaction? Hadn't she written to a friend that "I counted all the cost beforehand, and am so sure I am right that nothing that can be said or done moves me in the least"? She must have expected opposition, though she may have assumed it would come from the public accusing her and Henry of being free lovers. What she may not have expected was opposition from her sister feminists, for weren't they fond of quoting Walker's statement—"The merging of her name in that of her husband, is but an emblem of the fate of all her legal rights"? Hadn't they themselves taken a firm stand against the practice of calling married women Mrs John by insisting on being addressed by their own first name? Lucy Stone may well have expected that her sister feminists would champion the woman who took the next logical step and used her own surname. She must have been dismayed when she discovered most of her friends disapproved, feeling the way Antoinette Brown Blackwell did, that she would be "paying dear . . . for the minor point of a name," and not only Lucy Stone but the cause for which they were laboring. For people could now point to Lucy Stone, who in name was no different from those infamous free lovers, as proof of their contention that feminists wanted to undermine the institution of the family. When, as Lucy Stone discovered, their disapproval took the form of authoritarian repression—printing her name Lucy Stone Blackwell—no wonder she was upset and "her faith in human beings" lessened.

Yet if that had been the fundamental reason why she was upset, she would have been chiefly angry. Her feeling faint and sick and bursting out crying suggests it was more than feminist opposition that was upsetting her, that it was something deeper. Although she was aware of her conscious reason for wanting to keep her own surname, she was probably unaware of her unconscious reason. When she decided to be known by the surname Stone, she did not drop the title Mrs. On the conscious level her continuing to be "Mrs" was a concession to convention, the public acknowledgment of wifehood society demanded of women, and also an expression of her belief that just as boys graduate from the title Master to Mister, so girls should graduate from Miss to Mrs, regardless of marital status. Unconsciously, however, the name Mrs Stone may have meant something else to her. For if she were Mrs Stone, who was Mr Stone? "I have lost something," she felt when she saw the name Blackwell on the Convention Call, "that has darkened all my heavens." She had lost the heaven of the little girl—to be her father's wife, Mrs Stone. She may have burst out crying like a child when she saw the name Blackwell because a childish wish had been frustrated. But it was a wish that was taboo. By defying the convention that requires a woman to take her husband's name, her unconscious had to confront and struggle to keep repressed the early desire of little girls to marry their father. No wonder it took over a year before she could finally decide to be Mrs Stone not Mrs Blackwell.

It was an especially difficult struggle because it had to remain at the unconscious level since there was then no knowledge of children's Oedipal desires. However, perhaps she was finally able to become Mrs Stone because she gained some insight into her unconscious conflict. During the first year of her marriage she lived in Henry's home in Ohio where Henry's mother also lived. In that home, therefore, were two Mrs Blackwells, and when someone asked for Mrs Blackwell there must often have been a question of which Mrs Blackwell was wanted, Henry's mother or his wife. The confusion of identity of mother and wife must have made Lucy unconsciously aware of a further inequity in a male-dominant society. Custom, by requiring women to take their husbands' names, allowed men to act out the desire of little boys to marry their mothers, Mr

Jones' sweetheart after marriage becoming another Mrs Jones, just like mama. Mr Jones, however, can remain unaware of the fulfillment of his early desire because his wife, when she takes the same name as his mother, is merely obeying the dictates of convention. In a male-dominant society men build their unconscious desires into the structure of society, that is, a forbidden wish is transformed into a socially approved convention. In a female-dominant society, one in which girls could act out their unconscious desires, men would take their wives' surnames, thus allowing women the unconscious pleasure of being married to their fathers. By changing her name from Blackwell back to Stone, Mrs Stone, the woman who believed in equal rights gave herself an Oedipal satisfaction society normally allows only men to enjoy. However, Lucy Stone could not have the normal male unconscious pleasure, for not only did she have to suffer the pain of breaking a social convention, but the name of the beloved parent was not assumed by the person she loved, that is, Henry had not been nominally transformed into Mr Stone. Mr Stone remained her father. Mrs Stone's raw Oedipal desires must have come dangerously close to her consciousness.

That Lucy Stone was struggling with the unconscious desire of little girls to marry papa is further revealed by the difficulty she had naming the daughter she gave birth to in 1857. She agonized for months over the baby's name. Consciously, it was the baby's first name she could not decide upon, but that may well have been a screen for the decision she made without any agonizing, the decision that the baby should not be given the surname Stone. Henry felt that since she had been the one who had "suffered to bring the child into the world," she should have the right to give the baby her own surname. But she felt that would be unfair not only to Henry since it was his child too but unfair to the child since only illegitimate children bore their mother's name. She must also have had to realize that although she had a name that could mean she was her father's wife, to give her child a name that could mean it was her father's child was unthinkable. And yet nine months went by and the baby had no name. Finally, the baby was named Alice Stone Blackwell, that is, like other children she had her father's surname; her mother's surname, as was a common American custom, became her middle name.

Lucy Stone, Wife of Henry Blackwell

In the fall of 1856 Lucy Stone wrote to Susan B. Anthony that she now occupied "a legal position in which I cannot draw in my own name the money I have earned or give a valid receipt for it when it is drawn or make any contract, but am rated with fools, minors and madmen, and cannot sign a legal document without being examined separately to see if it is by my own free will, and even the right to my own name questioned." In regard to her name, she was probably thinking of an incident that had happened in Chicago that summer when she and Henry were engaged in buying land. As Myra Bradwell, a lawyer and the owner of the *Chicago Legal News,* recalled: "We remember when Mrs Stone, with her husband, appeared in the old court house, in the fifties, before Judge John M. Wilson, then of the Common Pleas Court, for the purpose of acknowledging a deed. At first the learned Judge objected, saying that, under the law, the wife must take the name of the husband in such conveyances; but after hearing Mrs Stone, and a few words from Mr Blackwell, he was convinced, and took the acknowledgment with the signature 'Lucy Stone' " (*The Woman's Journal,* November 11, 1893). But other judges, lawyers and bureaucrats would not accept the name Lucy Stone by itself and therefore in signing legal documents she was often forced to use the form, "Lucy Stone, wife of Henry Blackwell." Since "wife of" is merely an old-fashioned equivalent of Mrs, the law really required her to use two signatures—the one she insisted on using and Mrs Henry Blackwell, the name that legally counted. This compromise was apparently satisfactory to her, for not only did she not go to the law to establish the validity of the name Lucy Stone by itself, but she and Henry did not even register a symbolic protest by Henry signing legal documents, "Henry Blackwell, husband of Lucy Stone." In only one bureaucratic area did Lucy Stone not have trouble in having her name acknowledged—the states she lived in made no fuss about her name when she paid taxes.

One wonders if the form she had to use in signing many legal documents did not make her realize the law would not accept "Lucy Stone" only. For on April 22, 1858 she gave a lecture in New York in which, according to the *Times,* she imagined a husband proclaiming, "Your name shall be my name . . . And the children's name shall be mine also . . . We have legislated for that," as if the law compelled a wife to take her husband's name. Stone may have immediately added that no matter what a husband might think, the law did not force a wife to use her husband's name, but if the *Times'* summary of the speech is accurate, Stone discussed the wife's loss of her name as one among many inequities married women suffered because woman "has not granted to her the right of suffrage." From this speech one might suppose that Lucy Stone had come to the conclusion that a woman's legal right to her own name after marriage would be won only when women got the vote.

On the other hand, the following month she expressed the view that the law could not compel a woman to use her husband's name. In May 1858 at the annual Woman's Rights Convention, Stone was approached by a Mrs Julia

Branch who asked her why the convention was going to discuss only suffrage and not the "marriage question." According to Mrs Branch, Lucy Stone said the convention was not "a proper place . . . they wished the rights of women in regard to voting settled then and there, and *that* would settle all other rights." To which Mrs Branch retorted, "How can she [woman] have the right to vote, when she has not even the right to her *name* in the marriage bonds?" As we shall see, Mrs Branch was goading Lucy Stone; she knew very well that Stone was using her own name. But Lucy chose to ignore the attack and replied as if Mrs Branch were ignorant: "It is a mistaken idea that woman is obliged to give up her name and take that of her husband, by the ceremony. I have not given up mine, and no law can compel me to. I call myself Lucy Stone, and shall always." She did not tell Mrs Branch that in signing legal documents she was often forced to use the form "Lucy Stone, wife of Henry Blackwell."

Mrs Branch would have loved to know that fact since it supported her contention that, so far as the law was concerned, Lucy Stone was Mrs Blackwell. Branch would also have liked to know what Henry Blackwell revealed many years later (in the January 12, 1901 *Woman's Journal*), that "to avoid misunderstanding" at hotels, he and his wife registered as "Henry B. Blackwell and Lucy Stone, wife of Henry B. Blackwell." For Mrs Branch seems to have assumed that Stone, because she was well-known, did not have to establish her marital status at hotels. At least in the speech in which she recounted her conversation with Lucy Stone (a speech given in June at a convention in Rutland, Vermont), Mrs Branch imagined how it would "have been with Mrs Blackwell if she had kept the fact of the marriage ceremony a secret, and gone to a hotel with the intention of stopping a few days with Mr Blackwell and signing her name Lucy Stone? Would they have been permitted to occupy one room? What do you suppose would have been the astonishment of the virtuous landlord at such a proceeding . . . Mrs Lucy Stone Blackwell and every one else knows the act would be sufficient to denounce her in the eyes of society, an infamous woman."

But the well-known Lucy Stone, like famous actresses, was not able to retain her respectability at a hotel unless she added her husband's name to her own. Julia Branch felt that no woman would really be able to keep her name until a woman's respectability did not depend upon having society's seal of approval on her sexual relationships, that is, only when marriage was abolished. At the end of her speech, Mrs Branch introduced the following resolution to the Convention: "*Resolved*, that the slavery and degradation of woman proceeds from the institution of marriage; that by the marriage contract she loses the control of her name, her person, her property, her labor, her affections, her children and her freedom."

Julia Branch's speech occupied a column and a half of the front page of *The New York Times* for June 29, 1858, on which day the *Times* shocked and entertained its readers with a full account of the Rutland Free Convention in which not only marriage was repudiated but slavery, capital punishment, the authority of the Bible, the observance of the Christian sabbath and the "crime of an undesigned and undesired maternity." What must have been Lucy Stone's horror when she saw her name associated with such radicals and her position in regard to her name linked with Mrs Julia Branch, a professed believer in free love. Didn't she then have to admit that her sister feminists' objections to her using her own name had validity? For didn't the cause of women's rights suffer when her name was linked on the front page of *The New York Times* with the notorious Julia Branch? And for many years she and Henry, because of their different names, continued to be accused of being free lovers. In 1867 when they were campaigning for woman suffrage in Kansas, she wrote to Susan B. Anthony that "the papers here are coming down on us . . . and charging us with being Free Lovers. I have today written a letter to the editor, saying that it has not the shadow of a foundation." But when that campaign for woman suffrage failed, didn't she have to ask herself if her position in regard to her name had not had something to do with it?

Whatever her misgivings, she did not desist; she had the courage to go on calling herself Lucy Stone, Mrs Lucy Stone, and eventually she and Henry were no longer accused of being free lovers but were looked upon as an old married couple who had an idiosyncrasy about names. But though she stuck by her name, the right of a married woman to keep her own name ceased to be a cause she publicly proselytized for. Instead, she did what most of the early feminists did; she became a suffragist. As she had said to Julia Branch as early as 1858—when women get the right to vote, "*that* would settle all other rights." The right to vote became *the* right women fought for, the panacea for all women's ills, the theory being that when women could vote, they would create a society in which there was no more discrimination against women. Rights for which women had earlier fought were quietly dropped. For example, Amelia Bloomer, for whom the nineteenth-century pantsuit was named, not only stopped wearing bloomers but became an advocate of crinolines and in 1869 suggested to Dr Mary Walker, who had continued to wear pants, that "it would be well, in the present state of public opinion, if Dr Walker could conform to the fashionable style, or else make herself less conspicuous . . . . If a dress . . . causes another to . . . reject the great truths we bring before them, then let us sacrifice our own comfort and preference for the sake of the great cause in which we labor."

Lucy Stone did not sacrifice her name to the great cause of the vote, but with rare exceptions it became merely the silent testimonial of her beliefs. "Some insist upon dragging in their peculiar views on theology, temperance, marriage, race, dress, finance, labour and capital. No one can estimate the danger . . . the cause of woman's enfranchisement has already sustained by the failure of its advocates to limit themselves to the main question." Thus wrote Henry Blackwell on January 8, 1870 in an editorial that appeared in the first issue of *The Woman's Journal*, the feminist newspaper he and Lucy Stone were to edit for the rest of their lives. Though *The Woman's Journal* by no means restricted itself to the cause of woman's enfranchisement and published many items on temperance, marriage laws, race and dress reform, it rarely took up the cause of a married woman's right to her own surname. And during the first decade of the *Journal's* existence, one looks in vain for an editorial by Lucy Stone on the subject. The handful of items that deal with women's names are mostly about first names. For example, on July 30, 1870 the *Journal* printed a letter from a Mehitabel March who, among other things, complained about the fad of calling women Nettie or Maggie or Jennie, as if they were "giggling school-girls," and about the absurdity of calling married women Mrs Augustus or Mrs Peter. There were also short articles on such subjects as whether or not female doctors should be called "Doctress" (December 12, 1874). "Value of a Name," an article that begins, "There is a great deal in a name," turns out to be a discussion of the importance of female authors choosing mellifluous pen names (March 16, 1878).

Lucy Stone was surprisingly silent on the subject of married women's surnames. Although she and Henry wrote many editorials on equal rights in the marriage relation, they did not discuss a wife's equal right to her own name. "Marriage is really a permanent partnership of equals who have reciprocal rights and duties. Let it be so defined by the law," wrote Lucy Stone in *The Woman's Journal* for July 26, 1873, but she did not suggest that the co-partnership of marriage might be exemplified as it is in business by the partners calling themselves Smith & Jones. On August 16 of that year Henry illustrated "the true relation between husband and wife" from his personal experience. "Eighteen years ago my wife and I . . . declared our marriage to mean 'a permanent partnership of equals, with reciprocal rights and duties'," but Henry did not mention that they exemplified their equality by his wife's keeping her own name. Again on April 12, 1873 *The Woman's Journal* printed in full an important Illinois Supreme Court decision in which a judge decided a husband was no longer liable for the torts of his wife because the legal supremacy of the husband no longer existed. At one point in his argument the judge said that although husband and wife "are not one as heretofore," "they are one in name." One might have expected Lucy Stone would have used the occasion to point out that since in Illinois there was no statute compelling a woman to take her husband's name, a husband and wife need not be one in name either. But the *Journal* let the judge's statement that husband and wife "are one in name" stand without comment.

In that same year a minister referred to Lucy Stone in *The Universalist* magazine as Mrs Blackwell, insisting he would address her "by the only name the law gives her a right to use." The minister was corrected in *The Woman's Journal*, but not by Lucy Stone or Henry Blackwell. Instead "A Universalist Clergyman" who happened to be writing a series of articles for the *Journal* replied. "Hunt over your law books, Mr D. D.," wrote the Universalist Clergyman, "and see if you can find anything that requires a woman to take her husband's name! Whatever you find, publish, that we may know the truth." Here was another occasion when Lucy Stone herself could have written on married women's names, but she chose not to do so. More important, on May 10, 1873, *The Woman's Journal* reported the marriage of the Reverend Olympia Brown to Mr John Henry Willis and then made the following announcement: "We rejoice to learn that Olympia Brown retains her maiden name." But that was all that was said; Lucy Stone did not write an editorial on the subject and try to gain other converts; Olympia Brown's retention of her name was not mentioned again.

It is likely that Lucy and Henry decided not to use *The Woman's Journal* as a platform for advocating that wives keep their own surname because they did not want to endanger the cause of suffrage by associating it with an even more unpopular cause. They may well have felt justified in not expatiating on the subject because there were in fact no laws that compelled a woman to change her name to her husband's. Lucy's having to sign legal documents "wife of Henry Blackwell" may have seemed to them a trivial formality, not evidence that the law did not acknowledge the name Lucy Stone.

1879—A Married Woman Must Vote Bearing Her Husband's Surname

If Lucy Stone and Henry Blackwell did believe that since no law existed requiring a wife to assume her husband's name, lawyers and government officials would have to recognize the legal validity of the name Lucy Stone, they were disabused of their naiveté in 1879.

The New York Times, like other newspapers, did not approve of Lucy Stone's keeping her name and had often indicated its disapproval when it had occasion to mention her in its pages either by not calling her by her correct name or by subjecting her to mild ridicule. For example, on March 18, 1857 the *Times* reported that "Mrs Lucy Stone Blackwell delivered an address on Monday night . . . Mrs Blackwell—we beg her pardon—we believe she still insists on being called Lucy Stone." Again on February 11, 1858 the *Times* remarked that "Mr Henry Blackwell, in a brief address, introduced his wife, Mrs Lucy Stone. (The nomenclature of *this* married pair is peculiar . . .)."

The *Times*, ever on the alert, learned in March 1879 of a legal difficulty Lucy Stone had had because of her name and on March 15 published the following editorial:

> A grotesque illustration of the extremes to which "women's rights" may be run was lately furnished in a legal complication growing out of the refusal of LUCY STONE, wife of HENRY B. BLACKWELL, to assume her husband's name. To a deed from MR BLACKWELL, in which his wife was obliged to release her rights of dower, the lady signed her name thus: "LUCY STONE, wife of HENRY B. BLACKWELL." The purchaser of the property thus conveyed demurred to the signature, which he thought might not give validity to the instrument. Accordingly, as Mrs LUCY STONE, wife of HENRY B. BLACKWELL, firmly refused to write her name otherwise, BLACKWELL and WILLIAM B. STONE [Lucy's brother] were compelled to execute a bond to defend this property against all proceedings on the part of "said LUCY STONE, wife of said HENRY B. BLACKWELL" to recover her right of dower. This was a little awkward for the men, but Lucy had her own way.

To this editorial, Lucy Stone made the following reply, printed in the *Times* on March 23:

> Referring to an item in your paper of the 15th inst. permit me to say that during my married life of nearly 25 years my legal right to sign my own name has only been twice questioned, and each of these instances occurred more than 20 years ago. So this statement of any recent question about my name has no foundation whatever. On the contrary, there has been a most beautiful recognition all along of the propriety of my retaining the name by which I was known to the public.
> Lucy Stone

Boston, Thursday, March 20, 1879.

It is a strange reply. Does the sentence—"this statement of any recent question

about my name has no foundation whatever"—mean that the *Times'* account
of the land transaction was a total fabrication? In 1879 Henry was in the beet
sugar business and in financial trouble, so it is quite likely he and Lucy sold
some land. Or was Lucy denying a bond had to be executed because of the
buyer's doubt of the validity of the signature Lucy Stone? Again, why should
the *Times* have made up the story? What was more likely was that Lucy Stone
was not facing the facts, was trying to deny that her right to her name was not
recognized legally. But that she in part knew she had won only social acceptance of her name is revealed in the last sentence of her letter—"there has
been a most beautiful recognition all along of the propriety of my retaining the
name by which I was known to the public." In 1856 she would not have spoken
of "the propriety" of keeping the name by which she was well-known;
rather, she then claimed she would have kept her name even if she had been
entirely unknown because all wives ought to have a separate identity. Almost
twenty-five years later, however, she speaks only of her right to the name by
which she "was known to the public." If Lucy Stone needed further proof she
had gained only social recognition of her name, it was to come to her in the
next few months.

On April 10, 1879 Massachusetts passed a bill giving women the right to
vote for members of the school committee. Perhaps because the *Times'* March
editorial brought her refusal to use her husband's name to their consciousness
again, the Massachusetts Board of Registrars decided Lucy Stone would not be
allowed to vote under that name but only as Mrs Blackwell. Not knowing their
decision, however, Lucy went to the assessor's office to pay the $2 poll tax that
was a pre-requisite to voting. The clerk, who knew her only as Lucy Stone (the
name under which she had for years been paying taxes), took her money and
gave her a receipted bill in that name. She then took the bill to the Board of
Registrars and registered. The clerk there was new and had not been informed
of the ruling in regard to her name. When the Board noticed that the clerk had
unwittingly allowed her to register under the name Lucy Stone, it had her name
erased from the registration rolls and informed her she could not vote unless
she used the name Blackwell. On June 2, Lucy replied to the secretary of the
Board of Assessors:

> Replying to yours of the 28th ult., I will say that my name is Lucy
> Stone, and nothing more. I have been called by it more than sixty
> years, and there is no doubt whatever about it. If the use of a foot
> or cart-path for twenty years gives the right of way, surely the use of
> a name for three times twenty years should secure the right to its
> use. There is no law that requires a wife to take her husband's

name. I have signed many important legal papers, and the signature has not been questioned, and it has no reason to be in the case
of my vote.

She told the Board she was willing to use the form "Lucy Stone, wife of Henry
Blackwell," but the Board of Registrars insisted that she could vote only if she
signed her name Lucy Blackwell.

The Board did not approve of the new law that gave women the right to
vote in school elections; yet that was the law and they had to obey it. But the
Board was not going to further the equality between the sexes by allowing a
married woman to vote in her own name, thus establishing a legal precedent
that would allow other married women to do likewise. Although Massachusetts
had been willing to take taxes from Lucy Stone without quibbling about her
name, it now had the power without injuring its purse to punish Lucy Stone for
violating social custom and it did so.

It is most significant that during this humiliating controversy with the
Board of Registrars, a controversy that was reported at some length in Boston
and New York papers, it was never mentioned in *The Woman's Journal*. As
soon as the bill was passed giving women the right to vote in school elections,
Lucy Stone wrote editorial after editorial urging women to register to vote,
giving detailed instructions on how to register and objecting to the differences
in registration procedure required of women and men. She also wrote an
editorial about a woman who had been unjustly debarred from registering because she paid her taxes through a trustee, even though the law specifically
stated that taxes might be paid in that way. But she wrote no editorial on the
Board of Registrars' decision not to allow her to vote under the name of Lucy
Stone, even though Massachusetts had no law requiring a wife to use her husband's surname. *The Woman's Journal* not only did not register a protest
against that decision, but when the Board converted their decision into the
general ruling that "A married woman must vote bearing her husband's surname," the *Journal* in August quietly printed that ruling among the various
other voting requirements and made no comment.

Lucy Stone decided not to fight the Board's ruling and since she refused to
sign her name Lucy Blackwell, she lost her vote. She felt that voting for
members of the school committee was not worth the trouble and expense of a
court fight. She also felt the public was rapidly becoming more favorable
towards woman suffrage—hadn't the territories of Wyoming and Utah already
granted women municipal suffrage? hadn't Kansas, Michigan, Minnesota and
New Hampshire recently granted women school suffrage? It might not be long
before Massachusetts women were granted municipal suffrage. Then, she de-

cided, if she were not allowed to vote as Lucy Stone she would go to court and make a test case of whether or not the law could bar her from voting in the name she had used all her life. Lucy Stone also felt that public opinion was becoming more favorable towards equal rights for women in other areas besides suffrage. Hadn't that male stronghold, Harvard College, opened an annex for women in 1879? weren't the number of female lawyers, doctors and ministers increasing every year? Lucy Stone hoped that when Massachusetts women got municipal suffrage, public opinion would have so far changed that a wife's right to her own name would not be questioned.

But she was also undoubtedly afraid to fight. Her old unconscious Oedipal struggle about being Mrs Stone may have deprived her of the intense conviction of her rights a prolonged legal battle requires. And she of course may not have wanted to damage the cause of suffrage (a cause she felt would soon be won) by associating it with what most people regarded as a minor issue. She also had rational grounds for fearing she would lose her case. In 1872 Susan B. Anthony had tried to vote under the Fourteenth Amendment and had lost a court fight. Moreover, Myra Bradwell had been refused admission to the Illinois bar solely on the grounds that she was a married woman, a decision that in 1872 had been upheld by the United States Supreme Court. When Anthony lost her case, hadn't Henry himself said, "To appeal to the Courts to-day is, in my judgment, unwise, simply because it will result in establishing hostile precedents, which will have to be reversed hereafter."

Whatever her reasons, Lucy Stone chose not to fight in 1879. She did not live to see Massachusetts women get the right to vote in municipal elections; therefore, she never fought the Board of Registrars' ruling and never gained legal recognition of her name.

11

LUCY STONE v. THE STATUS QUO

Lucy Stone v. The Commonwealth of Massachusetts

A married woman must vote bearing her husband's surname. If Lucy Stone had decided to fight that 1879 ruling of the Massachusetts Board of Registrars, would she have won her case?

Lucy Stone would have had no trouble finding a lawyer willing to defend her right to vote in her own name. Samuel E. Sewell, one of the lawyers who checked the law for her when she decided to keep her name after marriage, was a friend of hers and a co-owner of *The Woman's Journal.* Sewell was an active feminist who, among other activities, had petitioned the Massachusetts legislature in behalf of woman suffrage and had written a pamphlet on laws relating to the legal condition of married women. If Mr Sewell had represented Lucy Stone, he would have argued much as follows:

In 1855, the year Mrs Lucy Stone married, there was no statute in Massachusetts that required a woman upon marriage to change her surname to her husband's. In 1879 there is no such statute in Massachusetts, nor is there in any state in the Union.

If in 1855 Mrs Stone had changed her name to her husband's, she would have done so not in obedience to any Massachusetts law. She would have changed her name because of the old common law right of any person to change his surname as he saw fit.

In 1859 when discussing the right of a person to change his name, Judge Daly of the Court of Common Pleas in New York remarked that the correct legal name of a person "is a subject to which legal writers have paid little attention" (2 Hilton's Reports 566). I might add that the correct legal name of a married woman is a subject to which legal writers have paid no attention, and that to understand the correct legal name of a married woman it is necessary to know something about the origin of surnames.

As the court is undoubtedly aware, throughout most of history it was deemed sufficient for people to have only one name. In England men and women were known as Beowulf or Wulfstan or Coulava or Eormenburg; they did not have surnames. It was not until about the eleventh century that surnames began to be used in England and it was not until the reign of Henry VIII that they became common. Surnames gradually came into common use because it became necessary to distinguish one William or John from another. What had happened was that the Christian church, as its influence deepened, dictated that members of the faith must give their children Christian names, that is, names derived from the list of canonized saints. Since there are relatively few of these, it came about that many children bore the same Christian name. It has been estimated that in the twelfth century thirty-eight percent of the men had either the name Henry, John, Richard, Robert or William. As a consequence, some means had to be devised to differentiate among several Henrys and Johns. The means that developed was the surname.

A surname, as the etymology of the word reveals, was a person's super-added name, the name written above the Christian name for the purpose of more accurately identifying the person. One's additional identification tag was either a father's name, a physical or mental characteristic, or an occupation or locality. This additional name, since it was an identification tag, could change as one's life changed. Thus a child who might at first be known as Tom John's son could later acquire the name Tom Black because of his dark complexion or Tom Cobbler because of his trade or, if he changed trades, become known as Tom Carpenter. As Chief Justice Coke said in 1628 in his Commentaries on Littleton (3,a[m]), though a man can have only one Christian name, "he may have divers surnames" and "divers names at divers times."

It was because of the original mutability of surnames that men had the right under the common law to change the surname given them at birth to another and to do so not by petitioning the courts but simply by use. It was because of man's common law right to change his surname at will that a woman had the right upon entering the state of matrimony to change her surname to her husband's, and the right, it must be made clear, not to change it. In an English will dated 1328 we learn that one Juliana Cross upon her marriage to Henry Box took the name Juliana Box, but upon Mrs Box's second marriage, to one John de Luda, she chose not to change her name again but continued to be known as Juliana Box. It was not at all uncommon until well into the seventeenth century for a woman to continue to use her maiden name after marriage.

Let me cite some examples. In the 1268 will of William de Beauchamp, he refers to his wife as "Isabel, my wife, Isabel de Mortimer." In the fourteenth century in the public records of the city of Norwich one finds such listings as the following from the year 1318: "Robert de Poswyk Taverner et Alicia Godesman ux' ej' [the Latin abbreviation for 'his wife']." In 1351 a woman named Isabelle Roll who lived in York sued John Bullock in order to get the Church court to declare him her legal husband, and the fact they had different names was not considered to be evidence that she did not regard herself as married. Whoever consults various Consistory Court Act books or Cause papers or Common Pleas plea rolls of the fourteenth and fifteenth centuries will find in cases involving divorce or the legality of a marriage that husband and wife often do not have the same surname. And whoever consults various public records will also discover that it was not at all uncommon for a husband to change his name to his wife's when his wife owned property. For example, in the fourteenth century after John atte Hethe of Cobham married Lucy atte Grene, he, so states the court book of Chertsey Abbey, Surrey, "is now called atte Grene."

During the reign of Elizabeth many a woman of the middle and upper classes chose not to take her current husband's surname. In 1577 in Leeds there was buried a "Mastris Anne Standish," wife of one George Baildon, and her mother was "My Ladye Hussye," widow of Thomas Falkingham. Indeed, the wife of the Chief Justice, Sir Edward Coke, did not use his name. The former Elizabeth Cecil had first been married to Sir William Hatton and after her marriage to Coke continued to call herself Lady Hatton, preferring that august appellation to Coke, which name, as if to remind him of his humble origins, she always spelled Cooke. Much as the Chief Justice must have disliked his wife's scorn of his name, he could not compel her to use it, for surnames, he well knew, were a matter of choice.

In the seventeenth century there were also women of the middle and lower classes who chose not to use their husbands' names. For example, one finds recorded in the Blackburn register such an entry as— "April 16, 1647 Peg Nance, wife of Thomas Sudell was buried." In America there were also wives who did not go by their husbands' names, and their maiden names were accepted as their legal names by the courts. Among the records relating to divorce in the state of New York one reads of an Anneke Adriaens who in 1664 sued for divorce from her husband, who is named as Aert Pietersen Tack, and in 1669 one William Bogardus was "freed from any further type of obligation of matrimony to the said Woijntie Cobrantz." At that time in New York there was also a merchant and ship owner, one Margaret Hardenbrook, who conducted all her business affairs in that name, her maiden name despite two marriages. And her maiden name was legally acknowledged; in a 1660 deposition she is described as "Margaret Hardenbroeck, living in the Manhattans . . . at present married to Pieter Adolphus, merchant there."

There were women living in England in the early years of this century who did not use their husbands' names. A judge in 1823 in a case that will be discussed later said he knew *"many living instances"* of women who had names different from their husbands'. There are regions today in England where it is the custom for wives to retain their names. A correspondent in the December 23, 1865 Notes and Queries *states that in Dorset "It constantly happens that a married female retains her maiden-name," and he adds, that name "also descends to her children and their descendants."*

Friends of mine who recently traveled to Scotland visited a David Barrie whose wife is known as Margaret Ogilvy, and many wives in the village of Kirriemuir are known by their maiden names. It is of course true that in most of Scotland wives are now known by their husband's surname; nevertheless, a wife's maiden name must be used on all legal records. Thus, when a Jean McNabb marries a Donald Douglas the law requires her to sign all legal documents as *"Jean McNabb or Douglas,"* Douglas, her husband's name, being regarded as a mere alias.

In Scotland all women used to retain their maiden names after marriage, and that was also true in many other countries. Such was the custom in Ireland, Wales, Iceland, Sweden, Norway, the Netherlands, Persia, Ethiopia, South Africa, the Hawaiian Islands and in many more countries. Such continues to be the custom in many of these countries and at the present time is also the custom in parts of Spain. That celebrated traveler, George Borrow *in his* The Bible in Spain, *published in 1843, tells how he arrived "at the door of Juan Lopez, the husband of Maria Diaz."* In other parts of Spain Maria Diaz after marriage would be known as Maria Diaz de Lopez, that is, she would add her husband's name to her maiden one. Just as custom varies in different parts of Spain and in England, so it varies from country to country.

It is true that in America the custom of the wife taking the husband's name is universal, but it is only a custom, and it is not the province of the courts to legislate custom. To compel Mrs Stone to do as other wives do and take her husband's name would be just as absurd as to compel the odd woman who resists fashion to conform to the now current fad of the bustle.

The custom of the wife changing her name to her husband's derived, as I have said, from the old common law right to use the surname of one's choice and change it if one desired. America received its common law from England, and that America is under the common law in regard to names has recently been reaffirmed by Judge Daly in the 1859 case previously cited, the Petition of

Snook. In that case, Judge Daly, after a learned discourse on the origin of sur-names and the law and usage respecting them, decided that John Snook had had every right to change his name to Pike and to do so merely by use, that is, without getting the permission of the court. For, said Judge Daly, as soon as a person is generally known in his community by a name, that constitutes his legal name. "All that the law looks to is the identity of the individual."

In cases involving married women, courts in England and America have also looked only to the identity of the individual woman and have accepted the name she was generally known by even though it was not the name of her hus-band. Indeed, in England in 1823 when the court had to decide whether Ann Lovick, a married woman who had reverted to her maiden name, could legally be married again in that name, Justice Best maintained "a married woman may legally bear a different name from her husband" (The King v. The Inhabitants of St Faith's, 3 Dowling & Rylands Reports 348). Our own courts have also upheld the legality of a wife's maiden name. In 1871 a Vermont court decided a suit could not be declared at fault because Augusta Jackson, a married woman, was described by her maiden name. She was, said the judge, "legally entitled" to bear the name of her husband, but since she was generally known as Augusta Jackson, her marriage being unknown, she could be sued in that name, for her identity was not in question (44 Vermont Reports 662). The Kansas Supreme Court in 1878 also affirmed that a married woman could be sued in a name that was not her husband's. Sarah J. Brown, a married woman, had run off with a lover and assumed his name of Clark. In that name she later brought an action against him to recover money he had borrowed from her. Mr Clark's lawyers argued she could not sue him as Sarah Clark because her true surname was Brown, the name of her legal husband. But the court did not agree; it maintained that since she was generally known as Sarah Clark, that was her name and she could bring suit in it. Said the court: "A person has a perfect legal right to call himself by any name he chooses, and so long as such name identifies him by reason of his being thus known in the community . . . he would have a perfect legal right to sue and be sued by such name" (19 Kansas Reports 522). Moreover, in South Carolina in the case of Converse v. Converse the court in 1856 recognized it had the power under the laws of its state to change the name of a wife even against the wishes of her husband, in other words, that a wife might have a name different from her husband's (9 Richardson's Equity 535).

Lucy Stone had a perfect legal right to call herself Lucy Stone after her mar-riage to Henry Blackwell, for under the common law a person has the legal right to use any name he chooses to, so long as he has not chosen to use that name to commit fraud. The name a person chooses to use, the name he is known by in his community, constitutes a person's legal name. This common law rule of names prevails unless there is specific legislation to the contrary. When Lucy Stone decided to continue using her own name after marriage, she quite properly consulted lawyers to ascertain if there was a law in Massachusetts that compelled married women to assume their husbands' names. The three lawyers she consulted all agreed there was no such law in Massachusetts, and one of those lawyers was the late Salmon P. Chase who later became Chief Justice of the United States Supreme Court. Chief Justice Chase informed Lucy Stone that "there was no law requiring a wife to take her husband's surname; it was only a custom." Lucy Stone, therefore, had a perfect legal right not to follow custom. She had a perfect legal right to choose to go by the name Stone, the name by which she had been known for thirty-seven years, the name by which she in this year of 1879 has now been known for sixty-one years, the name by which she is now known not only in her community but all over the world. There can be no question of her identity; there can be no question that her legal name is Lucy Stone.

In the light of this fact, when the Massachusetts Board of Registrars informed Lucy Stone she could vote only under the name Lucy Blackwell, it was ordering her to vote in a name she was not known by; it was ordering her, therefore, to vote in a name that was not her legal name. Not only was the Massachusetts Board of Registrars violating the common law rule of names, it was also violating a Massachusetts statute. Since 1856 Massachusetts has had a Married Woman's Property Act that gives married women control over their own property. Since courts have consistently decided that a name is a species of property, the Massachusetts Board of Registrars when it forbade Lucy Stone from voting in her own name, was attempting to deprive her of her property— her name—and was therefore in violation of the Massachusetts Married Woman's Property Act. May I add that the Board was also acting inconsistently, for Massachusetts has for years acknowledged that Lucy Stone's name is Lucy Stone since for years the assessor's office has collected taxes from Lucy Stone under the name Lucy Stone and not once did the state refuse to accept her taxes unless she signed her name Lucy Blackwell.

The Massachusetts Board of Registrars was not only acting inconsistently and in violation of Massachusetts law, it was also violating the Fourteenth Amendment, added to the United States Constitution in 1868, which provides in part that "No State shall make or enforce any law which shall abridge the privileges or immunities of the citizens of the United States; nor shall any State deprive any person of life, liberty, or property, without due process of law; nor deny to any person within its jurisdiction the equal protection of the law." The Massachusetts Board of Registrars, when it ruled that Lucy Stone could not vote in the name she was known by in her community, was clearly violating the Fourteenth Amendment of the United States Constitution, for it abridged the privilege of Lucy Stone as a female citizen of Massachusetts to vote in a school election; it tried to deprive her of her property—her name—without due process of law; and finally, it denied her the equal protection of the law, which in Massachusetts permits its citizens to use the name of their choice so long as it is not for a fraudulent purpose.

Lucy Stone should not have been deprived of her right to vote because she quite properly insisted on voting in her legal name. The Massachusetts Board of Registrars, when it ordered Lucy Stone to change her surname to her husband's, was not administering the law but whipping Mrs Stone for her nonconformity to custom, to paraphrase the words of our Massachusetts sage, Mr Emerson. And Mrs Stone's nonconformity to custom was not the caprice of an unruly child, but the careful and considered act of one who had consulted her conscience, the guardian of God within us, and at that shrine learned that respect for her individuality, for the God within each person, required her to keep her own identity when she married Mr Blackwell. Mrs Stone's long and happy union with Mr Blackwell provides us with a forecast of what all marriages will be like when husbands and wives deal with each other as equals. In that future time women when they marry will no longer sink into the existence of their husband but will remain separate and equally important existences. Even now that day is being prepared for us, even now in state after state courts and legislatures are deciding that wives are separate and distinct from their husbands and capable of acting on their own for many purposes. Eventually, the law will recognize that wives are capable of acting on their own for all purposes because mankind will have learned that women are the equals of men. When that time comes, when wives will have ceased to be the bondservants of their husbands, when man will have learned to treat woman as his equal, to summarize Mr John Stuart Mill's great essay on The Subjection of Women, *when that time comes every woman will be like Lucy Stone, every woman will have so profound a sense of self-respect and self-worth that she will no more think of giving up her identity when she marries than men do today. Lucy Stone is the morning star of that new day.*

If Lucy Stone had decided to fight the 1879 ruling of the Massachusetts Board of Registrars, her hypothetical lawyer would probably have used most of the above arguments, his chief legal argument being that under the old common law a person had the right to use whatever name he wished, which right had made it possible for wives to change their names or not to change their names, as many wives did not. In short, his chief legal argument would have been that Lucy Stone violated present day American custom, not law. The state of Massachusetts, therefore, would have had to prove that Lucy Stone violated law, not custom, when she did not take her husband's name. Consequently, a lawyer representing the Board of Registrars would have defended the Board's right to make its ruling in much the following way:

Although Mrs Stone's lawyer and even the late Chief Justice Chase assert that when Mrs Stone married in 1855 there was no law in the state of Massachusetts that compelled a woman to assume her husband's name, such a law, in fact two such laws existed, both of which had the effect of changing Lucy Stone's name as a matter of law to that of Lucy Blackwell after her marriage to Henry Blackwell.

Chapter 141 of the laws passed in Massachusetts in 1849 reads: "Whenever a married woman shall obtain a decree of divorce from the bonds of matrimony, it shall be in the power of the judge granting the decree, to allow said woman to resume her maiden name." Furthermore, Chapter 256, section 1 of the laws passed in Massachusetts in 1851 reads in part: "No lawful change of the name of any person, other than that of the wife in case of marriage or divorce, shall be made in this Commonwealth, except for sufficient reason consistent with the public interest, and to the satisfaction of the judge of probate of the county in which the party resides . . ."

Both of these laws presume that a woman's name as a matter of law is changed to her husband's when she marries. For would our legislators have specifically stated that a woman's change of name in case of marriage constituted a "lawful change" of name if they had believed her change of name was a mere matter of custom to be followed or not according to a woman's whim? Chapter 256, section 1 of the General Laws of Massachusetts definitively recognizes that when a woman marries, the law changes her name to her husband's. Chapter 141, which gives the judge granting a decree of divorce the power to allow a woman to resume her maiden name, also recognizes that the law changes a woman's name to her husband's when she marries, for could a judge have the legal power to divest a woman of her husband's name if the law had not originally given her that name? If it had been merely a matter of custom for a woman to take or not to take her husband's name, the law would not have had to devise special legislation to deal with the matter.

Whatever common law rights married women may once have had in regard to their names, legal bodies have long had special jurisdiction over them. Chapter 141 was enacted in 1849 to give to the courts the power previously delegated to legislatures, which had used to grant divorces and which consequently had used to have the power to allow a divorced woman to resume the use of her maiden or former name. To illustrate, in the first decade of this century, after Martha Codd was granted a divorce by the legislature of New York, she obtained an act from that legislature authorizing her to resume the use of her maiden name of Bradstreet. Similarly, in 1843 when the Connecticut legislature granted a divorce to the wife of Dr Christopher Yates, it at the same time gave her the right thereafter "to be known and called by her former name, Emma Willard." If Emma Willard or Martha Bradstreet had changed their names to their husbands' as a matter of choice then there would have been no need for them to appeal to their legislatures for a change of name. Their names changed at marriage as a matter of law and therefore their names could only be changed after marriage by the law.

Massachusetts is not the only state that has statutes recognizing that after marriage a woman's legal name becomes her husband's. According to The Revised Statutes of Kentucky for the years 1851-1852, Chapter 68, section 1: "Any person of the age of twenty-one years, and NOT A MARRIED WOMAN, may have his or her name changed by the county court in which he or she resides." Similarly, in 1863 Vermont passed An Act Relating to Changes of Names, No. 22, section 1 providing in part: "Any person of full age and sound mind, OTHER THAN A MARRIED WOMAN, who may wish to alter his name, may . . ." Such laws, by barring a married woman from changing her name but not barring a married man, establish the rule that a married woman's name must follow that of her husband. Mrs Stone's lawyer says that need not be the case in South Carolina, citing the case of Converse v. Converse in which the court held that the laws of South Carolina gave it the power to change a married woman's name from that of her husband, even against his wishes. But Mrs Stone's lawyer failed to point out that although the court had the power to do so, it did not, that the court refused to change the name of Mrs Converse, for, said the court, it seems "to be wrong in principle." "It is inconvenient," the court said later that wives "should have appellations different from husbands." The court further said that should a husband change his name, "that of the wife would also be changed, as a necessary consequence."

It may be that there are some Englishwomen who have the legal right to have a name different from their husband's, as the judge maintained in the 1823 case cited by Mrs Stone's lawyer. But these women must have been what the English call "peeresses in their own right" and such women have always been permitted to retain their noble names, just as Queen Victoria did not take the name of the late Prince Albert. But other Englishwomen do take their husbands' names; Ann Lovick, the woman in the 1823 case, reverted to that name only when her husband deserted her and immediately became Mrs Riggs when she married again. The Vermont woman Augusta Jackson used that name because she did not live with her husband, and Sarah Brown changed her name to her putative husband's. However, the courts never said Jackson and Clark were the legal names of these women, only that they might be sued in them. For a court may permit a married woman to sue and be sued in a name other than her husband's, but that does not mean the court is saying her legal name may be different from her husband's. In 1833 in the case of Scanlan v. Wright (13 Pickering [Mass.] 523) the judge decided a deed conveying land to Eliza Ann Castin was valid although she had subsequently changed her name by marriage to Eliza Ann Scanlan. In making that decision, the judge was not saying Mrs Scanlan's legal name could also be Castin; the assumption was her legal name was Scanlan, that of her husband. The court merely recognized she had a different name before her marriage, a name in which a deed of land had been conveyed to her. She was not to be barred from acquiring her land because she now had another name. The court's decision only recognized that women have one legal name before marriage and another after. In the handful of cases in which there has been a question about a married woman's name, the courts have invariably assumed her legal surname was her husband's. See, in addition to the above cases discussed, Bell v. The State 25 Texas Reports 574 and Warren v. Quill 8 Nevada Reports 218.

Case decisions as well as laws that deal with married women's names clearly reveal that husband and wife are considered to be one in name under the law. And this is so even though at the present time the older concept of the complete legal unity of husband and wife is breaking down, for married women are now treated as separate persons in certain matters relating to property and the bringing of suits. However, no court has gone so far as to suggest that a wife might destroy family unity by separating herself from her husband in name. On the contrary. As Justice Anthony Thornton of the Illinois Supreme Court remarked in 1872 in deciding the case of Martin v. Robson (65 Illinois Reports 129), "The unity of husband and wife has been severed. They are now distinct persons, and may have separate legal estates, contracts, debts and injuries." But, he added, although "they are not one as heretofore. They are one in name."

Mrs Stone's lawyer defines the law differently, contending that when Mrs Stone did not take her husband's name, she was exerting her common law right to use the name of her choice. But may it not be argued that since common law came into being as the result of long usage and since women for several centuries have assumed the names of their husbands, that common law as it now exists requires a married woman to change her name to her husband's? But even if that not be admitted, I think I have made abundantly clear that actual statutes and case decisions now legislate what a married woman's name must be.

Mrs Stone's lawyer, however, insists that the wife's taking the husband's name is a mere custom, and he has tried to prove that by showing how custom has varied from country to country. But his profuse illustrations of the great variety of appellations by which married women were designated seem to me to prove the opposite. For whether a woman were called Alice Jackwyf or Alice Goodman, wife of Jack Bullock, the name of her husband was always required in legal records. Therefore, it might be said that a husband's name was always a legal part of a woman's name.

Mrs Stone's lawyer has also tried to demonstrate that even at the present time it is not universal for a wife to assume the name of her husband. But hasn't he again proved the opposite of what he set out to? Hasn't he proved that it is now virtually universal for a wife to assume the name of her husband? Mrs Stone's lawyer has himself pointed out that in Scotland it is well nigh the rule for wives to assume their husbands' names, a rule that was greatly fortified by the passage in 1854 of the Registration of Births, Deaths, and Marriages Act, an act whose aim was to make uniform, regular and orderly Scottish record keeping, and which, therefore, listed married women under their husbands' names. For imagine a record keeping system that listed some married women under their maiden names and others under their husbands' names! Chaos would ensue. But to return to my main point, that it is now virtually universal for wives to assume their husbands' names. Mrs Stone's lawyer listed the Hawaiian Islands as one of the countries in which women did not take their husbands' names. He left unclear whether or not the Islands were among the countries in which women still do not take their husbands' names. He left that unclear because he did not think it expedient to mention that in 1860 the Hawaiian Islands passed a law that reads: "All married women now living, and all that may be married hereafter on these Islands, shall, from and after the passage of this Act, adopt the name of their husbands as a family name."

Native Hawaiian women did not used to take their husbands' names, but now that the race is becoming civilized, they do. For as civilization advances, men stop regarding their wives as concubines or as chattel. Rather when they unite themselves to a woman, the woman who is to be the undisputed mother of their children, they bind themselves to her for life, make her part of their household and family, which is signified by her being permitted to share the good name of her husband. Mrs Stone in her zeal for women's rights apparently thinks that when a woman takes her husband's name she is wronged, deprived of her property and individuality. But Mrs Stone fails to understand his-

tory. Man's permitting woman to share his name shows in what high regard he now holds woman, how under the shield of his name man now protects woman from the harshness of the world for which woman's constitutional delicacy unfits her. Moreover, when a wife is permitted to share her husband's name, she is thereby permitted to share whatever honors may accrue to that name. A wife, when she shares her husband's name, signifies the blessed unity of the family, the unity upon which the foundations of society rests, a unity which depends upon woman continuing to fulfill her God-ordained role as the keeper of man's hearth and as the mother of man's children, a role that all women, with the lone exception of Mrs Stone, are proud to acknowledge to the world by bearing the name of their husband.

It is because woman was destined by God to be a wife that Mrs Stone cannot contend that she was denied the equal protection of the law as granted to United States citizens by the Fourteenth Amendment to our Constitution. For Mrs Stone's lawyer must be aware of a recent decision by the United States Supreme Court. In December 1872 the highest court in the land decided that the state of Illinois was not violating the Fourteenth Amendment when it forbade Myra Bradwell from practicing law because she was a married woman. As Mr Justice Bradley explained, her rights as a citizen were not being abrogated; rather, Illinois was merely affirming the laws of God, from which the laws of man derive. To quote Justice Bradley: "The paramount destiny and mission of woman are to fulfill the noble and benign office of wife and mother. This is the law of the Creator. And the rules of civil society must be adapted to the general constitution of things, and cannot be based upon exceptional cases" (16 Wallace 130).

May it not also be said in Mrs Stone's case that her rights as a citizen have not been abrogated, that the ruling of the Massachusetts Board of Registrars was an adaptation of the law of God to the rules of civil society? Since the "paramount destiny and mission of woman" are to be a wife and mother, should not the laws of man, reflections of the laws of God, require a woman when she enters into her mission of wife to publicly acknowledge that fact by requiring her to assume the name of wife, that is, the name of her husband? Indeed, would we not soon live in a godless Gomorrah if every woman were to follow the example of Lucy Stone? For it would become impossible to tell a respectable woman bound in holy wedlock from a rank Free Lover! Morality alone demands that women take the name of their lawfully wedded husband.

I, of course, do not in any way wish to impugn Mrs Stone's moral character. No one doubts that she is legally married to Mr Blackwell. Nor does anyone doubt that she has every right to use her maiden name of Lucy Stone in her capacity as an editor and lecturer, just as actresses have stage names. The ruling of the Massachusetts Board of Registrars only affects the use of her name when she acts in her capacity as a citizen by voting. Then indeed she must use her legal name, that is, her own first name followed by the surname of her husband, the name the laws of civil society, derived as they are from the laws of God, decree must be the name of wives.

How would a judge have decided? It is most unlikely that in 1879 a judge would have decided in Lucy Stone's favor. Public opinion, though it had come to look somewhat favorably on Lucy Stone's work for women, nevertheless did not look favorably on her keeping her own name. The *Boston Post* on June 5, 1879, in the midst of her troubles with the Board of Registrars, wrote: "We yield to no one in our respect for the lady who has labored with so much devotion . . . to break down the barriers which she has believed kept her sex from its full rights and privileges . . . But . . . we hope there will be no change in the present custom by which the wife takes the name of her husband. Were this convenient arrangement to cease, almost endless family complications would ensue." The *Boston Post* felt the decision of the Board of Registrars was the only one possible, and since judges' opinions pretty much follow public opinion, it is almost certain that a judge who ruled in her case would have canonized the status quo by deciding that Lucy Stone's only legal name was Lucy Blackwell.

Her Maiden Surname Is Absolutely Lost

Lucy Stone almost certainly would have lost her case in a lower court. But what if she had appealed and taken the matter as far as the United States Supreme Court? It is again almost certain she would have lost and that the Supreme Court would have decided that Massachusetts did have the right to require married women to use their husbands' surnames for legal purposes.

And yet, after the Supreme Court decided Illinois had the right to prohibit Myra Bradwell from practicing law, Bradwell proceeded to get a law passed in Illinois that guaranteed all persons, regardless of sex, freedom in selecting a profession, for which reason the state of Illinois on its own initiative eventually issued Myra Bradwell a license to practice law. Moreover, on March 28, 1892 Bradwell was admitted to practice before the United States Supreme Court, the court that twenty years before had declared that the laws of man, since they followed the laws of God, must not permit a married woman to practice law.

It may be, then, that Lucy Stone ultimately might have got Massachusetts to pass a law permitting all persons, including married women, the legal right to use the name of their choice. But it is highly unlikely, for women were to get almost every other right before married women got the right to use a name not their husband's. Even before the 1879 Massachusetts ruling requiring married women to vote in their husband's surname, the tendency of American law had been to treat married women as if they had no common law rights in regard to names. As we have seen, Massachusetts, Kentucky and Vermont already had laws that could be interpreted as requiring married women to assume the name of their husband, and between 1880 and 1882 a revision of Vermont's law, additions to two legal treatises and a case decision further revealed that legislators and lawyers felt it was their right, not a wife's right, to decide what name she should use.

Sadly enough, the example of Lucy Stone cannot be discounted as the probable cause of these further restrictions of women's name rights. For Lucy Stone was famous and her refusal to use her husband's name was disapproved of, so much so that her name difficulties in negotiating a deed were thought worthy of an editorial in *The New York Times* and the decision of the Board of Registrars to bar her from voting in her own name was discussed in newspapers in several states. It is therefore possible that Lucy Stone's well-publicized difficulties influenced Vermont legislators, when revising their change of name law in December 1880, not only to again bar married women from changing their name but to further mandate that "if a married man changes his name," his wife's name was also changed, a virtual assertion that a wife's name must be the same as her husband's. That law so outraged Lucy Stone that in the January 22, 1881 *Woman's Journal* she broke her editorial silence on the subject and after printing the new law, bitterly remarked that she hoped reading it would fill women with a "wholesome discontent" so they would revolt against "the humiliation and helplessness of being a mere appendage."

The fearful example of Lucy Stone may also have induced two Boston attorneys to lay down nominal law when revising their books on marriage. Joel P. Bishop's *Commentaries on the Law of Marriage and Divorce,* first published in 1852, went through five editions without mentioning names, but in the 1881 edition Bishop added section 704a: "The rule of law and custom is familiar, that marriage confers on the woman the husband's surname." Similarly, James Schouler in his *Treatise on the Law of the Domestic Relations* did not discuss names until the 1882 edition when he included section 40: "Marriage at our law does not change the man's name, but it confers his surname upon the woman."

In addition, the Lucy Stone bugaboo may have incited a New York judge in 1881 to deliver the following dictatorial pronouncement:

For several centuries, by the common law among all English-speaking people, a woman, upon her marriage, takes her husband's surname. That becomes her legal name, and she ceases to be known by her maiden name. By that name she must sue and be sued, make and take grants and execute all legal documents. Her maiden surname is absolutely lost, and she ceases to be known thereby.

Read out of context, one would think the judge was laying down the law to another Lucy Stone, but the case, Chapman v. Phoenix National Bank (85 New York Reports 437), had nothing whatsoever to do with a woman who refused to use her husband's name. It concerned a Southerner who was trying to get back her shares of stock in the Phoenix National Bank of New York, stock that had been confiscated by the United States government during the Civil War. The judge, Robert A. Earl, felt the government had given the woman only the most perfunctory notice of the confiscation, which he additionally felt had been in a misnomer since at the time it was issued the former Verina S. Moore had married and changed her name to Chapman. It was at this point in his decision that Judge Earl categorically stated that a married woman could not be sued in her maiden name because at marriage her maiden surname was "absolutely lost," her husband's surname becoming her legal name.

However, Judge Earl's opinion that a married woman could not be sued in her maiden name was irrelevant to the case. In the first place, the question was academic since the United States government could not possibly have published the confiscation notice in the name Verina Chapman since Mrs Chapman had not informed the Phoenix Bank of her marriage and change of name. If there were a misnomer issue, it had nothing to do with the name in which a married woman should be sued but with the fact that an entirely wrong person had been named in the confiscation notice, one "Ver. S. Moore," who was alleged to be, among other things, an officer in the Rebel army and navy and a member of the Confederate Congress, an understandable mistake since several men prominent in the Confederacy bore the name Moore, among them a major in the army, a member of the Confederate Congress from Kentucky, and an Alabama governor who had equipped six regiments. But even the fact that a wrong person was named in the confiscation notice was not the most fundamental issue, for the Judge decided in Mrs Chapman's favor chiefly on the grounds that the Phoenix Bank, as the trustee of her stock, had surrendered it without making any effort on Mrs Chapman's behalf.

The case could have been decided without any discussion of married women's names, and yet in three sentences Judge Earl said five times that a wife "takes her husband's surname," "that becomes her legal name," "she ceases to be known by her maiden name," "her maiden surname is absolutely lost," "she ceases to be known thereby." One cannot help feeling that Judge Earl had read in the newspapers about Lucy Stone's not being able to vote in her maiden name, had, perhaps, even discussed the matter with other lawyers and decided to use the Chapman case as a vehicle for setting forth his belief that a married woman's legal name had to be her husband's, hoping he could thus give future judges and lawyers a precedent to cite should they have to restrain another Lucy Stone. For Judge Earl knew full well that it is a habit of the legal profession to cite such an off the cuff statement as his as if it were a summary of a case decision. But Judge Earl's pronouncement on married women's names was merely what in law is called a judicial dictum, a statement on a legal point other than the one a judge is deciding in a case. Since the legal point is not being reviewed and examined, the judge's words are not supposed to be treated as if they were a considered judicial decision. In practice, however, they often are; certainly, Judge Earl's dictum on married women's names was to be treated as if it were a commandment handed down from Mt Sinai, so much so that Chapman v. Phoenix National Bank came to be regarded as a case in which a judge had denied a married woman's request to be known by her maiden name. But that was many years later.

In the nineteenth century no such case came before the courts. However, there were a fair number of cases in which married women's names did become an issue, and why they did was anticipated by Elizabeth Cady Stanton, who, when she congratulated Lucy Stone for keeping her own name, had said: "Under our new property rights, married women may make contracts—buy and sell, and give deeds and mortgages. It becomes very important, therefore, that a woman should not change her name two or three times in one short life." But women did continue to change their names when they married and remarried, and their doing so was creating a new branch of the law that concerned itself with whether or not a married woman's *first* name had to be her own or could be her husband's, whether or not she could sue and be sued in her maiden name and whether or not she could resume the use of her maiden name after divorce.

There was a babel of opinions, there being no unanimity among judges about what name a married woman should be permitted to use. In regard to first names, we find one judge saying that a married woman had to be sued in her own Christian name not her husband's, as did a New Jersey judge in 1880 (Elberson v. Richards, 42 New Jersey Law Reports 69); on the other hand, in 1898 a judge in the Nebraska Supreme Court felt that since most married women were better known as Mrs John Jones, not Mary Jones, their identification would be more perfect and complete by the use "of their husband's first name, not their own" (Carrall v. The State, 53 Nebraska Reports 431). In regard to the name in which a married woman could sue and be sued there was also no agreement, not even among judges in the same state. For example, in May 1890 a judge in the Texas Supreme Court decided that a suit brought against a married woman in her maiden name was invalid (Freeman v. Hawkins, 77 Texas Reports 498), but the very next month, in June 1890, another judge in the Texas Supreme Court decided that a deed made out to a married woman in her previous name (that of her first husband) was valid (Wilkerson v. Schoonmaker, 77 Texas Reports 615). There was also no unanimity of opinion about whether or not a married woman should continue to use her husband's name after divorce. In 1892 Judge Braley of Lowell, Massachusetts decided that all women who obtained divorces in his court must retain their husband's name so as not to "complicate the records" (reported in the May 7, 1892 *Woman's Journal*). However, in 1897 a judge in the New York Supreme Court decided it was wrong for a woman "to identify herself with her former husband when all relations between them are so broken" and therefore ordered a divorced woman to stop using her husband's name (Blanc v. Blanc, 21 New York Miscellaneous Reports 268).

One finds so much contradictory opinion in part because judges were dealing with a new branch of the law, and an emotionally charged one. For judges felt married women ought not to be known by any other name than their husband's, but that feeling, especially when they had to decide whether or not a married woman could be sued in a former name, often led them to abandon common sense, and worse. For example, when Judge Earl in the Chapman case declared that the confiscation notice issued in the name Verina S. Moore ought to have been in the name Chapman, he failed to ask how the notice could have been issued in the name the former Miss Moore was currently using since she had not informed the Phoenix Bank of her marriage and change of name. Similarly, in the 1890 case of Freeman v. Hawkins the Texas judge did not ask how those who were suing the former Miss Robinson could have known her name had become Freeman since she had not changed the name under which she held title to her land. That obvious question was not asked until 1908 when a California judge decided that a suit to quiet title to land in the name Louisa Munro was not in a misnomer even though after Munro bought the land in question she married and changed her name to Emery. "There was nothing of record to disclose that Louisa Munro had ever changed her name," said the judge. "No steps, which a reasonable or prudent person might take . . . would serve to give a party desirous of commencing an action any knowledge that Louisa Munro had married or had in any other way changed her name" (Emery v. Kipp, 154 California Reports 83).

In making his decision, the California judge cited the Texas case of Freeman v. Hawkins as one in which "universally accepted" legal practice had been violated. For what the Texas judge violated, as did all the judges who ruled that a married woman could not be sued in a former name, was not only common sense but the law of contracts, according to which, a person is held to be bound by his contracts no matter what name he used in making them. As one New York judge explained: "If in making a contract a person uses a name, he will not be permitted to say that it is not his name" (26 New York State Reports 107). Otherwise, by changing his name a person could protect himself from suits on the grounds of misnomer. The Texas judge would not have permitted a Moses Freeman to contend that a suit brought against him in the name Moses Robinson was invalid because after he bought some land he changed his name. The Texas judge, Judge Earl and the others who held that a married woman could not be sued in a former name were obviously not categorizing women as people for whom the law of contracts applied as it did for men.

They perhaps did not because judges seemed to believe that the ceremony of marriage automatically and as a matter of law changed a woman's name to her husband's. The Texas judge who decided Mrs Freeman could not be sued in her maiden name declared: "On the marriage of Mary E. Robinson the law conferred on her the surname of her husband." The New York judge who ordered a divorced woman to stop using her husband's name thought she had acquired the right to use it "solely by the office of marriage," and another New York judge said of a married woman that "the marriage relation gave her the name she bore" (Rich v. Mayer, 26 New York State Reports 107). A Wisconsin judge similarly asserted that "since her marriage she is entitled to the name of her husband" (Lane v. Duchac, 73 Wisconsin Reports 646). But among the marriage laws of Wisconsin, New York, Texas or any other state there was none that said marriage gave, conferred or entitled a woman to her husband's name.

Judges perhaps thought it was common law not statutory law that changed a woman's name when she married. Judge Earl certainly did. "For several centuries, by the common law among all English-speaking people, a woman, upon her marriage, takes her husband's surname," said the judge, who may have assumed that a well nigh universal custom must be common law. Judge Earl in writing the Chapman decision seems not to have checked the common law of names, but to do so would have been easy since another New York judge in an 1859 case had discoursed learnedly on the origin of surnames and of a person's common law right to do what he wished with his name. That judge consequently decided John Snook had the right, merely by use, to change his name to John Pike (Petition of John Snook, 2 Hilton's Reports 566). But one suspects he would not have discoursed on the common law right to use the name of one's choice if the person before him had been a Lucy Stone, a suspicion that seems warranted when one looks at two cases in another state.

When the Texas judge in the 1890 case of Freeman v. Hawkins decided that a married woman could be sued only in her husband's name, he dogmatically asserted that "the law" conferred a husband's name on a wife, but in 1897 another Texas judge said otherwise. "There is nothing in our statute requiring or compelling the wife to take or assume the name of her husband. While this is generally the case, yet the wife might retain her own name. She might be married to the defendant and still be known by her maiden name, or some other name than his." The judge then quoted from the recently published *American and English Encyclopedia of Law* (1887-96): "By custom, the wife is called by the husband's name; but whether marriage shall work any change of name at all is, after all, a mere matter of choice, and either may take the other's name, or they may join their names together." This judge knew it was custom, not law, that gave a woman the right to take her husband's name, but one cannot help feeling that he displayed that knowledge because he was dealing with a man accused of raping a fifteen-year-old girl and pointing out that the indictment against him did not positively prove the girl was not his wife, for the fact she had a different name was not conclusive proof since the law did not compel a wife to assume her husband's name (Rice v. The State, 37 Texas Criminal Reports 36). If the judge had been dealing, not with a man, but with a Texan Lucy Stone, one suspects that, instead of quoting from the *American and English Encyclopedia of Law*, he would have quoted both Bishop and Schouler's statements that the law conferred the husband's name on the wife.

Most judges seemed to know nothing about the common law of names when they were dealing with married women, with even so minor a matter as a wife's use of her husband's first name. A judge in 1860 did feel that whether the defendant's name was Mrs George Bell or Sally Bell depended upon which name she was best known by (Bell v. The State, 25 Texas Reports 574), but most later judges would have felt it was their right to tell Mrs Bell whether she was Sally or Mrs George, even though the name they decided was her legally correct name was not the name she was commonly known by. When a judge in 1897 ordered a divorced woman to stop using her ex-husband's name, it did not occur to him he was abrogating her right to use the name of her choice. He discoursed only on why he had the right to so order her, explaining that since there was "no common-law jurisdiction on the subject of divorce," judges had to create precedents, in this case in regard to the name borne by a divorced wife. He offered several good reasons why women should not use an ex-husband's name. He suggested, for example, that her continued use of his name was a form of deceit since the public might think she was "still the lawful spouse" and she might well be extended credit by a store on that false assumption. He also expressed sympathy for the man who wished to remarry, since "the use by the former wife of his name might be a serious impediment in gaining the consent of some worthy woman who might not want to be one of two women bearing the name of the husband." He therefore enjoined Baroness Blanc, the former wife of Frederic Blanc, from using that name, entirely forgetting that although there was "no common-law jurisdiction on the subject of divorce," there was in regard to names. More important, it did not cross his mind he was depriving Baroness Blanc of a valuable property since under that name she had become well-known as an actress.

But the judge was not able to think of Baroness Blanc as a woman with a profession; he viewed her only as a wife. Similarly, the judges who refused to acknowledge the maiden names of married women were also refusing to see women except as wives, as was Judge Earl when he asserted that the name a woman used before marriage was, after marriage, "absolutely lost," as if her former non-wifely identity could by some legerdemain be obliterated from all records. In their denial of a woman's identity except as wife these judges were perhaps still bound by the older legal view of women, like that found in *The Lawes Resolutions of Womens Rights* (1632) where women were treated as potential or actual wives, as being one with a husband even before marriage. However, it is more likely that a judge's obliteration of a woman's non-wifely identity was a symptom of his opposition to the changing role of women. From that point of view, when Judge Earl declared that the name Verina S. Moore was "absolutely lost," he was expunging the independent woman who had worked as a schoolteacher and earned enough money to buy 150 shares of stock in the Phoenix National Bank and acknowledging her only as Mrs Chapman, a wife. Similarly, the refusal of judges to let wives have a separate identity probably reveals the general reluctance of the legal profession to accept the fact that the legal unity of husband and wife was being severed, that wives were more and more being treated as separate from their husbands. Most judges and lawyers wanted wives to remain one with their husbands, albeit in name only. They therefore maintained that the law compelled wives to be one in name with their husbands, for to have admitted that custom alone dictated what name a wife used would open the door to change. The legal profession in its insistence that women must be wives in name was no different from the public that called Dr Kate Hurd-Mead Mrs Mead, refusing to acknowledge that portion of her name that signified her profession and denominating her as if she were an ordinary wife. In like manner, the majority of judges declared that a married woman's name must be her husband's, disregarding the common law and arrogating to themselves the power to tell women what their names were.

To see how much power over married women's names American courts were arrogating to themselves, we need only look at the way England was handling the same problem. In 1879, the same year the Massachusetts Board of Registrars refused to allow Lucy Stone to vote in her own name, a similar case occurred in England. Florence Fenwick Miller, a member of the London School Board, had married Frederick A. Ford in 1877 and with his consent and by previous arrangement she kept her own name. In 1879 she was re-elected to the School Board, but her election was objected to on the grounds that her legal name was really Ford. Mrs Fenwick Miller, unlike Lucy Stone, proceeded to fight, preparing her case so well it never got to court, for the officers of the Crown were advised they could not win because the common law allowed any person, even a married woman, to use any name he or she chose.

America had always interfered more than England did with married women's names. It was the American Quakers who early in the eighteenth century added a phrase to their marriage certificate that compelled a wife to change her name. Thus, the last sentence of a 1798 Delaware Certificate reads in part: "And moreover, they the said William Warner, and Esther (she according to the custom of marriage assuming the name of her husband) . . ." The English marriage certificate does not have that phrase, and one cannot help wondering if it were added to the American certificate because some Quaker wife, guided by her own inner light, had decided it was wrong to go by the name of another and had refused to take her husband's name. Whatever the reason, American Quakers legislated custom and the English did not.

De Tocqueville had noticed that Americans were more emotionally bound by conformism than Europeans, and the legal profession was as conformist as the man in the street. As Oliver Wendell Holmes pointed out in his 1880 lecture on common law, more often than not rules of law derived from "the prejudices which judges share with their fellow men." Certainly, the law that developed in America in regard to married women's names was the validation of prejudice.

Lucy Stone was the first married woman to continue using her own name in private life and the first woman who as a consequence was deprived of her right to vote. Her experience was a forecast of the future, when the legal establishment was to act as the bulwark of the status quo.

12

A NAME OF THEIR OWN

Lucy Stone was not the only woman who practiced what Elizabeth Cady Stanton once called "the new gospel of individual sovereignty," a woman's right to a lifelong name of her own. The Englishwoman Florence Fenwick Miller, we have just seen, had troubles similar to Lucy Stone's because she too kept her own name after marriage, and a handful of other nineteenth-century women in America, England and Europe kept their name or got their husband to change his name to their own or to combine surnames. There was even one woman who stopped using not only her husband's name but her father's as well. Between 1855 and 1900 one finds here and there, sometimes in a place as unlikely as Kansas, one of these lonely rebels.

Lucy Stone is usually believed to be the first nineteenth-century woman who kept her own name in both private and public life, but she may not have been. She certainly was not the first woman to speak out against the custom. As early as 1839 the heroine of the German novel *Der Rechte* described the custom of the wife taking the husband's name as "barbarous," comparable to stamping property with one's name. The author of *Der Rechte* was Countess Ida von Hahn, who in 1826 when she married her cousin Count F. W. Adolph von Hahn, adopted the hyphenated surname Hahn-Hahn. One cannot help wondering if she did so because it was the only way she could demonstrate her separate individuality, for if she had continued to call herself simply Hahn, the public would have thought that, like an ordinary wife, she had adopted her husband's surname. Whatever her reasons for calling herself Hahn-Hahn, she spoke out against the barbarous custom long before Lucy Stone.

The woman who may have preceded Lucy Stone and been the first woman to keep her own name was a New York doctor, **Mary E. Walker**, who in November 1855 shortly after she received her MD, married Dr Albert Miller in a most unusual ceremony. The presiding minister was the feminist and abolitionist the Reverend Samuel May, the bride wore trousers, obey was omitted from the ceremony and after the ceremony the new wife continued to use her own name. Thus Dr Mary Walker may have preceded Lucy Stone as the first married woman in the nineteenth century who refused to change her surname to her husband's, for although Lucy Stone had been married in May of 1855, she probably did not consistently repudiate her husband's name until July of 1856. On the other hand, Dr Walker did occasionally sign her name "Dr Miller-Walker" or "Dr Mary E. M. Walker." But to whomever belongs the precedence, Lucy Stone remained married and for thirty-seven years defied society by living and traveling with Henry Blackwell under her own name. Dr Mary Walker, however, separated from her husband in 1859, and although she did not get divorced until 1869, almost no one knew she had ever married, so that the radical position she had taken in regard to her name remained unknown to her contemporaries. She did maintain an interest in married women's names, at least during a lecture tour in 1869 she objected to the custom of calling wives Mrs. If a wife must "let all the world know she is married" by assuming the title Mrs, she asked, then why aren't husbands required to announce their change of condition by adopting the title "Misterer"? Dr Mary E. Walker is now chiefly remembered for having had the courage to wear trousers from the early 1850s until her death in 1919. She ought also to be remembered for having had the courage to continue using her own name during the four years of her marriage.

Another highly unconventional woman who kept her own name was the sculptor **Elisabet Ney**. The Prussian born Ney, famous throughout Europe for her busts of Schopenhauer and George V of Hanover, married Dr Edmund Montgomery on November 7, 1863 on the condition that the marriage never be publicly acknowledged, for the bride refused to change her famous name to her husband's. Accordingly, until her death in 1907 Dr Montgomery referred to his wife as Fraulein or Mademoiselle or Miss Ney. Only once did she agree to be called Mrs Montgomery, and that was during the summer of 1866 when they were acting as spies for Garibaldi and did not wish to be conspicuous. Few people knew they were legally married; when they were living in Munich in 1868 she did not tell even her old friends. In 1871 when Ney and Montgomery emigrated to America, it was under separate names (but each had a separate cabin). In Georgia where they first stayed, only their hosts, Baron and Baroness von Stralendorff, were told they were married and probably only because Ney was pregnant. When Montgomery took her to a doctor because of the pregnancy, he introduced her as "Miss Ney, my sister." Of course the townsfolk thought Ney and Montgomery were living in sin and that the child was a bastard, as did the townsfolk in Hempstead, Texas where in 1873 they bought the Liendo Plantation under separate names. The local Klansmen once planned to run them out of town unless they could prove they were legally married (and unless Ney stopped wearing trousers), but friends talked the Klansmen out of the raid and for years they continued to live there, ostensibly in sin. They did not tell even the one son who survived childhood (and who was named Lorne Ney-Montgomery) that he was not a bastard. As the years passed everyone probably assumed they were married, but Elisabet Ney was accepted under her own name both locally and in Austin where she later built a studio. When she died Dr Montgomery had her gravestone inscribed as she would have wished: "Elisabet Ney, Sculptor." Ney said she denied she was married because she believed the law should have nothing to do with love, but if she had lived in a world that respected the autonomy of women and did not demand they submerge their identities in their husbands, she probably would not have objected to marriage and denied her own. She felt she could keep her unique identity— her famous name—only by pretending she was single, much preferring to be thought of as a sinful free lover than as Mrs Montgomery, a respectable wife.

Another woman who preferred to be known as a sinner than change her name was **Victoria Woodhull**. Born Victoria Claflin in 1838, she became the wife of Dr Canning Woodhull when she was fifteen and as Victoria Woodhull acquired a small reputation in the family traveling medicine show. In the early 1860s she met Colonel James H. Blood; they became lovers, divorced their spouses and on July 14, 1868 in Ohio took out a marriage license. Whether or not they were legally married has been disputed, for there is no record of the marriage being performed, but they both said they were married. What probably made the public and her biographers suspect they were not married was that Victoria did not change her name. She may not have because she was following the example of her sister, **Tennessee Claflin**, who had married John Bartels in 1866 and had not changed her name. But Bartels almost immediately disappeared from Tennessee's life and few people knew she had ever married, whereas Victoria and Blood lived together for ten years. It has been suggested that she did not change her name because she had strong convictions she would become famous and quite rightly judged the name Victoria Woodhull to have more public appeal than Victoria Blood. What has not been suggested is that Woodhull and Blood traveled in free love circles where it was far more respectable to seem not to be married. Besides, Victoria Woodhull was a woman who enjoyed defying convention. Moreover, if Lucy Stone could be married to Henry Blackwell and keep her own name, why couldn't she?

She did become famous as Victoria Woodhull. She and her sister were the first women to open a brokerage firm, a firm that was successful; they also ran a newspaper, *Woodhull & Claflin's Weekly*; and in 1872 Victoria Woodhull ran for President of the United States. She achieved great fame and was popularly known as "The Woodhull." By 1876, however, she had lost her popularity; she divorced Blood and moved to England. There, ill and defeated by life, she tried to become respectable; in 1883 she married a banker, John Biddulph Martin, and had cards printed that read: "Mrs J. B. Martin." However, she also used the name Victoria Woodhull-Martin and when she visited America the press as often as not called her Victoria Woodhull. Her sister Tennessee also gave up her famous name and turned respectable; in 1885 she too married an Englishman, Francis Cook, and after 1886, when her husband acquired a title, she was known as Lady Cook.

Much less famous than Victoria Woodhull but just as tenacious of her small fame was the Rhode Island lighthouse keeper **Ida Lewis**. Starting about 1858, she rescued several men from drowning by rowing out to them from the lighthouse she tended in Newport. But it was not until 1869 that another rescue brought her national fame when the story of her saving two soldiers from drowning was published in a New York newspaper and reprinted throughout the country. Visitors from far and wide came to visit her, she was written up in magazines, championed by Susan B. Anthony as an example of what women could do, presented with a new rowboat and a gold watch by the citizens of Newport, and even had a book written about her, *Ida Lewis, the Heroine of Lime Rock* by George D. Brewerton. In the midst of this celebrity, at the age of twenty-eight, she married William Heard Wilson, a sailor. She used the name Wilson during the short time she lived with her husband, but she soon left him. Not believing in divorce, she remained married, but she refused to be called Mrs Wilson. For the rest of her life she insisted on being addressed as Miss Ida Lewis, the name associated with her heroic feats.

Ida Lewis did not want to lose her famous name; it is most unlikely she had strong views or any views at all on the injustice of wives having to change their names. But the next married woman who kept her own name did have strong views on the subject. She has previously been mentioned; she was the Reverend **Olympia Brown**, a Universalist minister. In 1867 at an Equal Rights Association meeting in New York she met Lucy Stone. Brown must have had a deep interest in Lucy Stone's retention of her name because she took the trouble to ask her why she had kept it. "What she said impressed me much," she later wrote in her autobiography. "It is undoubtedly true that the custom of surrendering one's name upon marriage originated when woman was a mere chattel and marriage was a family arrangement based upon financial considerations. In this view of the subject we perceive that the name merely indicated the person to whom she belonged, as in slavery times when the negro changed his name on gaining a new owner, the purpose being to indicate who was his master and to what family he was attached." Lucy Stone's views so impressed her that in April 1873 when she married John Henry Willis, she too with her husband's full approval retained her own name. In a letter written less than a month after her marriage, one in which she agreed to speak at a conference of churches, she informed the minister in charge that her recent marriage was not to be announced and that she was to be "introduced to the audience as ever [the] Rev. Olympia Brown neither more nor less." She had, of course, to inform him her name was not Willis despite her marriage, and she once told Susan B. Anthony she spent a good deal of time telling people that her surname was her own not her husband's and why she had kept it. In the main she must have met with disapproval, but that could not have bothered her much since she had a low opinion of the average American woman who, she felt, was a "feeble, abject being," without education and incapable of forming independent opinions. Among such psychologically fettered creatures, she did not expect to find approval or understanding. But she quietly and steadfastly persisted in using her own name and her wishes were generally respected. Occasionally, of course, a smug journalist played games with her name. For example, in an article in the *Advocate* for April 15, 1883 she is referred to as Mrs Willis, the Rev. Mrs Olympia Brown Willis, Mrs Brown-Willis, Olympia Brown Willis and Olympia Brown. Even *The Woman's Journal* did not always respect her name; for example, on November 19, 1892 the *Journal* announced that "Rev. Olympia Brown Willis has lately taken charge of the Universalist church at Mukwonago, Wis." But until her death in 1926 she herself continued to sign her name either Reverend Olympia Brown, or, after she resigned from the ministry, Mrs Olympia Brown.

Another Midwestern woman who kept her own name was **Martha Strickland** of Michigan. She married Leo Miller in 1875 and refused to change her name because, as she said, she believed "in the individuality of women." She was the daughter of a lawyer, receiving her own law degree in 1883 and eventually becoming assistant prosecuting attorney in St Johns, Michigan and the first woman to argue cases in the Supreme Court of Michigan, where she won for Michigan women the right to hold the office of deputy clerk. She also lectured widely and wrote legal articles on such subjects as "Woman's Right to Hold Office" and "Women as Lawyers." Throughout her career and although she had a son who used her husband's name, she continued to call herself Mrs Martha Strickland.

One wonders how Strickland and Miller and other couples who kept separate names solved the problem of signing hotel registers. Late in his life Henry Blackwell recalled in an article in the January 12, 1901 *Woman's Journal* that he and Lucy "to avoid misunderstanding" signed the register "Henry B. Blackwell and Lucy Stone, wife of Henry B. Blackwell." Probably most of the women who kept their own name made the same concession to convention, but not Dr **Aletta Jacobs** of Holland, wife of Cornelis Victor Gerritsen, who signed hotel registers "Mr Gerritsen and Mrs Jacobs" and apparently had no trouble in European hotels. In America, however, a room clerk once refused to allow them to share a room if they signed the register with two names, so Gerritsen assumed her name and signed "Mr and Mrs Jacobs," for Dr Jacobs adamantly refused to use Gerritsen's name. They were an unusual couple. She was the first woman in Holland to become a physician and to attempt to vote and she later helped establish the Woman's International League for Peace and Freedom. Gerritsen, a member of the Netherlands Parliament from 1893 to 1897, shared Dr Jacobs' opposition to conventional marriage. In 1891 they were legally married only so any children they might have would not suffer the stigma of illegitimacy. Dr Jacobs remained fully independent after marriage; she continued to practice medicine and at the end of every year she and Gerritsen tabulated the household expenses, each contributing half; they also not only maintained separate names but each had separate quarters in their apartment.

It should not be surprising that women who kept their own name had other egalitarian views about marriage. It should also not be surprising that a few women who kept their own name developed even more radical views on names. Most women who kept their name simply continued to use the father's name given them at birth. But one woman felt this system unjust and used a combination of her mother's and father's surname. She was the Englishwoman previously discussed, **Florence Fenwick Miller**, who married Frederick A. Ford in 1877 and whose use of her own name was challenged by the London School Board in 1879, a challenge she successfully fought. Not only did she call herself Mrs Fenwick Miller, thus preserving her mother's as well as her father's name, at least one of her daughters, Irene Fenwick Miller, who became a suffragist, used her mother's name not her father's.

An American woman also defied the tradition of handing down only father's names to children. She was Elizabeth Oakes Smith, Oakes being an old family name she added to her husband's name in the late 1830s and under which she became famous, her *The Sinless Child* (1842) being hailed by Edgar Allan Poe as one of the great poems of the century. With the approval of her husband Seba Smith, she had the name of her sons legally changed to Oaksmith, a version of the name she had made famous.

Another woman who invented a name for herself, a name she chose to use instead of her husband's, was the woman born Alice Chenoweth. In 1875 when she was twenty-two she married Charles Selden Smart and changed her surname to her husband's. During the next few years Mrs Smart became a feminist and began to write on the subject, but she was so afflicted with conventional feminine modesty she at first refused to publish and then used various masculine pseudonyms. In the 1880s she came under the influence of the free thinker and agnostic Colonel Robert G. Ingersoll and in 1884 she published *Men, Women, and Gods*, a collection of lectures in which she denounced the Bible for its degradation of women. That iconoclastic book was published under the name **Helen Hamilton Gardener**, which was not to be another pseudonym but eventually became the name she used in private as well as public life and that she legally adopted, no longer using her husband's name. She probably chose to invent a name because she reasoned that to stop using the name Smart and go back to Chenoweth would merely mean using the name of her mother's husband not her own, that the only way for a woman to have a name that had not been imposed by a man on his wife was to invent her own name.

Helen Hamilton Gardener continued to use the name of her own invention for the rest of her life, which included a second marriage in 1902 to Colonel Selden Allen Day. During this marriage, she occasionally used the name Helen H. Gardener-Day when it seemed politic. A letter she wrote in 1917 to President Woodrow Wilson in regard to suffrage was thus diplomatically signed, lest Wilson be offended by a wife who totally ignored her husband's name. Ordinarily, she signed her letters Helen H. Gardener, and it was as Helen Hamilton Gardener that in 1920 she was appointed to the United States Civil Service Commission.

The women so far discussed had a profession or were famous and therefore might be said to have had a stake in keeping the name with which their work or fame was associated, even though most of them said they kept their own name for idealistic reasons, that is, to exemplify woman's equality in marriage. Lucy Stone, for example, said she would have kept her own name even if she had not been famous, for no woman, albeit a plain housewife and mother, ought to lose her identity when she married. Did the nineteenth century produce any such women, young women not established in or starting a career, women who intended to be plain wives and mothers, who kept their own name because they believed in the equality of women?

There seems to have been one. On Sunday September 19, 1886 in Valley Falls, Kansas **Lillian Harman** married Edwin C. Walker in a private ceremony at her home where she read a statement in which she said she would make no immoral promise to obey her husband, for she was retaining "the right to act always as my conscience and best judgment shall dictate. I retain, also," she added, "my full maiden name, as I am sure it is my duty to do." Lillian agreed with the advanced views on marriage held by her father Moses Harman, who advocated what he called "autonomistic marriage," marriage as a self-governing private contract between a man and a woman entirely free of "the rites and ceremonies of church and state." Harman thought legal marriage an immoral abomination "made by man for man's benefit, not for woman's," making man "the head and autocrat of the family" and requiring a woman to merge "her individuality as a legal person into that of her husband, even to the surrender of her name, just as chattel slaves were required to take the name of their master." Harman believed, on the contrary, that since "Dame Nature has placed the burden of maternity upon woman," marriage should be "woman's institution" and that wives, not husbands, "should have the first voice and control" and the paramount right to custody of the children. Moses Harman read his views on marriage as part of the ceremony establishing there was a marriage compact between his daughter and Edwin C. Walker, who also read a statement in which he repudiated conventional marriage. Whereas, he said, "in legal marriage, woman surrenders herself to the law and to her husband and becomes a vassal," in his marriage Lillian remains "free," "sovereign of herself" in every way, including sexually, and with the "right and duty to retain her own name."

Moses Harman was the editor of *Lucifer, The Light-Bearer*, a paper that advocated free love, for which reason, the day after their unconventional marriage ceremony, Lillian and Edwin were arrested for violating the Kansas marriage act, tried, found guilty and sentenced to jail, Edwin to serve seventy-five days, Lillian forty-five. They appealed their conviction, but the Kansas Supreme Court decided that although the marriage was a valid marriage (and, incidentally, that Lillian's use of her own name was legally acceptable), the state nevertheless had the right to punish them for violating prescribed state regulations that, among other things, required couples to take out a marriage license (The State v. Walker, 36 Kansas State Reports 297). They apparently served their sentences, but Lillian and her father continued protesting against institutional marriage, both of them later publishing pamphlets on such subjects as *Marriage and Morality* and *Love in Freedom*.

Lillian Harman, then, although she intended when she married to be just a wife and mother, was no ordinary middle class girl who had chanced to become a feminist. She was an outsider, a member of one of the groups of free thinkers and social and religious radicals that sprang up all over the United States during the nineteenth century. She and her father were, however, highly unusual in their radically feminist stand in regard to married women's names. For although there were Utopian communities in which women did not go by their husbands' names, in these communities there was either no marriage or no monogamous marriage. Married women who entered the Shaker community were required to stop using their husbands' names, as the eighteenth-century leaders Ann Lee and Lucy Wright had done, for the Shakers repudiated marriage and led celibate lives. In the Oneida community women who entered who were not already married remained Miss Theirowname because there was no monogamous marriage, each person being regarded as married to every other person of the opposite sex. Where there was conventional marriage, as among the Amish and Amanans, women changed their name when they married, as indeed women did where there was unconventional marriage. Among the polygamous Mormons, a husband might keep his several wives straight by calling them by their maiden names, as did John D. Lee in his *Journals,* but the wives themselves used the name of their husband. The dozens of wives of Brigham Young appropriated his name, signing themselves "Harriet E. C. Young," "Emily D. P. Young," "Margaret Pierce Young," "Succy B. Young," "Harriet B. Young," "H. A. F. Young," to list a few.

That a woman should keep her own name despite marriage was not a popular cause even among those who were opposed to conventional family life. However, another woman who decided to keep her own name after marriage did live for about a year in a so-called advanced community, the Ruskin Co-operative Colony in Tennessee. She was **Lydia Kingsmill Commander,** a native of Canada, who in 1897 served as the pastor of the Free Congregational Church in Baraboo, Wisconsin, but who resigned from the ministry in 1898 to join the Ruskin Co-operative Association. There she met Herbert Newton Casson, a former Methodist minister, who had become a socialist minister (the founder of the first labor church in America), then joined the Ruskin Colony, where he served as editor and Commander as associate editor of the colony magazine *Coming Nation.* When they were at Ruskin the Colony was breaking up, in part because of a division among the members about the practice of free love. Commander and Casson were not free love advocates, for they were married twice. The first time on March 5, 1899 on the stage at Ruskin. What that ceremony was like we do not know, but after leaving Ruskin and going to Toledo, Ohio they were married again on May 4, 1899 and the ceremony was so unusual it was reported in Midwestern newspapers. Like Lillian Harman and Edwin Walker, Commander and Casson each read "declarations of belief" before the judge who married them. Commander said, among other things, that although the lives of a married couple "should blend and harmonize," "each should preserve his or her own individuality." Casson also stressed that marriage should not mean "the destruction of individuality." In addition, he repudiated the rights the law gave him over his wife, for, he declared, "I wish to marry a free-hearted woman, not a slave" and he pledged himself "never to let this marriage interfere with the life work she has chosen."

Their declaration was signed "Herbert N. Casson" and "Lydia Kingsmill

Commander," for as they explained in a statement they wrote for the press, they did not believe a wife should take her husband's name. Their statement, as it was printed in the May 14, 1899 *St Louis Post-Dispatch*, reads as follows:

> Having been joined together in the holy estate of matrimony according to the ideas advanced so-called, that we both entertain, we respond to the invitation to place on record our views with regard to a union of hearts and lives in this age of enlightenment. We were agreed before our marriage that anything that fell short of soul-union was desecration. For the woman to give herself to the man in return for her support was to us a revolting idea. The rule that the woman change her name we regarded as another mark of the servitude of the wife to the husband; the very identity of the woman is lost and the name and title of the wife marks her degraded condition matrimonially, in that anyone can tell at once whether or not the woman is married and whose property she is. We were agreed that the equality of the sexes demanded that the woman retain her own name as an absolutely indisputable possession. With all this thoroughly understood between us, we agreed to unite our lives as man and wife.

Commander's keeping her own name was what the press regarded as the most unusual feature of their marriage. The *St Louis Post-Dispatch* headlined its story—WIFE WHO RETAINS HER MAIDEN NAME AND WON'T OBEY—and the first paragraph begins: "When Miss Lydia Kingsmill Commander married Rev. Herbert Newton Casson of Toledo, O., recently, she did not become Mrs Herbert Newton Casson. She remained Miss Lydia Kingsmill Commander."

Lydia Kingsmill Commander continued to use her own name for the rest of her life. Shortly after they were married in Ohio, she and Casson moved to New York where they both became social reform writers and lecturers. Commander wrote frequently about the new woman, her book *The American Idea* (1907) becoming so popular she was listed the next year in *Who's Who*. Commander was also active in the suffrage movement, being one of the founders of the militant Women's Political Union. Later in life she developed a summer colony and ran a farm in the Catskill Mountains. She and Casson continued to use different names during the sixteen years the marriage probably lasted, for about 1915 they separated or divorced, Commander continuing to live in New York and Casson moving to England.

Lydia Kingsmill Commander continued to call herself Miss after marriage, but most women who kept their own name changed their title to Mrs. Some, like Lucy Stone, felt that just as boys advance from Master to Mr so girls after they come of age should stop being called Miss and become Mrs. But Lucy Stone did not begin to call herself Mrs until after she married, nor did the others. They changed their title to Mrs because they wanted the world to know they were married, that they were respectable wives not immoral free lovers. However, since they were not Mrs the man they were living with, they were nevertheless suspected of living in sin. There was one way, though, that a woman could keep her own name and yet satisfy the social proprieties—by getting her husband to change his name to hers.

For a man to change his name to his wife's is not uncommon, particularly in Europe where an inheritance can depend upon a husband adopting his wife's name, usually because her father has no male heirs to carry on his name. Occasionally, a husband takes a wife's name when she has a title and he does not. Thus in 1881 when the American William Ashmead Bartlett married the Englishwoman Baroness Burdett-Coutts, he changed his name to hers. Once in a great while a man takes his wife's name because of her father's fame. In the 1880s and 90s the sons-in-law of General William Booth changed their name by Deed Poll to Booth-Clibborn, Booth-Tucker and Booth-Hellberg so their wives could continue to use the Booth name in their Salvation Army work. The Booth women did believe in women's rights and led active professional lives, but their husbands took the Booth name because Booth had made it famous, whereas the husband of a feminist changed his name in order to preserve the name a woman had made famous or did not want to lose.

Olive Logan started her career as an actress, in 1857 marrying Henry A. Delille, whose name she used in private life. She divorced Delille about 1865, and in 1868, as Olive Logan, she left the stage and started a new career as a lecturer. When she discovered that whereas the public had no objection to seeing her on stage acting but strongly objected when she appeared on stage lecturing, she became active in the feminist and suffrage movements. In 1871 she married for a second time and again adopted her husband's name socially and in part professionally, now publishing her books as "By Olive Logan (Mrs Wirt Sikes)." But when in 1892 she married a third time, she did not change her name; her husband changed his. Too little is known about her life to understand the reasons for her husband's decision, but Olive Logan was fifty-three and with a substantial reputation, whereas James O'Neill was twenty years younger and her secretary. Considering her superiority to him, she may have feministically decided he should take her name, or she may not have wanted to change for a third time the name she used in private life, or it may have been O'Neill himself who wanted to take her well-known name. Whatever the reasons, after the marriage he called himself James O'Neill Logan.

We know a good deal more about **Olive Schreiner's** agreement with her husband that he should take her name. When Schreiner met Samuel Cron Cronwright she was famous for her *The Story of An African Farm* (1883) and he was a South African farmer. After they decided to marry, she told him she wanted to keep her name because she was well-known. In a letter dated August 29, 1893 she explained: "I would like to take your name instead of mine if I married you, only I am known by mine everywhere. Do you think it would be strange if we were 'Cronwright Schreiner'? It would be so beautiful if we could have one name. People would understand that it was because I had written books." But she was not being honest with him. In the first place, she did not want to take his name because she "had written books." In a letter to her brother written on February 20, 1894, four days before her marriage, she said, "I have always resolved to keep my own name when I married," and shortly after her marriage she wrote to Dr Alice Corthorn, "I'm glad I'm still OLIVE SCHREINER. I couldn't have borne to give up my name." The woman who had long been a feminist, who was writing an historical study of women, must have felt strongly the injustice of the custom that required women to change their identities when they married. Cronwright understood her real motivation in keeping her name; in his biography of her he said "that something of her attitude towards the freedom of woman was behind her desire; I sympathized with that unexpressed feeling, and after all, names are useful merely as identification tablets."

Not only did she keep her name because of her feminism not her fame, she did not use the name Cronwright Schreiner, as in her August 29th letter she said she would. Shortly before her marriage she informed Havelock Ellis: "Address—Olive Schreiner. If you ever write to Cron address—Cronwright Schreiner, Esq." She informed other friends to address her as "Mrs Olive Schreiner." Only her husband changed his name, adopting the name Samuel C. Cronwright Schreiner, like the married women who tried to retain their former identity by continuing to use their own surname as a middle name. But around 1897 he tried to regain part of his original name by hyphenating Cronwright to Schreiner. Nevertheless, he had to endure ridicule because he had changed his name the way women do; a speech of his was once interrupted by a heckler who told him he should speak under his maiden name. After Olive Schreiner died in 1920, he continued to use the hyphenated name Cronwright-Schreiner, perhaps because of loyalty, perhaps because the name had become his identity, and perhaps because by keeping her name he could continue to share her fame.

Schreiner's original suggestion to Cronwright that they both combine surnames was appealing to other nineteenth-century couples, who could thus demonstrate their belief that husband and wife should be equal in marriage and yet satisfy custom that demanded husband and wife have the same name. The first couple to combine surnames because they believed in the equality of the sexes was probably **Charlotte Garrigue** and **Thomas Masaryk**. Garrigue was an American studying music in Leipzig when she met Masaryk, who was later to be the founder and first president of Czechoslovakia. During their courtship, they read John Stuart Mill's *The Subjection of Women*, and when they married in 1878 they decided to symbolize the cooperation and harmony of their relationship by Masaryk as well as Garrigue changing his name. Henceforth Masaryk used the name Thomas Garrigue Masaryk, just as his wife used the name Charlotte Garrigue Masaryk (and their children were also given the two names). But since they used Garrigue only as a middle surname, their gesture was largely symbolic, for they were commonly known as Mr and Mrs Masaryk, not Mr and Mrs Garrigue Masaryk.

An English couple later took the more radical step of hyphenating their surnames, so that both husband and wife had a new surname after marriage. The couple was **Annie Cobden** and **James Sanderson**. Annie was the daughter of the liberal politician Richard Cobden, who as early as 1845 had spoken in favor of women's right to vote. Annie grew up to be an ardent feminist and in 1881 when she met James Sanderson she converted him to her beliefs. On October 27, 1881 Sanderson recorded in his journal that he and Annie had argued "about women." On October 31 he bought a copy of John Stuart Mill's *The Subjection of Women* and was profoundly affected: "A whole social revolution yet to be made dawns before my eyes . . . Shall I not recognize that there is a right yet to be won before the world is older, that women should be put upon an equality with men?" In demonstration of his new belief, when he and Annie were married on August 5, 1882, he as well as Annie changed his name to Cobden-Sanderson. Once when the scientist John Tyndall asked him why he called himself Cobden-Sanderson, he explained "that my wife was a daughter of Richard Cobden, and that for her sake I had prefixed the name of Cobden to my own, that she might not altogether lose hers in it." To the economist Henry George he similarly explained "that my name Cobden was due to the fact that I had married one of Cobden's daughters, and that I had wished her to continue to bear her own and her father's name." From these explanations one would conclude that they combined surnames only because Annie's father had been famous, but it is likely that James offered the socially acceptable explanation for his change of name, preferring not to antagonize people with the more radical reason—that he and his wife combined names because they believed in the equality of the sexes. For there is no doubt he was a convert to feminism. He believed "all employment should be open equally to women as to men" and encouraged Annie in her feminist activities, even supporting her when she joined the militant suffragists and was sent to prison for demonstrating outside the House of Commons.

There were other feminist couples who combined surnames. In the January 12, 1901 *Woman's Journal* Henry Blackwell recalled that some ten or fifteen years before a Miss Berenice Morrison of St Louis, Missouri married a Mr Fuller and "by mutual agreement each took the other's name, and they have since been known as Mr and Mrs Morrison-Fuller." Elizabeth Cady Stanton also recalled in a letter to *The Woman's Journal* (October 13, 1900) that after Minnie D. Gurney's daughter married a Mr Sawyer, she had "her cards engraved Mr and Mrs Gurney Sawyer, thus recognizing the names of both members of the matrimonial firm."

There must have been not only other couples who combined surnames but other women who had the courage to keep their own name after marriage. *The Revolution* (a feminist paper edited by Elizabeth Cady Stanton and Parker Pillsbury) on May 8, 1869 printed a letter from an anonymous wife who had retained her name and was having difficulties: "As many persons cannot comprehend any change from the old custom, frequently I am called Mrs D_____, my husband's name. I let that pass, but when called upon to sign a legal document, I am told my name is not lawful without it has my husband's attached. Is it true? Please help me, and you will oblige one who cannot see why she should be obliged to change her name." Stanton told her that all she had to do was sign her name and then add "wife of Richard Roe," but as we have seen in the case of Lucy Stone even that concession to custom was sometimes not regarded as sufficient by lawyers and bureaucrats.

Such occasional legal difficulties and the frequent vexation of being addressed as Mrs Husband and either letting it pass or explaining that one used one's own name and why, in addition to the embarrassment of being suspected of living in sin must have made some women who decided to keep their name give up the attempt. In his note in the January 12, 1901 *Woman's Journal* Henry Blackwell mentioned three such women. One was Maria Persons of Boston, for some years secretary of *The Woman's Journal*, who married Leslie Miller and retained her own name while they lived in Boston, but when they moved to Philadelphia she adopted the more conservative custom of using a double surname, calling herself Mrs Persons Miller. Blackwell also mentioned Catharine Waugh of Illinois, a lawyer who on May 30, 1890 married another lawyer, Frank McCulloch. According to Blackwell, "she for some time retained her maiden name," but it could not have been for more than a year or two because in *A Woman of the Century*, an 1893 woman's *Who's Who*, she listed her surname as McCulloch and the name of the firm she shared with her husband as McCulloch & McCulloch.

We know a good deal more about the third woman Blackwell mentioned as retaining her name for some time. She was the woman now known as Carrie Chapman Catt. Born Carrie Clinton Lane, she in 1885 left her job as superintendent of schools in Mason City, Iowa to marry Leo Chapman, the owner and editor of a local newspaper. The now Carrie Lane Chapman met Lucy Stone at a suffrage convention held in Iowa that year and was so impressed with her speech she introduced herself and spent a long time questioning her about her life as a feminist. Whether or not Mrs Chapman asked Lucy Stone why she had kept her name is not known, but it is likely that she did and that Carrie Chapman, like Olympia Brown, was influenced by what Lucy Stone told her. For in 1890 when Mrs Chapman married for a second time, she and her husband-to-be, George W. Catt, wrote out a prenuptial contract, legally attested, in which it was agreed, among other things, that she would continue to use the name Carrie Lane Chapman, the name under which she was by then well-known as a suffrage leader.

It was as Carrie Lane Chapman that in the early 1890s she campaigned for suffrage in many states. It was Carrie Lane Chapman who was listed as toastmaster at a dinner given for the Mississippi Valley woman suffrage conference held in Des Moines, Iowa in 1892. It was Carrie Lane Chapman who spoke on "Evolution of Woman Suffrage" in May 1893 at the Chicago Columbian Exposition and who during the fall campaigned for suffrage in Colorado, playing an important part in Colorado women winning the vote that year. Her not using her husband's name was apparently not detrimental either to her career or to the cause of suffrage. Lucy Stone knew her only as Carrie Lane Chapman, and in the fall of 1893 when Stone was dying she wrote a letter commending "Mrs Carrie Lane Chapman" to a Denver suffrage leader and asked her husband to "send a hundred dollars to Mrs Carrie Lane Chapman. She has a level head."

But Mrs Chapman had for some time been planning to change her name, for she listed herself under Catt in *A Woman of the Century*, the biographies for which had been compiled in 1892. However, throughout 1893 she fulfilled all public engagements in the name Chapman. Perhaps she did not want to hurt Lucy Stone's feelings who, she knew, was dying. At any rate, after Lucy died in October 1893, Mrs Chapman began to make the transition to her new name. During the first few months of 1894 she used the name Carrie Lane Chapman-Catt, then she omitted Lane and called herself Mrs Carrie Chapman-Catt. Throughout 1895 she used the hyphenated surname, but after that year it was gradually dropped and she became simply Mrs Catt. In 1905 in an obituary for George Catt in *The Woman's Journal* an explanation was given for her change of mind: "At the time of their marriage it was agreed between them that Mrs Catt should retain her own name, under which she had become widely known as a lecturer but the practical inconveniences arising from their bearing different names proved so great that after a short trial they abandoned the arrangement, by mutual consent." Undoubtedly there were practical inconveniences, but as she came more and more into the national spotlight she probably feared her fuss about a name might injure the cause of suffrage. Whatever her reasons, from then on the now Carrie Chapman Catt would no longer publicly champion any other feminist cause except the right to vote. Indeed, some years later when, as we shall see, a young feminist gave a speech on a woman's right to keep her own name, Mrs Catt sent one of her deputies to personally rebuke her, telling her she had set back the cause of suffrage. Moreover, she saw to it that in her official biography, written by Mary Gray Peck, no mention was made of her having used her former name during the first years of her marriage to George Catt.

Carrie Chapman Catt nevertheless maintained a quiet interest in the subject. When she visited Burma and later wrote articles on "The Matriarchate," she did not fail to note that in Burma and other matriarchies "family names descend in the female line" and that women kept their own names after marriage. For although a woman might decide she must conform to convention, that did not mean she did not resent being deprived of her name. Indeed, the resentment some women must secretly have felt is revealed by the rapidity with which they divested themselves of their husbands' names after being widowed, separated or divorced. No sooner did Mrs Sarah Lowe Erwin of South Carolina leave her husband than she began to call herself Twiggs again, for she was proud of being the daughter of Major General Lowe Twiggs and the great granddaughter of General John Twiggs and the grandniece of two other generals of the name Twiggs. Similarly, as soon as her husband died, a Chicago physician, who had traced her ancestors back to the fourteenth century, resumed her former name of Corresta T. Canfield.

These women resented losing a family name they took pride in. Other women resented having to give up a name they had made well-known and, moreover, had no intention of continuing to use the name of the man they now disliked. The internationally famous educator Emma Willard married for a second time in 1838. Her husband, Dr Christopher Yates, soon revealed he was interested only in acquiring the fortune she had accumulated, so in about nine months she left him and stopped calling herself Mrs Yates or Mrs Willard-Yates and became Mrs Willard again, even though it was five years before she was divorced and got permission from the Connecticut legislature to resume the use of her former name. Eliza Farnham, well-known as a prison reformer and former matron of the woman's division of Sing-Sing prison, in 1852 took a second husband, William A. Fitzpatrick. The now Mrs Fitzpatrick left him a year and a half later and, although she was not divorced until 1856, she stopped using his name; it was Eliza Farnham who in 1854 was appointed principal of the common school in Santa Cruz, California.

Willard and Farnham had used their second husbands' names for a short period, but other women divested themselves of husbands' names they had used for many years. When Harriet McConkey divorced her husband for habitual drunkenness in 1867, she had used his name for almost ten years; nevertheless, she got the Minnesota legislature to pass a special law changing her name back to Bishop, the name under which she had originally been well-known as a missionary and teacher. The wife of Senator William P. Sprague had used his name for almost twenty years when she divorced him in 1882, but she had always resented having to use his name and eagerly became Kate Chase again. As Kate Chase she had been one of the most popular women in Washington DC circles, so popular that her name clung to her for some time after she married. One of her friends remembered that in 1866 "she was still called Kate Chase, in spite of the fact that she had married Senator Sprague three years previously." After her marriage, she signed her letters Kate Chase Sprague, disliking the then socially correct forms Mrs William Sprague or Mrs Senator Sprague. For she not only did not want to lose her own famous identity, she wanted people to remember she was the daughter of a man far more distinguished than her husband—the Chief Justice of the United States Supreme Court, Salmon P. Chase.

Kate Chase resumed the use of her own name in spite of having four children who continued to bear the surname Sprague, and other women were also willing to endure the social inconvenience of having a name different from that of their children. A Kentucky suffragist who divorced her husband in 1872 stopped calling herself Mrs Herrick although she had two sons and again became Mary Barr Clay. The archaeologist Zelia Pinart divorced her husband in 1888 and, although she had a daughter, became Zelia Nuttall again. In 1892 when Florence Kelley-Wischnewetzky got divorced and resumed the name Kelley, she avoided the difficulty of having a name different from her children's by getting the court to change their name to Kelley.

A few women who were not freed from their husband's name by divorce or widowhood continued all their married life to bitterly resent losing their own name. The most touching case was that of Julia E. Smith. She had become famous, at least in feminist circles, for having translated the Bible six times and for having forced Connecticut to sell her cows if the state insisted on taxing her without letting her vote. In April 1879, when she was almost eighty-seven, she married Amos Parker, and it seemed as if she were going to become a follower of Lucy Stone. In an account of the wedding published in the May 10, 1879 *Woman's Journal,* her husband expressed strong negative views on women being called by their husbands' names. Parker had noticed that congratulatory letters sent to his wife came addressed in a variety of ways. "Some of them not having any part of her name upon them, as 'Mrs Amos G. Parker'. Julia Smith Parker is a frequent form. On the pile of letters that came last night, no two were alike, and last of all . . . was one addressed . . . 'Julia Smith', as of old." Parker said he would not be surprised to hear his wife "chattering to herself . . . who am I?" "Her name, however," Parker firmly stated, "is not Amos. She prefers her own old name. Among all the things unreasonable . . . that have been handed down and fastened upon women from past tradition, there is no greater one than this of the name. She bears a dozen names if she marries a dozen times. How is one to keep track of her, or to know who or what she is? . . . Perhaps women will sometimes awake to the absurdity of this thing. It always seems as if a man were laughing in his sleeve when he hears his wife called 'Mrs John', or 'Mrs Peter', or whatever his name may be. If he does not laugh he ought to."

It is not clear if Parker objected merely to the custom of calling wives Mrs John, but he was obviously one who would have been sympathetic if his wife had decided to retain her own surname. And for awhile she did. A letter she wrote to *The Woman's Journal* in June of 1879 was signed Julia E. Smith. But her rebellion against custom did not last long. When she attended women's rights meetings, she was soon signing herself Julia Smith (Parker), then Julia Smith Parker. However, in 1886 after she died, a note was found on the flyleaf of the Bible she read everyday in which she asked to be buried with her sisters and that on her tombstone only Julia Smith be inscribed. She had cared very much about the loss of her name but could finally assert herself only from the grave.

If someone had asked the resentful Mrs Parker, "What's in a name?", she would probably have answered that if a rose by any other name would smell as sweet, why could she not have remained Julia Smith? why had custom forced her to change her name?

More profound than Shakespeare's endlessly quoted "What's in a name?" are the words of Elizabeth Cady Stanton: "There is a great deal in a name. It often signifies much, and may involve a great principle." The women who kept their own name knew there was a great deal in a name and refused to be mis-labeled, refused to be classified with the mass of wives who happily wore the name tag of the man they were serving as wife. The women who kept their own name were purists, women who were willing to endure the ridicule and harass-ment of a Victorian society because they wanted the world to acknowledge their separate individuality, to accept them as persons in their own right, as Lucy Stone or Dr Mary Walker or the Reverend Olympia Brown, not as Mrs the man they happened to marry.

Persevering in their lonely and courageous course, they must have felt very much ahead of their times, and of course they were. But in another sense they were most in tune with their times, most sensitive to the new forces at work in society, forces that were creating a world in which women would no longer have only the one role of wife but would have as many different roles as men and would therefore not wear the label "wife of." But that new world was at least a century away. The Elisabet Neys and Lydia Kingsmill Commanders were sports, rare examples of a new species that would some day proliferate but who in their own time were hardly noticeable among the multitude of Mrs Men.

13

THE MINOR POINT OF A NAME

Nominal History

> MARRIED WOMEN'S SURNAMES—Has any one historically
> investigated the rise and establishment in England of the custom of
> a married woman changing her surname for that of her husband?
> Has the custom ever been formally sanctioned by law, or is it merely
> a matter of popular usage, which the law tacitly recognizes? What is
> the first recorded instance of a married woman being called by her
> husband's surname, and when was it fully established?

The above query appeared in the August 13, 1887 *Notes and Queries* and was
signed E. D., who, one imagines, must have been a feminist. Yet E. D. may
not have been, for whenever women agitate for equal rights, even those con-
tented with the status quo grow curious about the phenomenon of women
taking husbands' names. Whereas feminists decide the custom is further proof
of woman's degradation, scholars do not condemn; instead they express their
awakened interest by examining the tribal custom through the telescope of history, and the scholars who read *Notes and Queries* became so interested that
items on married women's names appeared for two years, until September 21,
1889.

In the original query E. D. related what she or he knew about the
subject—that changing one's surname to one's husband's seems not to have
been fully established in England even as late as the early seventeenth century,
that in Scotland a woman's legal surname was her own with her husband's surname added as an alias, that in the United States "it appears to be customary
for a woman to add her husband's surname to her own, as in Mrs Harriet
Beecher Stowe," and that in Spain women combine their own surname with
their husband's and children are given the surname of both parents.

The first reply was printed on September 7: "E. D. has struck the note of an inquiry which has long demanded attention. England is, I believe, the only (so-called) 'civilized' country where a woman entirely loses her identity on marriage," a fact the correspondent, R. H. Busk, felt was unjust, particularly when a distinguished man has only daughters and cannot therefore pass on his famous name to future generations. Miss Busk and several others during the next two years told what they knew about the origin and prevalence of the custom in England, Ireland and Wales and the differences in custom in contemporary France, Belgium, Italy and Spain. It was again and again pointed out that women did not used to take their husbands' names and that in certain rural sections of England and in Ireland and Wales, they still did not, but no one knew when or why the custom started and there was a good deal of disagreement about what names married women actually used in Europe.

In general, there was no strong objection to women taking their husbands' surnames, though many favored women keeping their own surname as a middle name. The interest was not radical but historical; however, history itself was radical, for the average person thought God on Mt Sinai commanded women to take their husbands' names, whereas history revealed the custom was of fairly recent origin and varied from country to country. But those who were enlightened were the few scholars who read *Notes and Queries*.

More profoundly radical were the observations of an English historian of names, Harry Long, who in *The Names We Bear* (1877) and at greater length in *Personal and Family Names* (1883) discussed how society's belief in woman's inferiority was revealed in her names. Just as "writers on physiology say that woman is man modified," so the student of names discovers that woman nominally is a "maness," that is, that her names and titles are formed by "appending a feminine ending to masculine names."

Long went on to illustrate woman's nominal inferiority in regard to her first, last and married names. Women's first names were generally based on male ones and when etymologically examined were inappropriate for women. For example, Louisa derives from Louis and means victor, and Georgianna derives from George and means husbandman. Women's last names were equally inappropriate, for why should a girl go by the name Roberta Robert*son* or Henrietta Hard*man*? That women were nominally manesses was also revealed by their having to lose their own surname and take their husband's, a custom Long blamed on Christianity: "Obeying the spirit of its teachings, the bride signifies dependence upon her husband by renouncing her maiden name and adopting the name of him who adopted her. This helped consolidate family ties, but resulted in the loss of designations peculiar to women."

But the greatest loss of women's names was in history. "Who was Noah's wife?" Long asked. "Who were the sisters of Abel and Cain?" For every hundred men's names in the Old Testament, only five were those of women. Although there was a higher proportion of women's names in the New Testament, who knows the names of Christ's sisters, though his brothers' names were recorded? "As it is in the Bible, so it is in every national history and in all genealogies." Long understood that history recorded "only the deeds of the mighty," that "her-story," as it is now called, had not been written.

"Seeing the woman's rights section of the ladies are full sail on the franchise, they should take action on being merely nominal terminations of the rougher sex," concluded Harry Long, and he was not being entirely facetious. But the very fact that the woman's rights section of the ladies were full sail on the franchise made them feel they should not make a fuss about being merely nominal terminations of men. The few rebels who did make a fuss and refused to become Mrs the man they married were disapproved of by most of their sister feminists, who had convinced themselves that the right to keep one's name after marriage was an unimportant one and of no deep significance.

A Sort of Half-Established Individuality

It was not that most feminists did not realize that a woman's having to lose her name at marriage was an injustice. Married women's names immediately became an issue at the first women's rights conventions. At the very first one held in Seneca Falls, New York in July 1848, the sixty-eight women who signed the Declaration declaring women to be the equals of men refused to use the Mrs John Jones style and signed their own female first names, and the next month at the second Woman's Rights Convention Elizabeth Cady Stanton spoke at some length on the importance of a woman's having "a life-long name to mark her individuality."

But after Lucy Stone married in 1855 and decided to keep her own name, such vigorous protest disappeared. According to Susan B. Anthony, many women at the 1856 convention felt Lucy Stone's defiance of custom had "injured the cause" so that an attempt was made to pass a resolution "against a woman not taking her husband's name." Stone was felt to have injured the cause because even then the women's rights movement had narrowed to a fight for the vote, the male weapon by means of which suffragists believed the enfranchised women of the future would easily secure all their rights, including the right of a married woman to keep her own name. Not that most suffragists thought more than a few zealots would want that right. But be that as it may, suffragists felt it was certainly not prudent at the present time to demand that right since the public was constantly accusing them of wanting to destroy family life, and a woman who was living with a man under separate names seemed to be no different from those arch flouters of family life—free lovers. The suffragists were understandably vexed with Lucy Stone and they continued to regard her and the other women who kept their names as extremists who made themselves and the cause "pay dear . . . for the minor point of a name," to quote the sentiments of the Reverend Antoinette Brown Blackwell.

Needless to say, a woman's right to a lifelong name of her own never became a cause backed by any nineteenth-century woman's rights organization. Indeed, the subject was rarely mentioned at public meetings and almost always in a low-keyed way. Typical was the way in which a wife's loss of her name was brought to the attention of the delegates at the 1876 meeting of the National Suffrage Association. As part of the celebration of the centennial of the signing of the Declaration of Independence, the Association, according to the *History of Woman Suffrage,* displayed "framed copies of all the laws bearing unjustly upon woman—those which rob her of her name, her earnings, her property, her children, her person." Since there were no laws that actually stated a woman must take her husband's name, perhaps they displayed copies of the 1850 Kentucky and 1863 Vermont laws that barred married women from changing their names, or perhaps the statement from Timothy Walker's *Introduction to American Law* that the merging of a woman's "name in that of her husband, is but an emblem of the fate of all her legal rights."

A notable exception to the usual low-keyed handling of the subject occurred at the 1880 convention of the National Woman Suffrage Association when a resolution was adopted on an issue even more explosive than a woman's right to keep her own name after marriage:

> *Resolved,* That since man has everywhere committed to woman the custody and ownership of the child born out of wedlock, and has required it to bear its mother's name, he should recognize woman's right as a mother to the custody of the child born in marriage, and permit it to bear her name.

To demand that children be permitted to bear their mother's name was as bold a resolution as could have been adopted, striking as it does at the male dominance of the family. That iconoclastic resolution was probably on the agenda because in 1880 the Chairman of the Executive Committee was Matilda Joslyn Gage, who was much interested in what she called "The Matriarchate," the time before Christianity when children were given their mother's name and men sometimes took their wife's name. Gage blamed the teachings of the Christian church for woman's loss of status and she was then writing down her views in "Woman, Church, and State," which the next year was published in Volume I of the *History of Woman Suffrage* and which she later expanded into a book. Gage, a radical, had little patience with the conservative women in the suffrage associations and ultimately broke away and formed her own organization.

Another radical who scorned the conservatism of the suffragists was Elizabeth Cady Stanton. From her marriage in 1840 when she wrote to her friends to tell them not to address her as Mrs Henry B. Stanton until the end of her life, she continued to express her opinion that "there is much involved in this matter of a name" and to express herself with force, making no attempt to soothe the feelings of conventional women. For example, in *The Revolution*, the feminist paper she edited for two and one-half years, she on April 1, 1869 published a short piece on the absurdity of women taking husbands' names, the occasion being the fourth divorce of a Chicago woman, who therefore had five names trailing after her—Warren, Greendyke, French, Conners and Grant. Stanton's pithy moral for this marital fable was: "Let all women do like 'Lucy Stone,' honor her own name, and then keep it . . . There is no more reason in every wife taking a husband's name than in his taking hers." Stanton entitled the piece "Lucy Stone," for although she had quarreled bitterly with her, she never ceased to admire her for having had the courage to keep her name. In a letter read at the memorial services for Lucy Stone in February 1894, Stanton singled out that act for special praise: "Lucy Stone did a brave thing in keeping her name, and it is strange that so few women follow her example. It seems so pre-eminently proper that every individual should have a life-long name, especially when one has made her own distinguished."

Significantly, only Stanton and one other person among the many who paid tribute to Lucy Stone mentioned her keeping her name, for Stone's extremism on that point continued to be an embarrassment to most of her sister suffragists. And the other person who admired her for keeping her name did not, like Stanton, urge other women to do likewise. Instead, Josephine K. Henry of Kentucky spoke of Lucy Stone and Henry Blackwell as harbingers of the ideal future. "It has not yet been written in our ecclesiastical and civil codes that every woman shall own and dignify her own name through life," said Mrs Henry, "but civilization is drawing a pen now to issue this edict. The coming woman will not resign her name at the marriage altar . . . In the time to come, civilization will secure to woman her name and all human rights." For Josephine Henry, Lucy Stone's keeping her name was not an example of what every woman might at once do to assert her equality with her husband. It was, instead, a symbol of what "in the time to come, civilization will secure to woman."

And yet even that attitude was atypical. The average suffragist did not even want her name handed her some heavenly day on the platter of the vote. The average suffragist, like the average person, agreed with Wendell P. Garrison, who in an obituary in the October 26, 1893 *Nation* said: "In becoming a married woman, Miss Stone entered a protest against the convenient practice of adopting the husband's name, and continued to wear to the end the name imposed by her father upon her mother. The individuality of an actress or singer has some merchantable value, but, as Mrs Blackwell, Lucy Stone would have forfeited nothing of her power as a reformer." Indeed, it is not too much to say that the average suffragist felt *The New York Times* called Lucy Stone by the name she ought to have used when on October 22, 1893 it announced "The Death of LUCY STONE BLACKWELL."

The contemporary attitude of suffragists towards married women's names was reflected in *The Woman's Journal*, which we have seen Lucy Stone did not use as a vehicle for urging young women to keep their own names after marriage, for she knew if she did she would alienate most of her readers. The *Journal* did print an occasional exotic item, such as a paragraph on the fact that in South America a man sometimes takes his wife's name for business or social reasons, or that in England a "peeress in her own right" keeps her own name after marriage. In 1873 the *Journal* noted that the Reverend Olympia Brown had kept her own name, but later it did not inform its readers about other women who did. Moreover, most discussions about women's names were not in editorials or essays but were in letters sent by readers, and the majority of these letters merely complained about the contemporary fad of giving girls names like Nellie or Hattie, most correspondents feeling that such diminutives lacked dignity, the most perceptive criticism occurring in a letter printed on April 5, 1890 from Dr Marie Zakrzewska, head of the New England Hospital for Women and Children, who felt such pet names, since they were used when speaking to infants, were psychologically bad for women.

In her long letter Dr Zakrzewska also pointed out that in her native Germany women for all legal purposes maintained one name throughout life, they being required by law to sign their name on deeds and contracts as "Anna Eleanora Miller, wife of Baron von Ketzen" and that female doctors had to use their own name professionally, the sign on the street door of a dentist she knew reading, "Dr Henriette Pagelson, widow of Hirschfeld, wife of Tiburtius." Dr Zakrzewska wished that American doctors would do likewise because she had often been vexed when a former intern who married and changed her name asked for a recommendation in a name Dr Zakrzewska of course did not recognize. But Dr Zakrzewska was not advocating that women imitate Lucy Stone; she was careful to emphasize that she was recommending only that women doctors and lawyers maintain their own name professionally: *"Let me be understood,*—I do not mean to say that a woman should not in social life accept the name of her husband; I do not desire to overturn existing customs; and I think it is far more sensible to be 'Mrs Smith' in common social life than to be 'Dr Brown'."

The readers of *The Woman's Journal* were not desirous of overturning existing customs, at least not much. Occasionally, a reader wrote in to urge that girls be given their mother's maiden name as a middle name or that women retain their own name as a middle surname after marriage, but that was the height of their radicalism. Even Elizabeth Cady Stanton revealed in a letter printed in the December 22, 1884 issue that when she was in England in 1883 she had "labored unceasingly" only to get women to retain their maiden names as middle names, but undoubtedly that was all she urged because she knew it would have been labor in vain to urge them not to take their husbands' names. When in the November 5, 1898 issue Professor Ellen Hayes of Wellesley suggested that "self-respecting women" express their belief "in a woman's having an individuality of her own" by the names they used, she meant that a woman should not call herself "Mrs John Smith, when her real name is Jane Brown Smith." Almost all suffragists were content with what Thomas Wentworth Higginson in his essay "On the Desire of Women to be Individuals" called "a sort of half-established individuality."

The attitude of most suffragists towards the right of a woman to keep her own name was well expressed in a letter from England printed in the October 19, 1895 *Woman's Journal.* The author, M. A. B., in discussing the feminist movement in England, differentiated the level-headed "New Woman" from the zealots who were overly concerned with "unimportant particulars . . . as for instance, whether a married woman should be known by her husband's name or her own, whether 'Mrs' or 'Miss' be the most dignified title for an unmarried lady of a certain age, whether girls should be allowed latchkeys, etc." *The Woman's Journal*, like M. A. B. and almost all feminists throughout the world, regarded a wife's right to her own name as an "unimportant particular" that would easily be won by the few extremists who wanted it when women got the right to vote.

A *Plea for Mrs John Smith*

How far the woman's rights movement had strayed from its early idealism, how accommodating it had become to customs once abhorred is revealed by the change in attitude towards the Mrs John Jones form.

When in the 1830s and 40s it first became popular to call married women by their husband's full name, feminists strenuously objected and made a point of using their own first name. Some persisted, and as time passed such women made people angry. When a group of Kansas women founded an educational club in 1886 and listed themselves under their own first names, they were accused of being "bold" women. The founder of the club, Mary Elizabeth Lease (later to become famous as a Populist orator), submitted poems so signed to the Wichita *Eagle* and the editor Colonel M. M. Murdock disapproved: "I did not fancy the use of her Christian names, for she was known to us as Mary Elizabeth Lease and not Mrs Charles Lease." Good women, those who were modest and unassertive, were supposed to veil themselves with their husband's full name. When in 1860 Elizabeth Cady Stanton rebuked Wendell Phillips for sending her a letter addressed "Mrs H. B. Stanton," he became angry, and after saying he had a bad memory for women's first names (but he had known Elizabeth for twenty years), he said he would henceforth remember her name by associating her with Queen Elizabeth, "you know, red-headed and so jealous of her looks that she forbade (by proclamation) all but two painters to attempt her likeness—she will exactly bring you to mind." If it were vanity to want to be called by her own name not her husband's, Elizabeth continued to be vain, and she never ceased to inveigh against the Mrs John Jones form. For example, in Part I of *The Woman's Bible* (1895) she complained: "To-day the woman is Mrs Richard Roe, to-morrow Mrs John Doe, and again Mrs James Smith according as she changes masters, and she has so little self-respect that she does not see the insult of the custom."

Most women, even suffragists, could not see "the insult of the custom" because most people never question the customs of their community, especially when a custom has become correct etiquette, and certainly by the 1880s the Mrs John Jones form had achieved that eminence. *Manners That Win* (1883), a handbook for those who aspired to proper social behavior, unequivocally stated: "All married women are addressed by the names of their husbands. The use of the baptismal name means that the lady is unmarried or a widow."

To see how women who had first hated the Mrs John Jones form came to endure it and, finally, even to embrace it, one can again go to *The Woman's*

Journal. In its first years the *Journal* from time to time reminded people of the absurdity of calling women by men's names. For example, in the June 21, 1879 issue it printed a short paragraph from a New Hampshire newspaper in which John Scales pointed out that to realize "how nonsensical" it was to call women "Mrs David Ladd . . . or Mrs Ichabod Somebody" one need only reverse the sexes. Imagine reading in a newspaper that "Mr Mary Ladd was elected in Ward 4, and Mr Susannah Horne carried the election in Leathers City! Why not? if Mrs David is feminine, why is not Mr Susannah masculine? The one is really no more absurd than the other." *The Woman's Journal* continued to print objections to the Mrs John Jones form, but as time passed the objections were voiced in letters sent in by an occasional reader, generally by the persistent Elizabeth Cady Stanton. In 1898 a letter in which she rebuked women for "burying their individuality in the names of their husbands" aroused a few other women to similarly object, Fanny Bullock Workman writing all the way from India to say that "the sooner 'Mrs John Smith' is relegated to the rear guard with 'Mrs General' and 'Mrs Doctor Smith' the better."

The *Journal* democratically printed these criticisms, but it used both the Mrs John Jones and Mrs General forms itself. How could it do otherwise since as the years passed a larger and larger percentage of its readers were using their husband's full name and title, as were a considerable number of those who attended the suffrage conventions, for as women came to understand that voting once or twice a year would not change woman's traditional role as wife and mother, the cause of suffrage became increasingly respectable among the Mrs George Washington Joneses and Mrs General Smiths of society.

But *The Woman's Journal* did more than bow to changing custom; it condoned it. In the December 20, 1884 issue it published "A Plea for Mrs John Smith" whose purpose was "to deprecate the unqualified condemnation sometimes pronounced upon such expressions as 'Mrs John Smith'." The author did concede there were valid objections to the form, that it could not be a woman's legal name and that to call a woman Mrs John Smith "wipes out all trace of her former personality," for which reason the author advised a woman "who has been famous under her maiden name" not to "efface it entirely by calling herself 'Mrs John Smith'." The author was convinced, however, that the form Mrs John Smith did not, as some argued, signify that a wife was legally, politically and morally one with a husband. Such interpretations were overre- actions to a mode of address that was often "a mere matter of convenience." For "when John Smith is a distinguished person, and his wife is known to the world in general only as his wife, it saves time and trouble to speak of her as Mrs John Smith . . . It certainly is inaccurate; it may be vulgar; but it is so conven-

ient that a busy and hurried world will probably never consent to give it up."
Moreover, courtesy demands that individuals be called by the name they
prefer, and "many women prefer to be called Mrs John Smith."

"A Plea for Mrs John Smith," sensible but entirely accepting of the status
quo, was written by Alice Stone Blackwell, the daughter of Lucy Stone.

The Disgraceful Custom

A woman's right to a lifelong name remained an unimportant right to
most feminists, but there was another woman, besides Elizabeth Cady Stanton
and the bold women who kept their own names, who thought passionately on
the subject. She was Charlotte Perkins Stetson, whose "The Woman of John
Smith" was the strongest essay of protest against the custom of wives changing
their surnames that appeared in the nineteenth century. It is of some interest
that the essay was printed in the November 1, 1892 *Kate Field's Washington,* a
periodical of tiny circulation, and not in *The Woman's Journal*, to which Stetson may well have offered it since in 1892 she published other of her essays in
the *Journal*. Not only did *The Woman's Journal* not publish it, but although
the *Journal* directed its readers to feminist articles in other periodicals, including *Kate Field's Washington*, it did not call the attention of its readers to this
thousand-word condemnation of the custom.

When you call a woman Mrs John Smith, said Charlotte Perkins Stetson,
what you are saying is that she is John Smith's woman, in the same sense that
slaves used to be called "Mr Carter's Caesar." Who, she asked, most commonly
change their names? Men who receive inheritances on that condition, fugitives
from justice, nuns when they give up the world and "women when they
marry." A woman may consider it an honor when a man chooses her to be his
wife, but "there remains undeniable ignominy in the enforced loss of name.
The inconvenience resulting to even average women is unnoticed by them because they are used to it. The amount of hardship human creatures will bear
when they think it unavoidable is amazing." Among the hardships Stetson
listed were loss of property because of inability to trace descent in the female
line, loss of friends because of inability to trace them after marriage and the loss
of "honor and recognition for work done under the lost name." To illustrate
the latter, Stetson recalled being at a concert when someone said of a woman in
the audience, " 'She composed that herself.' . . . 'Why no!' said I, looking at
my program, 'It is another name.' So it was. One was the name she had owned
once and done good work under, the other a man's name—her sole distinction
now."

Stetson felt that the fact women were now composing music and in other ways making distinguished names for themselves would finally be the "cure of the disgraceful custom." "Heretofore our women have rested content under the sole distinction of belonging to such or such a man" and a woman was therefore known "accurately for all domestic and locally social purposes" for just what she was—the woman of John Smith. But the woman who does human work, the teacher, writer, artist, doctor—anyone who is useful to her fellows as an individual—such a woman needs a name of her own, has one, and in the very nature of things keeps it . . . Jenny Lind is Jenny Lind to all our memories, though she did marry someone long since. The advancing line of differentiated women will have permanent names whether they like it or not."

Stetson concluded that that time was far off and that most women would probably continue to be merely the woman of John Smith. She therefore suggested that each girl be given a number at birth so that when she changes her name she will be able to be traced. If people object because convicts are given numbers, then "how would a brand do? As the countless herds of Western ranches take each their owner's mark," so females would "be branded in infancy, and carry the mark always as a personal distinction no change of civil status could take away." Might it not be "simpler, pleasanter, and nobler," suggested Stetson, "to follow the line of development already entered upon by so many women—to do distinguishing work, and so win and keep an inextinguishable name"?

And yet after writing such an unqualified denunciation of "the disgraceful custom" and although the name Stetson became known all over the world, when Charlotte Perkins Stetson married again on June 11, 1900 she changed not only the name she used in social life but her professional name to Charlotte Perkins Gilman.

Protest against taking a husband's name was a feeble countercurrent against a tidal wave of conformity, ninety-nine percent of women transforming themselves into Mrs John Jones without a murmur, rather with a sense of their increased prestige. Enumerating what few protests there were exaggerates their importance. Yet in another sense it does not, for despite the overwhelming conformity the very existence of any protest had significance since it was not until the nineteenth century that a fair number of women began to feel that acquiring a husband's name had disadvantages, disadvantages from which by the end of the century they had to a considerable extent freed themselves.

At the beginning of the nineteenth century women had been completely in bondage to husbands' names. Theatrical performers acquired new stage names with every husband. Authors who dared put their own name on a title page felt obliged to change it when they married or remarried. But most authors had no name; they were "Anonymous" or "A Lady," and later in the century they hid behind male pseudonyms. There were no other professions in which women could make names for themselves, and the nonentity of wives was becoming total with the introduction of the Mrs John Jones style. Needless to say, there was no (recorded) protest against the custom of wives having to change their names.

By the end of the nineteenth century women had won a fair measure of nominal independence. Women in the theatrical professions had the right, a right most of them asserted, to keep a constant stage name regardless of the husbands' names they acquired in private life. No longer did authors feel obliged to be anonymous and fewer and fewer of them used male pseudonyms, most of them publishing under their own name or the name they used at the beginning of their career. Women had entered almost every profession and had become active in public life, making names for themselves they tried to preserve by retaining their own name as a middle name or by hyphenating it to their husband's. If at one extreme it had become correct etiquette to call wives Mrs John Jones, at the other a handful of rebels insisted on being known as Lucy Stone or Lydia Kingsmill Commander despite their marriages. Moreover, the right they boldly claimed was a right feminists recognized all women in the future would have as a matter of course. That it would be a right not easily wrested from a male power structure became clear in 1879 when the Massachusetts Board of Registrars refused to let Lucy Stone vote in her own name. But that the custom of women changing their names was also going to cause legal difficulties became clear in 1896 when, according to the September 29 *New York Times*, the marriage of a female notary public in Colorado forced the Attorney General to wrestle with a new legal problem—was her maiden name still valid on notarized documents or did she have to be recommissioned in her new name?

Charlotte Perkins Stetson had predicted that "the advancing line of differentiated women" would have permanent names whether they liked it or not. Certainly, the fact that women did not have permanent names was bound to become a greater and greater problem as more and more women stopped being only the woman of John Smith.

14

TWO NAMES ON A GREENWICH VILLAGE DOOR

The Changing Feminine Ideal—1901-1911

In the first decade of the twentieth century women continued to avail themselves of the nominal freedoms won by their nineteenth-century sisters and discontent with having to replace one's own name with a husband's was increasing. The emerging discontent as well as the established nominal pattern can be seen in the very first year of the new century.

In 1901 women in the theater and authors felt free to continue working under their own name despite marriage, but women in other professions did not. The California writer Eleanor Gates (the future author of *The Poor Little Rich Girl*) on January 26, 1901 married Richard Walton Tully and continued to sign her work with her own name. The journalist Winifred Black (also known as "Annie Laurie") on February 7 married Charles A. Bonfils, her second husband, but continued professionally to use the name Black (that of her first husband). The violinist Geraldine Morgan (the first American to win the Mendelssohn prize at the Royal Academy in Berlin) on June 2 married Benjamin F. Roeder and continued to tour the United States as the head of the Morgan String Quartette. The prima donna Fritzi Scheff (who had dropped her father's name and adopted that of her mother, the singer Hortense Scheff) also married in 1901 and notwithstanding a husband with a title, Baron Fritz von Bardeleben, she signified her marital status only by changing her title to Madame. But although a singer, a violinist and two writers kept their well-known names, a scientist did not. The astronomer Dr Dorothea Klumpke, who had received her PhD from the Sorbonne and who was the first woman to be elected to the Astronomical Society of France, in December 1901 married the celestial photographer Isaac Roberts and transformed herself into Dr Roberts.

The year 1901 also had its radicals, witnessing the marriage of an English couple who decided to combine surnames. Emmeline Pethick, a social worker, converted Frederick Lawrence to feminism during their courtship, and shortly after they were married on October 2, 1901 Frederick wrote to Emmeline's father requesting permission to add her family name to his own. "It was not only that he wanted me to keep my identity by retaining my maiden name," wrote Emmeline in *My Part In A Changing World*, "but he craved for himself the honour of being associated with the Pethick clan." For why shouldn't a man as well as a woman be able by marriage to acquire a well-known name? And in fact Frederick's nickname eventually became "Peth." As the Pethick-Lawrences they for many years devoted themselves to the cause of woman suffrage.

It was also in the year 1901 that another Englishwoman got the House of Lords to agree that she had a right to use whatever name she wished. Lady Violet, Countess Cowley was no feminist; she was a snob who wished to go on using the name and title of Earl Cowley despite her divorce from him and her remarriage to a commoner, R. E. Myddleton Biddulph. Earl Cowley disliked his ex-wife continuing to call herself Countess Cowley and asked the House of Lords to order her to stop using it, but the Lords refused because "the law of this country allows any person to assume any name" (Appeal Cases 450). Thus was a precedent established for future Englishwomen who might wish to retain their own name after marriage.

If in England it seemed to have been legally established that a woman had the right to have a name different from her husband's, there is evidence that women in other countries were becoming interested in having the same right. One of the equal suffrage associations of Paris, at a meeting held in December 1901, "adopted a resolution in favor of married women keeping their own names" (reported in *The Woman's Journal* January 11, 1902), and eleven months earlier, on January 12, 1901, Henry Blackwell, the aging husband of Lucy Stone, published an article in the *Journal* in which he listed eight nineteenth-century women who had kept their own name. He did so because he had been asked by a friend "to give the names of women who have retained their maiden names after marriage." The fact that a friend was interested and that Blackwell satisfied that interest by publishing an article in *The Woman's Journal* certainly seems to indicate that women were changing, that a subject conservative suffragists once thought best avoided was now beginning to be talked about more freely.

If that were not the case in 1901, it was by 1904 when *The Woman's Journal* on April 9 published "Women's Names" by the iconoclastic Charlotte Perkins Gilman. Twelve years before, "The Woman of John Smith," her attack on "the disgraceful custom" of changing women's names at marriage, had been published in the obscure *Kate Field's Washington*, but in 1904 the subject had become sufficiently acceptable so that the most widely circulated and conservative feminist paper was willing to print what Gilman now more calmly called a "clumsy and injurious custom." After comparing a wife's loss of her name to a Jewish bride's loss of her hair and a Japanese bride's blackening her teeth, Gilman repeated much of what she had said in "The Woman of John Smith," though with less sarcasm, again stressing that now that women were becoming "active members of the species . . . differentiated individuals with a use in the world beyond their general functions, names are essential to them."

Gilman felt "a new system of naming human beings" ought to be developed, one that would "not rest on the mistaken theory of masculine supremacy, or burden us with genealogical records, but which shall clearly and permanently distinguish individuals." She, however, did not think a new system would develop quickly since "racial habits take long to change."

But it seemed likely that some change would occur soon, for discontent with the old naming system was in the air. The radical Gilman was not the only one who was then feeling annoyed at the "clumsy and injurious custom." Her essay had been occasioned by an editorial complaint in the April *Current Literature*: "If only our artistic and literary friends of the feminine persuasion might change their domestic relationships without being obliged to change their names," said the editor, who was referring to Mrs Everard Cotes, whose *The Imperialist* the magazine was reviewing that month, and who was probably known to readers only under her former name of Sarah Jeanette Duncan, the author of two highly popular travel books.

The editor of *Current Literature* felt annoyed at her change of publishing identity because by 1904 it was becoming more and more uncommon for authors to let marriage change their professional name. The few women who did decide to change their name tended to be of an older generation, like Mary Wilkins who, marrying in 1902 when she was forty-nine years old, could not resist informing the world she had acquired a husband, so that, despite her fame, she changed her publishing name first to Mary E. Wilkins Freeman, then tried Mary Wilkins-Freeman and finally settled on Mary Wilkins Freeman. Occasionally, an author felt obliged to include her married name in parentheses, as from time to time did "Anne Douglas Sedgwick (Mrs Basil de Sélincourt)" and "Josephine Preston Peabody (Mrs Lincoln Marks)." But young writers rarely changed their professional identity. When Myrtle Reed married in 1906, she, despite her excessively sentimental views on marriage, continued to publish as Myrtle Reed. When Dorothy Canfield married in 1907 she had only a small reputation, but she did not change her publishing name.

That women were feeling more nominally independent of husbands was noticed by Laura Alton Payne, who remarked in an article on names in the January 25, 1906 *Independent* that "Hyphenated names and the wife's retention of her maiden name for a middle name are customs growing in favor in the United States and Great Britain." Between 1901 and 1910 these customs did grow in favor. For example, when the Unitarian minister Marie Jenney married she called herself Marie Jenney Howe, and when the civil engineer Nora Blatch (granddaughter of Elizabeth Cady Stanton) married she used the name Nora Blatch DeForest. Hyphenated surnames had a marked vogue. After the marriage of the Maryland physician Dr Patience Bourdeau, she became Dr Bourdeau-Sisco; after the marriage of the Minnesota English professor Anna Helmholtz, she became Professor Helmholtz-Phelan; after the marriage of the English suffragist Teresa Billington, she became Mrs Billington-Greig.

More women were using hyphenated surnames or retaining their own name as a middle name because women were changing, and more radically than the names they used would indicate. As early as 1901 *The New York Times* felt women were becoming dangerously unrestrained; in a February 27 editorial the *Times* described "the principal characteristic of the new woman" as "her exaggerated self-reliance," a mild way to speak of the new women who, according to the *Times*, had threatened "to wipe man out of existence" if Carry Nation were not released from jail for having wrecked the barroom of the Hotel Carey in Wichita, Kansas. That Carry Nation, a woman, had used violence to gain her teetotalitarian ends had an important effect on the woman's movement. Her use of violence influenced the English suffragettes to become militant in 1903, and the widely publicized militance of Nation and the suffragettes changed not only men's image of women but women's image of themselves, making them feel less like genteel ladies and more capable of assertion.

Women were also feeling more assertive because they were getting more education. By 1910 in America 70 percent of high school graduates and 44.1 percent of college graduates were women, which explains the great increase in the number of women entering professions or in other ways becoming active in public life. The increase was so marked that the American editor of *Who's Who*, John Leonard, projected the first *Woman's Who's Who of America*, a volume finally published in 1914 that contained the names of almost 10,000 women, a huge increase over the 1470 women listed in the 1893 woman's *Who's Who*, Willard and Livermore's *A Woman of the Century*.

There was not only a substantial increase in the number of women in *Who's Who*, there was a significant increase in the number of working women generally. Between 1901 and 1910 the percentage rose from 23.5 to 28.1, a rate of increase greater than had occurred in the nineteenth century and than would occur again for several decades.

With more women working and many at high level jobs women inevitably began to think that having a husband was less important. Not only was there a sharp increase in the number of women who decided to have a career and not marry, women who found their marriage unhappy were more inclined to walk out. The divorce rate almost doubled in ten years: whereas in 1896 42,937 divorces were granted, in 1906 the number was 72,062 and rising. That a woman's chief goal in life ought not to be marriage began to be generally discussed. In the conservative *Atlantic* in January 1902 William Salter described "The Real Emancipation of Woman" as her developing the feeling she was "an entity in herself," "not simply an appendage to mankind" for whom home is everything.

But the very institution of marriage was under attack and the ideas of the nineteenth-century free lovers were now being widely talked about. Whereas in the September 10, 1898 *Woman's Journal* Henry Blackwell had said that "to abolish legal marriage would be in the vast majority of cases to reduce women to a state of concubinage," now feminists were asserting that legal marriage was concubinage. Cicely Hamilton's *Marriage as a Trade* (1909) presented marriage as a socially respectable form of prostitution, as had George Bernard Shaw's *Mrs Warren's Profession*, first performed in New York in 1905. The sociologist Elsie Clews Parsons in *The Family* (1906) advocated trial marriage, and the anarchist Emma Goldman interviewed in a Chicago park with Alexander Berkman proudly admitted they were living together "in true spiritual love" and that each felt free to leave if love ceased (*The New York Times* May 26, 1906). Isadora Duncan was dancing semi-nude and having children out of wedlock and nevertheless becoming rich and famous, and young women were inspired by her uninhibited life to live with more exuberance themselves, to at least talk about sex and cut their hair and smoke and drink. By 1910 the novelist Margaret Deland, writing in the March *Atlantic*, felt "The Feminine Ideal" had changed, that young women were going to college, earning a living, not going to church and uttering their views on marriage and the birth rate without a blush, that whereas a generation ago achieving women were conspicuous because there were so few of them, now they were not noticed because there were so many of them, that, indeed, the New Woman was almost ceasing to be "new" because she was the norm, that most young women were now discontented and restless and that, unlike their mothers, their ideal was not selfless devotion to husband and children but devotion to themselves, to their own individual self-development and to the acquisition of political power in order to improve the world.

Among such a generation of individualistic women, eager to achieve, it was inevitable that a few would decide they did not want their individuality eclipsed by a husband's name. What could not have been predicted was there would be so many. No longer, as in the nineteenth century, does one chance upon an isolated rebel; starting in 1911 one finds many rebels, so many their number will never be known.

This Miss Wife—1911

In November 1911 a reporter for the New York *World*, walking along Charles Street in Greenwich Village, stopped at No. 83, for his eye had been caught by a prominent card on the mailbox that read:

IDA RAUH

MAX EASTMAN

The reporter probably thought he had a story about a couple unblushingly living in sin; he discovered something more sensational—a married couple who didn't care if the world thought they were living in sin, for they used their own names. On November 29 the *World* ran their story:

NO "MRS" BADGE OF SLAVERY WORN BY THIS MISS WIFE

Legally She is Mme Eastman,
but Maiden Name of Ida
Rauh is Still Used
by Her.

HUSBAND, A SUFFRAGIST,
FULLY AGREES WITH HER.

Max Eastman, then a philosophy professor at Columbia University, told the press his wife was continuing to be known as Ida Rauh because marriage ought to be "the union of two strong, independent persons." "I prefer to have my wife known by her own name rather than mine. I am far more insistent upon this than she is, and I get quite cross when she is simply called Mrs Eastman." Rauh said she preferred being called by her own name and their friends obliged, but with strangers "it is easier just to let it go." Not so Eastman, who felt as strongly as Lucy Stone that wives ought to retain their own identity. "I do not want to absorb my wife's identity in mine. I want her to be entirely independent of me in every way." Years later in his autobiography *The Enjoyment of Living* he said that "This pinning of your own name on the object of your love displays an egotism . . . comparable to the similar defacement of statues and monuments by small boys."

The *World* also printed Rauh and Eastman's admission that they had been legally married merely to placate convention and that their own marriage might well not be permanent. "All marriages these days under our laws are trial marriages," they declared. But apparently such radical views on marriage did not shock the public as much as Rauh's keeping her name. Not only did the *World*'s headlines feature "This Miss Wife," but in Elmira, New York, Eastman's home town, Rauh's not using her husband's name was what upset most people. A Colonel D. C. Robinson sent a letter of outrage to an Elmira paper in which he asserted that if Professor Eastman and Miss Rauh "are married and entitled to live together in the state of New York, their names are Mr and Mrs Eastman under its laws. If their names are Mr Max Eastman and Miss Rauh, they would be classed in the police courts under titles which politeness forbids me to put upon this page." Many a clergyman, merely because they used separate names, accused them of striking at the "sacredness of marriage." One clergyman, however, did come to their support. He was the Reverend Samuel Eastman, Max's father, who the next Sunday preached a sermon on "The Home and Its Defenses" in which he advocated the equality of men and women in marriage and the equal right of a wife to retain her own name.

The Reverend Eastman, when interviewed by reporters, revealed that his daughter Crystal had the same views as Max on marriage and had also kept her own name. Crystal Eastman, a lawyer who specialized in workmen's compensation laws and who in 1910 had published an influential book on work accidents, had been married on May 5, 1911 to Wallace Benedict, an insurance agent, and had moved to Milwaukee, Wisconsin. There, using the name Miss Crystal Eastman, she became active in the National American Suffrage Association, speaking at conventions under that name.

Whether or not she was bold enough to put the names Crystal Eastman and Wallace Benedict on her mailbox is not known. It certainly would have been harder to defy convention in Milwaukee than in Greenwich Village where many couples lived together openly without benefit of clergy. Eastman thought that he and Rauh were the first couple, married or otherwise, who had had the courage to put their full names (not just their surnames) on the mailbox, and perhaps they were. But by the time they were interviewed by the *World* reporter, another married couple had "Two Names on a Greenwich Village Door," to quote George Middleton. Middleton, a playwright, had been married in Washington DC on October 29, 1911 to Fola La Follette, the daughter of Senator Robert La Follette, and they had immediately moved to W. 12th Street in the Village where, as in every later home they shared, "our door . . . was always to bear two names. For Fola was never to take mine."

Fola La Follette was then a well-known actress and for her to have kept her own name professionally was a matter of course. But actresses did not keep their own name in private life. Fola kept hers because she was a feminist. Her mother, Belle Case La Follette, was a lawyer and a suffragist and a good friend of one of the nineteenth-century women who had kept her name, Olympia Brown, whose example undoubtedly influenced Fola. At any rate, before she married, Fola asked George "about keeping her own name," and George thought it a good idea. "I couldn't see why any woman, professional or otherwise, should give up her identification tag. I wouldn't have changed mine." They felt that the custom of wives changing their names often led to a woman changing her identity more often than a snake changes its skin. "Our prize exhibit . . . was a friend who had worn the names of four husbands, two pen names, plus the in-and-out maiden one she started with!"

Fola La Follette and George Middleton adhered strictly to nominal separatism. Not only did their apartment door and mail box bear their two names, they each had a bank account in her/his own name, and each had separate visiting cards. A card they both used that showed them sitting together *en ménage* bore their two names. Such cards and Fola's being called Miss La Follette occasionally resulted in a friend who knew them for years not realizing they were married. But they did not care what people thought, not even hotel clerks. They always made it a point to register at hotels under separate names. Once in Atlantic City when Middleton signed the register "Fola La Follette and George Middleton," the clerk suggested, "Don't you want two rooms, Mr Middleton?" to which Middleton shrewdly replied, "If we *weren't* married, would I have signed it that way?"

One had to scorn Mrs Grundy to marry and keep separate names. An Englishwoman who also married in 1911 and kept her own name had the same scorn of conventional morality as did La Follette and Middleton. She was Dr Marie Stopes, later to be notorious for founding Great Britain's first birth control clinic and for writing handbooks telling husbands how to make love to their wives. In 1911 Dr Stopes was a botanist and in late June or early July she married a fellow botanist Dr Reginald Gates and decided not to change her name. Shortly after her marriage Dr Stopes had a notice printed and sent to all her friends and colleagues in which she announced that "notwithstanding my marriage my legal name is Marie C. Stopes." Like Lucy Stone, she had had lawyers investigate the law of married women's names and, as she explained to her friends, she learned that a married woman's change of name was voluntary. "This is a very different thing from a woman's being 'forced legally' on marriage to take her husband's name. If she does not elect to take her husband's name no law in the land can compel her to do so, and her original name remains her legal name." All a woman had to do to retain her name was to use it consistently. She also informed her friends they need not be in difficulties about whether to address her as Miss or Mrs, for she had earned the title Dr and would use it. She acceded to social custom on one point only: "Privately, for the few friends who cannot escape the bonds of custom, I add the name of my husband by hyphen—Stopes-Gates," but she did not use Stopes-Gates for long. According to her friend Alymer Maude, there was a good deal of press interest, much of it unfavorable, in her retaining her name.

There was also another Englishwoman who in 1911 decided to keep on using her own name. She was Mary Macarthur, the women's labor organizer, who on September 21 of that year married William Anderson, and not wanting to confuse the country women she represented, she, according to her friend Mary Agnes Hamilton, "stuck to the name which had by now become a household word." But unlike La Follette and Stopes, Macarthur did not object to being called Mrs Anderson socially.

Probably other women who married in 1911 kept their own name. The Chicago surgeon and writer on sex education for the young Dr Edith B. Lowry on July 24, 1911 married Dr Richard Jay Lambert and certainly never changed her name professionally, always publishing and listing her name in *Who's Who*s as Lowry. Whether or not she was willing to be Mrs Lambert socially, I could not discover. Dr Lowry may have been one of the increasing number of women who, according to Charlotte Perkins Gilman, remained "Mary Smith to the trade" but introduced themselves socially "with modest pride, as Mrs Peter Saunders."

Gilman made that observation in yet another essay on the subject, this one entitled "Names—Especially Women's" appearing in the October 1911 issue of *The Forerunner*, the feminist periodical she was then writing and publishing herself. It was the second time in 1911 that Gilman had discussed women's names. Earlier in the year, in March, she had published in *The Forerunner* Chapter Three of *Moving The Mountain*, her novel about a Utopian community in which men and women are equal. In that chapter we meet Dr Ellen Robertson, a physician and president of a co-educational college, who is married to Owen Montrose but does not use his name. The community not only believes that wives should not take husbands' names, they also think all children should not be named after the father; accordingly, boys are given the father's name and girls the mother's. But the community thinks even this system unsatisfactory. "There's a strong movement on foot," says Dr Robertson, "to drop hereditary names altogether."

In her October essay "Names—Especially Women's" Gilman in the main repeated what she had said in her 1892 and 1904 essays, though here she insisted on spelling surname "sirname." She did so in order to stress that in our man-made world only "the desire to repeat the name of the father" is honored, that women never have "the distinction of a sirname, beyond the badge of paternity" because sirnames "descend in the male line only." "Men, being persons, had names. They must be distinguished from one another. Women, being female belongings, needed no badge save that of the man to whom they belonged." Gilman again said that now that women were becoming differentiated beings, not merely the daughters or wives of some man, having a name of their own would become important to them, that women in business and the professions would at least be reluctant to change an established "trade name." But Gilman's most radical point, one she had not discussed in earlier essays, was that it was none of society's business to know whether or not a woman was married. "You do not know whether a man is married or not, either by his name or by a glittering official ring." When a man is introduced as Paul Waterson, we don't instantly ask, " 'Are you a bachelor or married?' " but when a woman is introduced as Susan Mortimer, we immediately inquire, " 'Miss or Mrs?' "

Of course, the obvious reason for asking "Miss or Mrs?" was that it used to be the custom to address people one had just met by a title and their surname, and since there was no universal title for women, a person would have to know whether he should address Susan Mortimer as Miss or Mrs Mortimer. But what Gilman was fundamentally objecting to was that there was no universal title for women, that women were divided into the married and the unmarried. Lucy Stone and most of the other nineteenth-century women who kept their own name had also wished society did not classify women as Miss or Mrs; nevertheless, when they married they changed their title to Mrs, thus labeling themselves respectably married women. But their twentieth-century sisters remained Miss, feeling, like Gilman, that their marital status was none of society's business and not caring if Mrs Grundy thought they were living in sin.

What the Miss Wives had had the courage to do was to defy the sexual double standard. By remaining Miss Smith and refusing to become Mrs Jones they were acting like men, whom society did not compel to announce to the world the name of the one person they had acquired a license to sleep with. The Miss Wives wanted to live in a world in which they, like men, could have sex freely, without necessarily being married. Indeed, Edward Carpenter in *Love's Coming-Of-Age* (1911) felt that woman should be freer than man "to work out the problem of her sex-relations," that she should be "hampered as little as possible by legal, conventional, or economic considerations." And Emma Goldman in *Marriage and Love* (1911) also asserted that woman ought to be free to love and have children without being married. Goldman denounced marriage as an unholy "insurance pact" that in return for giving woman food, clothing and shelter deprived her of sexual freedom, of the freedom to work outside the home, and of "her name, her privacy, her self-respect, her very life." She felt, however, that times were changing, that "Now that woman is coming into her own . . . the sacred institution of marriage is gradually being undermined, and no amount of sentimental lamentation can stay it."

From the very beginning of the woman's rights movement society had feared that if women should achieve equal rights with men and could without social ostracism have sex and children outside of marriage that marriage and family life would be destroyed, and that fear was somewhat justified. For in a world without a sexual double standard marriage and family life would be, if not destroyed, radically changed. To allay such fears nineteenth-century suffragists had presented themselves as respectable family women, as did the early twentieth-century suffragists. Nevertheless, "A Lover of Home, Mother, and Sister" in a circular handed out before a meeting of the Woman's Political Union in New York accused them of being "destroyers of homes and families and the sacred ties of marriage," as proof of which, asserted the circular, "Suffragettes do not take their husband's name when they marry" (*The New York Times*, November 5, 1911).

"A Lover of Home, Mother, and Sister" was, of course, rebuking the wrong women. All the married women who spoke at that meeting used their husbands' surnames, many of them, indeed, speaking as "Mrs John M. Brannon" and "Mrs Raymond Brown" and "Mrs J. H. Rogers." It is true that a few older suffragists were using their own name: Lydia Kingsmill Commander had been one of the prime movers of the Woman's Political Union; Olympia Brown was working for suffrage in Wisconsin, as in Washington DC was Helen Hamilton Gardener, who had married again in 1902 and still called herself Mrs Gardener. But the younger women who were then devoting all their energy to getting the vote did not have radical views on marriage.

But although "Lover of Home" accused the wrong women of not "taking their husband's name when they marry," his accusation was significant, for it revealed that the existence of Miss Wives had become known to the public at large, which had become aware, not of one odd rebel, but of a group of women who were refusing to become Mrs Theirhusband. And starting in 1911 there began to be what can almost be called a movement among women to keep their own name after marriage.

Would the movement be successful? Would the public like "Lover of Home" frown upon them? Or would it be easy for the public, now there were so many women in business and the professions, to at least extend to them the same right accorded to women in the theater and authors and let them have their own name in public life? In 1911 the identity of singers and actresses was carefully respected in newspapers and magazines. The singer Emma Eames, having married for a second time on July 13, was given both her own name and her husband by referring to her as "Mme Emma Eames and her husband, Mr Gogorza." Or when on August 17 the actress Julia Marlowe married again, neither the public nor the press felt the sacred ties of marriage and the family were being destroyed by referring to her as "Miss Marlowe and her husband, Mr Sothern." It would seem an easy step to extend that custom to another group of women and refer to "Miss Crystal Eastman and her husband, Mr Benedict" or to "Dr Marie Stopes and her husband, Dr Gates."

In 1911 it also seemed as if the women who wanted to keep their own name would have no trouble with the law. For the year before, the New York Court of Appeals had eloquently upheld a person's common law right to use the name of his choice. In deciding that the late Maurice W. Mansfield had had the right to change his name without resorting to the courts, Judge Vann quoted many authorities both in England and America, all of whom affirmed that "one may legally name himself, or change his name, or acquire a name by reputation, general usage, and habit," and that the name by which one was "generally known in the community" was one's legal name (Smith v. United States Casualty Co., 197 New York Reports 420). Such opinions would seem to assure a woman's right to use the name of her choice and guarantee that the name she was generally known by would have to be adjudged her legal name.

That more and more women would want to keep their own name because more and more of them would be making their names well-known or would feel themselves to be the equals of men also seemed imminent in 1911, a year in which women made notable achievements, demonstrating their physical courage, their mental prowess and their political clout. Harriet Quimby, having in 1910 become the first person in the world to win a monoplane pilot's license under the revised rules of the International Aeronautics Club, on August 1, 1911 became the first woman to be issued a license in America. And on November 8 it was announced that a woman had achieved the highest honor in a field nineteenth-century men had thought women's brains could never master—Marie Curie was awarded the Nobel Prize in Chemistry. Moreover, when in October California women won the right to vote, it seemed as if women would soon be the political equals of men. For in the nineteenth century only four states had granted women that right, Idaho in 1896 being the last, after which for fourteen years no further progress was made. But in 1910 Washington granted women suffrage and with the victory in California in 1911 suffragists knew the movement was revitalized, and in fact in the next three years six more states and the territory of Alaska gave women the right to vote.

Since the vote was the means by which it was thought women would gain all their rights, it would certainly seem that so minor a one as the right to use the name of one's choice would not be denied.

Married but Not Renamed—1912-1920

When Floyd Dell moved to Greenwich Village in 1913 he immediately noticed the number of couples who were living together under two names. The more timid had a card on their door and mailbox that read "Brown-Nelson" so the postman and strangers would not be shocked, but others, said Dell, boldly proclaimed "that the apartment was occupied together by

> Miss Phyllis Wood
> Mr George Henderson."

Many of these couples were not married, but many were. From their names there was no way of telling which was which.

There had been a revolution in Bohemia. When Mary Wollstonecraft began to live with Gilbert Imlay in Paris in 1793, she called herself Mrs Imlay. When Eleanor Marx began to live with Dr Edward Aveling in England in 1884, she became Mrs Aveling. But in the late 1880s and early 90s when Lincoln Steffens was living with Josephine Bontecou in the Latin Quarter in Paris, they in 1892 sneaked off to England to get married and returned and lived in their Paris apartment under two names, telling no one of their marriage for fear of being drummed out of the unconventional corps. Greenwich Village in the 1910s was different; one neither had to pay obeisance to Mrs Grundy or thumb one's nose at her. It did not matter. If "Morality consists in being suspicious of other people's not being [or being] legally married," as Shaw defined it in *The Doctor's Dilemma* (1906), then the Village was developing a new morality.

The new morality, that a married woman should not be differentiated from a single one by a change of name or title, was practiced by many couples in the Village. After the social reformer and feminist Henrietta Rodman moved to the Village in 1910, she became a propagandist for the belief that a woman's marital status was none of society's business and when she married Herbert de-Frem in 1913 she practiced what she preached. Another convert was a friend and neighbor of Fola La Follette and George Middleton, Frances Perkins, whose wedding announcements read like the name cards on Villagers' mailboxes: "Paul C. Wilson and Frances Perkins / announce their marriage / September 26, 1913 New York City." Friends of Perkins and her husband (and also of Max Eastman and Ida Rauh) were the writers Susan Glaspell and George Cram Cook, and when they married in 1913 Glaspell remained Miss Glaspell. The professional free lover Harry Kemp in 1915 finally married the woman he was living with and Mary Pyne kept her name. In Kemp's autobiographical novel about Village life, *More Miles* (1926), he mentions two married couples living together under different names, one couple described as a settlement worker and a society man and the other as a playwright and a woman with no specified job. Most histories of the Village mention Grace Potter and Ernest Holcombe as a married couple who kept separate names.

In the 1910s it became so fashionable for Village women to be known by their own name that wives who had previously used their husband's name began to use their own again. The writer Neith Boyce, who in 1899 married Hutchins Hapgood and not only became Mrs Hapgood but occasionally published as Neith (Boyce) Hapgood, apparently stopped calling herself Mrs Hapgood in the 1910s, for those who wrote about her in that decade almost always called her Neith Boyce, and her husband dedicated his autobiography, *A Victorian in the Modern World* (1939) to "Neith Boyce." When Mrs Louise Trullinger came to New York and was exposed to the influence of the feminists in Greenwich Village, she stopped using her first husband's name and became Miss Louise Bryant, a name she retained after she and John Reed decided to legalize their union in 1916.

It was a Villager who spread the new gospel of nominal separatism to a national audience as a result of a speech she gave in New York on February 20, 1914. Fola La Follette, at the Second Feminist Mass Meeting, spoke for twenty minutes on a woman's right to keep her name, the first speech wholly devoted to the subject. "Should a man keep his own name?" La Follette boldly began. If, she said, the question seems absurd applied to men, it is, rationally considered, just as absurd applied to women. "If a woman is to change her name simply as an acknowledgment that she loves a man and has married him," she continued, "why should not the same sacrifice be made by him toward her?" La Follette felt, however, that women would soon stop sacrificing their names "The ready acceptance of the custom of a woman retaining her maiden name plus the name of her husband may be taken as a token of how in a very few years we may expect to see women in marriage keeping their own maiden name intact." And La Follette predicted that not only would all wives soon go by their own names but that members of a family would not "all have the same names." She did not think children should continue to be named only after the father. "The children could have either the combined names of their father and mother," or "let the parents pick the last name for the child the same way they select the first name . . . or, preferably, let the children take the mother's name." La Follette concluded her speech by advocating the abandonment of the title Mrs. "Why should the world know a woman is married or single any more than it knows a man is married or single? 'Mrs' is simply a survival of man's property sense towards women. Let us cease to label women as maids or matrons . . . If Miss is the form of address for women before marriage, let it be so after marriage too. Let the term acquire a large social significance. When women keep their own name, a woman will not have to explain her children by wearing the name of a . . . husband."

Fola La Follette's speech was the sensation of the evening. Five others were given at the Second Feminist Mass Meeting, some on subjects far more revolutionary, such as a woman's right to have babies and a full-time job too, and her right not only to get equal pay for equal work but "equal chance for promotion" and her right to ignore fashion totally, rights that if achieved would seem to create greater changes in society than wives keeping their own name. Yet it was La Follette's demand that aroused the public. The New York *World* headlined its account of the evening, "WHAT'S A NAME TO A MAN OR A FAMILY? WOMEN ASK," as if La Follette's speech were the only one given that night, and on February 23 *The New York Times* singled out her speech for a critical editorial entitled "A Grievance Hardly Intolerable," the *Times* feeling that "in a world so abounding in real troubles and hardships" Miss La Follette had spoken with "unnecessary stress of indignant emotion" about so small a matter as taking a husband's name. Moreover, on March 7 the *Times* printed a letter from a Brooklyn reader who suggested that what married women who called themselves Miss and did not wear a ring really wanted was "man's freedom to range unobstructed."

But although the press thought Fola La Follette was making a great fuss about a small matter, it nevertheless played up her speech, and the resulting publicity brought the new gospel to the attention of thousands of women and fell on many receptive ears, so much so that by 1915 the *Times* could no longer consider married women's names a small matter and in fact in that one year alone discussed the subject seven times.

Because "The question has repeatedly been raised whether a woman upon marriage is obliged by law to take her husband's surname" the *Times* on January 17, 1915 published a long and learned article on the law and married women's names. On April 7, again because the *Times* felt the subject was "not interesting to herself alone," it informed its readers in an editorial about an Oregon woman who had asked her state Attorney General "whether she was under any legal obligation to assume her husband's name." On April 10 and 20 the *Times* published two more editorials in which, after recognizing that only the "advanced members of the sex" would want to keep their own name, the editor urged other women to have sufficient respect for their personality not to submit to the "humiliating" custom of being called Mrs John Jones, a subject the *Times* returned to on December 8 when the editor again urged women not to be robbed of their "next to the last shred of nominative independence" and at least revolt against being totally submerged in their husband's full name. On December 3, after announcing on the 2nd that Brooklyn's first woman intern Dr Mary Merritt Crawford had married Edward Schuster and not changed her name, the *Times* published "Married But Not Renamed," an editorial on Dr Crawford's "departure from custom and convention" that ended with words that must have made Lucy Stone in heaven shout hallelujah: "For the wedded pair to use the same name is in many ways convenient, but it is not very clear why the woman, any more than the man, should be forced or even expected to make a change of patronymic on getting married." Ten years earlier such an editorial would have been inconceivable. The *Times* had indeed changed with the times as more and more women were "Married But Not Renamed."

How many women between 1910 and 1920 kept their name is impossible to discover, but the new "departure from custom and convention" was affecting women all over the United States, the little known as well as the famous. That the popular novelist Fannie Hurst should have kept her name after her 1915 marriage to Jacques Danielson or that the dancer Ruth St Denis kept hers after her 1914 marriage to Ted Shawn does not seem remarkable, but even a Los Angeles beautician, the twenty-two year old Marie Washburn, who was beginning her career as a specialist in the Marcel technique of hair waving, continued to be known as Miss Washburn to her friends as well as clientele after her marriage in 1912 to Loron Hilliker. Nominal radicalism was in the air in the 1910s, and many a couple "proposed to keep our names separate, however our lives were joined," to quote Francis Hackett, editor of *The New Republic*, commenting on his 1918 marriage to his assistant editor Signe Toksvig. Even Lady Randolph Churchill declared her nominal independence in this decade by not taking her third husband's name. After her second marriage in 1900 she had become Mrs George Cornwallis-West, but in 1914 after divorcing West, she legally resumed the name Lady Randolph Churchill, which she retained after her marriage in 1918 to Montagu Porch not only because she was a snob but because, as she wrote to a friend, "I have made a name for myself."

Other women who had made names for themselves on a lesser scale also held onto them after marriage. Among them were Colonel Kathleen Burke, internationally known for her work for the Allies in the first World War, Mary Elizabeth Evans, owner of a large candy business in New York, Gertrude Rand, Professor of Physiological Optics at Johns Hopkins School of Medicine, and Alice Chapman Miller, a girl scout leader in Milwaukee, Wisconsin and a trustee of the Milwaukee Downer College. There were also a fair number of women who took the more conservative course of hyphenation, like the sculptor and painter Lucy Perkins-Ripley and the Virginia physician Dr Cora Corpening-Kornegay. The most famous was the lawyer and suffragist Inez Milholland. A friend of Max Eastman and other Village feminists but also a socialite who liked the rich girl's life of parties and opera-going, she satisfied the radical and conservative aspects of her nature by adopting the hyphenated surname Milholland-Boissevain after her marriage in 1913 to Eugen Boissevain.

Some women who adopted double surnames had husbands who also adopted a double surname after marriage. When the writer Emanuel Julius married the actress Marcet Haldeman in 1916, they both took the name Haldeman-Julius, which was legally established by court order. Shortly thereafter they moved from New York to Marcet's hometown, Girard, Kansas, where the townsfolk probably at first thought Julius had annexed the Haldeman name because the family was rich and influential, Marcet's mother having been president of the State Bank of Girard. The town, however, must have soon learned they combined surnames to symbolize their belief in the equality of husband and wife. Another couple who combined surnames were Betty Gram and Raymond Swing. Gram had abandoned a stage career to become a militant suffragist and in 1919 had been arrested during a demonstration and jailed for eight days, after which she resumed her career and went to Berlin to study voice. There in 1920 she married the foreign correspondent Raymond Swing. She had wanted to retain her own name, but Swing, whose work required him to travel widely, felt embarrassed at the prospect of having to register at hotels as Betty Gram and Raymond Swing, for which reason he suggested a compromise—if she would take his name he would take hers. She agreed and they became known as Betty and Raymond Gram Swing.

The children of these couples had surnames that derived from both parents, and a few women who kept their names also gave their children combined surnames. Marie Stopes, who in 1918 took a second husband, Humphrey Verdon Roe, gave their son the surname Stopes-Roe. More radical was the New York physician Dr May Wilson, later to become an authority on rheumatic fever, who married Dr A. Albert Smernoff about 1918 and not only kept her name but had her son's name legally changed to Wilson before he entered school.

Fola La Follette's 1914 prediction that "in a very few years we may expect to see women in marriage keeping their own maiden name intact" and giving their children names that did not derive only from the father seemed by 1920 to be coming true. At least the new phenomenon was sufficiently widespread so that when Sinclair Lewis was writing *Main Street*, published in 1920, he felt free to say of a spinster who at long last married but who was still called by her maiden name that people did so because she still looked and acted like an old maid, not because she had "ideals about the independence of keeping her name." Lewis had lived in Greenwich Village and had in fact proposed to Frances Perkins, but he would not have included that remark if he felt the mass audience he wrote for would not understand what he was talking about.

Of special interest during this period was the decision of Ruth Hale to keep her own name. Hale, a Tennessee woman, had come to New York in 1910 and worked as a drama critic for *Vogue* and then as a writer for the Sunday edition of the *Times*. A friend of Fola La Follette, she, according to George Middleton, had given Fola "a raking down" for not changing her name when she married. She later came to believe that although it was theoretically right for a wife to keep her name, it was an unimportant matter; in *The Sun Field* (1923), the autobiographical novel of her husband, the woman who is obviously Ruth Hale is described as feeling, "Why do the poor dears fret about that while Armenians are dying?" Before she married Heywood Broun on June 7, 1917, Hale, as she later told her friend Doris Fleischman, had had no intention of keeping her name, but when she and Broun left the altar, a friend who was eager to be the first to call her by her new name said, "Hello, Mrs Heywood Broun," and Hale then and there underwent an instant nominal conversion experience, for she immediately and angrily replied, "I am *not* Mrs Heywood Broun! I am Ruth Hale. Don't *ever* call me Mrs Broun!" She had realized that Ruth Hale "was more than a name; it was me." From that day forward, keeping her name became almost an obsession. She and Broun spent the next six months in France where, as Alexander Woollcott on October 2 reported in astonishment to a friend, "She still insists on being known as Ruth Hale." When they returned to New York, the apartment she and Broun shared and later their house had, it goes without saying, two names on the mailbox. If someone phoned and asked for Mrs Broun, Hale gave them the number of Broun's mother. If an invitation arrived addressed to Mr and Mrs Heywood Broun, Hale took the position she was not invited. Invitations she and Broun sent out began, "Ruth Hale and Heywood Broun invite you . . . " The only one in her household called Mrs Heywood Broun was the cat. Unlike Fola La Follette, who never corrected anyone who called her Mrs Middleton, Ruth Hale never let it pass; she corrected even a casual stranger. She could also be rude; the publisher and drama critic George Oppenheimer recalled that at a Hale-Broun party, when a well-known singer was crooning the romantic ballad "Under the Bamboo Tree" and came to the line, "I'm gonna change your name," Hale began to hiss and hissed so loudly and so long he was forced to stop. Hale never let an occasion pass to proselytize for the cause, but her diatribes against the custom did not seem to impress her friends Jane Grant and Harold Ross until after they were married on March 27, 1920 and Grant was immediately addressed as Mrs Ross. "Jesus Christ, I don't think I like that 'Mrs Ross' stuff," said Ross as they walked through the churchyard to the street. "Maybe Ruth Hale's got something after all." And Grant later recalled that her "heart stood still at the realization that my own little name had dissolved when the minister finished the service." Deciding that her name was "too personal, too much a part of me to be summarily discarded by a wedding ceremony," Grant forthwith became a convert.

Jane Grant and Ruth Hale were among those who made up the Round Table of wits who had lunch at the Algonquin Hotel. Another regular was Dorothy Parker, Mrs Parker, for the former Dorothy Rothschild had married Edwin Parker in 1917 and abided by custom. Parker was a quiet man, so different from Dorothy she was once asked why she married him. She is supposed to have replied, "I married him to change my name," a reply we now think funny because she was so frankly admitting she wanted to change a Jewish name or was making light of marriage. But in the 1910s when Hale and Grant and other of her friends were marrying and making a loud point not to change their names, her reply had the humor of the perverse.

Secretly Proud of Being Mrs Riggs

In 1914 after Fola La Follette gave her speech on a woman's right to keep her name, the leader of the suffrage movement, Carrie Chapman Catt, was so furious she sent one of her deputies to personally rebuke Fola, who was told, "Your speech has put suffrage back twenty-five years." Poor Mrs Catt! She could not have forgotten that in 1890 she herself had felt so strongly about women having to lose their names that she had not taken her second husband's name. Three and a half years later, however, she had sacrificed her name to the cause of suffrage, and she still obviously felt other women ought quietly to conform to convention until the vote was won, the key that would open the door to all other rights. Mrs Catt was wrong. Fola's 1914 demand for a wife's right to keep her name did not hold suffrage back twenty-five years; women got the vote six years later. It was Fola's prediction that "in a very few years we may expect to see women in marriage keeping their own maiden name intact" that was wrong. Very wrong. Over fifty years later women were still eagerly becoming Mrs Him.

Even when she was delivering her speech at the Second Feminist Mass Meeting on February 20, 1914, Fola La Follette ought to have realized "a very few years" would not bring a nominal revolution. For three days before, at the First Feminist Mass Meeting, one of the speakers was Crystal Eastman Benedict; this former Miss Wife had become Mrs Benedict. Sometime in 1913, about two years after she married, Crystal Eastman had adopted her husband's name; it was as Mrs Benedict that in June 1913 she spoke in Budapest at the International Woman Suffrage Alliance. Her adoption of her husband's name was undoubtedly the first public sign her marriage was in trouble, for there are few husbands like Max Eastman who prefer their wives to have names of their own; most husbands feel slighted, and Crystal must have tried to mollify hers by becoming Mrs Benedict. It did not help; they were divorced in 1916. Shortly thereafter she married Walter Fuller, an Englishman, and then chose a more moderate nominal course; she remained Crystal Eastman professionally but in private life signed her name Crystal Eastman Fuller.

Many of the women who started out as Miss Wives soon became Miss on the job and Mrs at home. Being a 100 percent Miss Wife was too difficult; Frances Perkins thought it "absurd" to register at hotels as Mr and Miss, and as Elsie Clews Parsons had noted in *The Old-Fashioned Woman* (1913), no married woman "has found any escape from being addressed, at least by servants and shopkeepers, as 'Mrs'." Moreover, a woman with a husband more famous than she was had to forgo sharing his limelight. Louise Bryant, for one, could not resist flourishing her famous husband's name. In Washington DC in 1919 she introduced herself to a senator as "Louise Bryant, Mrs John Reed, you know," and in Russia she used the name Reed as often as Bryant. To be a 100 percent Miss Wife one had to have the convictions of a Ruth Hale, and there were few Ruth Hales.

The chief effect of the nominal radicalism of the 1910s was not a proliferation of Ruth Hales but the emergence of a large number of professional women who decided to keep their own name in public life. Women doctors, lawyers and businessmen had at last found the courage to follow the lead of actresses and authors and remain Miss Their Own Name professionally. When the owner of the Finch School of Design in New York took a second husband in 1913, she felt it would be bad business to stop being Miss Finch at the school, so she became Mrs Cosgrove only in private life. When Dr Phyllis Greenacre married Dr Curt Richter in 1919 she chose to remain Dr Greenacre at Johns Hopkins where they both worked, feeling that having two Dr Richters on the staff would be confusing. But in the nineteenth century these women would have changed their names and the practical consequences would not have been great. Dr Mary Putnam in 1873 became Dr Jacobi although her husband was also Dr Jacobi and her professional career survived the confusion. In the 1860s Delia Murphy's San Francisco Printing Office became Delia Dearing's Printing Office and the business survived. Indeed, actresses had used to change their name with every marriage and their popularity was not affected. Professional women in the 1910s began to keep their own name in public life not for practical reasons but because their numbers had so increased they felt less odd, less alone, and therefore could more confidently assert their professional identity.

But their personal identity was still shaky; they still felt a need to prove their femininity by becoming Mrs Him in private life. As Charlotte Perkins Gilman noticed in 1911, a woman who was "Mary Smith to the trade" introduced herself at parties "with modest pride, as Mrs Peter Saunders." Even the most famous woman in the world wanted to be Mrs MyMan at home. Mary Pickford on March 28, 1920 married Douglas Fairbanks who, at a dinner after the ceremony gave the men Havana cigars in souvenir boxes, boxes that Mary proudly signed "Mrs Douglas Fairbanks."

By becoming Mrs Fairbanks or who-ever-he-was in private life, these women revealed that despite their remarkable accomplishments and despite their earning as much money or working as hard as their husbands, they still felt they had to be wives, that is, that the responsibility for taking care of the home and children rested wholly on their shoulders. And if lawyers and doctors and world-famous actresses had the wife complex, women of average accomplishments might be said to have the wife psychosis. Floyd Dell recalled that in Greenwich Village in the 1910s "Any tenth-rate free-verse poet could find a capable and efficient girl stenographer to type his manuscripts, buy his meals and his clothes, pay his rent and sleep with him; the maternal emotion sufficed instead of a marriage ceremony." The maternal emotion sufficed even with a marriage ceremony. In Dell's story "The Button" a girl who comes to Greenwich Village to become a writer gets married instead: "She had always liked the name—Barbara Locke. In imagination she had seen it featured on the covers of magazines. She had intended to make that name famous. But now without a demur, she became Mrs Riggs. She felt secretly proud of being Mrs

Riggs . . . by some terrible alchemy . . . she was happy in just being that man's wife. She gave up her ambitions. She gave up her name. She lived in and through him. She had no life of her own."

"Between announcing that you will live your own life, and the living of it lie the real difficulties of any awakening," said Walter Lippmann in his 1914 "Note on the Woman's Movement" in *Drift and Mastery*. Lippmann thought that "so many emancipated women" were "only too glad to give up the racket and settle down" because they, like newly-freed slaves, did not know what to do with liberty. But the truth was women did not have liberty, and it was not that it was still difficult for women to get into professional schools or get good jobs, equal pay and equal advancement. It was that women were deficient in the psychological characteristic that might have made them capable of overcoming these difficulties. Being free means being able to assert oneself, and girls were still being taught that assertion was for boys and compliance for girls. A real woman was supposed to be self-abnegating not self-assertive, which meant that a surge of self-assertion would inevitably be followed by a backwash of self-doubt, a sexual identity crisis most women tried to resolve by acting womanly, serving some one else's interests not their own, which usually meant serving a man or children. As Elsie Clews Parsons observed in *The Old-Fashioned Woman* (1913), "Women try hard to live down to what is expected of them."

This conditioned response was, however, believed to be innate, a manifestation of what Floyd Dell called "the maternal emotion," an overwhelming drive that even most feminists then believed made women not only want to have babies but to baby men. And almost all men secretly believed that contact with a man inevitably generated the maternal emotion in woman, converting her, will-she nill-she, into man's devoted servant. It was the rare man, notwithstanding a theoretical feminism, who did not feel woman, no matter what her abilities, had been endowed by the Creator with the principal duty of serving him dinner and in every other way serving as a mother surrogate. The historian of science George Sarton, who married Eleanor Elwes in 1911, believed in women's rights, yet, as his daughter May recalled in *Journal of a Solitude* (1973), he "expected everything to be done for him, of course, by his wife" and he took it for granted that her life should revolve around his life, even when she was earning more money than he was. We do not know if Floyd Dell when he was a feminist shared the housework with the new women he lived with, but it did not take him long to frankly admit he no longer wanted an intellectual woman with a career. As he confessed in *Homecoming* (1933), he did not want "a girl who would . . . put her career before children—or even before me." The man who in 1913 had written *Women as World Builders* by 1919 wanted "a girl as simple and natural as a South-sea islander" whose "beautiful breasts were perfect for the suckling of babies." On February 8, 1919 Floyd Dell married B. Marie Gage, who of course became Mrs Dell, and who proceeded to produce sons, much to the relief of Dell's mother who had feared the Dell name would not be carried on.

Dell had reverted to the stereotypes—woman with a babe at her breast and man with brains working outside the home. But if woman's position in society were to improve, such stereotypes would have to be abandoned, mankind would have to realize, as George Middleton put it in his 1914 speech at the First Feminist Mass Meeting, "that men and women are made of the same soul stuff," that they therefore should be educated "according to temperament and not according to maleness and femaleness" and that girls should be educated "for work and not for sex."

But in the first two decades of the twentieth century women, in the name of emancipation, were being educated for sex more blatantly than they had ever been before. By 1910 it had become acceptable to wear low-necked dresses not only in the evening at operas and balls but during the day in restaurants as well as at home. By 1920 skirts had begun to rise and legs were becoming not symbols of woman's new strength and freedom but sex symbols. Moreover, women were routinely wearing make up as if they were actresses on stage. *Vogue* in 1912 had suggested that "the discreet application of a little paint would enhance a lady's appearance" and the paint got less and less discreet and was used by shopgirls as well as ladies. By 1920 women all over the United States were using make up and although students were expelled from school, teachers and office workers fired, there was no stopping it. Everywoman had come to believe make up made her beautiful, an aesthetic that was not to be seriously challenged for some fifty years. Even feminists managed to believe that by wearing make up they were wearing the colors of sexual emancipation; Sylvia Pankhurst's warning that lipstick was the mark of a slave was not understood. Instead, women, including feminists, were bedizening themselves as if they were inhabitants of a seraglio, using Sex Appeal not their minds to get ahead in the world, which meant women still wanted to support themselves not by work but by getting a man, becoming a mistress or a wife. When F. Scott Fitzgerald's daughter was born on October 26, 1921 he wrote to a friend: "We dazzle her exquisite eyes with gold pieces in the hopes that she'll marry a millionaire." The ordinary man, and Fitzgerald in his view of women was ordinary, still wanted girls to be legal courtesans, to pursue Mrs Astor's profession.

George Middleton's 1913 play *Nowadays* was about a new woman, Diana Dawson, who does not use Sex Appeal to get a man to propose to her; she proposes to him. She is, moreover, a sculptor who has won a contest for a group called Democracy that depicts a man and woman marching side by side, and both are holding the child. "I've broken away," she says, "from the old form that made the man lead far ahead with the woman trailing behind." Middleton's play should have been called *Some Day*. In the 1910s too few women felt comfortable marching side by side with a man; they felt more at ease in an ancillary position and were incapable of proposing to a man since they wanted to be chosen not to choose. As for men, almost none felt manly unless his woman was trailing behind, and they would have felt their manhood threatened if a woman proposed to them. So far as child rearing was concerned, almost all men and women still felt it was chiefly woman's work. The 1910s did not sufficiently change the roles of men and women.

The National American Suffrage Association at its 1915 convention accused those who said suffragists wanted to undermine the institution of marriage of "gross slander." "We believe," the suffragists declared, "the home is the foundation of the State; we believe in the sacredness of the marriage relationship, and further, we believe that the ballot in the hands of women will strengthen the power of the home and sustain the sacredness and dignity of marriage." In other words, the suffragists were saying that should women get the vote, the domestic status quo would not change. They were right. When women got the vote in 1920 they became more housebound than they had been in the 1910s. Although during World War I women had worked outside the home and at such "male" jobs as manufacturing explosives and armaments, after the war they went back to being wives. In 1920 women achieved political equality, not social equality.

Because women did not achieve social equality, because professional women were still as eager as the average woman to perform the job of wife, it should not be surprising that the few women who persisted in using their own name for all purposes had difficulties with that handmaiden of the status quo—the law. Even in England there was trouble. When Englishwomen got the vote in 1918, they also won the right to run for Parliament and two of the women who did were wives who used their own name—Mary Macarthur, who had married William Anderson in 1911, and Violet Markham, who had married Major James Carruthers in 1915. Before Mary Macarthur handed in her nomination papers, she had consulted lawyers who had told her her use of her own name was legal, but her returning officer (an election official) rejected the papers, ruling she could not go before the electors except in her married name of Anderson, and it was as Mary Anderson that her name was printed on the ballot. She tried to inform the women laborers in her district what had happened, but there was little time and many of them were barely literate and were confused when they saw the name Anderson on the ballot, not understanding she was the Mary Macarthur who had served them for ten years. She lost the election. But on the other hand, so did Violet Markham and she had succeeded in convincing her returning officer to print her own name on the ballot. Mary Macarthur, however, had had a much better chance of winning and should have taken the matter to the courts, where she eventually would have had her name acknowledged because there was a precedent, the 1901 case of Cowley v. Cowley that held that under the common law even a married woman could use the name of her choice.

American women had no such precedent behind them and that their battle would be long and difficult could have been predicted by mid 1919, serious legal troubles having started in November 1918, when New York women first won the right to vote. Many of the Miss Wives who tried to vote in their own name ran into trouble. According to Ruth Hale, "registrations were refused and a few women arrested for attempting to vote in their own names." And Frances Perkins a few months later had difficulty getting her own name acknowledged as her legal name by the New York Senate. As recounted in the November 1921 *Women Lawyers' Journal*, after Perkins was appointed State Industrial Commissioner in January 1919, the senators maintained that to confirm her in that name would be illegal since her legal name was Wilson, that of her husband. Perkins argued that since Frances Perkins was the only name she had ever used, she was indeed the individual named by the Governor to serve as Commissioner, and after lengthy discussions, the Senate finally did confirm her appointment.

But if the senators had known about a recently published legal article, Perkins might not have been confirmed in her own name, for in February 1919 the *Virginia Law Register* published the first legal article on married women's names. That the subject had been researched only because a sufficiently threatening number of wives had begun to use their own names is virtually certain; one suspects that a few lawyers, alarmed by the Miss Wives, decided to do what they could to stop the nominal rebellion, at least in legal actions. At any rate, "Proper Designation of Married Women in Legal Proceedings" unequivocally stated that "The law confers upon a wife the surname of her husband."

It was when the keep-your-own-name movement seemed to be dying, when legal and social pressure to conform to custom was becoming stronger that Ruth Hale and Jane Grant formed the Lucy Stone League, an organization whose aim was to revitalize the movement, chiefly by forcing clerks, bureaucrats and the legal profession to acknowledge that a married woman's own name could be her legal one.

15

THE LUCY STONE LEAGUE

Origins

Harold Ross is credited with being the father of the Lucy Stone League. According to Jane Grant and Dale Kramer (the biographer of Ruth Hale's husband), during the summer of 1920 because of a postwar housing shortage Grant and Ross shared Ruth Hale and Heywood Broun's apartment, where Hale and Grant talked so much about a woman's right to keep her name that Ross, sick of the subject, exploded, "Why don't you people hire a hall!"

But Hale and Grant would not have had to hire a hall nor would they have talked endlessly about keeping their names if it had not been so difficult to do. Jane Grant had been married only three or four months and she was still correcting people who insisted on calling her Mrs Ross and bearing the anger her unconventionality roused in them; as Grant recalled, "Men ridiculed me and married women raged." Such social harassment, however, could be overcome or ignored. What often could not be overcome was bureaucratic harassment—bank managers who maintained a married woman could not have a bank account except in her husband's name; real estate agents who declared a deed or mortgage was illegal if signed in a married woman's maiden name; hotel clerks who refused to rent a room to a couple who signed the register with two names. There were also, as we have seen, voting problems, New York women in 1918 not having been permitted to register or vote in their own name. Moreover, even prominent women like Frances Perkins could have their right to use their own name questioned by officials who believed the only legal name of a married woman was her husband's. Most important, the State Department refused to issue passports to married women in their own name; Ruth Hale had tried to get one in 1917 but had had to sail to Europe as Mrs Broun. In such real difficulties, not in Harold Ross's vexation, lay the origins of the Lucy Stone League.

The League may also have had unconscious origins in what Heywood

Broun called Ruth Hale's "curious collaboration" with him in his work. Hale was Broun's mentor, so much so that many friends thought Broun would have remained a sportswriter if he had not married Hale. Whether true or not, Hale and Broun discussed everything together—books, people, ideas, politics— Hale usually leading the way, being the tougher minded and more radical. Hale also criticized and corrected most of what Broun wrote and, as Broun confessed in a column written the day after Hale died, "A very considerable percentage of all newspaper columns, books and magazine articles which appeared under the name 'Heywood Broun' were written by Ruth Hale." But by 1921 Broun and Broun alone had become well-known for his column in the *Tribune;* Broun had just made *Who's Who*, but Hale's career was languishing. One therefore cannot help feeling that when Hale founded an organization whose aim was the recognition of a wife's name that what she was unconsciously demanding was the recognition due her own name, that, indeed, the League might not have been founded if the byline of Broun's column had read "Heywood Broun and Ruth Hale." At any rate, from about 1921 to 1926 when Broun was achieving fame, Hale channeled most of her energy into trying to force the public to acknowledge that a wife's name deserved equal recognition with a husband's.

Ruth Hale, probably in the latter half of 1920, began a systematic campaign to get a married woman's name accepted by banks, hotel clerks, the Passport Office and all the other functionaries who usually refused to let married women use their own name. As early as 1918 Hale had consulted Frances Perkins, who had managed to get life insurance in her own name because her lawyer had convinced the company it was legal. But in 1920 Hale's chief legal consultant was Rose Falls Bres, the author of *The Law and The Woman* (1917) and in 1921 editor of *The Women Lawyers' Journal*. Bres researched the law in New York and got lawyers in other states, among them Felice Cohn of Nevada and Paula Laddy of New Jersey, to do likewise. They typically discovered, to quote Laddy, "There is no law that I can find in our statute books which makes it compulsory that when a woman marries she must take her husband's name. Therefore she can do as she likes" (*The Women Lawyers' Journal*, November 1921). Hale also found out what she could about Lucy Stone, probably by writing to Alice Stone Blackwell, Lucy Stone's daughter who was then living in Dorchester, Massachusetts. Hale learned that Lucy Stone had also had lawyers research the law and that one of them had been Salmon P. Chase, later Chief Justice of the Supreme Court, who told her there was no law compelling a woman to take her husband's name. Hale also wrote or spoke to various New York jurists, among them Federal Judge Learned Hand, who, like other lawyers, told her "a woman's own name was entirely legal after marriage."

Armed with this knowledge, Ruth Hale, probably late in 1920, applied for a passport in her own name, perhaps feeling that if she were successful she would have no trouble with lesser functionaries. It is virtually certain she got other friends who used their own name to apply also and that, when they were all unsuccessful, she organized what seems to have been a proto Lucy Stone League, a club called The Woman Pays Club that was described in the February 3, 1921 *Tribune* as having been "organized recently" and consisting of women "authors, composers, playwrights, press agents and musicians" who "after some of the members discovered . . . they could not get passports except in their married name" at a luncheon on February 2 passed the following resolution: "Whereas, the question of nomenclature having been investigated, it has been found that no woman is legally bound to be known by her husband's name and may rightfully retain and use her maiden name or the name by which she is commonly known throughout life; and whereas, the woman's maiden name stands fully for her undiminished individuality and represents her work, whatever it may be, both of which are diminished when she merges her identity into that of her husband by adopting his name, now, therefore, be it resolved that all the members of The Woman Pays Club advocate the use and retention of their own names."

One of the signers of the resolution was Margaret Wilson, daughter of President Woodrow Wilson, who was guest of honor at the luncheon, her appearance most likely arranged by Ruth Hale, who was then a theatrical press agent and knew full well the meeting would not be covered by the press unless some prominent person was present. The meeting was reported in the *Times* as well as the *Tribune*, the *Times* on February 4 also publishing an editorial that was entitled "A Liberty Already Possessed" because the *Times* maintained the members of The Woman Pays Club were revolting "against custom rather than law." But the *Times* did not ask why, if the law did not compel a woman to change her name to her husband's, the State Department had refused to issue the members of the club passports in their own name.

Ruth Hale insisted on knowing why and in mid February revealed to the press she had returned her passport because it had been issued to "Mrs Heywood Broun, otherwise known as Ruth Hale," and had again asked that one be issued to her in the only name she had ever used and that Secretary of State Bainbridge Colby consider the question (*The New York Times*, February 18, 1921). Colby tabled the matter, so that with the advent of a new administration in March the new Secretary of State Charles Evans Hughes had to make the decision, and he too refused to issue her a passport in her own name. Hughes informed Hale through her attorney Rose Bres that "under the provisions of the Rules Governing the Granting and Issuing of Passports in the United States signed by the President on June 13, 1920, a passport is issued to a married woman in her own Christian name or names with the family name of her husband." He refused to discuss "the legal points raised" by Bres. He made his decision chiefly on moral grounds, arguing that a consular official would be "placed in a most embarrassing and difficult position" if he had to assist a man "travelling with a woman who does not use his family name yet claims to be married to him." Hughes apologized for Hale's having been issued a passport in the name "Mrs Heywood Broun" and offered her another in the name "Ruth Broun (otherwise known as Ruth Hale)," but Hale refused it (*The Women Lawyers' Journal*, November 1921).

Although unsuccessful with the Passport Office, Hale was successful in other areas. According to Hale, it was she who worked out the question of hotel registration with Roy Carruthers, managing director of the Waldorf-Astoria, so that a husband and wife could register as "John Smith and wife, Jane Brown." But Carruthers in an announcement of the new policy in the March 18, 1921 *Times* said the suggestion came to him from a young magazine writer who had lost business calls because she was registered under her husband's name and that he had also been "flooded with demands" from other professional women to have their own names registered in the hotel directory. It is not unlikely that Hale engineered the flood of demands, asking friends who used their own name to complain whenever they stayed at the Waldorf. But however the matter was brought to Carruthers' attention, he was pleased to comply, being very much aware he now had to do business with "many women writers, politicians, lawyers, physicians and those in other professions who gained their fame before marriage" and who, when traveling with their husbands, did not want to be inconvenienced by having mail, business and personal calls miscarry because only their husbands' names were registered. Apparently bank managers were also made to understand it would be bad business policy not to accommodate the many professional women who used their own name, for according to Hale, she easily got many banks to agree they would let wives have bank accounts and sign checks in their own not their husband's name.

Hale also succeeded in getting her own name incorporated in a real estate deed with the help of the lawyer Oscar Bernstein (husband of another woman who kept her name—Rebecca Drucker, a drama critic at the *Tribune*). Hale and Broun had bought a house on 85th Street and with Bernstein's aid had convinced the seller and registrar of deeds that it was legal to have the deed made out to "Heywood Broun and Ruth Hale, his wife." Hale contrived to have that transaction written up in the *Times* on May 15 under the headline "Maiden Names Score a Victory." She used the occasion also to announce the existence of the Lucy Stone League, "recently organized for the purpose of enabling women to maintain their maiden names after marriage," a League that already had fifty members and that would hold its first meeting on May 17 at the Hotel Pennsylvania.

If The Woman Pays Club were the original League, it henceforth had a separate existence. Sometime between February and May, Rule Hale, Jane Grant and others founded another organization whose name honored the first wife who kept her name and whose motto was Lucy Stone's words: "My name is the symbol of my identity which must not be lost."

The First Three Years

Ruth Hale presided at the first meeting of the Lucy Stone League, a meeting that was attended by many of the women who were then married but using their own names, among them Rebecca Drucker, Crystal Eastman, Susan Glaspell, Fannie Hurst, Freda Kirchwey, Anita Loos, Grace Potter, Ida Rauh and Signe Toksvig. Also present and also members of the Executive Committee were Charlotte Perkins Gilman, Zona Gale, Janet Flanner, Neysa McMein and three men—Oscar Bernstein, Heywood Broun and Francis Hackett.

At the first meeting officers were elected: Ruth Hale became President, Beulah Livingstone Vice-President, Ruth Pickering Editor of a monthly bulletin to inform women of their name rights, Rose F. Bres Legal Advisor. The League also adopted a constitution and decided that since there were no laws requiring a wife to use her husband's name, the purpose of the Lucy Stone League could not be to agitate to change law but to inform the public that wives had the legal right to use their own names. That was why the League immediately elected a publicity director, Grace C. Oakley. For if the public were to learn that wives could keep their names, the League's activities would have to get wide press coverage.

One device the League often used to get the press interested was to arrange for celebrities to attend their meetings. Their first meeting was reported at some length in *The New York Times* undoubtedly because two actresses, then at the height of their popularity, were present, actresses the *Times* featured in its account. One was Elsie Ferguson, who, the *Times* reported, was delighted to learn her bank and checking accounts could be in her own name and not in that of "Mrs T. B. Clark Jr." The other actress was Michael Strange, the current wife of John Barrymore. Strange, the former Blanche Oelrichs and Mrs Leonard Thomas, had adopted the name Michael Strange first as a pseudonym, then as the name she used for all purposes. She assumed, however, that when she was married her legal name was her husband's and she told the members of the Lucy Stone League that her lawyer had recently insisted she sign a contract "Mrs John Barrymore." She was pleased to learn that her legal name could be Michael Strange, the name she was well-known by.

The presence of celebrities was not the only reason the Lucy Stone League was to get wide press coverage. In trying to account for the "tremendous amount of publicity" the League got, Ruth Pickering (who had married Amos Pinchot in 1919 and kept her name) suggested that newsmen thought wives who kept their names were always good for a laugh. Another reason was "the able journalism of Jane Grant and the courage and persistence of Ruth Hale" (*Equal Rights*, March 21, 1925). However, the fundamental reason why the Lucy Stone League got a tremendous amount of publicity was that many of its members were journalists employed by New York newspapers and magazines. Heywood Broun was with the *Tribune*, then the *World*, Francis Hackett with *The New Republic*, Jane Grant with the *Times*, Ruth Hale, Rebecca Drucker, Janet Flanner, Solita Solano, Signe Toksvig and several others were working journalists, which was why Ruth Hale's getting her own name incorporated in a real estate deed managed to get reported in the *Times*. In addition, Doris Fleischman, Edward Bernays, Beulah Livingstone, Ruth Hale and others were in public relations. Because many of the League's members knew how to get press coverage, for the next five or so years the activities of the Lucy Stone League were regularly, prominently and in the main sympathetically discussed in the media and a married woman's right to her own name became a fashionable topic, so much so that a new phrase was invented for a person who believes a wife should keep her name—a Lucy Stoner, a phrase that eventually got into the dictionaries.

Because Francis Hackett was the editor of *The New Republic* the magazine in July 1921 featured "Have Women Names?" by the editor's wife Signe Toksvig. After announcing that the Lucy Stone League had "recently been formed in New York" to inform the public "there is no law compelling a wife to take her husband's name," Toksvig discussed why women take their husbands' names. She thought they did because wives used to be their husband's property and that a woman born Anna Maria Brown who became "Mrs Thomas Smith," then "Mrs Henry Green," and perhaps later "Mrs Richard Robinson" was still undergoing a process "reminiscent of cattle-branding." Toksvig felt that now that husbands no longer legally owned their wives that wives should demonstrate their new freedom by keeping their own names. She doubted, however, that many would; she was certain that most women would continue to be willing to sell their birthright for free "bed and board for life," for which they were willing to flatter the man by accepting "the stamp of his name."

Toksvig predicted the Lucy Stone League would not appeal to "Main Street wives" but only to the few women who "dislike the total immersion in marriage which the loss of one's name implies."

Although any sensible person knew Toksvig was right and that Lucy Stonism would appeal to few women, conformists are rarely sensible. Instead of ignoring the League, conventional editors felt they must attack it, which of course only increased the League's publicity. *The Bookman* in December 1921 published the conformist's response to Lucy Stonism, St John Ervine's "On Taking Your Husband's Name in Vain." Ervine could not understand why a woman "who is willing to be endowed with a man's worldly goods" should not also be willing to be endowed with his surname. Nor could he understand why a woman should "refuse to be known by the name of her husband" when she is known by the name of another man, her father. He further could not understand why a career woman who used her own name professionally should not want to use her husband's name in private life. Ervine did admit that since two people are joined in holy matrimony, it might be symbolically appropriate for them to join surnames. But if couples did, what would happen to the children? What name would Millicent Smith-Robinson and George Brown-Johnson take when they married and give to their children? In view of the progressive absurdity of such a naming system, Ervine felt it was best to retain the old custom. "Any custom which has survived for centuries has done so because the generality of mankind has found it to be a convenient custom." Married women should not think it an insult or disgrace to take their husbands' names; it is merely "socially convenient." "Millions of women for centuries have endured the indignity without noticing it is an indignity."

Ruth Hale immediately demanded *The Bookman* publish her reply, which it did in February 1922. Men, she said, always think it "socially convenient" for women to take their husbands' names, but they would not think it so convenient if the custom were reversed. Ask the first thousand men you meet if they would take their wife's name and "not one of them would be able to make a coherent sound in reply." Hale, like Toksvig, thought women took their husband's name because wives used to be their husband's property and that just as little boys like to write their names on fences, so grown men like to put their names on their land, houses, slaves, children and wives. And Hale, like Toksvig, was not optimistic; men had for too many centuries regarded wives as property not as partners with equal dignity, and mankind was highly resistant to change. Therefore, "A married woman who retains her name is issuing a challenge . . . It is a defiance, and as such is dealt with by society, under a hundred euphemisms, always with hostility."

But as yet the hostility was slight and the League was making converts. In

June 1921 the young Margaret Good Myers, about to start graduate work in Economics at Columbia University, married Haggott Beckhart and decided to keep her own name. Also in June Eleanor Jewett, art critic for the *Chicago Tribune*, married Godfrey Lundberg and kept her name. In December the former militant suffragist Doris Stevens married Dudley Field Malone and became an equally militant Lucy Stoner. December also saw the marriage of Elsie Hill, daughter of Congressman from Connecticut Ebenezer Hill, to Albert Levitt and in January she publicly announced she was retaining her own name (*The New York Times*, January 21, 1922). When the *World* questioned the legal validity of her doing so, Levitt, a professor of law, informed the paper that a name "is a trademark, a stock in trade, and a characterization. The law recognizes this as such, and protects it. It is a tangible property, and the right to a name is a tangible legal right" (January 28, 1922). On January 27 Elsie Hill further announced that the National Woman's Party, of which she was Chairman of the Executive Committee, had added to its Woman's Bill of Rights, a wife's right to her own name: ". . . a woman shall no longer be required by law or custom to assume the name of her husband upon marriage but shall have the same right as a man to retain her own name after marriage." Hill was careful to explain that the National Woman's Party understood the attainment of that right "involves no change of actual law," nevertheless she felt that when the Equal Rights Bill passed, it would "protect by law the right of every woman to retain her own name." Thus for the first time the right of a wife to keep her own name became one of the official goals of a national feminist organization.

Ten months after its first meeting the Lucy Stone League had doubled its membership and was continuing to educate the public by getting its meetings reported in the newspapers. *The New York Times* on March 13, 1922 covered a particularly interesting one. The League, like a religious sect, first welcomed a new convert, "a Lucy Stone bride," Theresa Jackson, an advertising writer, who had married Milton Weill on March 9 and was keeping her name. There then followed a debate between Heywood Broun and Arthur S. Roche on Lucy Stonism, Broun arguing that a girl should hold on to her name and Roche that a woman's new state required a new name and title. Jane Grant then read replies from notable people to whom she had written asking for their views on wives keeping their names. Charles W. Eliot, President Emeritus of Harvard, felt genealogical records would be too confusing if wives kept their names, for it would lead to children being given either the father's or the mother's name, and children ought to be given the father's name because he was the one who earned the money transmitted to descendants. The editor Hamilton Holt was also concerned about what name the children would bear if the wife kept her name—"After the father or mother or neither?" "Isn't it, after all," he concluded, "the old question of whether a rose will smell any better if it has a different name?" The inventor Henry Wise Wood was opposed to the League because his mother's "personality was so merged with that of my father that in all things the two seemed one." Their son, therefore, could not respect the principle of "marital separation" Lucy Stonism implied. David Belasco, on the other hand, agreed with the League, for "when the wife takes the husband's name she bows to the ancient tradition of slavery." Belasco, however, thought children should continue to be named after the father. Belle da Costa Greene of the J. Pierpont Morgan Library felt it was "the indisputable right and privilege of every woman to retain the personality of her own name after marriage if she so desires," and John Emerson, Anita Loos's husband, wrote that "he couldn't see any reason for a bride taking the bridegroom's name except for sentimental reasons." Only former President Woodrow Wilson thought the subject did not deserve a reasoned reply. His secretary wrote to Grant: "Mr Wilson wishes me to say in reply to your letter of March 1, that he does not approve the object of your league."

Certainly, most people did not approve of the League's object, but because of the publicity the League got, more and more professional women discovered they did approve and the keep-your-own name movement that seemed to be dying in 1920 took on a new and vigorous life. During the first three years of the League's existence many women upon marrying decided to be Lucy Stoners. Among those who married in 1922 were Bella Cohen, a reporter at the New York *World*; Helen Koues, an associate editor at *Good Housekeeping*; the economist Faith Williams, then a research assistant at Columbia University; the reporter Ruby A. Black, then teaching journalism at the University of Wisconsin. In 1922 there was also a male Lucy Stoner. The public relations counsel Edward L. Bernays, when he married Doris E. Fleischman (a former journalist at the *Tribune*), had been a member of the Lucy Stone League for over a year; it was he who after the ceremony convinced his wife to sign her maiden name to the register at the Waldorf-Astoria where they spent their honeymoon, a registration duly noted in the September 18 *Times*.

In 1922 a Lucy Stoner spread the gospel of nominal independence to California. Phyllis Ackerman, after earning her PhD in Art History from the University of California at Berkeley, had lived in Greenwich Village with Arthur Upham Pope, her former professor. Returning to California in 1922, she revealed in an interview printed in the October 1 *Oakland Tribune* that she and Pope had secretly married "several years ago" and that she had kept her name. "The day when a woman was compelled to merge her individuality with that of her husband and to symbolize it by substituting his name for her own," she optimistically asserted, "is gone forever."

If in 1877 the well-known Christian Scientist Mary Baker Glover changed her name upon marrying again, in 1922 the well-known advocate of birth control Margaret Sanger did not. Having become famous under her first husband's name, Sanger chose not to adopt the name of her second husband, J. Noah Slee, the president of an oil company. Sanger and Slee not only kept their names separate, they, like Fannie Hurst and her husband, had separate apartments and kept their marriage secret for some time. After 1924 when the marriage was discovered, Sanger did use the name Mrs Slee on some social occasions, but she was almost universally known as Mrs Sanger and even her husband referred to her as Mrs Sanger.

In the past women in the theater and authors were eager to be Mrs Current husband in private life, but in the 1910s a few actresses and authors, like Fola La Follette and Susan Glaspell, had kept their own names in their private as well as professional life. With the advent of the Lucy Stone League the number of such women increased. Perhaps the most famous one was Isadora Duncan. On May 2, 1922 she married the poet Sergei Essenin in Russia, where after the Revolution a law had been passed permitting married couples either to retain their names, adopt the husband's or wife's, or combine surnames. When asked at the Registry Office what surname they intended to use, Duncan and Essenin both said "Duncan-Essenin," which pleased Sergei, who after the ceremony shouted, "Now I am Duncan!" Isadora did not shout, "Now I am Essenin." She was no Mary Pickford, pleased to play the role of Mrs Douglas Fairbanks, just a wife in love. She did not use the combined surname, nor in fact did Essenin, who the next month, after they were married a second time in Germany, seemed to take conventional male pleasure in writing to a friend, "Now she is no longer Duncan-Essenin, but simply Essenin." But Isadora never became Mrs Essenin in name. A letter written by both of them in July 1922 was signed: "S. Essenin. Isadora Duncan."

A famous writer who kept her own name in private life was the poet Edna St Vincent Millay, who on July 18, 1923 married Eugen Boissevain (the former husband of Inez Milholland-Boissevain). Millay, unlike Duncan, was a conscious Lucy Stoner, probably a member of the League. No one was permitted to call her Mrs Boissevain, and she bought property and paid taxes as Miss Millay. She also registered at hotels in her own name; in 1926 in New Mexico she had an amusing altercation with a hotel clerk when she told him Eugen Boissevain was arriving and would share her room. The clerk of course said that was impossible, and Millay at first refused to tell him Boissevain was her husband, but when the clerk remained adamant Millay admitted they were married. "Why didn't you say so in the first place?" asked the clerk, to which Millay, resting on her laurels, replied, "My dear sir, don't you know famous women always use their own name."

Another writer who used her own name in private life was Rita Weiman, so well-known in the early 1920s that her marriage made the front page of *The New York Times*. On November 27, 1924 she married Maurice Marks and announced she was keeping her name. Like Millay, she registered at hotels under her own name but did so more diplomatically. At the hotel where she spent the first night of her honeymoon, she "registered as Miss Weiman above her husband's name, and in parentheses opposite the names she wrote 'Mr and Mrs'." A writer much less well-known who kept her name was Ella Winter, who in 1923 married the famous Lincoln Steffens and chose not to share his famous name. Steffens in his letters calls her Ella Winter or Peter (his nickname for her), never Ella Steffens. Lucy Stonism may also have affected the once popular novelist Laura Jean Libbey, who had been content not only to be Mrs Stilwell in private life but to list herself in *Who's Who* as Laura Jean Libbey Stilwell. But after her death in October 1924 her will revealed she wanted her own name "only" carved on her tombstone (*The New York Times*, November 7, 1924).

A Lucy Stoner in spite of herself was the then famous illustrator Neysa McMein. Although McMein had been a member of the Lucy Stone League and was indeed on its first Executive Committee, after her marriage to John G. Baragwanath in 1923 she had no objection to being called by her husband's name. However, no one except the Passport Office did and many of her friends did not know she was married. At one of her parties some years after her marriage Marlene Dietrich, having discovered to whom she was married, said to Baragwanath, "I didn't know you were Neysa's husband," to which he replied, "That's all right. Nobody does."

The majority of women who kept their own names in the early 1920s were not famous. Some of them had substantial local reputations, like Mary Elizabeth Dillon, Acting General Manager of the Brooklyn Borough Gas Company, or the astrologer Evangeline Smith Adams, or the Foreign Trade Consultant Lucy A. Goldsmith, all of whom married in 1923. Other Lucy Stoners were just beginning to be well-known. When Georgia O'Keefe married Alfred Stieglitz in 1924 she had just begun to acquire a reputation as a painter. Many Lucy Stoners were very young and not yet launched on their careers. When Constance Glass, who was to become a Los Angeles attorney, married in 1923 she was only twenty and a student at Western Reserve University. Dorothy Whipple, later Dr Whipple, was twenty-two when she married Ewan Clague in

1923 and had just received her B.A. from the University of Wisconsin. She re-called keeping her name not because she had heard of the Lucy Stone League but because "My name meant ME. I could not bear to see Dorothy Whipple go into oblivion." She thought she was not "copying anyone," and it is true that many women kept their names solely because of a personal inner conviction. But in the 1920s Lucy Stonism was in the air as a result of the publicity the League managed to get, and most of the women who kept their names would not have if the League had not existed. Margaret Mead recalled that in the early 1920s Lucy Stonism was so well-known that a conventional cousin who disliked Margaret's mother said that if Mrs Mead were marrying then "she'd even keep her own name!" When Emily Fogg married in 1900 she had merely retained her own name as a middle name, but when her twenty-one-year old daughter married Luther Cressman in 1923 she remained Margaret Mead. Mead was about to start graduate work at Columbia, having just graduated from Barnard, where Lucy Stonism was especially popular. Clara Eliot, who started to teach in the Economics department in 1924, recalled having heard "plenty" about the Lucy Stone League and that some of her friends then "thought it wrong to take a husband's name."

During the first three years of its existence the Lucy Stone League not only made many converts, it also forced various business and government officials to acknowledge a wife's own name, especially in New York. The League arranged several transfers of property in which the wife signed her own name. For example, when Jane Grant and Harold Ross bought a house on West 47th Street in 1922, Grant signed her own name to the deed, which so disturbed the registrar half the words in the deed concerned this unusual practice. The League also got various companies to agree to allow wives to open accounts in their own name. The New York Telephone Company agreed to, as did several department stores (if the wife could show independent financial records), and a few insurance companies issued policies to wives under their own name. Amus-ingly enough, the League met the greatest resistance from the New York Public Library system, which at first absolutely refused to issue library cards to married women in their own name. However, the Library finally succumbed to the League's pressure and the ruling that a wife could be issued a card in her own name was published in the Library's journal. The League had far less trouble persuading the New York Board of Elections to allow wives to vote in their own name. When women first voted in New York, many were not allowed to regis-ter under their own name, but the League got the Board to change its ruling and to agree that married women who continued to use their maiden names could vote in those names, a ruling that eventually became a New York election law. The wide promulgation of the fact there was no law compelling a wife to take her husband's name helped Lucy Stoners in other states vote in their own name. Attorneys General of Maryland and Michigan in 1921 and 1923 issued Opinions advising their state's Election Board that a woman registered under her maiden name was not required to reregister after marriage. And the Wisconsin Attorney General in 1923 and 1924 issued Opinions that a woman notary public or county clerk who married during her tenure might continue to act under her maiden name, for although "a married woman generally takes and uses her husband's surname, there is nothing in the laws of this state that affirmatively requires it."

The Lucy Stone League had made so much progress by mid 1924 that *The Nation*, believing that "women are doubtless destined more and more to stick by their maiden names," felt the question of what prefix to use for Lucy Stoners must be settled. Should it be Miss or Mrs? (July 2, 16). Almost all American Lucy Stoners preferred Miss. Ruth Hale felt that since in England and America the tradition had developed of calling female actors and writers Miss regardless of their marital status, Lucy Stoners should follow that established custom. Miss was also preferable because Mrs implied a Mr who was bearing the same name and because there was no more reason to know if a woman were married than a man. Hale hoped that a new form of address would come into being that would mean "the woman, professional or otherwise, who had not relinquished her surname at marriage," and one member of the League, Nora Golden, an advertising executive, suggested the prefix "Mion." A few English Lucy Stoners, like Helena Normanton, used the prefix Mrs, feeling it was more dignified, and *The Nation* preferred Mrs, although it suspected that eventually titles would be abandoned for both sexes and a woman would be referred to "as Mary, as Mary Smith, [or] as Smith" (July 16).

Another social matter not yet settled was what to name the children of Lucy Stoners. For the League it was not a problem since it had officially adopted the conservative position that at the present stage of social evolution children should continue to be named after the father since that was their guarantee of legitimacy and of their legal rights of inheritance. Almost all Lucy Stoners gave their children their own name as a middle name and the father's name as a surname. Ruth Hale's son was named Heywood Hale Broun; Doris Fleischman's daughter Doris Fleischman Bernays. The League did hope custom would change, and most thought children in the future would be given the combined surname of their parents. The daughter of Elsie Hill and Albert Levitt, born November 15, 1924, was named Elsie Hill-Levitt. But what if, as St John Ervine feared in 1921, an Elsie Hill-Levitt married a John Grant-Ross? Would their child be given a quadruple name? *The New York Times* once asked that question of Harriot Stanton Blatch, suggesting that "after a generation or two" the hyphenated names would "pyramid to an unwieldy size." Blatch had an answer; she felt the children "would always have the right of selection" (September 28, 1924). But most people felt the pyramiding problem was insoluble, and from time to time newspapers printed letters from worried citizens who feared that if wives retained their surnames and children were given hyphenated surnames, *their* children would have quadruple surnames and so on to absurdity.

Of course most people were not worried about what name Lucy Stoners would give their children or whether they should be called Miss or Mrs. The average person simply did not approve. The average woman, like Mary Roberts Rinehart, professed herself "proud" to have taken her husband's name. "I do not understand women who think otherwise" (*The New York Times*, April 24, 1925). The average man, like George Wickersham (a former United States Attorney General), felt it was a veritable "glory" for a woman to share her husband's name (quoted in *The Nation*, March 21, 1923). *World's Work* in its November 1924 issue argued that the wife's taking the husband's name was "an eloquent sign of woman's improved status in civilized society," for, the editors reasoned, when women did not, they were savages who had sex so promiscuously the father of a child was unknown. But when the sex drive was controlled and the father was known, children and wives took the father's name. The wife's taking the husband's name was, therefore, an eloquent sign of a higher order of morality.

Such editors could only insult Lucy Stoners by implying they wanted to be sexually promiscuous, but lawyers and government officials could try to destroy the Lucy Stone movement by invoking imaginary laws and thus forcing women to use their husband's name. An experience of Margaret Myers was typical. When she married in June of 1921 she was working at the Federal Reserve Bank in New York and as soon as she informed the bank of her marriage her paycheck was made out to Margaret Beckhart. She protested and was referred to the bank's attorney who told her the law of New York required the paycheck of a married woman to be made out in her husband's name, and Myers, then ignorant of the law, thought she had to submit. The Lucy Stone League later did help many women get their own names accepted by their employers, but Myers' experience in 1921 was a forecast of how the legal profession would try to quash the Lucy Stoners, and it was in the area of payroll checks that the League late in 1924 suffered its first major defeat.

Comptroller General McCarl

When Dr Marjorie Mason Jarvis, who was on the staff of St Elizabeth's Hospital (a Federal Hospital near Washington DC), married Charles L. Hutson on May 24, 1924 she decided to keep her name. But after notifying the hospital of her marriage, Dr Jarvis found her paycheck was issued in her husband's name and she was requested to sign Marjorie Hutson to the payroll. Dr Jarvis refused, maintaining her name had not changed. She consulted an attorney, Olive Lacy, who informed the Superintendent of the hospital that Dr Jarvis had every legal right to continue using her own name. The Superintendent did not agree and considered the matter so serious he brought it to the attention of the Secretary of the Interior, who on July 17 wrote to the United States Comptroller General J. R. McCarl, asking him to decide the issue. On August 8 McCarl announced his decision. In "(A-4176) Pay Roll Signatures—Married Women Employees" McCarl ruled that "When a woman employee in the Government service marries her legal surname becomes that of her husband and such surname is to be used by her in signing the pay roll instead of her maiden surname." McCarl maintained that legal encyclopedias and case decisions all held that upon marriage a woman's name is changed to her husband's. "The law in this country that the wife takes the surname of the husband is as well settled as that the domicile of the wife merges in the domicile of the husband." A wife "may have an assumed name, but she has but one legal name. The separate legal entity of the wife is not so generally recognized as to accept the maiden name rather than the surname of the husband."

The Lucy Stone League immediately denounced McCarl's ruling as "contrary to existing legal facts." "The right of women to their names after marriage has been firmly established in many court decisions," said Ruth Hale, and the League's attorney Rose Bres told the *Times* that "so far as the law goes, no married woman need be known by her husband's name unless she voluntarily wishes to be. In Louisiana, for instance, the law makes the interesting requirement that a woman be referred to as 'Jane Smith, wife of John Brown,' the latter phrase being added only for the purposes of better identification" (August 15, 1924).

Not only did the League condemn McCarl's ruling, so did the major New York newspapers. The *World* accused McCarl of violating the civil liberties of women, for a woman "should have the right to sign herself as she pleases," an opinion the *World* held even though it felt wives ought to take their husbands' names, for which reason it pointed out to McCarl that although he may have hoped his ruling would stop the Lucy Stoners, "he could have chosen no better method to fan the Lucy Stone agitation to a fine flame" (August 15). The

Times also said the ruling would be "sure to increase the now small number of women who see no reason why marriage should change their names any more than it does those of men." The *Times* professed not to understand why women should not want to observe so old a convention, but the *Times* flatly asserted, taking the husband's name was only a convention; McCarl "had no warrant in law for his ruling" (August 18). The *Tribune* also pointed out that the Lucy Stone League had searched the law books and found no law that forbade a married woman from using her maiden name. "Names are for identification in the eyes of the law. In business transactions a married woman's signature in her maiden name is valid. She is under no compulsion to take her husband's name." The *Tribune* labeled McCarl's ruling "an impertinent exercise of control" (August 19).

Even newspapers outside New York City condemned McCarl's ruling. The *Buffalo Express* felt that if a woman wanted to receive her pay envelope as "Miss Dill Pickle" not "Mrs John Dough" that was her affair, and although *The Philadelphia Inquirer* disapproved of "the new woman," it felt McCarl's ruling was "one of those bureaucratic exercises of power for which there is no legal justification." As far away as Kansas editorials were written on McCarl's ruling. *The Kansas City Star*, although it felt with some bitterness that modern wives "take everything a man has except his name," advised McCarl to "let the matter drop" (editorials reprinted in *The Literary Digest*, September 6, 1924).

McCarl did not let the matter drop nor did Dr Jarvis. The National Woman's Party decided to help her fight her case. Alice Paul sent a letter of protest to the Secretary of the Interior Dr Hubert Work together with a brief prepared by the Party's attorney Burnita Shelton Matthews. Matthews pointed out that in no case cited by McCarl in his decision was "the right of a married woman to retain her maiden name . . . before the court." On the contrary, "no statute or court decision exists in any State supporting the principle that a woman must take her husband's name . . . the law allows anyone, man or woman, to assume any name he or she chooses" (*Equal Rights*, September 20, 1924). The Secretary of the Interior did not reply to the arguments presented in the brief; he flatly stated that "the decision of the Comptroller General is binding and controlling in this department, and no good reason is known for requesting a reopening of the case." Alice Paul then asked for an appointment with Dr Work, the Lucy Stone League sent an official letter of protest and some fifty women representing the League, the Women's Bar Association, the medical profession and government clerks planned to send a deputation to the Secretary.

On September 28 *The New York Times* reviewed the case at length and printed the views of prominent women on a wife's right to keep her own name.

Said Alice Paul: "Why should a woman renounce the name under which she has been for many years established? Professionally it is injurious to her career, legally it is unjust. It is unfair discrimination against sex . . . When, under a national equal rights bill, the sexes will be on an equal social, political and economic basis," "a married woman will act as she pleases in regard to the name she lives under." Harriot Stanton Blatch, then campaigning for the Equal Rights Bill, said: "If I had my life to go over again, I would carry my name to the grave. It is important to live consistently from the beginning to the end, to keep one's individuality from start to finish." The *Times* article concluded: "New York State, officially, takes a liberal view of women's right to their maiden names. Miss Frances Perkins may be mentioned in illustration. Miss Perkins was a member of the State Industrial Commission from 1919 to 1921 and is now on the State Industrial Board. Though married, she has consistently used the name under which she made her reputation."

As both the *World* and the *Times* had predicted, McCarl's ruling, far from suppressing the Lucy Stoners, gave their cause national publicity. The publicity was so great, so many editors felt McCarl's ruling was an illegal and arbitrary exercise of power that the Secretary of the Interior gave in. Dr Work wrote a letter to Ruth Hale informing her the case would be reopened.

It was not. For reasons now unknown, Dr Jarvis chose not to fight. She left the government service and the case was dropped. Her decision not to fight was unfortunate. Not only did McCarl's ruling stay on the books, but it is virtually certain she would have won her case because a few months later the Lucy Stone League and the National Woman's Party succeeded in getting the State Department to issue passports to married women in their own name.

Passports

During the McCarl controversy the unfairness of the State Department's policy in regard to passports had been much discussed in the newspapers, particularly its absurdity in regard to famous women. Alice Paul had remarked that no matter how well-known a woman was, "she must go under her husband's name when she fares abroad . . . Mme Melba would have to sail as Mrs Armstrong. Mme Nordica would have to sign as Mrs _____, was it Smith or Brown?" Fannie Hurst, then at the height of her fame, told of the ritual she went through when she wanted a passport: "Religiously, as a protest to the Government, I write the name under which I have elected to live, and each time I see the officials pass the wink and hear them tell me to add my husband's surname. I am, however, not enough of a martyr to the cause to refuse such passports as they will give me" (*The New York Times*, September 28, 1924).

The growing impatience of the Lucy Stoners with the State Department and their frustration at Dr Jarvis's decision not to fight McCarl's ruling was channeled into constructive action when it was learned that Helena Normanton, the first woman barrister in England, had succeeded in getting the British Foreign Office to issue her a passport in her own name. Normanton had been married in 1921 to Gavin B. Clark and had retained her own surname as her legal and only name. A year after her marriage, when she was called to the bar, her fellow barristers were bitterly opposed to her practicing under her maiden name. The Joint Council of the Four Inns of Court considered the question for about eight months, her husband in the meantime preparing to temporarily change his name to his wife's so she could continue to practice under the name Normanton. That proved unnecessary. Normanton had spent weeks researching the law and had discovered the common law of England was strongly on her side, so that the Joint Council was forced to agree she had the right to use her own name. However, late in 1924 when she applied for a passport to the United States, she was told first by the tourist office and then by the Foreign Office that her passport had to be in her husband's name. She then, according to her own account, "went to the Chief of the legal department of the Foreign Office who said that as I had won recognition from the benchers of the Middle Temple to be a barrister at law in my maiden name I was entitled to a passport. I received it in due course and had no difficulty in getting the document visaed at the United States Consulate."

Normanton's account of her fight to get a passport in her own name was published in *The New York Times* on January 7, 1925, the day after her arrival in the United States, where she had come to give a series of lectures. On January 20 she was the guest of honor at the fourth annual Lucy Stone League dinner where she told the over 300 people present—members, women lawyers and guests—about her fight to win the right to use her own name and delivered a lecture on "The Institution of the Surname" in which she gave many examples of women who as early as the twelfth century did not use their husbands' surnames. She ended by rallying the League to action: "You are allowing individual officials to tamper with your surnames in a way that has never been tolerated or permitted . . . Find some way of bringing it home, possibly in a heavy action for damages against any State official who dares to crash right through the common law" (*Equal Rights*, March 7, 1925).

After her speech Ruth Hale announced that the League was in fact planning to fight, that it was bringing suit against the Secretary of State for his "refusal of a passport to a young married woman under her maiden name" (*The New York Times*, January 21, 1925).

The woman chosen for the test case was Ruby A. Black, the journalist who had married Herbert Little in 1922 in Wisconsin and who was in 1924 living in Washington DC, trying unsuccessfully to crash through the we-don't-hire women policy of Washington newspapers. Black had applied for a passport in her own name and had of course been told by the State Department she could be issued one only in the name Ruby Little. Black refused it, saying she "did not want to travel to Europe under any assumed name." Black, acting together with the National Woman's Party, appealed to the Chief of the Division of Passport Control and on April 17, 1925 she was granted a hearing before Secretary of State Frank B. Kellogg.

At that hearing Black's case was argued by Burnita Shelton Matthews, Margaret Whittemore, Isabella Kendig, Olive Lacy, Millie Roerher and Helena Normanton. Their main argument was that "a regulation depriving a woman of her own name without her consent was contrary to the supreme law of the land as well as the English common law." Normanton informed Kellogg of what the common law was in England and that since surnames began to be used "Englishwomen who so desired had used their own names regardless of those that came to them by marriage." Kellogg replied that he himself could do nothing since passport regulations could be changed only by the order of the President; he would, however, make a concession "in Miss Black's case." "He would issue an order that a passport be issued in her maiden name with the statement that she was a married woman, and with the understanding that Miss Black would sign the surname of her husband to the papers" (*The New York Times*, April 18, 1925).

The night of April 17 at a National Woman's Party dinner in Washington DC Helena Normanton revealed that although her passport was issued in her own name, her husband's name was included on the page reserved for observations and that this was done in order to prove her nationality (*Equal Rights*, May 2, 1925). But the next day Ruby Black announced she would not accept a passport "on the conditions imposed by Secretary Kellogg. I will not accept a passport except on the same basis as one would be issued to my husband. There is no more use of requiring me to describe myself as the wife of Herbert Little than for him to disclose that he is the husband of Ruby A. Black. We will continue to fight to secure complete equality on the passport matter" (*The New York Times*, April 19, 1925).

Secretary Kellogg had asked the Legal Department of the National Woman's Party to submit a brief and he promised he would present the case for the abolition of the rule to President Coolidge. The National Woman's Party

did so on April 20 and at a press conference maintained that the regulation that
deprived a married woman of the use of her own name deprived her of "a legal
right, without due process of law" (*The New York Times*, April 21). That day
the *Times* published an editorial in favor of giving women passports in their
own name, saying that in other matters women were "using what name they
please, and no harm, so far as known, has resulted, though the pillars of society
no doubt were much strained by the change of custom. The change, as it happens, was not an innovation, but a revival, a fact which its opponents always ignore, talking usually as if the woman's taking the husband's name was a
custom as old and as sacred as the Ten Commandments." And that night
Helena Normanton, in a radio talk sponsored by the *Washington Post*, told listeners in and around Washington DC that the custom of taking the husband's
name was not an old one (*Equal Rights*, May 2, 1925). On April 30 the New
York State branch of the National Woman's Party adopted a resolution calling
upon the Secretary of State "to rule that henceforth any married woman may
be granted a passport in the name by which she chooses to be known, under the
exact condition by which a married man is granted a passport" (*The New York
Times*, May 1, 1925). On May 1 President Coolidge at a news conference announced "he would give careful consideration to the question of abolishing the
rule requiring every married woman to sign her husband's family name to her
application for a passport, regardless of whether or not she has assumed that
name" (*Equal Rights*, May 9, 1925).

Ruby Black had refused a passport in which she would have been described
as "Ruby Black, wife of Herbert Little," but early in May another Lucy Stoner
did not. The writer Esther Sayles Root, about to marry the famous columnist
Franklin Pierce Adams and spend her honeymoon in Italy, applied for a passport in her own name, explaining to the clerk at the New York office that after
her marriage on May 9 she was retaining her name. Her request was promptly
denied. But being a member of the National Woman's Party, Root phoned
Burnita Shelton Matthews, who with Margaret Whittemore called upon the
head of the passport control division of the State Department, who in turn
notified the New York office of the oral ruling in regard to Ruby Black which,
he said, could be applied to Esther Root and all other Lucy Stoners. According
to the National Woman's Party, Root was issued a passport in the form "Esther
Sayles Root, wife of Franklin Pierce Adams" (*Equal Rights*, May 23, 1925). According to Ruth Hale in *The First Five Years of The Lucy Stone League*, she was
allowed to retain her old passport with "Wife of Franklin P. Adams stamped on
the back." The National Woman's Party felt it had won a victory; a picture of
Esther Sayles Root appeared on the cover of the June 13 issue of *Equal Rights*
and Root was described as "the first married woman in America to go abroad in

a passport issued in her own name." The Lucy Stone League did not consider the Root passport a victory; it petitioned the Secretary of State to permit married women to confine the information about their husbands to the regular application blank.

And the next month a Lucy Stoner did receive a passport in her own name with no "wife of _____" tagged to her name. She was Doris Fleischman, who had married a male Lucy Stoner and been converted to the cause. In June 1925 she applied for a passport in the name Doris Fleischman at the New York office and was refused. She protested and a sneering clerk told her if she was not satisfied, "Write the Secretary of State." Fleischman did, at once, on her application blank, simply requesting she be issued a passport in the name she had used all her life. "Since there is no law compelling a woman to use any but her own name," wrote Fleischman, and since passports were for the purpose of identification, she was sure the Secretary would not wish her "to travel under a false name." She was successful; she received her passport in her own name with no mention of her husband's name whatsoever. She thus became the first married woman in the United States to get such a passport, and when she sailed for Europe news photographers were at the dock and her historic sailing was reported in the papers.

Shortly thereafter several other married women applied for passports in their own name and they were all granted. It would seem then that President Coolidge had finally issued a ruling permitting married women who did not change their name to their husband's to get passports in their own name. According to the English *Law Journal* of November 21, 1925, it had been an open secret in Washington that the Departments of State, War and Navy and the President were greatly opposed to giving married women such passports and that the President had issued the ruling only because the Secretary of State had convinced him that in regard to names American law derived from English common law that had always allowed a person to use any name he wished so long as it was not for a fraudulent purpose. English lawyers therefore believed "the right of married women to use their maiden surnames as their legal name has been recognized" by the United States government.

By the end of 1925 the Lucy Stone League must have felt triumphant; the League in fact must have felt it had achieved its purpose, that since a married woman's own name had been recognized as her legal name by the State Department it would have to be recognized by other officials of the government and that Comptroller General McCarl would be compelled to change his ruling.

The League had other reasons for feeling triumphant in 1925. Its membership had quadrupled since its founding. The 1925 edition of *Women of Today* listed the membership as 250 and there were of course a great many other Lucy Stoners who were not members. Most of the original officers were still serving. Ruth Hale was still President, Beulah Livingstone Vice-President, Jane Grant Secretary, and Charlotte Perkins Gilman had been made Honorary Vice-President. Most of the original members had remained loyal, many who had attended the first meeting of the League in May 1921 were present at the dinner honoring Helena Normanton in January 1925, among them Elsie Ferguson, Ruth Pickering, Freda Kirchwey, Anita Loos, Fannie Hurst, Grace Oakley and of course Heywood Broun. Other old timers were there—Fola La Follette, Doris Stevens, Edward Bernays, John Emerson. Alice Paul and Harriot Stanton Blatch also attended and so did Franklin Pierce Adams, who wrote about the dinner in the next day's *World*. Also present were many distinguished lawyers, among them Emilie Bullowa, President of the National Association of Women Lawyers, Reba Swain, Deputy with the Labor Bureau in New York and Rose Rothenberg, then serving on the New York Court of General Sessions (*The Women Lawyers' Journal*, January 1925).

Rose Rothenberg was soon to become a Lucy Stone bride. In July she married M. W. Goldstein and kept her name. She was one of many other 1925 Lucy Stoners, among them Evelyn Smith, President of the Amawalk Nursery in Westchester New York, Bernice Fitz-Gibbon, advertising writer for Macy's, the Pennsylvania psychologist Phyllis Blanchard, the Massachusetts painter Helen Sawyer, the Chicago dancer Ruth Page. Lucy Stonism may also have caused a divorce that year. According to the February 12 *New York Times*, Mrs Park Abbott of California obtained a divorce because she wanted "to retain her maiden name and give it to her son." But according to the November 15, 1924 *Equal Rights*, Joan London Abbott, the daughter of Jack London, merely wanted to use her famous surname in signing her writing, which her husband would not permit her to do. Other husbands, however, were liberal in the extreme. The Englishman Dr E. Jeffrey Samuel not only wanted his wife, Dr Edith Summerskill, to keep her name, he wanted her to pass her name on to their children. Believing it unfair that children were always given the father's name, he wanted, he said, to make his "small contribution to redress the balance."

The author Vera Brittain, another 1925 English Lucy Stoner, was in America that year, having accompanied her husband George Catlin to Cornell, where he had a job. In the November 14 *Equal Rights* she published an account of the difficulties she experienced because she kept her name and dared accuse women who took their husbands' names of pursuing "a policy of militant inferiority, for which they imagine the loftiest moral sanction," which was why they subjected Lucy Stoners to "insidious and perpetual harassment." Brittain nevertheless urged English and American women "to enter into this particular aspect of the struggle to be regarded as complete human beings." The next month Ruth Pickering, speaking on station WGBS on December 21, also urged women to keep their names after marriage and to support the National Woman's Party campaign for equal rights between men and women (*Equal Rights*, January 23, 1926).

1925 began with Helena Normanton's triumphant arrival in America with a passport in her own name and ended with American women winning the same right. The very last day of the year gave Lucy Stoners another victory. On December 31 the Assistant Attorney General of Minnesota ruled that women who married did not have to reregister to vote. Although "social custom and usage have resulted in a married woman assuming as her name the name of her husband," wrote Rollin L. Smith, "there is no law preventing her from retaining her maiden name and voting under it if she so desires."

By the end of 1925 the Lucy Stone League did indeed seem to have succeeded in educating government officials, from President Coolidge to Attorneys General, that there was no law compelling a woman to take her husband's name, and an increasing number of women were willing to keep their names and combat the "policy of militant inferiority" of rank and file wives. Ruth Hale, in the concluding paragraph of *The First Five Years of The Lucy Stone League*, believed the future of the League was bright, that, as time passed, the League, acting in its "role of adviser and friend to all women who want their own surnames . . . will be increasingly in demand."

Chaos in Women's Names—1926

During the summer of 1926 Ruth Allison Hudnut went to England with her husband Hayes Baker-Crothers to do research. She needed the permission of Boylston Beal, counselor at the Embassy, to use the Public Records Office, but although her passport was in her own name, Beal refused to give her a permit except in the name Baker-Crothers. Hudnut got in touch with Burnita Shelton Matthews and Helena Normanton, both of whom were fortunately in London that summer, and they argued with Beal, but he was impervious to all their knowledge of the law. "The idea of any married woman retaining her own name was so abhorrent to him that he was determined to thwart it if he could find any excuse, passport or no passport." Hudnut did finally succeed in getting a permit in her own name but only because Beal had been maneuvered into agreeing that if the Public Records Office would accept Hudnut under her own name he would acquiesce, and the Public Records Office had had no objection. Beal remained highly displeased and refused to assure Matthews and Normanton that he would not do the same thing again (*Equal Rights*, November 6, 1926).

Boylston Beal was, alas, a common type of official, who cared not one whit what the law was when a woman who used her own name came under the sphere of his authority. Comptroller General McCarl was such another, for despite the decision of the State Department to recognize a married woman's own name, he continued to insist married women must sign their husbands' names to the payroll. Indeed late in 1925, fearing Lucy Stoners were not reporting their marriages, he threatened to discharge women who did not immediately do so and have their names changed on the payroll. Moreover, the District of Columbia at about the same time ruled that women teachers would henceforth have to sign their husbands' names to the payroll(*Equal Rights*, November 7, 1925). Similarly, H. S. Brimhall, county clerk of Tillamook county Oregon, displeased by the number of women who after getting married were not reregistering to vote in their husbands' names, asked the Secretary of State if he had the right to remove their names from the registration files. In June 1926 the Oregon Attorney General decided he did not have that right, but late in 1926 the Copyright Division of the Library of Congress decided it did have the right to force married women to conform to custom and passed a regulation to henceforth require married women to get copyrights in their husbands' names. Accordingly, Virginia Douglas Hyde, although she had been obtaining copyrights in her own name for some twenty years, in December 1926 was informed by the Assistant Registrar of Copyrights that no further copyrights would be issued to her except in her husband's name (*The New York Times*, December 20, 1926). The Lucy Stone League and the National Woman's Party protested, the latter sending a delegation to Thorvald Solberg, Registrar of Copyrights, who immediately made a concession, saying that if a married woman attached to her application an explanation of her reasons for wanting to use her own name, she would receive her copyright in that name. The National Woman's Party would not agree, believing that no explanations should be required of married women, and Fannie Hurst told the press she "had always taken out copyrights under her maiden name" (*The New York Times*, December 21). On December 21 Representative Sol Bloom of New York introduced a resolution into Congress providing that "registration of claims to copyright by married women shall not be held invalid by reason of being made or having been made in the maiden name of the author." The flurry about copyrights quickly died;

in January the National Woman's Party received a telegram from Virginia Douglas Hyde announcing she had received a copyright in her own name (*Equal Rights*, January 29, 1927), and married women continued to be able to get copyrights in whatever name they wrote under, and without explanation.

But the fact that the Copyright Division tried to get women to conform to custom illustrated that government officials were no different from the conservative women Vera Brittain complained about who insidiously and perpetually harassed a wife who used her own name. Government officials, however, almost always disguised their prejudice as obedience to law. The Copyright Division asserted it had instituted its ruling to be "in accordance with the generally recognized practice of all Government offices as well as all courts." It was able to assert that not only because McCarl's ruling was very much in force but because McCarl's position had been buttressed in 1925 by an *American Law Reports'* Annotation on "Correct name of married woman" that had upheld the position that "the law confers on the wife the surname of the husband," an Annotation that had had an immediate effect on a Massachusetts judge who in May 1926 declared that the only "legal surname of a woman after her marriage is that of her husband" (Bacon v. Boston Elevated Railway Co., 256 Massachusetts Reports 30).

A legal backlash was obviously underway, although other judges continued to uphold the Lucy Stone League's position. The very month the Massachusetts judge said a married woman's legal surname must be her husband's a Federal judge in New York, in the suit of Maria Jeritza against Cohen Bros for using her name in a cigar ad, said "married women are free to use their maiden or their married names, as they please" (*The New York Times*, May 26, 1926). Commenting on these two conflicting decisions, the National Woman's Party felt order must be brought "out of chaos in the matter of women's names" (*Equal Rights*, June 26, 1926).

The chaos in the law was a manifestation of the struggle in society between the conservative forces clinging to the status quo and the radical forces trying to liberate woman from her old role. Judges would ultimately be able to compel reluctant women to wear the label "wife of" only if a substantial number of Lucy Stoners gave up and became willing to be in fact and hence in name old-fashioned wives. And 1926 saw the first public recantation of a former Lucy Stoner. On April 14 *The New Republic* published the anonymous "Confessions of an Ex-Feminist," who movingly narrated how she who had been "one of the most ardent of the feminists," who had earned more money than her husband, who had insisted "upon being called by my own name, no 'Mrs' allowed," after a few years of marriage and the birth of a child, had become a "squaw," the servant of her baby and husband. She now, therefore, did allow "the butcher and baker to call me Mrs W without a protest. That is as it should be. Since the creature that was once me is no more, why cavil about the name of that deceased person. I *am* Mrs W, just my husband's wife."

And yet, although Mrs W gave up, there were at that time young men who actually wanted their wives to use their own name. Florence Guy Seabury in "By Any Other Name" (*The New Republic*, May 5, 1926) reported that one or two men "about to marry celebrities have stipulated recently that the bride's public career, at least, be carried on under her own flag," which made sense, said Seabury, even when a man did not marry a celebrity, for now that women were performing other roles in society besides that of wife, husbands were much better off when their wives did not go about "masquerading" in their names. What often happened was that a Patrick O'Toole, candidate for sheriff, found himself running against "Mrs Patrick O'Toole," or Leonard Swift, an eminent lawyer, found himself as "Mrs Leonard Swift" discussed in the newspapers as an advocate of birth control, a subject he himself thought "extremely distasteful." "There is a rumor" going about, Seabury concluded, "that a group of men, determined to preserve their identities after marriage, are already organizing a Henry B. Blackwell League, named after Lucy Stone's husband . . . Their idea is that the time has come when men must unite and insist upon keeping their names exclusively for themselves." Seabury was writing tongue in cheek, but when women did lead active public lives outside the home, it made practical sense for husbands and wives to have separate names after marriage.

In 1926, however, it was uncertain whether a substantial number of women would continue to think of themselves as complete human beings who had the right to lead full, not merely domestic, lives or whether social and psychological forces would transform them, like the Ex-Feminist, into "Mrs W, just my husband's wife." Before the Reverend Olympia Brown died on October 23, 1926, she may well have thought that the right for which she and Lucy Stone had endured the hostility of society was soon to become a right freely enjoyed by any woman who wanted it. But if she could have read her obituaries she would have taken pause, for on October 24 newspapers refused to give her her own name intact; instead they announced the death of "Mrs Brown-Willis."

1927-1934

In 1927 Lucy Stonism was in full vigor. Almost every other month women's names were in the news. In January in the "Information" column of the *Washington Daily News* and other Scripps-Howard newspapers women were told they were required by "no law, statute or court decisions" to take their husbands' names (*Equal Rights*, February 12). In March the Lucy Stone League met with the Zonta Club and debated "Shall a woman retain her own name after marriage?" (*The New York Times*, March 25). In April there was news that a modified form of Lucy Stonism had traveled to Germany, for the Prussian diet, having been petitioned by a number of women's clubs, introduced a bill that would permit women (if their husbands consented) to use hyphenated names after marriage (*The New York Times*, April 8). In June Ella Graubart, a Pennsylvania lawyer, having obtained help from the Lucy Stone League and the National Woman's Party, petitioned the Pennsylvania State Supreme Court for the right to practice law in her maiden name and her petition was granted (*The New York Times*, June 10). On July 20 an editorial in the *Times* treated Lucy Stonism as an accepted fact of life and suggested that Lucy Stoners in business letters indicate what title they used by typing under their signature Miss or Mrs and their name, an adaptation of army regulations. In December Ruth Allison Hudnut, in a discussion of the treatment of women as inferior beings in the modern novel, expressed the view that a woman did not merely have "the right to keep her name . . . it was essential to woman's progress and self-respect" (New York *Sun*, December 10).

1927 also had its full quota of Lucy Stone brides, among them Calm Morrison Hoke, chemical engineer and a founding Fellow of The American Institute of Chemists; Nancy Dorris, Food Editor of the News Syndicate Company in New York; Marie Wessels, a Chicago physician; the twenty-one year old Ruth Benson Freeman, recently graduated from the Mt Sinai Hospital School of Nursing; the forty-eight year old Rose Pastor Stokes, a socialist and communist leader, who upon marrying a second time did not again change her name. Of particular interest was the marriage of Clarence C. Dill, Senator from Washington, to the lawyer Rosalie G. Jones, who announced she was retaining her name, so that for the first time a Lucy Stoner was among senatorial wives.

Among the 1927 Lucy Stone brides was the Washington DC physician Dr Winifred G. Whitman, who to make sure her own name would be legally acknowledged, petitioned the court to have her name "restored" to her, but in 1928 a judge in the District of Columbia Equity Court informed her she had no need to petition the court, that since she had continued to use her maiden name since her marriage, "she had not lost it" (*Equal Rights*, July 14, 1928). In

1928 other lawyers continued to believe married women were not legally obliged to take their husbands' names. The Assistant Attorney General of Washington in an Opinion issued on January 20, 1928 said that when a woman takes her husband's name she is following custom and "custom is not binding upon anyone." "In the matter of the choice of name for a person, it is fundamental law that any person may use any name he sees fit," an Opinion the Attorney General of New York was to agree with in 1931.

There also continued to be many Lucy Stoners. Among those who married between 1928 and 1934 were the novelist Zona Gale and the Vice Chairman of the National Woman's Party Anita Pollitzer, both of whom made a point of registering at hotels with their husbands as Miss and Mr. Others were the writer Ayn Rand; the artist Charmion von Wiegand; Dr Irene Boardman of Connecticut; Lois Donaldson, a Chicago advertising manager; Eleanor Tupper, Dean of Endicott Junior College; Olive Huston, Director of Physical Education of the Dayton Ohio High Schools; Alice Hackett, an associate editor of *Publishers Weekly*; Berthe-Louise Karstensen, a San Francisco business executive; the journalists Naomi Buck, Ruth Finney, Doris Fleeson, Bess Furman, Gertrude Lynahan, Ruth Mugglebee, Hortense Saunders, Mary Zoretskie and many many more. The most famous Lucy Stoner of the early 1930s was Amelia Earhart, who married George Palmer Putnam in 1931 and decided "she should continue . . . to be called by her own name," to quote Putnam, who was in full agreement. Although a newspaper would occasionally call her Mrs Putnam, Putnam said he could not "remember introducing her even once as Mrs Putnam."

According to the biographer of Ruth Hale's husband, the Lucy Stone League at its peak had 5000 members, which seems too high a figure. But whatever the exact number, in the 1920s and early 30s more American women than ever before were deciding to retain their identity after marriage, the vast majority keeping their own name intact, a few preferring to hyphenate their name to their husband's, among them the New York suffragist Portia Willis who became Mrs Willis-Berg after her marriage, the Iowa professor Florence Busse who became Professor Busse-Smith, the geologist Katharine Fowler who became Dr Fowler-Lunn. Lucy Stonism was, moreover, an international movement, although there were proportionally fewer Lucy Stoners in England, and European women tended to favor hyphenated names. However, when Irène Curie, the daughter of Marie Curie, married Frédéric Joliot in 1926, they both took the name Joliot-Curie. As late as 1933 Maria Vérone, President of the French League for Women's Rights, noted that "more and more women lawyers, writers, doctors and others do not now assume their husbands' names on marriage" (*Equal Rights*, November 18, 1933). When one compares the

1915 *Woman's Who's Who of America* (ed. John Leonard) with the 1935 *American Women* (ed. Durward Howes), one finds that the number of married women (excluding actresses and authors) who chose to present themselves to the world under their own name had roughly doubled.

Would the number of such women again be doubled in another twenty years? Would women in substantial numbers continue to choose to be Lucy Stoners? that is, would professional women? For needless to say Lucy Stonism appealed only to the much less than one percent of married women who wanted to be more than a wife, and the women who wanted to be more than wives had by the late 1920s become different from their sisters in the 1910s and early 20s. The anonymous Ex-Feminist who defected in 1926 had been married about 1921 and as a matter of principle had kept her name, but for a woman who married late in 1927 Lucy Stonism had become an ideal she could not live up to. Dorothy Miller, writing in the January 1928 *Century Magazine*, admitted that although "deep within me beats a Lucy-Stoney heart," "I haven't the courage of my convictions." She told how shortly after her marriage she decided to open a savings account for her own earnings in her own name, but when her husband quietly said, "No dear, you'll use your *full* name here-abouts—Dorothy Miller Tweedledee," she at first rebelliously signed Dorothy Miller but then paused and meekly added Tweedledee. Dorothy Miller submitted to her husband not only because "the sweetest words" he knows "are Mrs Tweedledee'" but because a part of her "gloried in" being Mrs Tweedledee. She felt that so long as most women were proud of being wives the Lucy Stone League would not prevail.

Dorothy Miller intended to continue using her own name professionally, but a woman who characterized herself as "Feminist—New Style" not only used her husband's name professionally but predicted that feminists in the future would do likewise. Dorothy Dunbar Bromley, in her sketch of the new feminists in the October 1927 *Harper's Magazine*, singled out the Lucy Stone League for special attack, denouncing its "constant clamor about maiden names . . . [as] the most inane of all" the demands of the old feminists. Mrs Bromley accused the Lucy Stoners of keeping their names because they were not sure how long they were "going to remain married" and of registering at hotels as "Miss Jones and Mr Smith" solely to get "free publicity." Mrs Bromley believed that only the few women who had proved "their individuality—and their independence of their husbands—by some sort of real achievement" had the right to keep their names, and then only if "the woman has made a name for herself in a business or profession before marriage." "What's in a name?" Mrs Bromley asked. "Madame Curie managed to become one of the world's geniuses even though she suffered the terrible handicap of bearing her husband's name."

But despite her "What's in a name?" names were important to Mrs Bromley and the Feminists New Style who, Mrs Bromley was pleased to note, were not deep-voiced, badly dressed, ambitious amazons like Feminists Old Style. Rather, they were soft-voiced, chic and, except for the rare woman of genius, had given up "the masculine ideal of commercial success." They did believe in work, for work was essential to "a rich and full life," but they were not wholeheartedly committed to a profession because their primary commitment was to a husband and children. Without denigrating the balanced life style she advocated, how different Mrs Bromley was from the Crystal Eastmans and Frances Perkinses. Feminists New Style had lowered their sights. They were no longer striving for a name and fame; whatever else they might do, they wanted, first and foremost, to be Mrs WifeandMother.

That women had become less ambitious is also revealed by the education statistics. In 1930 there were four percent fewer women in college than there had been in 1920, seven percent fewer female physicians than in 1910, and the number of female PhDs and college professors had begun to decline. Moreover, the younger generation of women were going to be even less ambitious than Mrs Bromley predicted, who was after all over thirty. In Mary McCarthy's *The Group*, which describes women who were at Vassar from 1929 to 1933, none of the Group has a serious professional commitment. Kay, the most ambitious, wants to be "the wife of a genius," not a genius herself. All except one plan to get married and the exception proves to be a lesbian. The Group are repeatedly differentiated from their mothers, who are described as "Lucy Stoners and women's rights fighters," women who dared to register at hotels as "Mr and Miss," women who had been interested in work more than in being wives.

Not only were the younger generation of college women eager to become Mrs Whoevercamealong, the older generation of Lucy Stoners were being subjected to increasing legal pressure to use their husbands' names. When Elsie Hill ran for Congress from Connecticut in 1932 (the first woman from her state to do so), protests were made that she could not legally run or hold office in the name Hill but must run under the name Levitt, her husband's name. These objections were answered by Burnita Shelton Matthews, the attorney for the National Woman's Party, and although Elsie Hill lost the election, she ran in her own name (*Equal Rights*, October 8, 1932).

Hill's skirmish with officialdom was, like Frances Perkins's in 1919, not serious, but in 1931 Massachusetts Lucy Stoners had had a major confrontation with government officials and lost. It began when Representative Martha N.

Brooks of the Massachusetts Legislature, after her marriage to Major Walter Brookings, continued to use her own name, which so displeased her fellow Representatives they instituted an action against her and in January 1930 the General Court of Massachusetts ordered Brooks to change her name to her husband's. To make sure no other female office holder did likewise, in January 1931 a bill was introduced into the Legislature that would require women in public office who married to notify the Secretary of State of their change of name. The Massachusetts branch of the National Woman's Party protested, realizing the bill would be interpreted to mean married women in public office must use their husbands' names, and they tried to get the bill laid aside or amended. To no avail. The bill became Chapter 30, section 78 of the General Laws of Massachusetts. In an attempt to counteract it, Representative Marion C. Barrows in March introduced a bill that would give married women the right to run for public office in their maiden names, but the bill was killed before it got to the Senate floor (*Equal Rights*, February 28, April 4, 1931). Nothing further was done.

Massachusetts Lucy Stoners had at least rallied and put up a fight, but New York Lucy Stoners were strangely passive when the New York Board of Education in 1930 ruled that married women teachers must use their husbands' names and when in 1931 the trustees of Hunter College followed suit, adopting the resolution that "Married women teachers . . . will hereafter be required to appear on the payrolls only under their married names" (*The New York Times*, January 6, 1931). The Lucy Stone League apparently did nothing to challenge these rulings, perhaps because Rose Bres had died in 1927, perhaps because Ruth Hale was seriously depressed, believing as she did that "a woman is through after forty."

"Ten years from now no one will question the right of a woman to keep her own name after marriage," Anita Pollitzer had predicted in an interview with the Baltimore *Sun* on March 30, 1929. But long before 1939 judges were acting as if the Lucy Stone League had never existed, as if the legal necessity of wives taking husbands' names was and always had been a settled matter. "Under the law of New York," declared Federal Judge Knox, "a woman, at her marriage, takes the surname of her husband" (In re Kayaloff, 9 Federal Supplement 176). The judge made that pronouncement in December 1934, three months after Ruth Hale died. Thereafter for many years to come the Lucy Stone League existed in name only.

16

DWINDLING INTO A WIFE

Are the Twain No Longer One Flesh?

Sinclair Lewis's *Main Street*, an attack on small-town values, was a national bestseller in 1920. The Lucy Stone League, organized in 1921, was part of the same revolt against middle-class conformism. But it was far more than a few flappers thumbing their noses at the bourgeoisie by having names that made them indistinguishable from women living in sin.

The League was, fundamentally, part of a general movement in the 1920s to acknowledge wives as separate from and equal to their husbands. With the ratification of the Nineteenth Amendment in 1920, the husband was no longer the one political entity in a household; the wife now had a vote in her own right. Similarly, with the passage of the Cable Act in 1922 a woman who married an alien no longer became one in citizenship with her husband; she now could retain her own citizenship. Moreover, during the 1920s several states granted wives the right to a separate domicile for voting purposes, and more states granted them equal property rights and equal guardianship of the children. The passage of an Equal Rights Statute in Wisconsin in 1921 and the introduction of an Equal Rights Amendment into Congress in 1923 were also part of the movement to force the law to treat wives as no longer one with their husbands, as was most obviously the Lucy Stone League, which advocated that a wife no longer become one in name with her husband but remain in name separate and equal.

The Lucy Stone League was also an expression of the wife's new sense of herself as independent of her husband. In Somerset Maugham's *The Constant Wife* (1926) Constance discovers she has been constant to her husband not because she still loves him or tolerates his affair but because he is paying for her keep. As soon as she finds a job and makes enough money to keep herself, she announces her independence to her husband and leaves him, going off to have an affair of her own. Constance, like Nora in *A Doll's House*, walks out on her husband, but it was far easier for her to leave than it had been for Nora because it was much easier in the 1920s than in the 1870s for a woman to support herself. Opportunities for women to work at interesting and lucrative jobs had increased greatly, which was one reason why there were so many Constances—the divorce rate doubled in the 1920s. Moreover, Constance could have her affair with much less fear of social disapproval than a Nora could and with much less fear of getting pregnant, for contraceptive devices had been improved and were more easily available. Sexually, economically and politically women were approaching much more closely to the status and freedom of men, so that marriage need no longer be a food-clothing-shelter necessity. It need be merely what it was for men—one event in a full life. Wives who had their own jobs, their own money, their own affairs, their own votes were in fact no longer wives in the old sense; they were, in more than name only, Miss Myownself.

It was widely believed that this New Woman, because of her economic independence of men, would cease to be psychologically dependent on her husband and that a new relationship, an equal relationship, between husband and wife would inevitably develop. Beatrice Hinkle in "Marriage in the New World" (1926) said that women were finally "awakening from their long sleep—a sleep in which they were unconscious of themselves as individuals," that a wife was no longer "the shadow" of her husband but had "her own ego" and was demanding "recognition of herself as an individual separate and distinct from man." Hinkle believed that psychologically "the twain are no longer one flesh—the man being 'the one'—but instead they are two distinct personalities."

But were women no longer psychologically merged with their husbands? Of course some wives did hold on to their own personality, but the failure of the Lucy Stone League movement was a significant sign that women were still psychologically merged with their husbands, and when one looks at the lives of some of the members of the League, it becomes clear that the Lucy Stone League had put the cart before the horse, given a wife a separate name when she was in fact not separate from her husband, when she was in truth "Mrs Heywood Broun," for Ruth Hale herself, unhappily and against her will, became one with her husband.

According to Broun, when he and Hale married, Hale had been "the better newspaperman of the two," and in 1917 their careers were more or less on a par. But after marriage Hale's career languished. Broun felt what held her back was "biological"—she had a baby within a year. However, that was not the reason, for Broun was willing, nay eager, to help with the baby and by 1921 they had a competent full-time housekeeper. Hale also had as much privacy as she wanted: she had her own separate floor in their house in New York, a separate house in the country and later her own apartment.

Hale insisted on being physically separated from Broun in order to better deny her almost total intellectual fusion with him. For as Broun confessed in a column published on September 19, 1934, the day after Hale died, they had had "a curious collaboration." Broun in a fundamental way had been Hale's mouthpiece. Originally, Hale had been the more radical of the two, the un-compromising idealist who fought for what she believed was right, the one in-terested in books and ideas, whose discussions with Broun were the basis of many of Broun's columns and who herself wrote, as Broun admitted, "a con-siderable percentage." She could not stop herself from her course of "vicarious expression," although, said Broun, she was filled with "a vast rancor," "the inevitable bitterness of the person who projects himself through another." But her bitterness also came from a truth she had to face—she wrote best under Broun's byline, but Broun could write his best without her.

Their "curious collaboration" not only made her bitter, it made Broun feel guilty so that he once confessed to the editors of *Judge*, a magazine for which he wrote a movie column, that Ruth Hale was the one who actually wrote it. But Hale in this case was *not* the author; she loathed the movies and never went to them. A part of Broun wanted to give Hale credit and a part did not, so he gave her credit for something she did not write. He never did what he ought to have—signed the columns she wrote "Ruth Hale" and the ones they both wrote "Heywood Broun and Ruth Hale."

His guilty gratitude to Ruth undoubtedly accounts for his impassioned eulogy of Leora, the selfless wife of Dr Martin Arrowsmith in Sinclair Lewis's novel published in 1925. Leora was a nurse who abandoned her career and dedicated her life to making her husband "a great man." "I haven't any life outside of you," she once says, "I might've had, but honestly, I've been glad to let you absorb me."

A female reader of Broun's review of *Arrowsmith* asked him how he who had advocated "careers for women and independent lives" could praise a woman who had no life of her own. Broun could because Leora reminded him of Ruth who, though in a different way, had let her husband absorb what was best in her, who had lived through her husband and who, finally, could not live without him. In 1933 they were divorced, and although Hale was the one who wanted it, hoping divorce would give her a separate identity, she died less than a year later, from all accounts willing herself to die, for there was nothing organically wrong with her. Broun too found it difficult to live without Hale. He soon married Connie Madison, an ex-chorus girl, who of course became Mrs Broun and who functioned as a traditional wife. But Broun needed another

Ruth Hale, a spiritual and intellectual authority; he joined the Catholic Church in 1938.

Ruth Hale and Heywood Broun were not the only Lucy Stone couple who had a "curious collaboration" in which the wife did not get the credit she deserved. Doris Fleischman and Edward Bernays were partners in a supremely successful public relations firm, a firm that was named only after Bernays and in which Fleischman from the first functioned as a silent partner. She did because Bernays felt their clients would find it demeaning to be told what to do by a woman. Therefore, Fleischman's ideas were presented by Bernays, who got all the credit. Bernays, like Broun, felt guilty; he always introduced her as "Miss Fleischman, my partner" and dedicated his books "To my wife and partner, Doris E. Fleischman." But he did not rename the firm "Bernays & Fleischman," nor did he let Fleischman present her own ideas to clients. How important Fleischman was in bringing about the success of the firm does not become clear in Bernay's autobiography. Bernays undoubtedly did have the greater genius in public relations, but Fleischman undoubtedly did not get the credit she deserved. She remained relatively unknown.

In Fleischman's autobiographical *A Wife Is Many Women* she admitted that her "personality and courage" had been softened by the force of Bernays' personality. Indeed, Bernays had originally been the Lucy Stoner, bringing "a reluctant Doris with me," a Doris he wanted to remain Miss Fleischman because he felt a Mrs attached to his name "would take away some of my liberties as an individual"; a slogan he once coined for the Lucy Stone League was "The Freedom for Husbands Society." Not having a "Mrs Bernays" perhaps did give him some playboy freedoms; it certainly gave him all the fame, there being no Mrs Bernays even to share the limelight of her husband's famous name. After twenty-seven years Fleischman found the courage to become in name what she in reality had always been—Mrs Bernays. In the February 1949 *American Mercury* she announced she was abandoning "the struggle against the married name. I'd like to be Mrs Edward L. Bernays. I'm proud of him and of his name."

Mrs Bernays accused the Lucy Stoners of grasping "for a symbol—a name—instead of developing personalities of our own," and certainly she was not the only Lucy Stoner who had a remarkable ability to subordinate her personality to her husband's. Another such was Anita Loos, who had married John Emerson in 1919, kept her name and become in 1921 one of the original members of the Lucy Stone League. But in 1925 she committed the unpardonable wifely sin—she became internationally famous after the publication of *Gentlemen Prefer Blondes*. Her fame drove Emerson almost mad with jealousy; when he was once mistakenly called Mr Loos, he tried to strangle her. He promptly developed an hysterical illness which his doctor told Loos could only be cured if she gave up her career. Instead of leaving this childish egomaniac, Loos, without a regret, gave up her career. "Nothing could have been easier," she said. In the first place, she took no pride in being an author because she did not think "anything produced by females was, or even should be, important." In the second place, she thought "authoresses" should be "women first of all," and she proceeded to be a woman. After completing *But Gentlemen Marry Brunettes*, which she maneuvered Emerson into helping her with and that she published under both their names, she retired into wifehood, becoming Mrs John Emerson. In 1928 when she was listed in *Who's Who* for the first time, it was under Emerson and with no cross-reference under Loos, so that anyone wanting to learn something about the author of *Gentlemen Prefer Blondes* would not have been able to find her.

Few Lucy Stoners gave up international fame in order to indulge in the masochistic delights of catering to a jealous husband. Most Lucy Stoners dwindled into a wife because they were afflicted with a cultural not a personal neurosis, because they had been brought up to believe they were inferior to men and that husbands were the sun around which wives ought to revolve. When Julie Harpman, a reporter for the *New York Daily News* married the sportswriter Westbrook Pegler on August 29, 1922, she vowed she would not be dragged down into domesticity and got Pegler to agree that she would continue her career and that they would "remain individuals." But Pegler soon became discontented, then morose; he complained that she did not spend enough time with him, that he needed "more woman hours out of her." Undoubtedly, Pegler's real complaint was that her career was then more successful than his, but it was Harpman who gave up her career. After 1926 Miss Julie Harpman became Mrs Westbrook Pegler.

Most commonly, a Lucy Stoner dwindled into a wife because, almost without knowing what was happening to her, she found the burden of taking care of the house and the children resting entirely on her own shoulders. Typical was the experience of the anonymous Ex-Feminist who confessed her failure in the April 14, 1926 *New Republic*. Although her husband theoretically believed men ought to share domestic tasks, in practice he managed to be too incompetent to make a piece of toast or diaper a baby. The Ex-Feminist sometimes thought that if they had had enough money to hire a housekeeper and nurse, she would not have become "Mrs W, just my husband's wife." But she was not sure, for ultimately she blamed her failure on herself, on the fact she was a woman and had "a damnable maternal instinct" that not only prevented her from being as ruthless as men in the pursuit of her ambitions but made her want to coddle not only her baby but serve her grown-up baby—her husband—"coffee in bed!"

What women called their maternal instinct, their inability to be as assertive as men, was in 1931 diagnosed by Lorine Pruette in "Why Women Fail." It was not a maternal instinct that dwindled women into wives. It was conditioning, being taught that it was "greedy and grasping" for a woman to be ambitious but noble to help a man greedily grasp at success. Women failed because they did not have husbands who devoted their lives to bolstering their egos and who freed them from the petty details of daily life. Women failed because it was not a disgrace to fail. On the contrary, the woman who failed was more pleasing to men than the woman who succeeded, and women had been conditioned to please men, who had always praised most highly the woman whose only ambition was to help her husband achieve success.

A successful wife's "happiness . . . came in furthering the husband's happiness and success" was the conclusion of the guests at a dinner party on August 26, 1934. Among the guests, and the one who reported the conversation, was Franklin P. Adams, who was there with his wife, the former Esther Sayles Root, who in 1925 had sailed to Europe on her honeymoon triumphantly brandishing a passport in her own name. But wifehood and maternity had soon transformed her into Mrs Franklin P. Adams, just her husband's wife.

In Franklin P. Adams' "The Diary of Our Own Samuel Pepys" (one of his columns in the *World*), he had noted on April 16, 1924 that he went "to Miss Ruth Pickering's to dinner." In 1935 when Adams published the diary as a book, he appended a footnote to her name: "Mrs Amos Pinchot, but in those days a militant Lucy Stoner." So the woman who had been an original member of the Lucy Stone League, who had been elected editor of the monthly bulletin on women's name rights, who had given radio talks on a woman's right to her own name, by 1935 had become Mrs Amos Pinchot. As early as 1926 Anita Loos had become Mrs John Emerson, and though Doris Fleischman retained her name for many years, she had in fact always been Mrs Edward Bernays, as in her strange way Ruth Hale had been Mrs Heywood Broun.

In "Marriage in the New World" Beatrice Hinkle had said that wives in the year 1926 were no longer the shadows of their husbands but had their own egos. But most women who started marriage with an ego of their own soon found it had become one with their husband's ego. Marriage in the New World rapidly became like marriage in the Old World.

Swallowed Up by a Man

Pope Pius in 1930 condemned "the false liberty and unnatural equality of the New Woman," but the New Woman was doing a thorough job of condemning herself and was hastening to become indistinguishable from the Old-Fashioned Woman.

Tess Slesinger's novel *The Unpossessed* (1934), which was dedicated "To My Contemporaries," was her condemnation of the New Woman, "the girls [who] keep the names they were born with," who "sleep for a little variety with one another's husbands," who forget "to empty the pan under the icebox," and, most important, who do not want to have babies. Margaret Flinders, a reluctant New Woman, thinks the Sex-Equality movement made her generation of women "too mannish," gave them jobs and cigarettes instead of the babies a woman needs to make her a woman. And *mirabile dictu*, when Margaret accidently becomes pregnant she acquires a halo like the Madonna. "You've got such a big light where your face used to be," says her husband. But when he finds out pregnancy has produced the beautiful transformation, he fears a baby will interfere with their work and urges her to have an abortion. She does and afterwards, lying in the maternity ward surrounded by unintellectual women happily breeding, she despises her husband for not being a man and herself for being "a creature who would not be a woman." A view of woman identical with Benito Mussolini's, who in 1934 was also maintaining that women who worked lost their "generative powers," which was why he decreed that in Italy only men should get the jobs; women should stay at home and produce many babies.

Similarly, in Sinclair Lewis's *Ann Vickers* (1933) Ann does not become a woman until she has a baby. Ann had been a New Woman in the 1910s, ambitious and sexually liberated, who in order not to interrupt her career as a social worker had an abortion. She later married another social worker, a weak man whose name she almost never used. Her career was successful; she became the head of a woman's reformatory. But she felt unfulfilled and continued to until she fell in love with the virile Barney Dolphin and had his baby. Before her abortion she longed to have a daughter whom she planned to name Pride to symbolize the character of future woman. But Proud Woman was not yet to be; in 1930 Ann had a son who was named after Barney's father, and Ann herself was certain to become Mrs Barney Dolphin.

Ann Vickers was dedicated to and was inspired by Sinclair Lewis's second wife, who not only called herself Mrs Sinclair Lewis in private life but after their marriage in 1928 appropriated his famous name professionally. In June 1929 she published a series of newspaper articles on prohibition that were signed "Mrs Sinclair Lewis (Dorothy Thompson)." Nineteenth-century writers who felt obliged to publicly profess their wifehood, signed their names, for example, "Florence Marryat (Mrs Ross Church)," but Dorothy Thompson, despite her own solid reputation, put her husband first and herself in parentheses.

Ambitious women in the 1930s felt they had to prove they were women by such acts of subordination and by managing to believe that a real woman wanted a superior man to whom she could subordinate herself. "The reason why modern women are so unhappy and why they unconsciously hate men," wrote Dorothy Thompson in her diary in 1927, is that it is difficult to find a man worthy enough to "swallow them up." "I will give my body, soul and spirit to a man who can use it up to make a Damascene blade." Thompson had those feelings after rereading Lewis's *Arrowsmith* and reflecting on the character of Dr Arrowsmith and his wife Leora, who, she felt, were the "ideal of the truly dynamic and creative male" and of "the real woman" who is "swallowed up by a man" and is thus "transmuted into something" better than herself.

"The highest task of woman is to inspire man," Maxim Gorki had said in the March 26, 1924 *Nation*, giving twentieth-century utterance to an ancient male myth that even an intelligent woman like Dorothy Thompson swallowed whole. Thompson was rereading *Arrowsmith* when she and Lewis were in love, and when she married him she tried to be another Leora, putting his work and his wishes first, establishing a home for him, and even having a baby when she was almost thirty-seven. She tried, in short, to be a real woman, to be swallowed up by her husband, to become Mrs Sinclair Lewis.

But Dorothy Thompson was no Leora. The woman who signed herself Mrs Sinclair Lewis was fundamentally an ambitious journalist. Lewis's first wife, Grace Hegger Lewis, had insisted on having even her dentist address her as Mrs Sinclair Lewis because she was so greedy to share Lewis's fame. But Dorothy Thompson wanted her own fame, and her use of Lewis's name helped her get better known, especially after 1930 when Lewis was awarded the Nobel Prize. She did not again sign herself "Mrs Sinclair Lewis (Dorothy Thompson)," but she did use "Dorothy Thompson (Mrs Sinclair Lewis)," and then "Dorothy Thompson . . . who in private life is Mrs Sinclair Lewis." In 1936 when she began to write her own column for the *Herald Tribune*, Lewis's name was mentioned only in an advertisement announcing the column, but she was then, and for some time, more famous than he was. Never again did she use his name in connection with her work. Dorothy Thompson finally stood alone.

She soon became famous, but the more famous she got, the more she protested she was really a woman, that is, chiefly interested in serving the man she loved. In 1939 when Alexander Woollcott suggested to her that *The New Yorker* should do her profile, she told him she did not want to be presented as a famous journalist but "as a female," as "almost a perfect wife"—"a hell of a good housekeeper" and a good cook. She said she was tired of being told she had the brains of a man, and not because she thought women's brains were as good as men's but because she thought women's brains were not as good, at least her brain was not; she felt her male colleagues were all better journalists than she was, that her own reportorial strength was "altogether female," consisting in being "a receptive audience." She described herself as "still susceptible to the boys" and her career as having been conditioned by the man she was currently involved with and said she would "throw the state of the nation into the ashcan for anyone I loved." Woollcott may well have thought he was interviewing the current Miss America.

When Dorothy Thompson married the next man she loved, she did not throw even her career into the ashcan, but she still tried to be a real woman. In 1943 she married Maxim Kopf, a minor painter, and although she did not commit the folly of becoming Mrs Kopf professionally, she did delight in being Mrs Him in private life. An invitation she sent to a New Year's Eve party in 1952 read: "Mr and Mrs Maxim Kopf (Dorothy Thompson) request the pleasure of your company . . . "

How Maxim Kopf endured having a wife more famous than he, he did not record, but Sinclair Lewis had bitterly complained about being "Mr Dorothy Thompson." Men in the twentieth century could no more bear to be Mr Woman than could men in the nineteenth century, and their wives suffered as much if not more than they did. When Pearl Buck was awarded the Nobel Prize in 1938 she agonized because she was in the limelight and her husband, the publisher Richard Walsh, had to be in a "secondary position." "It was all the harder for me than it was for Dr Fermi," she recalled. "His wife was with him, but it was easier to be known as the wife of Enrico Fermi than it was to be known as the husband of Pearl Buck."

If Pearl Buck and Dorothy Thompson had been real women like Leora Arrowsmith, they would have given up their careers, understanding that a successful wife could ruin her husband, even cause his death, at least so went the gospel according to Hollywood. In *A Star is Born* (1937) as Vicki Lester's star rises, that of her husband, the actor Norman Maine, declines. As she becomes famous, he becomes a drunk. When her hands and feet are being immortalized in the cement in front of Grauman's Chinese Theater, he is committing suicide. Told of his death just before she is about to speak to her cheering fans, she reveals she is a real woman by repudiating her own famous name and announcing, "This is Mrs Norman Maine." Real life was true to fiction. The telegrams in which a famous actress announced her marriage on July 4, 1940 were signed, "Love from Mrs Richard Stoddard Aldrich, theatrically known as Gertrude Lawrence," and she once told her husband that she wanted "more than anything else in the world to be Mrs Richard Stoddard Aldrich."

In and Out of Names

In 1924 at the height of the Lucy Stone League's popularity, Laura Jean Libbey's will revealed she wanted her own name only to be inscribed on her tombstone, but in 1933 at the beginning of the cult of wifehood *über alles*, Sara Teasdale's will revealed that despite her divorce she wanted her tombstone to be inscribed with her married name—Sara Teasdale Filsinger. In 1922 when Lila Bell Acheson and her husband DeWitt Wallace founded *The Reader's Digest*, she used her own name on the masthead, but in March 1938 she changed it to Lila Acheson Wallace.

We are again in an era when women in the professions feel it is more important to profess their womanhood by taking a husband's name than to hold on to a professional identity. We are again in an era when women change their professional name with every marriage, even in a profession in which the tradition had long been established to keep a constant name. So intense was the cult of wifehood that Ernest Hemingway asked his wife-to-be, who was also a writer, to publish under his name after their marriage in 1940. Martha Gellhorn refused, but other women were so eager to certify their female credentials they changed their publishing name. The poet Laura Riding, who had continued to be Laura Riding during her first marriage, acquired a second husband in 1941, after which, despite her fame, she changed the name she published under to Laura (Riding) Jackson. Although Dorothy Canfield continued to publish her bestselling novels under her own name, using Dorothy Canfield Fisher (the husband's name she more and more preferred) chiefly for books on children and education, by the 1930s she was publishing in magazines and lecturing as Dorothy Canfield Fisher and eventually she came to be generally known under her husband's name. Such a shift in a woman's publishing name was rare, but just as rare was the woman writer who did not delight in being Mrs Manofthemoment in private life. From 1933 onwards Mary McCarthy was to change her wife name to Mrs Johnsrud, then to Mrs Wilson, then to Mrs Broadwater, and then to Mrs West, and without a protest.

Mary McCarthy at least held on to her professional identity, but women who were not writers or actresses found it difficult to withstand the pressure to conform and many found themselves changing their professional name in mid career, even against their will. Ruth Bryan Owen, who had served Florida in Congress from 1928 to 1932, was in 1933 appointed American Minister to Denmark, the first woman to hold such an appointment. Three years later, in July 1936, Mrs Owen announced she was taking another husband, Captain Borge Rohde of the Danish Royal Guards, but that she would "continue to use the name Ruth Bryan Owen in her official and literary work" (*The New York Times*, July 11, 1936). And it was "Ruth Bryan Owen and her husband, Captain Borge Rohde" who were honored at a reception of the Danish American Women's Association early in August. But late in August, having been forced to resign from the ministry because under Danish law her marriage had given her dual citizenship, the name Owen began to slip away from her. From 1938 on she allowed *Who's Who* to list her under Rohde, and she herself signed her books "Ruth Bryan Owen (Mrs Borge Rohde)." But in 1944 she insisted that *Current Biography* list her under Owen. In 1949, however, it was Mrs Rohde who was appointed alternate United States Delegate to the General Assembly of the United Nations and in 1954 *Current Biography* published the notice of her death under Rohde. If Mrs Rohde had been male, she could have profited from the name of a very famous father—William Jennings Bryan. Having been born female, she had to become Leavitt, then Owen, and at the age of fifty lose the husband's name she herself had made famous and take the name of a man who was unknown.

Ruth Bryan Leavitt Owen Rohde, who was a friend of Frances Perkins and whose matron of honor at her last marriage had been another Lucy Stoner, Fannie Hurst, made some effort to hold on to her famous name, but most prominent women shed a famous name as if it were an outmoded dress. Dr Mildred McAfee, President of Wellesley College, was appointed Director of the Waves in 1942, but it was a Captain Horton who retired from the service in 1946, for Captain McAfee married in 1945 and without a moment's hesitation changed her name to that of the Reverend Dr Douglas Horton. When Shirley Temple married Charles Black in 1950 she retired from the movies and assumed the role of wife, happily becoming Mrs Charles Black. In 1932 Elsie Hill ran for Congress from Connecticut in her own name, but in 1942 the second woman to run for Congress from that state ran under her husband's name, changing her name to her husband's for just that purpose.

The woman born Clare Boothe had been in and out of names since her marriage in 1923 to George Brokaw, whose name she continued to use, even professionally, after their divorce in 1929. It was Clare Boothe Brokaw who wrote for *Vogue* and *Vanity Fair* and published *Stuffed Shirts* in 1931. It was Clare Boothe Brokaw's play *Abide with Me* that opened on Broadway on

November 21, 1935 and ignominiously failed. Two days later Mrs Brokaw married Henry Luce and became Mrs Luce socially but for professional purposes resumed the use of her maiden name. The name Miss Clare Boothe erased the recent failure of Mrs Brokaw; it also soothed the feelings of Mr Luce, who would have disliked having a wife who continued to use another husband's name; in addition, it would seem less like favoritism if a Miss Boothe not a Mrs Luce wrote for Luce's *Time* and *Life*. At any rate, it was as Clare Boothe that she not only published her later plays and a newspaper column but in 1939 traveled to Europe as a special correspondent and visited foreign dignitaries, among them, the French Minister of Labor and his wife, who called her Mlle Boothe. Even her husband in his introduction to her play *Margin for Error* (1940) called her "my dear wife, Miss Boothe." It was Clare Boothe who debated Dorothy Thompson in 1940, whose life was sketched in *Current Biography* in 1942 and whose career was covered by *The New York Times*. But in 1942 when she decided to run for Congress, she changed her name to Clare Boothe Luce. She undoubtedly felt it was a political advantage to run under her husband's more famous name; she had also probably been advised by lawyers that she had to run under her only legal name—her husband's. But the most important reason why she became Mrs Luce was not to offend American housewivery, who would disapprove of a wife who presumed to call herself Miss Herownname. A woman politician was a sufficient offense against the status quo; a wife who did not present herself as a wife would offend fatally. Similarly, when a former actress first went into politics, she used the name Miss Helen Gahagan and under that name became the Democratic Committeewoman from California in 1940. However, when she decided to run for Congress in 1944, she filed her nomination papers as Helen Gahagan Douglas.

So women continued to shed old names and acquire new ones, an experience that at long last taught one woman she ought to have a name of her own. Mrs Dorothy Hall served on the Social Service Committee of Bellevue Hospital in 1931, but in 1932 that committee member had become Mrs Dorothy Backer, who in 1937 also served on the New York Board of Child Welfare and who in 1939 bought the New York *Post*. Mrs Backer became the *Post*'s publisher and president in 1942, but in 1943 the president had become Mrs Thackrey, under which name she won a place in *Current Biography* in 1945. She remained Mrs Thackrey until 1952, when she again divorced her husband. Mrs Hall Backer Thackrey, having learned the hard way that conforming to the convention of becoming Mrs Whoeverhewas had deprived her of a name she could permanently call her own, resumed the name she had been given at birth, and despite a fourth marriage in 1953, remained Dorothy Schiff.

The disadvantages of changing one's name at marriage were also experienced, one is pleased to discover, by a male Lucy Stoner. Raymond Swing in 1920, as a compromise with Betty Gram who would have preferred to retain her name, added his wife's surname to his own and he and Betty both became Gram Swing. When they were divorced in 1942, Raymond felt he was no longer entitled to the Gram in his name and dropped it. His radio network and close friends followed his wishes and called him Raymond Swing, but the general public refused to break an old habit. Swing was seriously annoyed and was sorry he had changed his name when he married, but he expressed no such concern for Betty Gram nor for the women he later married, both of whom became Mrs Swing.

Almost invariably, when men who had been married to Lucy Stoners married again, it was to women who became, and who were eager to become, Mrs Them. Heywood Broun's second wife became Mrs Broun; Harold Ross, after his divorce from Jane Grant, married two more times and both his wives became Mrs Harold Ross; Senator Clarence Dill, after his divorce from Rosalie G. Jones, married a woman who was happy to become Mrs Dill. Even men who seemed sincerely to believe in Lucy Stonism did not require a Lucy Stoner as a second wife. When Frederick Lawrence married Emmeline Pethick in 1901 they had combined surnames because they both believed in equality in the marriage relation, but in 1957 when Frederick Pethick-Lawrence took a second wife she became Mrs Pethick-Lawrence. When Emmanuel Julius and Marcet Haldeman married in 1916 they combined surnames for the same reason the Pethick-Lawrences did, but when Emmanuel Haldeman-Julius took a second wife, he did not drop the Haldeman and replace it with his second wife's surname; she became Mrs Haldeman-Julius. Even Max Eastman, who had been as ardent a Lucy Stoner as Ruth Hale, whose second wife, Eliena Krylenko, had also kept her name, married a young girl in 1958 who was eager to become Mrs Eastman.

Not only did the former husbands of Lucy Stoners take non Lucy Stoners as second or third wives, rarely did the daughter of a Lucy Stoner follow in her mother's footsteps. Dr Edith Summerskill's daughter did remain Shirley Summerskill after her marriage, but Vera Brittain's daughter became Mrs Williams, Frances Perkins' daughter became Mrs Coggeshall, Elsie Hill's became Mrs Latham, Margaret Mead's became Mrs Kassarjian, and Doris Fleischman's two daughters became Mrs Held and Mrs Kaplan. Indeed, Fleischman's daughters and their teen-age friends found their mother's Lucy Stonism incomprehensible and offensive. Said one of her daughters, "I'd be proud to take my husband's name. I'd want everyone to know I was married." Said her friend, "If my husband didn't let me use his name, I'd think he didn't love me." As if Lucy Stoners had not used their husbands' names because their husbands forbade them! Young girls in the forties and fifties were blindly pursuing what Vera Brittain had called "a policy of militant inferiority" and had no comprehension that they were proud to take a husband's name because they could not feel proud about themselves until they had acquired the identity of one of the superior sex. Young girls in the 1950s were as eager as girls in the 1850s to become Mrs George Washington Jones because women still believed they were inferior to men.

Needless to say, only the rare person then understood that taking a husband's name meant women had an inferiority complex. On the contrary, in the 1950s and later those who remembered there had once been such oddities as Lucy Stoners accused them of having had an inferiority complex. Elsdon Smith in *The Story of Our Names* (1950) maintained that Lucy Stoners kept their names because they were exhibitionists who fundamentally doubted they were the equals of men. How a strong sense of one's identity could be a sign of an inferiority complex Smith of course did not ask. Lucy Stoners were also accused of having been simply silly, and by a man who had once been an ardent believer. Edward Bernays, who in 1922 had convinced his wife to become a Lucy Stoner, in 1965 could no longer understand how "thoughtful men and women could have concerned themselves with such foolishness."

This Nominal Obstacle Race

Lucy Stonism seemed to be a cultural sport that quickly died in an atmosphere that became increasingly thick with injunctions to women to find their identity in being a wife. But although many Lucy Stoners defected, many did not, a few managing to hold on to their names and not dwindle into conventional wives.

Vera Brittain, for one, had the courage to set up a most unconventional marriage. When she married George Catlin in 1925, he had a teaching job at Cornell and she expected she could establish herself as a writer in America as she had begun to do in England. But it proved to be far more difficult to break into publishing in America and she grew unhappy, feeling she had either to give up writing and become just a wife or divorce her husband and return to England where she could find work. Instead of either of these drastic alternatives, she and Catlin decided on a "semi-detached marriage." They spent about half their time away from each other, Catlin in America and Brittain in England, an arrangement they maintained for several years, during which Brittain managed to have two children and laid the foundations for a solid writing career. Her marriage not only survived the separation but proved to be unusually good because, Brittain believed, she had not chosen "between personal relationships and the work for which she was fitted" but, like a man, had had "the best of both worlds."

Most Lucy Stoners who persisted did not have to overcome such difficulties; they managed with much less strain to have the best of both worlds. Dr Edith Summerskill had an excellent relationship with her husband, two children and two careers—as a physician and as a Member of Parliament. Margaret Mead married two more times—in 1928 and again in 1936—and though she had a child, she maintained her own work, personality and name, as did Frances Perkins, Elsie Hill, Ruby Black and many others. Fola La Follette, Fannie Hurst, Edna St Vincent Millay, Helena Normanton, Rita Weiman, Anita Pollitzer, Calm Morrison Hoke, to name a few, remained Lucy Stoners till they died. If almost all ex-husbands of Lucy Stoners took second wives who were eager to become Mrs Him, many Lucy Stoners who took second husbands remained Miss Theirownname. Doris Stevens kept her name through two marriages, as did the psychologist Dr Lorine Pruette, the photographer Margaret Bourke-White, and Dr Theresa Wolfson, Professor of Economics at Brooklyn College. Jane Grant had a highly successful second marriage and, as Margaret Case Harriman put it, she kept "the Lucy Stone flag flying." Invitations to her parties always read "Jane Grant and William B. Harris," and she so firmly continued to use her own name that "if anyone spoke of her as 'Mrs Harris' even to her closest friends, the automatic reply would be, 'Who?'"

But the Jane Grants, the women who were totally uncompromising, were rare, and one suspects that even Jane Grant when she divorced Harold Ross came before the court as Ross v. Ross. The decision to be a Lucy Stoner immediately thrust one into what Doris Fleischman called "this nominal obstacle race," and it took a woman of extraordinary dedication to keep up the struggle against nominal convention and not yield on one point or another, and most Lucy Stoners yielded on many points.

Most Lucy Stoners from the very beginning of their own free will became Mrs Theirhusband when they registered at hotels. Jane Grant did not, nor did a handful of others, but the rest chose to conform because, as Dr Charlotte McCarthy put it, "Hotel clerks are VERY conventional." For the same reason, most Lucy Stoners tended to use the title Mrs when they became pregnant. Occasionally, against their will. Alice Mendham, a social worker for the American Birth Control League in New York, continued to call herself Miss Mendham, but she noticed that when her pregnancy became highly visible her colleagues began to address her as "Mrs" Mendham. It took a woman of great fortitude to go to a hospital to have a baby as Miss. Cornelia B. Rose Jr, a Washington DC economist, did and was not frowned at by the nurses, but Doris

Fleischman was frowned at, and most Lucy Stoners, afraid nurses would think they were having an illegitimate child, became Mrs Wedlock at maternity hospitals and on the baby's birth certificate. Doris Fleischman in 1929 did succeed in getting the New York Department of Health to let her own name appear on her daughter's birth certificate, but her husband had had to argue at great length. A few Lucy Stoners, without arguing, got their own name recorded on their children's birth certificates, but most, to avoid anticipated trouble, did not use their own name.

Nor did Lucy Stoners as a rule give their children their own name. One or two did, like Dr Edith Summerskill and the psychologist Flanders Dunbar, who married George Soule in 1940 and gave their daughter the hyphenated surname Dunbar-Soule. By giving her children her own name or part of her name, a Lucy Stoner made it easier for herself to keep her name and made life easier for her children. For mothers traditionally took children to doctors, dentists and to school and signed report cards and went to PTA meetings and other school functions where having a surname different from one's children always required explanations and was embarrassing for the children. To help her children feel less different, most Lucy Stoners became Mrs Daddy on such occasions.

A Lucy Stoner not only became Mrs Legitimatewife at hotels and maternity hospitals and on birth certificates and report cards, she also generally lost her name on passports. For despite the Lucy Stone League's success in 1925 in getting the State Department to issue Lucy Stoners passports in their own name, clerks at the various offices almost invariably told a woman who asked for such a passport that it was impossible. Whether or not the Washington office instructed them to do so will probably never be known, but unless a woman made a fuss and/or happened to know there was a regulation that specifically permitted her to get a passport in her own name, she did not get one. When Jane Grant applied for a passport at the New York office in 1948, she was told by "a prejudiced clerk" who "made his own rules," as Grant put it, that she could not have one in her own name. She spoke to the head of the New York office, and he was equally adamant. Grant had to travel to Washington DC and give the passport officials hell before she got a passport in her own name. But the average Lucy Stoner, face to face with an imperious clerk, herself ignorant of the passport regulations, felt it was "a losing battle," "it never seemed worth the effort." And so the passports of most Lucy Stoners were in their husbands' names.

So were mortgages and deeds, for, again, face to face with a real estate agent certain the law required a wife to sign her husband's name to such contracts, most Lucy Stoners capitulated, convinced it would somehow be illegal to sign their own name. Of course some Lucy Stoners knew better; Frances Perkins, Jane Grant and several others always held property in their own name. But the few women who bought property with their husbands as "John Jones and Mary Smith, his wife" were, as often as not, sent tax bills in their husband's name. Even a woman who had received bills in her own name for years could, upon the advent of a new clerk who thought he had discovered an error, be billed in her husband's name. Edna St Vincent Millay, after paying taxes on her property in Maine for twenty-seven years in that name, in 1950 received a bill made out to "Mrs Eugen Boissevain." Being ill, she asked a friend to inform the tax collector that she "never used Eugen's name," that "(*Miss*) etc. is my correct and legal name."

Voting was another area in which a Lucy Stoner was likely sooner or later to lose her own name, usually when she moved to another town or state and had to reregister. But even when she continued to live in the same district, she could lose her name. During the Second World War Dr Margaret Good Myers, who had been known at Vassar as Myers since she joined the faculty in 1934, went to her polling place to vote and was told by the faculty wives in charge of the registration books they had put her name under Beckhart, her husband's name. Myers was furious; she also knew the New York Election Board specifically permitted a married woman to vote in her own name, but because she "did not want to make a scene in front of them all and my husband" she said nothing and from then on voted as Beckhart. As another Lucy Stoner expressed it, "With a job, a husband and four children, I was not making my name a *cause célèbre*."

But most Lucy Stoners did manage to find the energy to outwit those who tried to take away their professional identity. Dr Charlotte McCarthy could not get her bank to let her open an account in her own name, the bank manager insisting it had to be in the name Josephs, her husband's name. But she did not tell her patients to make out their checks to Josephs and when all the checks arrived at the bank made out to Dr Charlotte McCarthy, the bank manager was forced to yield to common sense. Similarly, the Comptroller at Vassar College at first refused to acknowledge Dr Margaret Myers' name; all bills were sent to Mrs Beckhart. However, by paying her bills with a check signed Myers and omitting to enclose the bill made out to Beckhart, Myers so confused the Comptroller's office she eventually was billed in her own name.

Dr Myers' colleagues addressed her by her own name, but other women were harassed by their colleagues. After Dr Marie Stopes' first marriage, her fellow scientists insisted on addressing her at meetings as Dr Gates and printed in their proceedings what they determined was her correct name, so that Dr Stopes more than once had to threaten legal action to get her name acknowledged. Lorine Pruette and her husband Douglas Fryer, after a trip to France in 1925, wrote an article on French psychologists they submitted to *Applied Psychology*. The editor wrote back that since it was obvious they had been traveling together, Pruette would have to use the name Fryer; otherwise readers would think she and Fryer had been living in sin. Pruette told the editor he could either use her own name or drop it entirely, and the editor summoned up his courage and printed the two names. Shortly after the marriage of Calm Morrison Hoke, she attended a meeting of The American Institute of Chemists, of which she had been a prime mover. The first president, Dr Byers, in a speech on the founding of the Institute, omitted any mention of her work, for which he later apologized, explaining that he had wanted to give her credit, but he did not know her husband's name and could not bring himself to use her own name. Hoke was, understandably, livid.

Election to high office was no guarantee a woman's right to use her name would not be challenged. When Dr Edith Summerskill was elected to Parliament in 1938, her fellow parliamentarians, distressed by her use of her own name, got Sir Stafford Cripps to question her concerning its legal validity, but she easily convinced him Summerskill was her legal name by pointing out that were she to sign a death certificate in any other name than Edith Summerskill it would be invalid. Cripps spoke to Summerskill in private, but when Frances Perkins was appointed Secretary of Labor in 1933, she did not get her name acknowledged without a public debate. Just as the New York senators in 1919 debated whether she could hold the office of Industrial Commissioner in her own name, so on February 25, 1933, three days after her appointment, Congressman Ralph A. Horr of Washington arose to declare there was "a pitfall in the pathway of the newly elected Secretary of Labor," that in view of Comptroller General McCarl's 1924 ruling, "the lady Secretary from New York" would have to sign the name Frances Wilson to the payroll in order to get paid. Representative John O'Connor of New York replied that "under the laws of the State of New York any person, whether married or single, may adopt any name he or she chooses," and on March 6 *The New York Times* announced that the new Secretary of Labor would sign the payroll Frances Perkins.

Although one could not tell a member of the President's Cabinet what her name was, lesser women working for the government could be dictated to, for despite Frances Perkins' victory, other women continued to be required to sign their husband's name to the payroll. In 1934 when Cornelia B. Rose Jr reported her marriage to the Treasury Department where she was then employed, her next pay check was made out to Cornelia B. Ecker-Rácz. Rose refused to endorse it and protested to her employer, asking why if Frances Perkins could be paid in her own name, she could not. The Treasury Department felt she had a point and took the matter to the Government Appropriation Office, which following the bureaucratic principle that some people are more equal than others, insisted that notwithstanding Miss Perkins, Rose could only be paid as Mrs Ecker-Rácz. Needing the money, Rose was constrained to capitulate, but she scribbled illegible tracks on the back of the check, then legibly signed her own name and had no trouble cashing the check. Indeed, she would have had trouble if she had signed her husband's name since her bank account was in her own name. Interestingly enough, in her next Federal job, with the Rural Electrification Administration, Rose had her own name accepted at once, even though she told them the Treasury Department had not accepted it. However, Lucy Stoners working in most government agencies continued to be required to be Mrs Husband in order to get paid. In addition, most school teachers, when they were not forced to resign upon marriage, were required to teach in their husband's name, for many school boards, like the New York School Board in 1930, adopted resolutions requiring married women to conform to nominal convention.

Nevertheless, the majority of Lucy Stoners, since they were self-employed or in high status jobs, did continue to use their own name professionally and, unlike Doris Fleischman, felt the struggle to keep it had been worthwhile. It was "a positive benefit to my ego," said one. "It meant I was a person in my own right," "It strengthened my personal identity," said others. Their egos were strong enough not to mind having a husband who was more prominent or less prominent than they were. Said one Lucy Stoner: " At first I had more reputation that he and did not want to give it up. Then he had more than me and I did not want to ride on his coattails." Said another: "What reputation I have, I acquired through my own efforts. My husband is a prominent person, but I have never traded on his reputation. We have been able to operate in the community and in our jobs without living in each other's shadow. We have had the experience of being introduced to each other at functions to which we had each been invited."

But though a Lucy Stoner thoroughly enjoyed having a separate professional identity, one could never be sure that she might not finally decide to be Mrs Him. Frances Perkins, who since 1913 had run the nominal obstacle race with far more than the usual endurance, died in 1965 and at her own request had her tombstone inscribed: "Frances Perkins Wilson." It may be that in her old age she too succumbed to the cult of wifehood and wanted the world to know she had been a wife, despite having held the "masculine" job of

SECRETARY OF LABOR OF U.S.A.
1933-1945.

Lucy Stoners from the 1930s through the 1960s acquired double identities fundamentally because they had double jobs. In addition to their work, they were as a rule solely responsible for the children and running the house, a second job their husbands did not have. Edward Bernays admitted he saw little of his children, that even when he set up a few drinks for guests he was "ready for a rest." Since his wife seemed not to be exhausted, he concluded that "women must be born with a catering gift." Under the comfortable delusion that women were born with the capacity to set up drinks and wash dishes and diaper babies, most husbands guiltlessly let their wives, despite their full time jobs, do all the work at home. And most women took on the double job because they felt it was the price they had to pay to have a profession and because, as time passed, they were living in a world in which the cult of wifehood had become almost fanatic.

It was a world in which the few young women who took up professions were, unlike feminists in the twenties, eager to do their own housework and tend several babies as well. Feminism had not died out, but it was, to say the least, not making headlines. As for Lucy Stonism, it had been almost totally forgotten. As Cornelia B. Rose recalled, "I used to tell people I was a Lucy Stoner until one day I was called Miss Stone." Most young women had never heard of Lucy Stone, not to speak of an organization that had once fought for a wife's right to have a name of her own. From about the 1940s onward, young doctors and lawyers who married and chose to keep their own name professionally—and a fair number did—regarded their own name as a sort of alias, assuming that their legal name, as an instant effect of marriage, had become their husband's. Their assumption was well founded. Lucy Stoners had run into more and more obstacles, had had their right to use their own name challenged in more and more areas because the legal profession had been busy making it more and more difficult for a married woman to go by any other name than wife.

17

The Lucy Stone League was founded in 1921; Emily Post's *Etiquette* was published in 1922. The League maintained that a wife was not compelled by law to bear her husband's name; *Etiquette* decreed that "A wife always bears the name of her husband." The League thought it had convinced lawyers and judges that its position was legally correct, but it was not many years before etiquette became law.

Correct Name of Married Woman

The proliferation of Miss Wives in the 1910s had sufficiently disturbed the legal profession so that in 1919 the *Virginia Law Register* issued, as it were, the first legal bull, a pronouncement on married women's names that decreed: "The law confers upon a wife the surname of her husband." The tremendous publicity the Lucy Stone League managed to generate, the few thousand wives it influenced to break with custom so alarmed the majority of the legal profession it issued a series of rulings, annotations, case decisions, Attorney General Opinions and laws that eventually made it difficult and often impossible for a married woman to use her own name except in her profession, and not always there. Just as Lucy Stone's attempt to vote in her own name in 1879 brought about an election regulation compelling married women to vote in their husbands' names, so a few nonconformists in the 1920s brought about the legislated conformity of all women.

The legal backlash against the Lucy Stone League began in August 1924 when Comptroller General McCarl ruled that married women employed by the Federal government must sign their husbands' names to the payroll. Since the Lucy Stone League's chief argument had been that there were no laws compelling married women to use their husbands' names, McCarl's chief counter-argument was that most states had such laws already in their codes, laws that presumed "the name of the woman is changed to that of the husband on contracting the marital relation." These laws were divorce laws that gave courts the power to restore the maiden name of the wife upon divorce, McCarl's reasoning being that a married woman "must have lost her maiden name, otherwise it could not be restored." McCarl further argued that legal reference works and case law both established that a wife's legal name was her husband's. He quoted from Schouler on Domestic Relations—"Marriage at our law does not change the man's name, but it confers his surname upon the woman"—and cited seven cases in which he said that rule of law was sustained. McCarl concluded: "The law in this country that the wife takes the surname of the husband is as well settled as that the domicile of the wife merges in the domicile of the husband. A wife . . . may have an assumed name, but she has but one legal name."

A month after McCarl's ruling, Burnita Shelton Matthews, the attorney of the National Woman's Party, pointed out that most of the cases cited by McCarl involved decisions about a married woman's first name not her surname and that in no case was "the right of a married woman to retain her maiden name . . . before the court" (*Equal Rights*, September 20, 1924). In November the *University of Pennsylvania Law Review*, in an analysis of McCarl's ruling, argued that statutes permitting the court to restore a divorced woman's maiden name were merely permissive since a divorced woman could change her name without a court decree, just as any person in America and England could change his name without one, such decrees being merely a convenience, a way of making a change of name immediate and public. The *Law Review* further argued that under our law a name "is not a matter of law, but of fact," that is, a legal name is the name a person in fact uses. Women who change their name at marriage establish that name by using it; the change does not occur because any law compels it. Women do customarily assume their husbands' surnames, but custom is not law. The *Law Review* was therefore "forced to conclude that the basis of the Comptroller-General's ruling is unsound."

But these objections to McCarl's ruling had as little influence on the legal profession as the State Department's 1925 decision to let Lucy Stoners have passports in their own name had on McCarl. Just as McCarl did not rescind his ruling but strengthened it by threatening to fire any woman who did not report her marriage to her employer, so in 1925 *American Law Reports* published an Annotation on "Correct name of married woman" whose purpose was to buttress the position of the Comptroller General and like-minded "administrative officers" for whom the correct form of a married woman's name "might be of practical as well as academic importance." Needless to say, the legally correct surname of a married woman proved to be the surname of her husband.

American Law Reports, according to the Forward in its first volume (1919), was founded in order to annotate "new and difficult cases" being decided in "our highest courts." Had such a case relating to married women's names occurred in 1924? In 1923 a case germane to Lucy Stonism had occurred. A Wisconsin schoolteacher, the former Elsie Dickerhoff, had been fired because after her marriage she had continued to sign her maiden name to the payroll in violation of a schoolboard regulation that "a married teacher shall be known by her married name on all school records." And yet despite that regulation, the judge decided she ought not to have been fired, technically because the regulation did not specify when a woman had to report her marriage but probably because the judge had doubts about the validity of the regulation since in 1921 Wisconsin had passed an Equal Rights Statute (State ex rel. Thompson v. School Directors, 179 Wisconsin Reports 284). But this unusual decision that did deal with "new and difficult" problems relating to married women's names was not chosen for annotation in *American Law Reports* for 1924. What the editors decided did merit an Annotation was a 1924 Minnesota case, Brown v. Reinke, in which it was held that a summons served on Mrs Charles Wallace ought to have been in the name Harriet Wallace. But such a case was neither new nor difficult; many times before judges had had to decide whether or not a married woman could be summonsed or sued in her husband's first name. Moreover, as a vehicle for establishing that a married woman's surname had to be her husband's, Brown v. Reinke was singularly awkward since the judge made no statement at all about a married woman's surname and in fact had merely said: "In law a person's name consists of a given or Christian name and a family surname." However, the Syllabus of the case (the summary of a case's key points) went beyond the words of the judge and stated that "A married woman's name consists of her Christian name and her husband's surname, the prefix 'Mrs' being a mere title." Perhaps because of that inaccurate summary, but chiefly because cases involving married women's names occur infrequently and *American Law Reports* wanted to act quickly, Brown v. Reinke was used as the vehicle for establishing that a married woman's surname must be her husband's.

Since Brown v. Reinke was a case in which there was a decision only about a married woman's first name, *American Law Reports'* Annotation on "Correct name of married woman" had to deal with married women's names generally in order to say what it wanted about surnames. Accordingly, the Annotation listed cases from 1860 to 1924 that dealt with married women's first names, middle names and surnames, whether the title Mrs could be part of a legal name, and whether or not married women could sue or be sued in their maiden surnames.

In the section that dealt with "the correct form of the surname of a married woman," the author of the Annotation, George Van Ingen, said there was "no dispute as to the correct form . . . because as stated in [the six cases cited] the law confers on the wife the surname of her husband." In some of the cases cited judges did make such statements, but the inference was they made them in cases that involved the right of a married woman to retain her own surname. None of the cases did involve such a decision and most of them were barely relevant. Indeed, one case (Lane v. Duchac, 73 Wisconsin Reports 646) could have been and later was used by those who wanted to argue that a wife did not have to use her husband's surname, for in that case a judge told a married woman who (probably for purposes of fraud) had signed her maiden name to a mortgage that she could be sued in that name. Said the judge: "True, since her marriage she is entitled to the name of her husband, but we are aware of no law that will invalidate obligations and conveyances executed by and to her in her baptismal name, if she choose to give or take them in that form." Another case cited in this section was, like Brown v. Reinke, a decision about a married woman's first name, whether she should have been named in a legal document as Mrs William Rogers or Mrs Lucy Rogers (Uihlein v. Gladieux, 74 Ohio State Reports 232). Two other cases involved divorce: in one a judge told a divorced woman she had the right to resume the use of her own name by common law (Rich v. Mayer, 26 New York State Reports 107), and in the other a judge ordered a divorced woman to stop using her ex-husband's name (Blanc v. Blanc, 21 New York Miscellaneous Reports 268).

Van Ingen felt he could cite such cases because a judge either implied that the ceremony of marriage was the legal act that changed a woman's name or because a judge, as in the Ohio first name case, actually stated that "At marriage the wife takes the husband's surname." In the two remaining cases cited in this section, judges made very strong statements to the same effect: in Freeman v. Hawkins (77 Texas Reports 498) a judge decided a woman could not be sued in the name under which she had bought property because she had later married, by which act "the law conferred on her the surname of her husband"; and in Chapman v. Phoenix National Bank (85 New York Reports 437) the judge said that "a woman upon marriage takes her husband's surname. That becomes her legal name . . . Her maiden surname is absolutely lost."

Chapman v. Phoenix National Bank, as we have previously seen, had nothing whatsoever to do with a married woman who was using her maiden name, but dealt with Verina S. Chapman's attempt to recover shares of stock that had been confiscated in the Civil War. Mrs Chapman's name was not at issue until the judge incidentally remarked that he felt the confiscation notice had been in a misnomer since it was in Mrs Chapman's maiden name (notwithstanding that she had bought the stocks when she was single and had not informed the bank of her change of name). The case was decided in Mrs Chapman's favor on grounds other than misnomer, but whatever the relevancy of the misnomer issue, the judge's statement that a married woman's legal name was her husband's was only that, a statement, not a judicial decision on married women's surnames. It was what in law is called a judicial dictum, a pronouncement by a judge on a point of law other than the one being decided in the case. Such pronouncements, or dicta, are off the cuff opinions of what a judge thinks the law is; they are not decisions derived from an examination of laws and precedents. In Chapman v. Phoenix National Bank and in the other cases cited in the Annotation there was no examination of what the law actually was in regard to names, surnames or married women's surnames. The cases were cited either because they contained a judge's assertion or assumption that a married woman's surname was her husband's or merely because the woman in the case used her husband's surname, as they all did. The right of a married woman not to use her husband's surname was never at issue.

American Law Reports' Annotation on "Correct name of married woman," so far as it concerned surnames, was based entirely on judicial dicta. It did not establish that "the law confers on the wife the surname of her husband" unless one believes a judge's mere statement has the same force as a statute. Nevertheless, the Annotation had a powerful influence, for it gave the legal profession an authority to cite. "35 American Law Reports 417" was cited again and again in State codes, State Digests, case decisions, Attorney General Opinions and legal encyclopedias as offering proof that a married woman's surname had to be her husband's. In addition, the Annotation contained a stockpile of precedents lawyers could draw on, and just as theologians used to cite I Corinthians 11, 3 to prove husbands had to be the heads of households, so lawyers would cite Freeman v. Hawkins 77 Texas 498 or Chapman v. Phoenix 85 New York 437 to prove that according to the Bible of the Law a married woman's legal surname had to be her husband's.

In 1926, a year after *American Law Reports'* Annotation, a Massachusetts judge cited the case of Chapman v. Phoenix National Bank after asserting that "as matter of law" a woman's surname was changed to her husband's when she married (Bacon v. Boston Elevated Railway, 256 Massachusetts Reports 30). The history of the case suggests that the judge felt he was laying down the law to a would-be Lucy Stoner. What had happened was that in 1923 Alice Bacon bought a car and registered it under the name Alice Willard, her maiden name. Why she did was not explained, for after her marriage in 1921 she apparently did change her name to her husband's and used it for all purposes, except in 1923 when she bought a car. However, her husband did name her as "Mrs A. W. Willard-Bacon" in a report he filed with the highway commissioner after the automobile was involved in an accident with a streetcar. Perhaps Alice had read about the Lucy Stone League and decided she wanted her own name back, or at least a hyphenated surname. But whatever her reason for registering her car under her maiden name, she and her husband were to pay dearly. For although it was determined that no fraud was intended since Alice gave her correct address and was easily identified, and although the motorman, not Alice, had been negligent, she and her husband were not allowed to sue for injuries they received because the judge decided the car was illegally registered since the registration was in Alice's maiden name. In Massachusetts the law did require a person to register his automobile in the name he was commonly known by, but if Alice had been commonly known by the name Willard, if she had never used any other name but Willard, it is doubtful the judge would have decided in her favor, for he categorically declared: "As matter of law after her marriage in 1921 her legal name was Alice W. Bacon. See G. L. c. 208, 23. *Chapman* v. *Phoenix National Bank of New York*, 85 N. Y. 437, 449."

We know that the statement about married women's surnames in the Chapman case was a mere dictum, but what was Chapter 208, section 23 of the General Laws of Massachusetts? Had Massachusetts passed a law that required wives to take their husband's surname? The law referred to reads: "The court granting a divorce to a woman may allow her to resume her maiden name or that of a former husband." The Massachusetts judge was following the lead of Comptroller General McCarl who in his 1924 ruling had held that such laws presumed that a woman upon marriage lost her own name and acquired her husband's. As a result of this case, the following note was added to Chapter 208, section 23 of the General Laws of Massachusetts:

> Legal name of married woman—In view of this section, as matter of law, after her marriage, a married woman's legal name becomes that of her husband.

Massachusetts thus became the first state then in the Union to put in its code a statement that a woman's legal name after marriage was her husband's.

Bacon v. Boston Elevated Railway was to have a wide ranging effect. In 1927 *American Law Reports* reprinted the case with an Annotation on names and the registration of automobiles. After citing its own 1925 Annotation on "Correct name of married woman," the 1927 Annotation stated that in Massachusetts "registration in the maiden name of the owner was held illegal." As a result of the publicity the case received because of the Annotation, many other states were also to decide that a married woman could neither register her automobile nor have a driver's license except in her husband's name.

By 1927 the law was well on its way towards establishing that a married woman's legal name was her husband's. McCarl's 1924 ruling, the 1925 Annotation on "Correct name of married woman," the 1926 Massachusetts case, the 1927 Annotation on names and the registration of automobiles were the first steps in the process. It is true that in 1925 the Passport Division permitted married women to get passports in their own name and that in 1926 Federal Judge Thacher in the case of Maria Jeritza maintained that a married woman's name did not have to be her husband's. It is also true that Attorney General Opinions in various states had acknowledged and for a while continued to acknowledge that a married woman had the right to use her own name. But simple reliance on the common law right of any person to use the name of his choice, plain recognition that there were no statutes compelling a married woman to use her husband's name almost disappeared. Instead, divorce laws, automobile registration laws and voting registration laws were interpreted as marriage laws mandating a name change, judicial decisions about married women's first names were cited as decisions about their surnames, and dicta were piled on dicta as judges and other officials, confronted by a woman who wanted to use her own name, followed the lead of the Massachusetts judge in 1926 and peremptorily and autocratically told her what her name was.

Redefining Legal Name

In New York in 1934 a Federal judge told a woman that if she wished to become an American citizen, her naturalization "certificate must issue in the surname of her husband." Anna Kayaloff, a professional musician, had wanted her naturalization certificate to be in the same name as her musicians' union card, her own name, but Judge Knox told her that "Under the law of New York, as pronounced in Chapman v. Phoenix National Bank, a woman at her marriage, takes the surname of her husband. 'That,' it was there said, 'becomes her legal name . . . Her maiden surname is absolutely lost, and she ceases to be known thereby.' " That doctrine, he asserted, "in my opinion, is sound policy and should be upheld." But the judge was not really telling Kayaloff her own surname was absolutely lost; he had no objection to her continuing to use her own name professionally and told her so; rather, he was informing her there was a difference between the name a married woman might be commonly known by and her legal name, that although everyone might know her as Kayaloff, her legal name nevertheless was Mersliakoff, her husband's name (In re Kayaloff, 9 Federal Supplement 176).

Four years later, in 1938, the Pennsylvania Board of Law Examiners told a lawyer her legal name was her husband's name. Marjorie Hanson, despite her marriage, had continued to practice law in that name (although she did use her husband's name socially). But when she asked the Board of Law Examiners to issue her a certificate recommending admission to the Supreme Court, it was issued in the name "Marjorie Hanson, now Marjorie Matson." Hanson objected, but the Board would not change its mind, so she appealed their decision on the grounds that the denial was "a deprivation of property without due process of law and a denial of the equal protection of the law." Hanson lost; the Appeals Court upheld the Board of Law Examiners, but solely on the grounds that the Board had the right "to formulate such rules as it sees fit . . . to admit persons to practice" (Hanson's Appeal, 330 Pennsylvania State Reports 390). The Appeals Court felt the Board had the right to formulate a rule requiring married women to use their husband's name even though the Court recognized that "the common law rule that a married woman may use her maiden name for many purposes" obtained in Pennsylvania and even though that same year a Pennsylvania court decided a divorced woman could reassume her maiden name without a judge's permission because of every person's common law right to use the name he wished (Appeal of Egerter, 52 York 40). In denying Marjorie Hanson the right to use the name of her choice, the Appeals Court and the Board of Law Examiners not only abrogated common law, they forgot precedent. In 1927 the Pennsylvania Supreme Court had granted the petition of Ella Graubart to be admitted to the bar in her own name. Feminists then thought Pennsylvania women lawyers would henceforth have the right to practice law in their own name despite marriage, but a decade later that right apparently no longer existed.

In 1938, the same year Marjorie Hanson unsuccessfully tried to continue the practice of law in her own name, Doris Carlton, an employee of the Social Security Board in Washington DC was struggling with the United States Comptroller General to get her own name accepted where she worked. Doris Carlton, unlike Marjorie Hanson who used her husband's name socially, was a thorough Lucy Stoner. Ever since her marriage on August 10, 1937 she had used her own name for all purposes, graduating from law school as Doris Carlton, paying premiums on life and fire insurance and maintaining checking and savings accounts as Doris Carlton and signing that name on her daughter's baptismal records. But when she was hired by the Social Security Board, Doris Carlton would not do. Because of the 1924 ruling of Comptroller General McCarl that all married women employees of the Federal government had to sign their husband's surname to the payroll, her pay checks were drawn in her husband's name. Carlton objected and in November 1938 wrote a memorandum describing at length her consistent use of her own name for all purposes and requesting she be paid in the only name she had ever used. In March 1939 her request was refused; the next month she asked for reconsideration of the question or that a special ruling be made in her case. In August Comptroller General Brown issued his decision (A-84336). Although he did agree to make an exception in Doris Carlton's case and permit Carlton and any other married woman to be paid in her own name if her administrative officer did not object, Comptroller General Brown did not concede that Doris Carlton was Doris Carlton's legal name. He regarded it as an assumed name. He maintained that her legal name, despite the fact she never used it, was her husband's name: "A woman upon her marriage legally acquires the surname of her husband regardless of whether she does or does not elect to use it."

Comptroller General Brown, in permitting Doris Carlton to be paid in her assumed name, was unusually lenient. Judge Knox had not permitted Anna Kayaloff to be naturalized except in the name he said she had legally acquired at marriage. The Pennsylvania Board of Law Examiners had not permitted Marjorie Hanson to practice before the Supreme Court except in the name the Board said she had legally acquired at marriage. And in 1945 an Illinois judge ruled that a married woman could not vote except in the name he said she had legally acquired at marriage.

In February 1944 Antonia E. Rago, an attorney who had been practicing law in Chicago since 1938, married William C. MacFarland and with his full approval continued the practice of law under her own name. Shortly thereafter, the Chicago Board of Election Commissioners, having learned of Rago's marriage, informed her that in order to continue to be a legally registered voter she must reregister under the name of her husband. The Board maintained that unless she did so she would be violating an election law that read: "Any registered voter who changes his or her name by marriage or otherwise, shall be required to register anew."

Rago protested, contending that that law did not apply in her case because she had not changed her name when she married. She also pointed out that since her birth she had been known in her community as Antonia E. Rago, that she had practiced law and been active in politics in that name, for which reason, if she were not permitted to vote in the only name she had ever been known by, her professional reputation would suffer substantial damage. In April 1944 a Superior Court Judge agreed with her and ordered the Election

Board to restore her name to the registration files and to cease and desist from demanding she register anew in her husband's name. The Election Board appealed that decision and in November 1945 it was overturned by the Appellate Court of Illinois. "We hold that her name was changed by marriage," said Presiding Judge Friend. "By the fact of marriage alone a woman changes her name so that her maiden name is lost and her new name consists of her own given name and her husband's surname." Judge Friend asserted that the Illinois election law "expressly recognizes a change of name by marriage," for which reason Rago could not maintain she did not have to reregister because her name was unchanged, for whether she wished to or not, her name as a matter of law had been changed when she married (People ex rel. Rago v. Lipsky, 327 Illinois Appellate 63).

In every case that dealt with men's names a legal name was defined as the name by which a person could be identified, the name by which he was commonly known in his community. But women, as the Supreme Court had decided again and again, were not persons in the same sense men were. It is therefore not surprising that "legal name" as it applied to married women acquired a different meaning. It came to be defined not as the name the woman was commonly known by but as her own first name and her husband's surname.

During the thirties and forties there continued to be women who wanted to keep their own name after marriage, women, moreover, who were willing to fight for that right. But judges and other officials looked upon them much as a Rabbi of an eastern European shtetl might have regarded a wife dragged before him by an outraged husband because she refused to shave off her hair and wear a wig. The wife might have argued she had as much right as her husband to keep her hair after marriage, but the Rabbi would have found a passage in the Talmud that, properly interpreted, contained a commandment from God that wives must shave off their hair. So during this period legal practitioners, confronted by an odd wife who did not want to give up her name, consulted their law books and discovered laws that, properly interpreted, required wives to give up their names and assume their husbands'.

Redefining Common Law

During the 1920s and into the early 1930s, when an attorney general was asked if a married woman could use her maiden name for various purposes, his answer almost always was Yes and was based on the common law view of names. Said the Attorney General of Washington in a 1928 Opinion: "In the matter of the choice of a name for a person, it is fundamental law that any person may use any name he sees fit . . . The custom of persons taking names from their male parent is merely a custom and is not binding upon anyone, and the same may be said of the custom of a woman taking her husband's name." But the common law was in conflict with the new view that the legal name of a married woman had to be her husband's, which at first confused attorneys general, who felt they had to reconcile the two views.

The Michigan Attorney General was asked in 1930 if a probation officer who married could continue to hold office in her maiden name, and in a five page Opinion he managed to keep one foot in the common law and the other in the new view that a married woman's legal surname must be her husband's. He at first set forth the new view, quoting from the *Corpus Juris* (a compendium of case decisions) that "At marriage the wife takes the husband's surname," and citing old and new cases to support that position. He then used McCarl's 1924 argument that although his state had no "statute compelling a woman to take the name of the husband at the time of marriage, nevertheless our statute indirectly recognizes this fact when it provides that in the divorce her maiden name may be restored to her." So far, he held to the new view that a married woman's legal surname must be her husband's. But he could not forget that various cases had held that a married woman might sue and be sued in her maiden name, which implied that the probation officer should be able to hold office in her maiden name. But could her maiden name be her legal name if marriage had given her her husband's name? It could become her legal name, he reasoned, for common law gave a person the right to change his name, that name becoming his legal one when he was generally known by it. The Attorney General therefore decided that since "a married woman may adopt any name she chooses" and "under her adopted name enter into contracts," the probation officer might hold office in her maiden name.

The argument that a woman's name was legally changed to her husband's when she married but that common law gave her the right to adopt her own name again was made by another Michigan Attorney General in 1935. He had been asked by Judge Lila M. Neuenfelt, who had recently married and not taken her husband's name, if she might run for re-election in her maiden name. He decided she might because "there is no law which forbids a woman from continuing to use her maiden name in all business dealings." But he felt he must add, "Assuming, however, that by marriage a woman's name is changed, there is nothing in our law which forbids her from changing her name to her maiden name," a name change he felt did not have to be affirmed by court order.

But the trouble with that position was it gave married women the freedom to use their own names and the whole point of changing the definition of legal name was to take that freedom away from them. That was why the Oregon Attorney General in 1940 after deciding a married woman could not be issued a real estate license except in her husband's name, added that she could not work under an assumed name, thus preventing her from adopting her own name under common law. But even to mention common law was awkward, since common law meant the freedom to choose one's name. It therefore behooved the legal profession to redefine common law when married women were spoken of and make it mean what the good Lord must have intended it to.

Just as legal name stopped meaning the name one was generally known by, so common law stopped meaning the right to use the name of one's choice, a redefinition made possible by the fortunate pronouncement of Judge Earl in an 1881 case: "For several centuries, by the common law among all English-speaking people, a woman, upon her marriage, takes her husband's surname. That becomes her legal name." After Chapman v. Phoenix was brought to the attention of the legal profession in *American Law Reports'* 1925 Annotation, Judge Earl's definition of common law was cited again and again by judges and other officials who were eager to believe that although the common law gave a man the right to adopt any name he desired, the common law compelled a woman to take her husband's surname. When Judge Friend in 1945 denied Antonia Rago the right to vote in her own name, he quoted Judge Earl on common law and later again referred to "the long-established custom, policy and rule of the common law among English speaking peoples whereby a woman's name is changed by marriage and her husband's surname becomes as a matter of law her surname." Similarly, when in 1952 the Oregon Attorney General decided a married woman could not be issued a license to conduct a collection agency in her maiden name, he not only quoted Judge Earl on common law but also Judge Friend. And both the Oregon Attorney General and Judge Friend added that since their state was under the common law of England, married women must abide by common law and take their husband's surname. Thus was the common law twisted out of its original meaning; instead of giving women the freedom to take their husbands' names, it became a legal compulsion to do so.

Neither Judge Friend nor any other judge or attorney who held that English common law compelled a wife to change her name to her husband's had consulted English law books. Their authority was Judge Earl, who had himself not bothered to check English law. If judges had consulted even the most basic reference works, they would have found stated without ambiguity that under the common law a wife was free not to adopt her husband's surname. For example, in Halsbury's *Laws of England* it was recognized that when a woman changed her name to her husband's, she acquired "a new name by repute," that is, in the same way any person changed his name by common law. "The change of name is in fact, rather than in law, a consequence of the marriage . . . On her second marriage there is nothing in point of law to prevent her from retaining her first husband's name." Indeed, in 1945, the same year Judge Friend asserted that under English common law a woman's surname at marriage was "as a matter of law" changed to her husband's, a judge in England was saying, "There is, so far as I know, nothing to compel a married woman to use her husband's surname, so that the wife of Mr Robinson may, speaking generally, go by the name of Mrs Smith if she choose to do so" (In re Fry, 1 Chancery Division 348).

American judges and attorneys were, perhaps, so anxious to suppress non-conformist wives they became paralyzed, physically incapable of opening Halsbury's *Laws of England* lest they find that the facts of English common law did not conform to their desires. At any rate, their ignorance was for many years canonized in American case decisions, Attorney General Opinions and legal reference works.

The Great Weight of Legal and Judicial Precedent

When Judge Friend forbade Antonia Rago from voting in her own name, he was able to do so not only by redefining legal name and common law but by twisting an Illinois voter registration law into a law mandating a name change for women who married. Just as Comptroller General McCarl in 1924 reasoned that laws giving judges the power to restore the maiden name of a wife upon divorce could be construed as laws requiring women to change their names, so Judge Friend in 1945 reasoned that Illinois' election law that required "Any registered voter who changes his or her name by marriage or otherwise . . . to register anew" could be construed as a law requiring women to adopt their husband's names when they married.

Judge Friend argued that the Illinois legislature included the word marriage in the law because it recognized a compulsory name change when women married and wanted to make sure married women voted in their only legal name. The Illinois election law was passed in 1936, and it may be that the memory of the Lucy Stone League was still so vivid the legislature used a voter reregistration law as a means of suppressing them. But if that were the intention of the legislature, it would have made more sense to pass a marriage law that flatly stated women must adopt their husbands' surnames when they marry. Illinois did not, nor did any other state. More likely, the Illinois legislature and the legislatures of the many states that passed similar laws included the word marriage not to mandate custom but in recognition of the fact that virtually all women did change their name at marriage. 99.99 percent of wives did not have to be ordered to take their husbands' names; they were eager to do so. The trouble was many of them did not bother to reregister to vote in their changed name; the legislatures, therefore, included the word marriage in the laws to force them to do so (presumably to insure that a woman did not vote twice—in both her maiden and married name). If the legislatures had intended these laws to serve as laws compelling women to adopt their husbands' names, they would have worded them differently, for it is perfectly possible to read them as requiring a woman to reregister to vote only if she in fact has changed her name.

On the other hand, the legislatures of a few states did pass reregistration laws that indeed seemed to mandate custom. Maryland, Maine, South Dakota and a few other states passed laws that required the county clerk to report the names of women issued marriage licenses to the registrar of voters, who cancelled their registration and informed them that in order to vote they must reregister in their husband's name. Perhaps these watchdog laws were not meant to legislate custom, but that was their effect. For when a newly married woman received a notice from her Election Board that her registration had been cancelled and that if she wished to vote she must reregister in her husband's name, such a woman would have no doubt that marriage had automatically and as a matter of law changed her name.

Although it is also possible to read these watchdog laws as requiring a woman to reregister only if she has changed her name, they were not thus read. And as a result of the 1945 Illinois decision, on the few occasions when a state had to deal with a nominal nonconformist, it could interpret its voter reregistration law as a marriage law mandating a name change. When the Oregon Attorney General in 1952 refused to permit a married woman to get a business license in her maiden name, he, after quoting at length from the Illinois case, said that Oregon's reregistration law furnished "substantial proof that the legislature regarded marriage as changing a wife's name." When the Attorney General of Nevada in 1966 decided a married woman could not run for office in her maiden name, he too argued that since Nevada's voter reregistration law specifically mentioned marriage, it mandated a name change: "It must be presumed that the Legislature had some motive and purpose in enacting the statute. The only logical purpose would be to have the married person reregister under the new name or changed surname (that of her husband)."

A judge or attorney general not only could use his state's divorce law and voter reregistration law as virtual marriage laws, he could similarly use an automobile registration law. Just as the 1945 Illinois case was largely responsible for the conversion of voter reregistration laws into marriage laws, so the 1926 Massachusetts case previously discussed converted automobile registration laws into laws compelling wives to use their husbands' surnames. Bacon v. Boston Elevated Railway had been reprinted in the 1927 *American Law Reports* with an Annotation on names and the registration of automobiles, where it was stated that in Massachusetts "registration in the maiden name of the owner was held illegal." That decision guided other states to follow suit. For example, the Idaho code (R 7-801) specifically stated that an automobile registered in the maiden name of a married woman "is not a compliance with the statute requiring it to be registered in the name of the owner. Bacon v. Boston Elevated R. Co. 256 Mass. 30." Or when the Connecticut Attorney General in 1934 informed the Commissioner of Motor Vehicles that proper identification required "registration of motor vehicles owned by a married woman to be applied for and issued in her married name," he too cited the Massachusetts case. By extension, any law that said a driver's license must be in "the owner's name" or not in "a false or fictitious name" could be and was interpreted as requiring a married woman to have a driver's license in her husband's name.

Other laws made to serve as laws mandating a name change for married women were change of name laws. Kentucky, Vermont and Iowa had long had change of name laws that barred a married woman from changing her name, and such laws were interpreted as presuming that a married woman's legal name had to be the same as her husband's. When in 1948 Michigan added to its change of name law the provision that a judge in the order changing the name of the husband "shall include the name of the wife," the law was not interpreted as a convenience for the average wife who wants to have the same surname as her husband but as a law recognizing that a wife may not have a surname different from her husband's.

During this period, several states passed laws that required female notaries public or office holders to notify their state agency of their change of name by marriage. That these laws were passed with the express intention of compelling female office holders to use their husband's name we saw in Chapter Fifteen when discussing the 1931 Massachusetts law that was passed to suppress a Lucy Stoner in the Massachusetts legislature. But such laws did more than force a particular female office holder to use her husband's name; they could also be cited as yet another law that recognized women were legally compelled to change their name at marriage.

Between 1924 and 1957 the states of Minnesota, Florida, Alabama and Nebraska managed to include in their State Digests (summaries of a state's important cases) actual statements that a married woman's legal surname was her husband's. "A married woman's name consists of her Christian name and her husband's surname," stated the Minnesota Digest. "The wife takes the husband's surname at marriage, but otherwise her name is not changed," declared the Florida Digest. "In a strict sense, a married woman's name consists of her own Christian name and her husband's surname," asserted the Alabama Digest. "A married woman's name consists, in law, of her own Christian name and her husband's surname, marriage conferring on her the surname of her husband," maintained the Nebraska Digest.

Reading these summaries, lawyers as well as laymen would assume the judges had decided a married woman's surname must be her husband's. But when one reads the cases themselves one finds the judges were making decisions only about married women's first names. In the 1924 Minnesota case, Brown v. Reinke (the excuse for *American Law Reports'* Annotation on married women's names), a judge decided Mrs Charles Wallace ought to have been sued as Harriet Wallace. In the 1930 Florida case, Carlton v. Phelan, a judge decided Mrs Francis K. Phelan Sr ought to have been named as Katherine E. Phelan. In the 1937 Alabama case, Roberts v. Grayson, a judge had to decide whether or not a claim against the estate of a Mrs J. C. Jones was valid, even though she ought to have been named as Hattie W. Jones. In the 1957 Nebraska case, Kelle v. Crab Orchard Rural Fire Protection District, a judge decided married women who signed a petition for the formation of a rural fire protection district ought to sign their own Christian name and not their husband's, that is, that they should sign Mary Jones not Mrs John Jones. In all these cases judges were telling women they must use their own, not their husband's first name. They did not decide whether or not a woman had to use her husband's surname, for all the women did; their surnames were never at issue. Whatever the judges did say about married women's surnames was dicta, but by summarizing these decisions as if they had also been decisions about surnames, Alabama, Florida, Minnesota and Nebraska were able to maintain that under the law in their state a married woman was obliged to adopt her husband's surname.

In the Louisiana State Digest one finds something different:

> Louisiana 1931. In law, widow retained maiden name and bore husband's name as matter of custom. Succession of Kniepp, 172 La. 411.

In Succession of Kniepp a judge had to decide whether a widow's signing a marriage license in her maiden name was proof she had not been married to her first husband. The judge held it was not proof because under Louisiana law a married woman's legal name continued to be her maiden name and she bore her husband's name only as a matter of custom. For Louisiana was under civil law, and according to *West's Louisiana Statutes Annotated*, "Under the civil law, a woman does not lose her patronymic name through marriage; and her legal name never varies with a change of her marital status. Socially, a wife is known by the name of her husband, but under the civil law she never acquires his name." Since Louisiana was under civil law, one would think the state could never require married women to use their husbands' names for any legal purpose. But the fact that in 1931 a widow's use of her maiden name was regarded as illegal and that its legality had to be determined in court reveals the times were changing; and Louisiana was in the process of forgetting its own civil law. Subsequently, the state not only passed an election law requiring married women to reregister to vote in their husband's name, it also passed a watchdog law to enforce it.

The times so changed that in 1963 a Supreme Court judge believed that in Louisiana a married woman's surname had to be her husband's. In the case of Wilty v. Jefferson Parish Democratic Executive Committee the question of the correct first name of a married woman once more came before the courts. Vernon J. Wilty Jr, the Assessor of the Parish of Jefferson, petitioned the court to prevent his wife (from whom he was separated) from running against him for Assessor under the name Mrs Vernon J. Wilty Jr. Wilty contended that his wife's first name was in law her own first name, not Vernon, and Justice Hamlin agreed with him. But in granting Wilty's petition, the judge revealed his ignorance of Louisiana civil law. Having apparently consulted neither the Annotated Statutes of Louisiana nor the Louisiana Digest, he said, "There is no definite law or decision in Louisiana as to what is the legal name of a married woman," and that therefore he would follow the common law as stated in the *Corpus Juris Secundum* (a compendium of American case decisions) and quoted their statement that a married woman's name consists of her own Christian name and her husband's surname. However, one judge who sat on the case was not ignorant. Justice Sanders in a concurring opinion pointed out Justice Hamlin's error: "The common law fiction of merger between husband and wife, from which a change of the wife's legal name arises, has never obtained in Louisiana. Rather, this state has followed the civil law doctrine. After marriage, the legal name of a woman continues to be her maiden name, or patronym. The surname of the husband is used only as a matter of custom to indicate the marital status of the wife."

Yet notwithstanding Justice Sanders' correction, in the Syllabus of the case the decision of the court in regard to married women's names reads: "Designation or appellation of married woman should be that of her Christian name and her husband's surname . . ." Justice Sanders might as well have not bothered to point out Justice Hamlin's error. Every Louisiana woman who married continued to receive a notice from her Parish Registrar informing her that her voter registration had been cancelled and that if she wished to vote she must reregister in her husband's name. For all practical purposes Louisiana abrogated its own civil law.

At the same time Louisiana was abrogating its civil law and other states were redefining legal name and common law and twisting voter and automobile registration laws into marriage laws and misciting cases in their State Digests, the State Department was in effect abrogating the 1925 regulation that permitted married women to get passports in their own name. That regulation stayed on the books and on March 31, 1938 was reaffirmed by Executive Order 7856 as Part V (20) of the United States Passport Regulations and read: "A married woman desiring a passport issued in her maiden name must submit with her application the affidavits of two or more persons to the effect that she used her maiden name exclusively, has used it exclusively for a stated period of time, and is known by such name in the community in which she resides." But despite Part V (20), clerks in the various Passport Offices confidently asserted it was against regulations for a married woman to have a passport in her maiden name, and a woman had to make a fuss or know about the regulation before she could get a passport in her own name, and sometimes not even then. Jane Grant in 1948 could not get one from the New York office and had to go to Washington DC. She there so belabored the head of the passport division that henceforth clerks at the New York office "remembered" the regulation when confronted by a Lucy Stoner, but in other offices clerks continued to act as if Part V (20) did not exist. And in August 1966 by Executive Order 11295 the authority for making passport regulations was transferred to the Secretary of State, who in October of 1966 issued new regulations that omitted Part V (20). That Executive Order had a savings clause providing that all previous rules and regulations were to remain in force until revoked, and Part V (20) was apparently not revoked. But the Passport Office acted as if it had been. The Department's official position, as stated in a 1971 letter to a married woman who had requested a passport in her own name, was that "passports are issued in the legal name of the applicants. The legal name of a married woman is her husband's surname. According to the weight of federal and state legal and judicial precedent the wife at marriage loses her maiden name and assumes her husband's surname."

The great weight of legal and judicial precedent that had accumulated since the mid 1920s can be seen by comparing the *Corpus Juris* (a many-volumed compendium of American case decisions) with its second edition, the *Corpus Juris Secundum*. In the *Corpus Juris* married women's surnames were discussed in volume 30 (published 1923) in the section Husband and Wife and consisted of one sentence supported by three case citations. In the *Corpus Juris Secundum* married women's names were discussed in volume 65 (published 1966) in a separate section on "Name of Married Woman" that was three paragraphs long and supported by three columns of citations.

The *Corpus Juris Secundum*'s view of married women's surnames was that of Judge Earl in Chapman v. Phoenix National Bank, whose 1881 pronouncement was in part literally restated at the head of the section "Name of Married Woman":

> At marriage the wife takes the husband's surname and the surname of the husband, so taken at marriage, becomes her legal name. Her maiden surname is absolutely lost, and she ceases to be known thereby.

The section included many of the cases cited in *American Law Reports'* 1925 Annotation with the addition of new cases, among them the 1945 Illinois decision that a married woman must reregister to vote in her husband's name, a case that was cited three times. Strangely enough, the 1963 Louisiana case that decided Mrs Vernon J. Wilty should run for office under her own first name was given great prominence, being cited at the head of the section as upholding the position that a married woman's legal surname was her husband's and being cited nine additional times in the case notes. In no place was it pointed out that in the case itself it had been noted that Louisiana was under civil law, which meant that the legal name of a wife continued to be her maiden name. In addition, the 1931 Louisiana case, Succession of Kniepp, was cited as giving only widows the right to use their maiden name, whereas in the actual case the judge was speaking of all married women.

One of the stated purposes of the *Corpus Juris Secundum*, according to the Preface in the first edition, was to report "conflicting and inconsistent decisions." But the fact that no mention was made of the inconsistency in Louisiana law would make one suspect that cases might not have been cited that were in conflict with the position that a wife's legal name had to be her husband's. And in fact two such cases had occurred.

Ohio, like many other states, had passed a law requiring those who changed their names "by marriage or otherwise" to reregister to vote. Ohio had in addition passed a watchdog law, so that the names of women who married were filed with the election board, which notified them their registration had been cancelled and they must reregister in their changed name in order to be eligible to vote. In 1941 Gertrude A. Bucher, who had been practicing law since 1933, decided to run for the office of City Commissioner of Dayton, Ohio and duly filed her petition to have her name placed on the primary ballot with the Board of Elections. Her petition, however, was refused on the grounds that since her marriage to Charles L. Marshall in February of that year she had not reregistered to vote in her new name. Gertrude Bucher, as Antonia Rago was to do four years later, contended she did not have to reregister because she had not changed her name. She said that before her marriage she and her husband-to-be had agreed she would retain her family name for all purposes, the name in which she practiced law and was known in her community. On August 5, 1941 Judge Mills of the Court of Common Pleas in Montgomery County decided in her favor.

In a lengthy opinion (almost ten pages), much of it concerned with the origin of surnames and the long established common law right to change one's name at will, Judge Mills pointed out, first, "that there is nothing in the General Code of Ohio that says when a marriage contract is entered into . . . that the wife should acquire at the time of marriage, the husband's name"; second, that when a wife changes her name to her husband's she is exerting her common law right to change her name since she is not legally obliged to do so; third, that marriage is a civil contract, which means a husband and wife have every right to contract between themselves that the wife should continue to bear her own name, and that such a contract (unless it was for a fraudulent purpose) is not "against public morals, or against public policy." Judge Mills noted that Gertrude Bucher was among many professional women who during the past half century had entered public life and made names for themselves, and he specifically mentioned Frances Perkins. Since women had been given the right to vote, to sit on juries and could "exercise any and every right that the opposite sex are given under the law," women had the same rights in regard to their names as men did.

As a result of this case, the General Code of Ohio was amended; the following case note was appended to the reregistration law:

> Where a woman does not change her name at the time of marriage and is otherwise legally registered, it is not necessary for her to reregister under the provisions of this section: State ex rel. Bucher v. Brower 21 00 208 (CP)

Twenty years later, in 1961, there was a similar case, also in Ohio. An attorney, Blanche Krupansky, wanted to run for Judge of the Municipal Court, but the Board of Elections refused to print her name on the ballot on the grounds that her legal surname was Vargo, the surname of her husband, in which name, said the Board, she had also failed to reregister to vote. Krupansky pointed out that the 1941 case had established that she need not reregister to vote if marriage had not changed her name, that she and Frank W. Vargo had entered into a written contract before their marriage in which they had agreed she would continue to use her own name after marriage, that she had informed the Board of Elections both before and after her marriage she was not changing her name and a note to that effect had been put on her registration card, and finally, that since her marriage she had continued to use the name Blanche Krupansky for all purposes.

Blanche Krupansky, like Gertrude Bucher, won her case, two judges in the Ohio Appeals Court agreeing she had every right to continue using her own name after marriage. Judge Kovachy again pointed out that "It is only *by custom*, in English speaking countries, that a woman, upon marriage adopts the surname of her husband," that "Ohio follows this custom but there exists no law compelling it," and that the purpose of a name is to identify a person, for which reason, since "Blanche Krupansky can be identified by no name other than that of Blanche Krupansky" that is her name. Judge Skeel added that although some might argue it was a matter of "public policy" for a woman to be bound by the custom of taking the husband's surname even though there was no statute requiring it, "it should be noted that the trend against the loss of the identity of a woman by marriage has received common acceptance" (State ex rel. Krupa v. Green, 19 Ohio Opinions [2d] 341).

It is extraordinary that these Ohio cases, heard in higher courts and printed in State Reports, were not cited in the annual Pocket Parts of the *Corpus Juris* or in the *Corpus Juris Secundum*. George Balluff, the Managing Editor in 1973, thought their omission was a simple oversight, but the cases were in fact known to previous editors, for they were cited under Elections section 48 in volume 29, published in 1965, a year before the volume that contained the section on married women's names. Moreover, the section on women's names had many cross-references to motor vehicle laws, the serving of processes, divorce and even to Elections section 113b, but there was no cross-reference to Elections section 48. The two Ohio cases were also not cited in *American Jurisprudence* nor in the various updatings of *American Law Reports*' 1925 Annotation on "Correct name of married woman."

The omission of the Ohio cases from legal reference works meant that decisions upholding a married woman's right to use her own name for all purposes remained unknown. If, during the forties, fifties and sixties, a lawyer had been consulted by a woman who wanted to keep her own name after marriage, he most likely would have turned to the *Corpus Juris Secundum* to get a quick overview of what the law was in regard to married women's names. The *Corpus Juris Secundum* is no final authority and in fact has a reputation for being incomplete, but in an area of law considered to be of minor importance its authority would generally have been regarded as sufficient. Since, moreover, neither *American Jurisprudence* nor *American Law Reports* cited the Ohio cases, 9,999 lawyers out of 10,000 would have told a would-be Lucy Stoner that "in the United States, the change in a woman's name upon marriage . . . appears to be generally required by law," that "in those instances where for some reason or another married women have expressed a desire" to use their own name "the courts have uniformly rejected the effort." That was the conclusion of Leo Kanowitz when he researched married women's names for his textbook on *Women and the Law* (1969). Kanowitz could not have known about the Ohio cases unless he had undertaken the task of checking the Digests or Codes or Reports of the fifty states and thus chanced upon them. Antonia E. Rago, the Chicago lawyer who in 1945 was barred from voting in her own name, obviously did not know about the 1941 Ohio case, for if she had she would have quoted from it at length since her situation and that of Gertrude Bucher were almost identical. If she had cited it, it would have been far more difficult for Judge Friend to have decided against her, and the history of the law in its treatment of married women's names might have been far less repressive.

It is hard to believe the Ohio cases were not cited in the *Corpus Juris Secundum* and other legal reference works because of a simple oversight. More likely, their omission was deliberate, an attempt to keep unknown cases that were in conflict with the position of the legal establishment. At any rate, the suppression of these cases was in line with the tendency of the law since the mid 1920s when, as a reaction against the successful work of the Lucy Stone League, comptrollers general, attorneys general, legal researchers and judges made use of a variety of dubious means to try to establish that married women must as a matter of law take their husbands' surnames. But that contention, based as it was on legal chicanery, was a mere *fiat lex*—"Let that be the law because I so decree it." Prejudice was converted into a legal truncheon that deserves the bitter words of Eliza Farnham: "Legal power is masculine power. It is but a step above physical power, which is pure barbarism" (*Woman and Her Era*, 1864).

It is fitting that during this period of legal repression Hawaii became a state. Admitted to the Union in 1959, Hawaii was the first state with an actual statute requiring married women to assume their husbands' names. Chapter

574-1 of the Revised Statutes of Hawaii read: "Every married woman shall adopt her husband's name as a family name." That law, originally passed in 1860, then read: "All married women now living, and all that may be married hereafter on these Islands, shall, from and after the passage of this Act, adopt the names of their husbands as a family name." What the original wording reveals is that Hawaiian women did not used to take their husbands' names. For example, the mother of Emma (a nineteenth-century queen) called herself Fanny Kekelaokalani Young although she was married to George Naea. The 1860 law was passed by a culture that wanted its citizens to conform to the customs of Western society. And by 1970 the other forty-nine states, frightened by a flurry of women who wanted to defy Western custom, had apparently succeeded in compelling legislative conformity to social custom.

In 1933 Frances Perkins was appointed Secretary of Labor and despite a Congressional dispute served in her own name. In 1970 Dorothy Andrews Elston, Treasurer of the United States, married a second time and promptly changed her surname to Kabis, thus forcing the Bureau of Engraving and Printing to change the signature in the left-hand corner of United States paper currency, needless to say at great taxpayer expense. But since the American legal profession had decided a married woman's legal surname had to be her husband's, perhaps there was some doubt the legal tender of the United States would be legal if it were not in the legal name of the Treasurer, that is, in the name of her husband.

18

MANNERS MAKE LAWS

The New Lucy Stone League

When Jane Grant had to go to Washington DC in 1948 before she could get a passport in her own name, she must have realized the work of the Lucy Stone League had been seriously undermined, for she again proceeded to propagandize for the cause. She wrote a letter to *The New York Times*, printed on September 27, 1948, in which she informed the public that the Lucy Stone League had "established legally that it was not necessary for a woman to take her husband's name at marriage," that the Passport Bureau, despite a few prejudiced clerks who made their own rules, did allow married women to get passports in their own name, that it was "a breach of civil rights for organizations such as the Waves and Wacs and other agencies arbitrarily to oblige women to change their names at marriage," and that the public should not think it so strange that women wanted some of the same privileges as men, among them that of "keeping their identity."

Jane Grant then began to reorganize the Lucy Stone League, getting in touch with former members, among them Doris Fleischman whom, despite her public recantation in early 1949, Grant succeeded in reconverting to Lucy Stonism. Fleischman attended the first meeting of the new League, held on March 22, 1950 at the Sherry-Netherland Hotel, gave a speech on the tribulations of keeping one's name and became vice-president. She and Jane Grant, who was president, together with twenty-one former members, were the nucleus of the new League (*The New York Times*, March 23, 1950). Jane Grant immediately took on the Census Bureau and the Marines. In April she got the Census Bureau to agree that for the purpose of census taking a married woman had the right to have her maiden surname officially recognized as her real name (*The New York Times*, April 10, 1950). In December Colonel Katherine A. Towle, Director of the Women Marines, responding to an inquiry from the

Lucy Stone League, announced that a woman marine who married could continue to use her own name if she so chose. Jane Grant informed the press that "it was the first time any branch of the armed forces had taken this position officially"(*The New York Times*, December 14, 1950). For the next few years the Lucy Stone League's activities were from time to time covered in the *Times*, so that occasionally a reader learned that the League sponsored the right of married women to use their own name "on all legal documents and for other general purposes."

But in items about the Lucy Stone League, readers rarely read about women's names, for the League quickly became far more than an organization dedicated to advancing the cause of a married woman's right to use her own name. Indeed, at the first meeting Harrison Smith, associate editor of *The Saturday Review of Literature*, spoke on the general subject of the ways "men belittle women." Jane Grant must have realized why the original League failed, that women would not keep their names until they regarded themselves and were regarded as men's equals. At any rate, the new League, virtually from its inception, was a proto National Organization for Women that concerned itself with sex discrimination in general. For example, Doris Stevens, at a meeting in 1952, moderated a forum on the press treatment of women that protested treating women's news as "cute" and advocated that important news about women not be put in a special section (*The New York Times*, March 17, 1952). In 1953 the League urged the John Peter Zenger Foundation to honor Anna Zenger equally with her husband since Anna was as responsible as her husband in establishing the freedom of the press in early America (*The New York Times*, April 22, 1953). That year the League also protested the Supreme Court's continued decisions that women were not persons under the Fourteenth Amendment and urged the passage of the Equal Rights Amendment (*The New York Times*, May 29, 1953). Among other activities, the League established scholarships at the Wharton School of Finance and at other colleges for women who wanted careers in business and set up feminist libraries in high schools. In a 1965 brochure the Lucy Stone League characterized itself as "A center of research and information on the status of women," "open to both men and women interested in achieving the goal of both sexes as complete partners in our society."

The brochure listed eleven rights women (and men) had to work for, the eighth on the list being

The Right to One's Own Identity—

Although the law recognizes the right of a woman to keep her maiden name (and thus preserve her identity) our society constantly harasses the woman who attempts to do so.

But in 1965 it could hardly be said that the law recognized "the right of a woman to keep her maiden name." The League was pretending the law was no different in 1965 than it had been in 1925. It is true that no state except Hawaii had a statute that compelled women to adopt their husbands' names, but the League was ignoring the case decisions, the Attorney General Opinions, the voter and motor vehicle reregistration laws, among other things, that were achieving the same effect in most states. Instead the League in its various brochures, information sheets and bulletins continued serenely to maintain, to quote from a fact sheet issued about 1968, that "There is a great body of legal opinion, all, without exception, upholding a woman's legal right to her name." That fact sheet cited the nineteenth-century dictum of Salmon P. Chase and opinions of judges in the early 1920s and a few dubiously relevant cases. The only contemporary judge cited was Judge Burnett Wolfson of the Los Angeles Superior Court who in 1965, when he granted the petition of Ivy Baker Priest Stevens to change her surname back to Priest, said "I know of no law that compels a woman to adopt her husband's name." And the League learned about that statement only because a former United States Treasurer's change of name was of sufficient importance to get into the newspapers (*The New York Times*, December 9, 1965). The 1968 fact sheet did not cite the 1941 and 1961 Ohio cases that had upheld a married woman's right to keep her name. The League, when it became a general women's rights organization, largely ceased to keep up either with favorable or unfavorable decisions or legislation that affected married women's names.

Perhaps the League did not because most of its members, almost from its reinception, did not have a passionate interest in keeping their names. At the first meeting of the new League Dr Mildred H. Clark merely advocated that wives "use their maiden names first with their married names after it, in brackets." Doris Fleischman, after serving as vice-president and hosting meetings at her home for three or four years, again recanted and again became Mrs Bernays. The League itself became conservative about names, recommending to prospective members a bulletin put out in 1961 by the Women's Bureau that in effect told women they could use their own name only professionally. "It should be borne in mind," stated *Right of Married Women to Choice of Name for Legal Purposes*, "that for administrative and other purposes where uniformity is desirable, or strict proof of identity is required—such as election laws governing registration and balloting or regulations governing the issuance of passports— official rules may be adopted which require specific identification through the use of a woman's married name," in other words, that a woman could use her own name, but not for voting and not in her passport nor whenever an official rule required "strict proof of identity." The Women's Bureau was upholding the position of the legal establishment that a married woman was not accurately, not legally, identified except in her husband's name.

The League perhaps cited the Women's Bureau bulletin because the majority of its members were doing what the bulletin recommended. Robey Lyle, the 1972 president of the League, said that she and most members were "binomials," women with two names—a professional name and the husband's name they used for legal purposes and sometimes socially. Moreover, many of the members used their husband's name for all purposes. Needless to say, Jane Grant never conceded an inch socially or legally, but in the 1960s only a minority of the members of the Lucy Stone League were true Lucy Stoners.

Of course, despite the conservatism of most of its members, the Lucy Stone League remained the only organization from which a woman who wanted to keep her own name could receive encouragement and advice. Unfortunately, the women who needed encouragement and advice were not likely to know about the Lucy Stone League. After 1956 the Lucy Stone League's activities were for many years not covered by the newspapers. It is not too much to say that in the early 1960s the Lucy Stone League was known only to a couple of hundred women, most of them over fifty.

A Creampuff Cause

Despite the Lucy Stone League's remaining largely unknown, a fair number of women from the mid 1930s to the late 1960s decided to keep their own name, and a surprising number, as we have already seen, felt so strongly about their right to retain their identity, they were willing to fight for their names in the courts—Anna Kayaloff, Marjorie Hanson, Gertrude Bucher, Antonia Rago and Blanche Krupansky, besides the women who forced attorneys general in various states to decide whether or not they could use their own names in running for office, on business licenses, as probation officers and in other ways.

Many other women chose not to take their husbands' names. Among those who married in the latter half of the 1930s were the pilot Jacqueline Cochran; the Texas lawyer Marguerite Rawalt; the New York lawyer and later judge Nanette Dembitz; the head of the Henry Street Settlement House Helen Hall; the Virginia economist Irene Till; the publisher of the Schenectady *Union-Star*

Carolyn Williams Callanan; and the sociologist Dorothy Swaine Thomas. Among those who married in the 1940s were the nuclear physicist Chien-Shiung Wu; Director of the South Carolina State Board of Health Dr Hilla Sheriff; surgeon at the New York Memorial Cancer Center Dr Isabel Scharnagel; the Oklahoma librarian Leta Sowder; and the Executive Director of the Family Service Bureau in New Brunswick, New Jersey Doris Dean Swain. Among those who married in the 1950s and 60s were the California lawyer Margaret E. Hoyt; the psychiatrist Judianne Densen-Gerber; the biologist Dr I. Dorothea Raacke; assistant Commissioner of Education Regina Goff; and the Ambassador to Napal Caroline Laise.

The majority of these women used their own name only professionally, some because they wanted to balance the "masculine" credential of Doctor or Lawyer with the "feminine" credential of Mrs, others because they found it too difficult to combat the social harassment. Most used their husbands' names for voting or on their drivers' licenses, passports and mortgages because they thought to do otherwise "would not be legal," to use the words of Dr Barbara Moulton of West Virginia. A few, generally lawyers like Judge Nanette Dembitz, did use their own name for all legal purposes. Some had no trouble with registrars of voters or passport clerks because they had their names changed by court order. The psychologist Flanders Dunbar did so in 1940 and before Ivy Baker Priest Stevens ran for Treasurer of California in 1965, she legally divested herself of her second husband's name. Another California woman, Mildred Lillie, Associate Justice of the Los Angeles State Court of Appeals, in 1969 had her name legally changed from Falcone (her second husband's) back to Lillie (her first husband's), the name under which she had become well-known.

The years between 1935 and 1970 were by no means a period of total nominal conformity. In fact, women who had once been afflicted by the cult of wifehood came to their senses. Dorothy Dunbar Bromley, who in 1927 had lashed out against the Lucy Stoners, calling their "clamor" about keeping their own names "inane," decided to keep the name Bromley when in 1947 she married a second time. Mrs John Emerson at last shed the veil of wifehood, becoming first "Anita Loos (Mrs John Emerson)" and then her own self again. Even the arbiter of etiquette Amy Vanderbilt, who had used her own name only professionally through three marriages and divorces, by 1967 was using her own name socially as well (*The New York Times*, February 7, 1967).

Starting in the early 1960s one again begins to hear women speaking out against the custom of taking the husband's name. In a radio broadcast in Berkeley, California in 1963 the movie critic Pauline Kael explained to a critical listener that although she was known as Miss Kael, she was in fact married but preferred not to have her name reflect her "marital vicissitudes," and she accused her critic, who had signed her letter "Mrs John Doe," of having been brainwashed by the Freudians into being "complacently proud" of her married state. Eve Merriam in *After Nora Slammed the Door* (1964) decided that although feminists laughed at Lucy Stone's keeping her name, calling it "a ridiculously creampuff cause," it might not be such a small matter and she devoted several pages to names, reasoning that the loss of a woman's name upon marriage was evidence of the long history of male domination of women, that taking a husband's name generally meant a woman identified with her husband's goals in life and had none of her own, which might be why there were so few women in the Hall of Fame. But Merriam only went so far as to suggest that women hyphenate their husband's name to their own. Totally radical was the female Don Juan in Una Stannard's *The New Pamela* (published in 1969 but written in 1963), who indignant at the custom, declared that were she to marry she could never take her husband's name because "it signifies woman's secondary position, her lack of identity, her willingness to absorb herself into the man."

But most feminists and feminist organizations in the 1960s thought that to fight for the right to keep one's own name was a "creampuff cause," much ado about not much. The Lucy Stone League was of course an exception. Another exception was Open Door International, an organization working for equal rights for women workers, that at its July 1966 London Conference adopted as one of its resolutions the right of a married woman "to choice of name." More typical was the National Organization for Women. When it was founded in June 1966 the right of a married woman to a name of her own was not among the rights NOW was then demanding. Betty Friedan was not interested in the subject and seems to have had the conventional view that taking a husband's name was a sign of love, at least in *The Feminine Mystique* (1963) she said of Lucy Stone that "though she loved him [her husband] and kept his love throughout her long life, she never took his name," and Mrs Friedan did not advocate that young women, as part of their fight to get out of suburbia and develop identities of their own, keep their own name after marriage.

In 1969 when Leo Kanowitz published *Women and the Law*, he said that American women were "not clamoring for the right to be known by their own names after marriage," and that was true of most feminists also, but a year later the clamor was to begin.

A Grass-Roots Movement

At its National Convention in March 1970 the National Organization for Women adopted resolutions against the oppressions of marriage, and Resolution 12 demanded that "the wife should be able to keep her own name." Starting in 1970 most of the newsletters put out by the local chapters of NOW contained articles on married women's names that ranged from the moderate suggestion that wives get a separate listing in the phone book under their own first name to legal advice on how a married woman could resume her own surname by court order. In newsletter after newsletter women declared that taking a husband's name was a sign of the wife's inferior status, of her being regarded as a man's property, and that if a woman really thought of herself as equal to a man she would not take his name when she married.

But the new keep-your-own-name movement had not originated in NOW; rather, NOW had been swept into a movement that already existed, a grass-roots movement, the sudden appearance of individual women from all over the country who spontaneously and independently decided they did not want to be nominally one with their husbands. The idea came to most of them as a personal revelation, for very few at first knew of other women who were doing likewise and had never heard of Lucy Stone, not to mention the Lucy Stone League. Nor were they typically members of NOW nor of radical feminist groups which, since they repudiated marriage as a form of institutionalized slavery to be abolished in the socialist state of the future, were above such bourgeois trivia as husbands' names. Oddly enough, most of the new Lucy Stoners denied they were "women libbers," as feminists were called by the press in the 1970s.

Whenever a feminist movement arises, it follows as invariably as day follows night that some women will feel deeply the injustice and humiliation of having to give up their names at marriage. Whether it is an isolated woman, like Lucy Stone or Elisabet Ney or Lydia Kingsmill Commander, or a group of women, like the Greenwich Villagers in the 1910s or the Lucy Stoners in the 1920s, feminist movements have always produced and always will produce women who decide they must keep their own name as a symbol of their equality with their husbands. Because the feminist movement in the early 1970s was larger and more widespread than previous movements, the number of women who felt they must keep their own name was also larger and more widespread. What was unusual about the grass-roots movement was that the women involved were not mainly doctors or lawyers or other highly trained professionals who might have been motivated by a desire to maintain a constant professional identity. Rather, a majority of the women had jobs like bank

WIFE WHO RETAINS HER MAIDEN NAME AND WON'T OBEY

Advanced Marriage Described by Two Daring Citizens Who Have Entered Into the Relation.

WHEN Miss Lydia Kingsmill Commander married Rev. Herbert Newton Casson of Toledo, O., recently, she did not become Mrs. Herbert Newton Casson. She remained Miss Lydia Kingsmill Commander. She made no promise of obedience. She read a statement of her position; the groom likewise read a statement setting forth his ideas of advanced matrimony and after the Judge, who listened, performed a civil marriage ceremony, they walked from the room equals, as they had entered, united, yet with names unchanged.

In view of the widespread interest aroused by their unusual contract, the bride and groom have written and made public the following separate and joint statements:

The Conditions.

"Having been joined together in the holy estate of matrimony according to the ideas advanced so-called, that we both entertain, we respond to the invitation to place on record our views with regard to a union of hearts and lives in this age of enlightenment. We were agreed before our marriage that anything that fell short of soul-union was desecration. For the woman to give herself to the man in return for her support was to us a revolting idea. The rule that the woman change her name we regarded as another mark of the servitude of the wife to the husband; the very identity of the woman is lost and the name and title of the wife marks her degraded condition matrimonially, in that anyone can tell at once whether or not the woman is married and whose property she is. We were agreed that the equality of the sexes demanded that the woman retain her own name as an absolutely indisputable possession. With all this thoroughly understood between us, we agreed to unite our lives as man and wife.

"By civil ceremony, then, there were married the Rev. Herbert N. Casson and Miss Lydia Kingsmill Commander. When the words were pronounced by the Judge who performed the ceremony, 'By the power of the authority vested in me, I pronounce you man and wife,' there walked from the hall, not the Rev. and Mrs. Herbert N. Casson, but Rev. Herbert N. Casson and Mrs. Lydia Kingsmill Commander. Both were equal when they walked to the hall. That equality was preserved when they left it and will be to the finish of the chapter. This has been carefully arranged for in the following declarations of belief read by us at the marriage ceremony:

The Bride's Statement.

"I believe true marriage to mean a deep affinity of heart and mind and soul existing between a man and a woman who find in each other the inspiration of all that is best, highest, noblest and purest in character. I believe that the lives should blend and harmonise, making together one perfect whole, and yet that each should preserve his or her own individuality, developing all that lies within the nature to its highest capabilities, neither demanding aught of the other, but each seeking the welfare and happiness of the other.

"Believing that such affinity of heart and mind and soul does exist between us, and that such will be our lives together, I, Lydia Kingsmill Commander, do, in presence of these witnesses, pledge myself as the wife

MISS LYDIA KINGSMILL COMMANDER.

of Herbert Newton Casson, promising to share with him whatsoever the changes and chances of life may bring, to stand by his side in sorrow as in joy, in sickness as in health, when the world smiles and when the world frowns, come grief, come pain, come joy, come gladness, through all the varying fortunes of life, so long, and only so long, as love shall bind our hearts, and our souls are blended as one.

"Self-reverent each and reverencing each, distinct in individualities, yet like each other, even as those who love."

The Groom's Statement.

"So high is my ideal of a true and lasting marriage that I regard it as far beyond the mere link which is forged by law. Marriage is the union of two lives attracted by congeniality and welded together by love. It is not the destruction of individuality, but the union of liberty and co-operation. I do not, by virtue of this ceremony, claim any right which love does not freely give.

"I wish to marry a free-hearted woman, not a slave.

"With all the confidence of love, I yield every right that a man should yield to a woman. I do not wish to compel affection or obtain a claim by any legal device. Un-

less love is spontaneous and free it is not love. I desire to be loved as long as I am lovable, and no longer. I will never be sent to chain the life of another being to mine in any irrevocable way.

"So, then, I declare, before these witnesses, that I, Herbert Newton Casson, take Lydia Kingsmill Commander as my wife so long as love and wisdom unite us.

"I pledge myself never to let this marriage interfere with the life work she has chosen, nor with the development of her larger powers for good.

"I will help her to make herself. Her own, to keep or give, to live and learn, and be all that develops highest womanhood.

"We shall both continue our life work, each seeking to help the other, one in heart and mind and purpose; free from the objectionable thralldom that modern marriage usually means to the woman, endeavoring always to be useful to the community and believing that the tie that binds us will be forever free from irksomeness and conducive only to mutual happiness and advancement.

"HERBERT N. CASSON.
"LYDIA KINGSMILL COMMANDER.
"Toledo, O., May 4."

NO "MRS." BADGE OF SLAVERY
WORN BY THIS MISS WIFE

Legally She Is Mme. Eastman, but Maiden Name of Ida Rauh Is Still Used by Her.

HUSBAND, A SUFFRAGIST, FULLY AGREES WITH HER.

They Think Marriage Should Be Robbed of Idea of Support and Commercialism.

IDA RAUH

MAX EASTMAN

"I prefer to have my wife known by her own name rather than mine. I am far more insistent upon this than she is, and I get quite cross when she is simply called Mrs. Eastman."

Prof. Max Eastman, professor of philosophy at Columbia, a prominent Socialist and worker for woman suffrage, said that yesterday. His wife, Ida Rauh, was formerly the Secretary of the Women's Trade Union League. She has been identified with the suffrage cause and various public movements for the good of working people. She has independent means.

The marriage of the two last July was a surprise to all their friends, who did not know of it until cards reached them from the couple, who were in Europe on their honeymoon. They returned to America in September and have been in their present home at No. 33 Charles street for about two months. On the door of the apartment is a card with "Rauh" in large letters. Just under it is "Eastman" in letters the same size.

What's in a Name.

The wife told a reporter for The World that she did not care much whether she was called Mrs. Eastman or Miss Rauh.

"I would prefer, of course, to be called by my own name, but it is almost impossible to carry it out," said she. "Our friends accede, but to strangers an explanation has to be made, and as so many of them do not understand it is easier just to let it go."

"I do not want to absorb my wife's identity in mine," explained Mr. Eastman. "I want her to be entirely independent of me in every way—to be as free as she was before we were married."

Mr. Eastman is young, of fine physique, with hair slightly gray, and clear, hazel eyes. Mrs. Eastman—no, Miss Rauh—has an interesting personality. She looks as if she had Russian blood. She has dark brown hair, coiled over her ears. Her eyes are blue, and she speaks with an air of conviction.

"Our attitude toward the marriage service," Miss-Mrs. Rauh-Eastman said, "is that we went through with it; then we can say afterward we don't believe in it. It was with us a placating of convention, because if we had gone counter to convention, it would have been too much of a bother for the gain. We both have too much work to do, so that if we had decided to dispense with the legal service there would have been such a hue and cry raised that it would have interfered with our work. We would always have had to overcome that obstacle in people's minds before we could have interested them in our real work in life."

"Then your idea was that, as long as the legal service didn't matter, with you one way or another, you might as well go through with it for the sake of convenience?" the reporter asked.

"Exactly. It seems to me that the world should be interested in the work people are doing, what they are, not whether they are bound by a legal tie or not, but, as people choose to interest themselves in that tie, we are willing to conform and satisfy them."

"Would you call your marriage a trial marriage?" was asked.

"All marriages these days under our laws are trial marriages," she retorted. "Everything one does in life is an experiment. There is no finality about any step one takes. But if you mean a trial marriage with the features of a time limit, I should answer, decidedly not."

"We have no theories about marriage. We simply wanted to be together. It was the natural thing for us to want to do, so we went about it. It is the other people who have the theories. We have none. We simply think for ourselves, and live perfectly naturally."

Works as She Did Before.

"I wish you would say, if you are going to say anything," said Mr. Eastman, "that my wife works just as regularly at the Women's Trade Union League for the things she is interested in as she did before marriage. She has her regular hours of work, and devotes herself as zealously as she ever did."

"Doesn't that tend to interfere with her attention to her home?" the reporter asked.

"Not at all," he answered. "Men are able to carry on their work without neglecting their homes, so why shouldn't women? The ideal is to make women economically independent. Then we shall have a perfect home and perfect marriage."

"What is wanted," said the possessor of two names, "is for women to have the freedom to choose. If a woman is domestic and wants to stay at home and be supported, then she should be free to do that. If she takes care of a home and rears children she is self-supporting, just as much as if she worked outside for a salary. But the woman who wants to work at something else, who has a talent or a liking for something outside her some, should be free to do so. Women were not born with pans tied around their necks as a sign that it was their destiny to wash them.

End of Commercial Marriage.

"If women could have this freedom in marriage it would raise the standard of marriage. If only marriage could be robbed of the idea of support, of commercialism, of gratitude, it would mean a wonderful advance in its status."

"You don't think the independence of the woman would tend to weaken the solidarity of the home?" was asked of Mr. Eastman.

"No, far from it," he replied. "It would work the other way. The ideal of the home is two perfectly developed persons, both working for the home and bringing something into it. Heretofore people have thought of a marriage as being the completion of two imperfectly developed beings. Now it seems to me that it is the union of two strong, independent persons."

"What is your conception of marriage?" Miss Rauh was asked.

"I think it is merely a legal status," she replied. "Most thinking people consider it so, I believe. There may be some who still feel that it is a sacrament, but the idea is passing away."

U. C. 'Co-Ed' and Former Professor Keep Marriage Secret
Day of Woman's Serfdom Is Long Past, Declares Wife

Use of Husband's Name Relic of Marital Slavery, Holds Modern Partner.

Economic, Social Reasons Urge Woman to Retain Own Public 'Label.'

"The day when woman was compelled to merge her individuality with that of her husband and to symbolize it by substituting his name for her own is gone forever," declared Miss Phyllis Ackerman, wife and professional associate of Professor Arthur Upham Pope, in her apartment in San Francisco last night.

"The taking of a husband's name upon marriage is one of the strongest influences toward ever making anything of herself or for getting her share of credit for it if she does," Miss Ackerman asserted.

"It completely destroys, so far as the public is concerned, the personality that she has been building up for twenty or more years. Also it tends strongly to destroy her sense of her own individuality. Time was when this was exactly what was expected of a woman—she simply became one of the many serfs of her feudal lord, and ceased thereafter to have any recognized existence apart from his.

WOMEN NOW ABLE TO MAKE OWN PLACES.

"That time has, fortunately, gone by. Women are now able to take places of their own in the world and, what is even more important, to go through their lives relying on their own individuality.

"Under such a condition the taking of a husband's name becomes an empty symbol and an absurdity."

Miss Ackerman declared that there were three principal advantages that she had found in keeping her own name since her marriage to Professor Pope several years ago in New York. They are:

1. The economic advantages.
2. The attitude of the world toward the woman.
3. The attitude of the woman toward herself.

"The economic advantages," Miss Ackerman declared, "are numerous, although different in individual cases. Take, for instance, the case of a woman writer. It is of great financial importance to her to be able to continue her work under the name with which the public has become familiar.

"Let her suddenly change to a new name and it is much the same as though an established business concern has abandoned its well known trade-mark. The greater part of her following drops off and she has the labor of building it up all over again.

LOSS OF OWN NAME HURTS IN BUSINESS.

"This is equally true in the case of every woman whose name has become a business and professional asset to her and such women are becoming more and more numerous every day.

"Then there is the important consideration of the world's attitude toward the woman who has suddenly dropped the name that throughout a great portion of her life has become a symbol of her distinctive personality.

"When they think of her as a new name, she loses much of the charm of individuality which they have grown to associate with her former name. There are many instances of this that could be cited among women with whom the public has become familiar.

"One of the most striking of these is the case of Alice Roosevelt, who although she was one of the first American women to give up the practice of wearing a wedding ring, nevertheless took the name of her husband.

"Now, although the name Alice Roosevelt conveys something very definite and distinctive to virtually every American, that something is scarcely recalled, if at all, upon hearing the name of Mrs. Nicholas Longworth.

"Furthermore, there is the very important consideration of what becomes of the woman's attitude toward herself after she takes a totally and utterly new name.

"The psychological effect upon her on such an act is to make her feel that she is in some way a different person; that she is now merely a sort of appendage to the original owner of the name and that something of her individuality and independence has gone from her forever.

Married in All But Name

MISS PHYLLIS ACKERMAN, who has emulated Fannie Hurst, the author, in that she has chosen a mate in PROFESSOR ARTHUR UPHAM POPE (below), but who is retaining her own name—thus upsetting conventions at the University of California, where both are well known.

Oakland Tribune October 1, 1922
(Reproduced by permission)

Wedding Several Years Ago Admitted by Her Mother After Couple Return.

Campus Romance Developed in East; Both at Work on Art Exhibit.

The secret has been divulged.

Phyllis Ackerman, brilliant University of California alumna, is the wife of Professor Arthur Upham Pope, erstwhile head of the philosophy department at the institution.

But Miss Ackerman has not taken the name of her husband in accordance with the time-honored custom. She does not wish to merge her individuality with that of any man.

Wherefore the element of the unusual has been added to the marriage, which was performed in New York several years ago, but just came to the attention of friends of the couple in the Eastbay district.

News of the wedding, which has been kept a dark secret, came to light today in an informal announcement by Miss Ackerman's mother, Mrs. John D. Ackerman of 2733 Tenth avenue.

"Yes, my daughter is the wife of Professor Pope," said Mrs. Ackerman. "They were married several years ago in New York, but my daughter has retained her own name.

"My daughter does not believe in merging her individuality with that of any man. She will continue to be known in the art world as Phyllis Ackerman and not as Mrs. Arthur Upham Pope."

WEDDING NEWS SURPRISES FRIENDS.

The wedding announcement came as a surprise to the friends of the couple here, who have heard nothing of them since they, together with Pope's first wife, dropped from the university world and went east.

Recently Miss Ackerman and her husband, Professor Pope, arrived in San Francisco to take charge of a tapestry exhibition at the Palace of Fine Arts. She engaged an apartment at the Clinton Court apartments at 455 Stockton street.

Miss Ackerman has been delivering three lectures a day at the Palace of Fine Arts and has been dividing her time between the apartment, the exhibit and her society friends.

HUSBAND ACTS AS BUSINESS ASSOCIATE.

Professor Pope is the associate of his wife in the business of research and lectures on Oriental rugs, tapestries, Mohammedan art and antiques, and is here as the special representative of three eastern art periodicals reporting the events of his wife's art exhibition.

The beginning of the romance between the professor and his present wife, which took place on the campus while she was a student and he was a member of the faculty, caused no little comment at that time.

Professor Pope gained considerable notice when, following the Panama-Pacific Exposition, he purchased the French building, moved it to this city and remodeled it into a home. There he and the first Mrs. Pope were host and hostess at many social affairs.

Previous to this Professor Pope became the center of no little comment when he launched on this coast a movement to end the European war. This was in October, 1916, and the movement was one in which Jane Addams and other persons of national reputation were interested.

It was known as the International League of Neutral Nations.

SORORITY ACTS AFTER DISCUSSIONS.

During the discussions concerning the alleged interest which Professor Pope was taking in the success of his pupil, Miss Ackerman, a climax was reached when the Gamma Phi Beta sorority, of which she was a member, requested her resignation. This she refused, it

Married, she'll not be Mrs.

COUPLE TO KEEP OWN NAMES

By GWENYTH JONES
Minneapolis Star Staff Writer

Deonne Parker and Lynn S. Castner plan to be married Sunday, but the bride will not become Mrs. Castner.

Ms. Parker and Castner have signed a marriage contract (antenuptial agreement in lawyers' language) that she will keep her own name, not take his.

Both of them are lawyers, and extensive research convinced them that the contract really is not necessary—that a woman can retain her maiden name when she gets married without formal action. But, Castner said, they signed the nine-line contract to prevent any complications.

Antenuptial agreements are not really rare—forms for them are in the lawyers' "standard forms books"—but they almost always concern property settlements. The forms read "in consideration for (the woman) marrying (the man)" he promises certain financial settlements.

Castner, former executive counsel of the Minnesota Civil Liberties Union, said this amounts to a woman "selling her body." He wrote the contract for himself and Ms. Parker to read: "In consideration of each of the parties (to the contract) marrying each other," they agree that there will be no change of name.

Appellate courts agree that a person can use any name he wants so long as it is not used for fraudulent purposes. A Minnesota attorney general's ruling said the purpose of the "change of name" statute was to make a legal record of the change, but that an action in court under the statute is not necessary.

The question of a woman's right to keep her maiden name has seldom reached appellate courts, whose records are kept in law libraries. However, there is an organization called the "Lucy Stoner League," after Lucy Stone, a 19th-century feminist, who (with her husband's agreement) never used his name.

What the lawyer's call the "leading case" on the question comes from Ohio. There a woman, who had practiced law for 11 years before her marriage and had become prominent in civic and political activities, filed for municipal judge under her maiden name a year after her marriage.

Supporters of her opponent filed a lawsuit to require her to use her husband's name, which was virtually unknown to the public.

The Ohio Supreme Court ruled in her favor, holding it is only "by custom" that in the English-speaking countries a woman takes her husband's

name. No law compels it."

It noted that she and her husband had signed a contract that she would always use her maiden name, and that she had "scrupulously used no other." (She won the election.)

Ms. Parker has no present plans to run for public office, but she does feel she wnts to "remain herself" after marriage.

She is a member of the legal editorial staff at West Publishing Co., and went through Indiana University Law School on the GI bill of rights. She earned that through a year's service in Korea with the Army Medical Specialists Corps.

Ms. Parker, who was elected to the board of the Minnesota Civil Liberties Union Dec. 11, wrote the MCLU brief in the case challenging the Minnesota abortion law in the Minnesota Supreme Court.

Castner and Ms. Parker plan to affirm their agreement at their marriage Sunday, and have the minister who marries them sign the contract as a witness that they did.

The Minneapolis Star   December 17, 1971
(Reproduced by permission)

clerk, librarian, grade school teacher, publisher's reader, social worker, or were undergraduates or graduate students with no job. And most important, a great many were housewives with children, women who had originally taken their husband's name but who now decided to reassume their own name. Nor did these women come chiefly from large metropolitan areas; at least half came from small towns.

In Anniston, Alabama when Wendy Forbush and Ronald P. Carver married on September 21, 1970 they agreed she would keep her own name "to demonstrate the equality of contract and commitment that they felt in the marriage." On the other side of the country in another small town, Kirkland, Washington, a married woman who had taken her husband's name decided she ought not to have done so because the custom made the wife seem like the husband's property. Her husband agreed with her; accordingly, on December 9, 1970, as a twenty-ninth birthday present he petitioned the Superior Court of Seattle to permit her to change her name from Francia Nathanson back to her birth name of Francia Leussen. Other women, feeling that the social and legal complications of having a name entirely different from their husband's would be too great, merely hyphenated their own surname to their husband's. Thus Anne Siefert, a graduate student in Epidemiology at the University of California at Berkeley, after her marriage in 1970 became Anne Siefert-Hoyt.

During the next two years thousands of women kept or resumed their own name or combined surnames with their husbands. In Wisconsin in July 1971 Kathleen Harney and Joseph Kruzel married and Kathleen determined to keep on using the name Harney. In Virginia in November 1971 Mary E. Stuart and Samuel H. Austell Jr married and as "a symbol of her independence" Stuart did not change her name. In Minnesota in December 1971 Deonne Parker and Lynn S. Castner married and their minister signed their antenuptial contract in which it was agreed Parker would keep her own name. Other couples signified their equality by combining surnames. In Berkeley, California in September 1971 two students preparing for the ministry at the Pacific School of Religion married and both henceforth bore the double surname Hambrick-Stowe. About a year later in Orono, Maine another young couple petitioned the court to have their names changed to Littleton-Taylor, their combined surnames. In addition, a great many married women petitioned the courts to have their name changed back to their birth name. In Indiana in January 1972 Elizabeth M. Hauptly, after having used her husband's name for four years and although she had a son who would continue to use her husband's name, filed a petition to have her name changed back to Howard. In Utah in the spring of 1972 Marcia Wilson, having used her husband's name for two years, petitioned the court to have her name changed back to Greenwold. In Washington DC in June 1972 a Congressional librarian, after having been Mrs Schwab for three years, petitioned the court to have her name changed back to Joiner. In Illinois at the same time a wife who had two children and had used her husband's name for eight years was petitioning the court to have her name changed from Terri Weiner to Terri Tepper.

These are just a tiny sampling of the thousands of women who between 1970 and 1972 decided to retain or resume their own name or combine surnames with their husband. According to *The Militant* of December 4, 1970, twenty-five percent of the four hundred teen-agers at a YWCA leadership conference felt women should not take their husbands' names. Undoubtedly, a much smaller percentage actually did keep their names when they married, but keeping your own name became sufficiently common so that when Marcia Seligson was traveling through the United States in 1971 and 1972 observing weddings for her *The Eternal Bliss Machine* (1973), she chanced upon one in which the couple announced in the middle of the ceremony they would be keeping separate names. And Khoren Arisian in *The New Wedding* (1973) outlined a model wedding ceremony for the bride who keeps her name.

In feminist books published in 1971 and 1972 women complained, often at length, about having to lose their names at marriage. In *Out of My Time* (1971) Marya Mannes revealed that although she had used her various husbands' names only in private life, even then she resented it, "breathing freely only under my own name." In *Liberated Marriage* (1972) Kathrin Perutz said it was not only legally unjust that women should have to lose their name at marriage but that it made women feel their lives were no longer their own responsibility but their husband's. She hoped wives in the future would keep their names. Nena and George O'Neill in *Open Marriage* (1972) suggested that wives, as an aid in developing their own identity, use their own first name on their checks and stationery, or, if they "feel it matters enough," go back to using their maiden name or start using a hyphenated name.

In 1972 women made public confessions of their conversion to the new philosophy of nominal independence. An eminent lawyer, Herma Hill Kay, who had taken her husband's name because she felt losing her name was a small matter, admitted in May 1972 in a speech given at the California Conference for Women State Legislators that her students had raised her consciousness so that she now felt it was important for women to maintain one identity throughout life. In September 1972 *Glamour* published the protest of Gena Corea, a young married woman who asked, "What's in a name?" and answered, "Me," all she had thought and done, a past she felt had been obliterated when she married and was called Mrs her husband. The new feeling that it was psychologically important to have an identity of one's own affected even women who had long followed correct etiquette. The editor of the *Radcliffe Quarterly* in the March 1972 issue admitted that women's liberation was liberating her and that one form it took was deciding to sign her name Aida K. Press, with no Mrs and no Mrs Newton Press in parentheses underneath. "One day last fall," she said, "it suddenly seemed to me as irrelevant to identify myself in my professional correspondence as the wife of Newton Press as it would be for him to add parenthetically that he is the husband of Aida Press." She further reported that her feeling was shared by a growing number of Radcliffe Alumnae who were taking the trouble to request that their mail be addressed to them in their own first name not their husband's.

Although it took courage for these women to stop being socially correct, theirs was for the times a mild gesture of independence. For when in 1848 the women at the first women's rights convention signed the Declaration of Sentiments with their own first name, they were a handful of rebels in the vanguard of the feminist movement, whereas in 1972 Aida K. Press and the Radcliffe Alumnae in their stand for half their individuality were timid late comers, the spume on the wave of a movement that wanted to dispense with husbands' names entirely.

The new surge towards nominal independence not only affected conservative women, it revitalized the Lucy Stone League. Starting in 1969 the League began to receive an increasing number of queries from women who wanted to know if it were legal to keep their names after marriage, and the number was so great the League's attorney, Kathleen A. Carlsson, began to prepare a new pamphlet on married women's legal right to use their own surnames. Because the new keep-your-own-name movement was so widespread, the formation of additional organizations was inevitable. In February 1971 *Female Liberation*, a Boston feminist newspaper, announced the formation of a Boston Lucy Stone League, which seems not to have become active. But other organizations flourished, most notably, the Center for a Woman's Own Name in Illinois, founded in 1973, and its offshoots, Name-Change in Massachusetts, the Olympia Brown League in Wisconsin and the Name Choice Center in San Francisco.

The increased interest in the subject was further evidenced by the inclusion of a whole chapter on names in Susan C. Ross's *The Rights of Women* (1973), by the publication of Una Stannard's *Married Women v. Husbands' Names* (1973), and the Center for a Woman's Own Name's *Booklet for Women Who Wish to Determine Their Own Names after Marriage* (1974). In addition, several chapters of NOW and of the American Civil Liberties Union and local groups of feminist lawyers prepared state fact sheets for women who wished to keep their name. These publications were meant for a lay audience, but, starting in 1971 one law journal after another also began publishing articles on the law and married women's names.

The number of women who were retaining or resuming their name became so large the press had to take notice of the new phenomenon. Starting in 1972 *The New York Times*, *The Wall Street Journal* and *The Christian Science Monitor* all printed long articles on the increasing number of women who were rebelling against social custom, as did many local newspapers all over the country. In addition, on August 20, 1973 *Newsweek* described the new trend in "The Name of the Dame"; in December 1973 *Ms* suggested married women give themselves their own name for Christmas and printed three short articles on the subject; on May 13, 1974 *Time* focused on "The Name Game" and in the same month so did *McCall's* in "My Maiden Name . . . Till Death Do Us Part."

The Legal Stone Wall

But how could these thousands of women put their belief in nominal equality into practice? No one of course could stop them from using their own name socially and in most cases professionally, but what happened when they registered to vote or applied for a driver's license or a passport, and would a judge grant the petition of a married woman who wanted to relinquish her husband's name? As the formation of several name change centers and the publication of fact sheets on the law and married women's names indicate, many women ran into the legal stone wall.

Shortly after Wendy Forbush's marriage in 1970, she applied for a driver's license in her own name, but the officials at the Department of Public Safety in Calhoun County, Alabama refused to issue it. Forbush was told that some thirty-five years ago Alabama had adopted the common law rule that upon marriage by operation of law the wife acquired the husband's surname, for which reason the Department of Public Safety required married women to have drivers' licenses in their legal, that is, their husband's name.

Mary Stuart had a similar experience. A few months after her marriage in November 1971, she and her husband moved from Virginia to Columbia, Maryland where on March 2, 1972 Stuart registered to vote, disclosing to the registrar that she was married but used her own name for all purposes, and her registration was accepted. But on March 16 she received a letter from the Board of Supervisors notifying her that under Maryland law "a woman's legal surname becomes that of her husband upon marriage" and therefore she must reregister to vote under her husband's name or her registration would be cancelled. Stuart refused to reregister and on April 4 her registration was cancelled. William A. Morris, State Administrator of Election Laws, had consulted Maryland's Attorney General who informed him that it was "a settled principle of common law that marriage automatically operates to change a wife's surname to that of her husband," and that Stuart could vote in her own name only if she had her name changed by court order. Stuart challenged that decision, but in May Judge T. Hunt Mayfield decided against her, repeating that according to Maryland law her legal surname had become her husband's when she married and that if she wished to vote she must reregister in her legal name. Meanwhile, the Maryland State Motor Vehicle Administration, having learned of Stuart's rebellious behavior in the newspapers, searched its files and discovered it had issued her a driver's license in the name Stuart. The Administration forthwith informed her she had violated the law, that unless she had her name changed by court order or got a new license in her husband's name, her driver's license would be revoked.

A great many women had trouble voting in their own name. In Connecticut, Margo Custer and Jane Holdsworth tried to register under their own names but were not allowed to. The registrar of voters consulted Connecticut's Attorney General who in September 1972 issued the opinion that a married woman could vote only in her husband's surname. In Milwaukee, Wisconsin in 1972, Thaddeus C. Stawicki, Executive Secretary of the City Election Commission alarmed by the number of married women who wanted to vote in their own name, announced they were forbidden to do so. The majority of women, confronted by such edicts, did not, like Mary Stuart, try to fight the legal establishment. They voted or got a driver's license in their husband's name. Some lied, that is, did not admit they were married. Others proceeded to try to get their names changed by court order, which was why so large a number of women in the early 1970s petitioned the courts for a change of name.

But here again women frequently met a hostile judge. In May 1972 the petition of Elizabeth Hauptly to change her name back to Howard was denied by a Circuit Court in Indiana; moreover, when she appealed that decision her right to change her name was again denied by the Court of Appeals, the State calling her "a sick and confused woman" (Petition of Hauptly, 294 North Eastern Reporter 2d 833). In July 1972 Circuit Court Judge William Winston denied the petitions of two Virginia women, of one to change her name from Barbara Ann Osterman back to Aiello, of the other to remain Kathryn P. Scott despite her marriage, the judge holding that a woman's name automatically became her husband's when she married and only divorce could change it. In Milwaukee, Wisconsin Kathleen Harney also had her petition to change her name refused. After Harney's marriage in 1971, she had been informed by the Milwaukee school board who employed her as an art teacher that she either had to use her husband's name or have her name legally changed back to Harney. Harney therefore proceeded to petition the court for a change of name, but in February 1973 Judge Ralph J. Podell refused to grant her petition, insisting that the common law compelled married women to adopt their husband's surname and that family unity "requires that all members bear the same legal name." For similar reasons, judges in Florida, Maine, Missouri, New Jersey, New York and Virginia in 1973 and 1974 refused to permit married women to resume their maiden names, and judges in California and South Dakota refused to permit divorced women to resume their own names.

Unless a woman did have her name changed by court order, she generally could not get a passport in her own name. In October 1971 Karla Simone and Nancy Hermann of Washington DC, who had used their own names for all purposes since marriage, were told by the Passport Office that passports could be issued to them only in the name of their husbands. In 1973 Kathleen Hewett of Florida could not get a passport in that name until she got a court order changing her name from the husband's name she had never used.

Women also had trouble getting credit cards, bank accounts and mortgages in their own name. Some women had special problems. For example, a Texas woman, Kathy Sheley, tried to get a military identification card in her own surname and did not succeed until she got her Senator to apply pressure to the Navy Department, which finally issued her a card, but only as an exception and without acknowledging that Sheley was her legal name. Most women had trouble with the Internal Revenue Service, for although a couple filed their income tax return under separate names, the Service would issue refund checks to John and Mary Husbandname. The majority of women endorsed such checks by signing their own name and then their husband's name, but a few stubborn women refused to. When Gail Griffin of Boulder Creek, California refused to and asked the Internal Revenue Service to reissue the check in her correct name, she was told that only if she and her husband filed separate returns could the refund be issued in two names, in other words, that they would have to pay a larger tax in order to get her name acknowledged.

Such were the sorts of trouble that married women often encountered when they tried to use their own name in the early 1970s. On the other hand, a great many women had no trouble or very little. Since most states did not have a watchdog law that automatically cancelled the voting registration of women who married, women simply continued to vote in the name they were already registered under. They also continued to drive with the license they had. A woman was likely to run into trouble only when she moved to a new state and had to reregister to vote or apply for a new driver's license. Moreover, many judges granted the petitions of married women who wanted to use their own name again. A Washington judge permitted Francia Nathanson to change her name back to Luessen. In 1971 when Judge Maloney of the Circuit Court of Madison, Wisconsin granted a married woman permission to resume her maiden name, he said there was no law in Wisconsin requiring a woman to use her husband's name (In re Smuckler, No. 134057). Similarly, in 1972 when Judge Cooney of Illinois permitted Terri Weiner to become Terri Tepper again, he said, "Your name is what you say it is"because according to common law, every person has the right to change his or her name at will. But name change petitions were granted at the whim of the judge, and one judge would grant such a petition and another in the same state would not, and the same judge would grant one petition and deny another. For example, although in 1972 Judge William Winston of Virginia denied the petition of Barbara Osterman to change her name, in 1971 he had granted such a petition.

That many judges refused name change petitions, that many women were denied the right to vote or have a driver's license in their own name is not surprising. What is surprising is that many women had little or no trouble, for in the early 1970s it was generally the opinion not only of the legal establishment but of most feminist lawyers that a married woman's legal surname was her husband's.

The first published legal discussion of married women's names associated with the women's liberation movement was in Leo Kanowitz's *Women and the Law* (1969) where Kanowitz concluded that in the United States a woman's change of name upon marriage "appears to be generally required by law." For some time feminists and feminist lawyers repeated that opinion. In an article in the *Yale Law Journal* (April 1971) Barbara Brown, Thomas Emerson, Gail Falk and Ann Freedman stated that the merger of a woman's legal identity into her husband's was "firmly entrenched in statutory and case law," but that these "legal barriers" would be removed by the passage of the Equal Rights Amendment, which "would not permit a legal requirement, or even a legal presumption, that a woman takes her husband's name at the time of marriage." Attorney Regina Healy in the October 1971 newsletter of the Boston Women's Collective informed Massachusetts women that in order to retain their own surnames after marriage they had to petition the court for a change of name. Marija M. Hughes, in an article in *The Hastings Law Review* (November 1971), also said that "in order to legally retain her maiden name," a wife must have her name changed by court order because "it is almost a universal rule in this country that upon marriage, as a matter of law, a wife's surname becomes that of her husband." It is no wonder that in September 1971 when *Glamour* in an editorial asked, "Can you keep your MAIDEN NAME after you're married?" the answer was "the only legal name you're entitled to is your husband's" and that you must go to court to reacquire your maiden name. The lawyers *Glamour* consulted had been of that opinion and very few lawyers would have had a different one.

If it had not been assumed that the law required a married woman to change her name to her husband's, feminists would not have introduced bills into various legislatures whose purpose was to permit women to retain their own name after marriage. As early as 1969 such a bill was introduced into the Wisconsin legislature, and in 1971 similar bills were introduced into the legislatures of California, Illinois, Massachusetts and Washington. The bills were not taken seriously. The Massachusetts legislature tossed its bill aside as "too ridiculous for words" and the Judiciary Committee of the California Assembly killed its bill amid laughter. Only the Wisconsin bill passed, but in January 1970 it was vetoed by Governor Warren P. Knowles. Moreover, the hostility the bill aroused may have been responsible for a slight backlash. At least in 1971 Wisconsin belatedly passed a law that required all electors to reregister to vote whenever their "name is legally changed, including by marriage or divorce," the sort of law that had been commonly interpreted as mandating a name change for married women.

In 1971 not only did several states refuse to pass laws that would have permitted married women to retain their names, in September of that year a Federal Court upheld a state's right to require married women to use their husbands' names on their drivers' licenses. When Wendy Forbush of Alabama was refused a license in the name Forbush, she hired a lawyer who brought a class action suit against the state, arguing that its unwritten regulation requiring married women to have drivers' licenses in their husbands' names was a violation of the Fourteenth Amendment since it deprived married women of their property (their name) and thus denied them the equal protection of the law. The State of Alabama contended that because it required its citizens to have licenses in their legal name and because it had "adopted the common law rule that upon marriage the wife by operation of law takes the husband's surname," the Department of Public Safety was compelled to require married women to have licenses in their legal, that is, their husband's name, a requirement that prevented fraud since it prevented women from getting licenses in two names.

On September 28, 1971 a three judge Federal Court decided in favor of Alabama. The Court held that state laws have generally not been considered in violation of the Fourteenth Amendment if they could be shown to have a rational basis connected with a legitimate state interest, and the Court felt "the state law requiring a woman to assume her husband's surname upon marriage has a rational basis," rational because "the state has a significant interest in maintaining close watch over its licensees" and a regulation requiring drivers to have licenses only in their legal name did prevent fraud by preventing drivers from obtaining licenses in any number of names. The Court therefore held that Alabama's regulation was not in violation of the Fourteenth Amendment. The Court further held that it would be far more inconvenient and costly for the state to change its regulation than for Forbush to comply with it and that the injury to her was minimal since "the State of Alabama has afforded a simple, inexpensive means by which any person, and this includes married women, can on application to a probate court change his or her name" (Forbush v. Wallace, 341 Federal Supplement 217).

In 1971, then, a Federal Court upheld a state's right to have laws that required a married woman to assume her husband's surname, a decision that in March 1972 was affirmed, but without briefs and without hearing arguments, by the United States Supreme Court.

Common Law Revived

On March 22, 1972, shortly after the Supreme Court upheld a state's right to require a married woman to use her husband's surname, the United States Congress passed the Equal Rights Amendment, and in the latter half of 1972 the tide turned; courts began to affirm a married woman's right to do what she pleased with her name. This change was in part an effect of the passage of the Equal Rights Amendment, for it made courts feel that legal equality for women was inevitable and imminent. But courts were to reverse their former policy not fundamentally on equal rights grounds. What happened was that feminist lawyers, many from the American Civil Liberties Union, began to do the basic legal research and rediscovered what the common law actually was in regard to married women's names.

In Forbush v. Wallace the Federal Court had noted without question Alabama's adoption of "the common law rule that upon marriage the wife by operation of law takes the husband's surname." Two months later, in May 1972, when Judge T. Hunt Mayfield of Maryland decided against Mary Stuart's right to vote in her own name, he too maintained he was following common law. "The use by the wife of the husband's surname following marriage is now based on the common law of England, which has been duly adopted as the law of this State," said Judge Mayfield, who cited the 1945 Illinois case in which

Judge Friend, when denying Antonia Rago the right to vote in her own name, said he was following the common law of England that had been duly adopted in his state, and Judge Friend in turn had cited the source of sources—Judge Earl's dictum in Chapman v. Phoenix National Bank: "by the common law among all English-speaking people, a woman upon her marriage, takes her husband's surname." This dictum by constant repetition had become a hallowed precedent, an unquestioned truth, so much so the case was not looked up and was actually described by Leo Kanowitz in *Women and the Law* as one in which a judge denied a woman's request that she be permitted to be known by her maiden name after marriage.

Chapman v. Phoenix was at long last read and Judge Earl's words were discovered to be a dictum in a case that had nothing to do with a woman who wanted to use her own surname. More important, the basic reference works of English law were consulted—Halsbury's *Laws of England*, J. F. Josling, *Change of Name* (London, 1950), M. Turner-Samuels, *The Law of Married Women* (London, 1957)—all of which, plus cases like Cowley v. Cowley (1901) and In re Fry (1945), uniformly maintained that under the common law of England any person, including a married woman, had the right to assume any name and that when a married woman changed her name she was asserting her common law right to change her name, that no law was compelling her to do so. Feminist lawyers not only rediscovered what the common law of names was in England, they also discovered the 1941 and 1961 Ohio cases (suppressed from the *Corpus Juris Secundum* and other legal reference works) that had upheld a wife's right to continue using her own name for all purposes.

Using this knowledge and these precedents and also invoking the equal protection clause of the Fourteenth Amendment, lawyers from the American Civil Liberties Union and the Women's Law Center of Maryland, among others, prepared briefs in behalf of Mary Stuart's right to vote in her own name, and on October 9, 1972 the Maryland Court of Appeals (the state's highest court) in a six-to-one decision reversed the lower court's decision and upheld the right of married women to use their own name. In his decision, Chief Judge Robert J. Murphy stressed the common law right to use the name of one's choice: "Under the common law of Maryland, as derived from the common law of England, Mary Emily Stuart's surname . . . has not been changed by operation of law to that of Austell solely by reason of her marriage to him . . . we hold that a married woman's surname does not become that of her husband where, as here, she evidences a clear intent to consistently and nonfraudulently use her birth given name subsequent to her marriage . . . [Although] long-standing custom and tradition . . . has resulted in the vast majority of married women adopting their husbands' surnames as their own—

the mere fact of marriage does not, as a matter of law, operate to establish the custom and tradition of the majority as a rule of law binding upon all" (Stuart v. Board of Elections, 266 Maryland Reports 440).

The Maryland Attorney General who had maintained early in 1972 that "marriage automatically operates to change a wife's surname to that of her husband" in November, a month after the Stuart decision, was constrained to rule that a wife who had not changed her name did not have to reregister to vote. In state after state other attorneys general began issuing opinions upholding a wife's right under the common law to continue using her own name for all purposes. The Virginia Attorney General in June 1973 issued the Opinion that "if, *in fact*, a married woman had consistently maintained her maiden name since her marriage, then it is my opinion that she may register to vote in that name." The Pennsylvania Attorney General in August 1973 ruled that a married woman did not have to have a driver's license in her husband's surname if she did not use his name: "It is our opinion . . . that a married woman has the right to continue to use after marriage the name given her at birth," for "there is no statutory authority mandating that a woman change her name to her spouse's on the date of marriage. It is strictly a social custom that has evolved over the years." In 1974 attorneys general in Arkansas, California, Delaware, Illinois, Maine, Massachusetts, Montana, South Carolina, Texas and Vermont followed suit, all maintaining that since their state was under common law women could not be compelled to change their name to their husband's and therefore might vote or register an automobile or be issued a driver's license in their own name. The Vermont Attorney General, for example, in February 1974 said: "The law of Vermont is guided by the common law which provides that absent fraudulent intent, a woman can retain or change her name, by consistent usage, to one of her own choosing without regard to social custom." In the 1920s attorneys general had upheld a married woman's common law right to choose to be known by a name different from her husband's; from the mid 1930s through the 1960s attorneys general maintained that a married woman's legal surname had to be her husband's; in the early 1970s attorneys general were again upholding a woman's common law right to continue using her own name after marriage.

Judges were no different from attorneys general; under the new light of the common law they now interpreted reregistration laws differently. Whereas in 1945 Judge Friend had insisted that the Illinois law requiring persons to reregister to vote when their name was changed "by marriage or otherwise" mandated a name change for married women, in 1972 Judge Murphy in the Stuart case felt there was nothing in the language of Maryland's similar election law that "purports to compel *all* married women to register to vote in their husband's surname," that it applied only to women who had in fact changed their name. Similarly, in January 1974 Judge Stapleton of the Hartford Superior Court interpreted Connecticut's reregistration law as merely recognizing that most women do assume their husband's surname but as not transforming a "social custom into a rule of law" (Custer v. Bonadies, 30 Connecticut Superior Court 387). The Supreme Court of Tennessee in 1975 also decided that neither its voter nor automobile reregistration laws requiring a person to reregister "after he changes his name by marriage or otherwise" mandated a change of name for married women, for under common law a woman's name is changed to her husband's only if she elects to use it (Dunn v. Palermo, 522 South Western Reporter 2d 679), and a virtually identical decision in regard to drivers' licenses was made by a Florida Appeals Court in 1976, again on common law grounds (Davis v. Roos, 326 Southern Reporter 2d 226).

Laws that require persons to reregister whose names are changed "by marriage or otherwise" can without a strain be read as applying only to women who do change their names, but even laws that clearly mandated that a wife must have the same name as her husband were now, under the new light of the common law, interpreted as permitting her to have a different name. For example, Vermont's change of name law provided that when "a married man changes his name . . . such change shall change the surname of the wife," a law that had been interpreted as meaning a wife's name must follow her husband's. But in his 1974 Opinion the Attorney General said that since in Vermont every person has the right to use the name of his choice, that law "does not nullify a married woman's right to keep her surname." Even the Hawaiian statute that dictated that "Every married woman shall adopt her husband's name as a family name" was in 1973 interpreted by the state's Attorney General as permitting a wife to change her name to one different from her husband's because "the common law, unless changed by statute, obtains in the United States," which law gives all persons, including married women, the right to change their names.

Not only were laws reinterpreted, laws were changed. In 1972 Iowa deleted from its change of name law the phrase that barred married women from changing their name, Kentucky repealed its similar law and its voter reregistration law, and a Kansas judge declared unconstitutional a law that cancelled a woman's name from the voter registration books until she reregistered in her husband's name (Gallop v. Shanahan, No. 120-456, Shawnee County) Moreover, in 1973 New York added a section to its divorce law making it mandatory for a judge to permit a married woman, if she so chose, to change her name upon divorce, and in 1974 California passed a law "declaratory of existing law," that is, affirming that nothing in its statutes, including the law that gave a court the right to restore the birth name of a wife after divorce and the change of name law, could "be construed to abrogate the common law right of any person to change one's name."

Starting in 1974 married women who had been denied the right to resume or establish their maiden names by lower courts began to have these decisions overturned by higher courts, usually on common law grounds. Appellate or Supreme Courts in California, Florida, New Jersey, New York, Missouri, Virginia and Wisconsin in 1974 and 1975 decided that lower courts had abused their discretion when they denied married or divorced women the right to change their name. For example, the Appellate Division of the New Jersey Superior Court in April 1975 held that a woman "is not compelled by law to assume her husband's surname as her legal name" (Application of Lawrence, 337 Atlantic Reporter 2d 49). The Supreme Court of Virginia in December 1975 similarly held that under "English common law . . . a person is free to adopt any name," which means a married woman "is under no legal compulsion" to adopt her husband's name (In re Strikwerda, 220 South Eastern Reporter 2d 245). A Wisconsin judge, moreover, told Kathleen Harney in March 1975 that since she had never used her husband's name, she had had no need to have her name changed by the courts (Kruzel v. Podell, 67 Wisconsin Reports 2d 138).

Not all states granted married women the right to use the name of their choice on clear common law grounds. When the Supreme Court of Indiana in June 1974 decided Elizabeth Hauptly did have the right to change her name, it nevertheless maintained that "under the common law . . . a married woman assumes the surname of her husband." However, the court also held that the common law gave her the right to change her name and "without any legal proceedings" (Petition of Hauptly, 312 North Eastern Reporter 2d 857). Or when the Maine Supreme Court in July 1975 decided Susan Reben had the right to change her name, it did so chiefly on the grounds that the Maine legislature "did not intend to exclude married women" from using the change of name statute, a statute, the Court suggested, that probably abrogated common law (In re Reben, 342 Atlantic Reporter 2d 688).

The Maine Court did not decide whether a woman's name was as a matter of law changed to her husbands's at marriage, and a few states continued to maintain that under the common law it was changed. The Attorneys General of Georgia and North Carolina both held in March 1974 that in their states a woman "takes the surname of her husband by operation of law," but following the lead of Alabama in Forbush v. Wallace, they nevertheless permitted married women to reassume their own names by court order.

Despite a few obstinate attorneys general and judges, English common law was finally understood in the United States. Between 1972 and 1976 over thirty states, either by Attorney General Opinions, decisions in higher courts or legislation, acknowledged that when a woman takes her husband's name, she does so under the old common law right to use the name of one's choice, that married women, therefore, cannot be compelled to use their husbands' names for any purpose. Even the Passport Office stopped requiring married women who had never used their husband's name to fill out change of name affidavits in order to get passports in their own name. Starting in December 1973 women only had to swear and present proof they had continued to use their own name. A cynic might say a married woman's right to use her own name received ultimate acceptance when in January 1976 a California Appeals Court held that a wife who used her own name during marriage was entitled to sue for divorce in her own name (Weathers v. Superior Court of Los Angeles, Appellate 126 California Reporter 547).

It would seem, then, that married women won the right to keep their names on common law grounds without the ratification of the Equal Rights Amendment. Indeed, when regulations requiring women to use their husbands' names were challenged on equal rights grounds, the cases were lost. Wendy Forbush of Alabama lost her case in 1971 and so did Sylvia Scott Whitlow in an almost identical case in Kentucky, a United States Court of Appeals in 1976 deciding that requiring women to have drivers' licenses in their husbands' names did not violate their civil rights under the equal protection clauses of the Fourteenth Amendment. Interestingly enough, the Court said state courts should determine if under the common law of Kentucky a woman's legal name was changed to her husband's at marriage, which suggests that if Whitlow's case had been argued on common law grounds at the state level, she would, like many other women, have won the right to use her own name (Whitlow v. Hodges, 539 Federal Reporter 2d 582).

But despite the failure to win name cases on equal rights grounds, feminists are certain that the ratification of the Equal Rights Amendment will guarantee that "no woman can be compelled to change her legal name each time she marries," to quote Priscilla MacDougall (*Women's Rights Law Reporter*, Fall/Winter 1972-73). But would it? Wisconsin in 1921 passed an Equal Rights Statute giving women "the same rights and privileges under the law" as men, a statute that in 1962 was interpreted as giving married women the same rights as single women. Yet that Equal Rights Statute obviously did not give married women the right to use their own name, otherwise a bill to give them that right would not have been passed in the Wisconsin legislature in 1969, a bill vetoed by the Governor not because under Wisconsin's Equal Rights Statute women already had that right but because it seemed, he said, "to give women the right to retain their maiden name as a matter of equality with men." Moreover, although Hawaii passed its own Equal Rights Statute in November 1972, the Statute did not automatically make the Hawaiian law requiring women to adopt their husbands' names null and void. Far from it. Bills were introduced to amend the law by replacing the word "shall" adopt the husband's name with "may" adopt, but the proposed change was considered extremely controversial and the bills did not get past the hearing stage. As a consequence, in 1974 the American Civil Liberties Union was constrained to file a suit challenging the law as violating the Equal Rights Statute, and at long last, in February 1975, the law was declared unconstitutional (Cragun and Spiller v. Hawaii, Civil Judgment No. 43175).

But if past history is any judge, the Hawaiian law could have been declared not in violation of the state's Equal Rights Statute. When a New York judge refused to grant the petition of a married woman to retain her maiden name, he insisted he was not discriminating against her on account of sex, even though he admitted he would have granted a married man's petition for a name change. Her petition was denied, he emphasized, "not because she is a woman" but because "even though it be the era of the women's liberation movement and the Equal Rights Amendment . . . it is still assumed that a woman, upon becoming married, will follow established custom . . . and adopt the surname of her husband" (Application of Halligan, 350 New York Supplement 2d 63). If such reasoning seems beyond reason, it is far from unique in the annals of male legal prejudice. According to Article 3 of the Italian Constitution, "all citizens . . . are equal before the law without distinction of sex." Nevertheless, Article 559 of the Penal Code sentenced a wife to jail for adultery but not a husband (unless he kept a mistress in his own house or in a public or notorious way). In 1961 two women challenged the constitutionality of Article 559, but the fifteen judges on the Constitutional Court ruled that Article 559 did not contradict Article 3, that the provision that "all citizens . . . are equal before the law without a distinction of sex" did not oblige the state "to provide equal discipline for all." An Equal Rights Amendment would not absolutely guarantee that women would have the same nominal rights as men.

Neither would the present general acceptance of common law be an absolute guarantee, for that view of the law changed in the past and might change again. "As manners make laws, so manners likewise repeal them," observed Samuel Johnson, and should another cult of wifehood supervene and 1970s Lucy Stoners, like their sisters in the 1920s, defect and stop insisting on their name rights, common law might again be abrogated. England, with its greater acceptance of eccentricity, managed to tolerate Lucy Stoners without turning its law inside out. But American judges, to force a few wives to conform to custom, did turn the common law inside out and should the times change would most likely do so again. On the other hand, perhaps America has become sufficiently mature to tolerate the still less than one percent of married women who keep their names. Judge Stapleton, when deciding married women in Connecticut could vote in their own name, said that although "the vast majority will continue to follow the social custom of our times and adopt their husbands' surnames," law should not mandate custom, for "some hear a different drummer and step to the music which they hear, however measured or far away."

Of course, the best guarantee of a married woman's right to keep her name would be a society in which it was the custom for all wives to keep their names. But before that society can come into existence, mankind will have to understand why so seemingly minor a right as the right to keep their own name after marriage should have been one of the last rights women won; mankind will have to understand why society was so hostile to Lucy Stoners and why, to quote Harvard Law Professor Frank Sander in a speech at the 1972 Radcliffe Conference on Women, American legislators and judges have been "so hung up on the question of women's names."

What's in a Married Name?

"I would advise Mrs Banks that a rose by any other name is a rose just the same. It doesn't make any difference what your name is," said Judge Joseph Kennedy of the San Francisco Superior Court in June 1973, whereupon he denied Janice Banks, upon the dissolution of her marriage, permission to call herself Janice Christensen again (In re Marriage of Banks, 42 California Appellate Reports 3d 631). But if "it doesn't make any difference what your name is," why not let Banks go by the name Christensen? "What's in a name?" may be the most popular quotation when names are discussed, but a married woman by any other name than her husband's has not been "just the same" for many a judge, lawyer and legislator who, when confronted by a wife who wanted to dispense with a husband's name, have frequently, like Judge Kennedy, suffered a lapse of reason or manifested some other symptom of deep emotional disturbance, an irrational state virtually admitted by Maine Judge Lloyd LaFountain who, when asked why he had denied Kim Matthews and Susan Hirsch the right to resume the use of their own names, said "that he ruled with his heart, not with his head" (*Maine Women's Newsletter*, April-May 1974).

So emotional have members of the legal profession become they have even sunk to invective. You are an "oddball," "a sick and confused woman," whose need is "not for a change of name but a competent psychiatrist" ranted the State of Indiana through its Attorney General merely because Elizabeth Hauptly wanted to resume her own name (In Petition of Hauptly, Indiana Appellate 3d 294 North Eastern Reporter 2d 833). And when the Supreme Court of Indiana finally reversed the decision of the Appeals Court, Judge Prentice in a dissenting opinion was so upset by Hauptly's being given the legal right to change her name to one different from her husband's that he said the decision was ushering in a period of nominal license when "the village drunk may legally change his name to that of the circuit court judge, and the village whore may change hers to that of the judge's wife" (312 North Eastern Reporter 2d 857).

When a bill to permit married women to retain their names was introduced into the California legislature in 1971, the Judiciary Committee of the Assembly was reduced to "joshing and giggling" (*Skirting the Capitol*, May 3, 1971). In a radio interview on "Capitol Cloakroom" in March 1972 Senator Birch Bayh compared women who keep their names to radicals who blow up banks, and Senator Bayh was one of the chief supporters of the Equal Rights Amendment, but in his fear of Lucy Stoners he was no different from the Amendment's chief opponent, Senator Sam Ervin, who was so distressed by the *Yale Law Journal*'s prediction that the Equal Rights Amendment would mean wives need not take husbands' names that in a Senate Minority Report (92-689, March 14, 1972) he devoted two and one-half pages of small type to upholding "the wisdom of allowing a state to determine that a wife's legal name shall be that of her husband."

The frightening prospect of married women liberated from husbands' names has turned many a male brain to jelly, at least men seem to have lost their reasoning power. When Comptroller General McCarl in 1924 began with the premise that a court upon granting a divorce may restore a woman's maiden name and from that concluded that all women were legally compelled to take their husband's name, he violated the most elementary principles of logic, as did the many judges and legislators who repeated his argument. Similarly, when Judge Friend in 1945 turned a voter reregistration law into a marriage law mandating a name change for wives, he too violated the principles of logic, as did the many members of the legal profession who thought his argument sound. It also seems muddle-headed to believe, as did some judges and attorneys general, both that under the common law a woman was legally compelled to change her name to her husband's and that under the common law she had the freedom to change her name back again without any legal proceedings. Moreover, when one analyzes the arguments most frequently put forward for opposing Lucy Stoners, one quickly realizes they spring from emotion not sound reasoning.

Again and again lawyers have contended that if wives kept their own names record keeping would become impossibly complicated. When Governor Knowles vetoed the Wisconsin bill that would have given wives the right to keep their names, he said such a law would create insurmountable difficulties in regard to the service of papers, the determination of titles to land and the ability of law enforcement agencies to determine the whereabouts of women. Senator Birch Bayh also felt that unless wives took their husbands' names record keeping would be chaotic, with which Senator Sam Ervin agreed. In his Minority Report he said the problems would be "staggering." "Imagine an attorney searching a land title with this type of last-name system."

But difficulties in the search for land titles occur because women who buy land under one name change that name when they marry or marry again. The difficulties can become so great that a few states, like Connecticut, passed laws that require married women who sell property bought before marriage to record the name in which it was originally bought so that both names can be cross-indexed. Reason is not on the side of those who argue that record keeping is simple and unchaotic under a system in which women change their name with every marriage. Record keeping was simple only when there were virtually no records to keep, that is, when married women had no rights and could not buy property and sue and be sued, when, therefore, they rarely appeared in any records and then most likely were without a name at all, as in "John Jones and wife." It is because women do have rights and yet continue to change their name that it is difficult to track them down and that record keeping is burdensome. It is because women do change their name that the Passport Office has to issue them new passports, Motor Vehicle Bureaus new drivers' licenses, banks new pass books and checks, stores new credit cards and Election Boards have to reregister them to vote. In an era when divorce and remarriage are so widespread record keeping would be greatly simplified if women kept the name they were given at birth as their legal name throughout life.

But lawyers fear that if wives did keep their names, they would be tempted to commit fraud. The Federal Court in Forbush v. Wallace felt that Alabama's regulation requiring wives to have drivers' licenses in their husbands' names prevented women from obtaining licenses "in any number of names." When the Maine Attorney General in April 1974 ruled that married women who used their own name could vote in that name, the Deputy Secretary of State immediately issued a warning that dual registered voters would be prosecuted "vigorously." But the fact is, since no state retains cross-references to old names, it would be easy for any person intent on fraud, male or female, married or single, to register twice. And common sense suggests it would be easier for a woman who changed her name to her husband's to have dual or treble identification (if she had married two or three times) than it would be for a woman who had only one set of identity papers because she had used one name throughout life. Do judges and officials really fear Lucy Stoners want to keep their names because they want to have two drivers' licenses or vote twice? That fear is so absurd, the warnings of vigorous prosecution so emotionally charged that one suspects the fraud men fear Lucy Stoners want to commit is not the fraud of voting twice but another fraud. Perhaps the fraud of passing themselves off as single in order to indulge in the same sexual license as men. "Man's freedom to range unobstructed" is what wives who keep their name really want, a worried citizen wrote to *The New York Times* after Fola La Follette's 1914 speech on names. Or to put it another way. It may be men fear that a wife who was not clearly labeled as belonging to some man might deceive other men into treating her as if she were fair game, that is, that men fear their property rights would be less secure if wives did not wear the name tag of the man who owned them.

Be that as it may. Men plainly and simply do fear a world in which wives would no longer be one in name with their husbands, which means, paradoxically, that men really want women to commit fraud, want women to go on pretending the husband is the one head of the family when the truth is we are living in a world in which woman's emerging equality with man is changing the monarchical structure of the family. That men want the old-fashioned family unit to stay the same becomes obvious when judges, upon denying a wife's name change petition, say, as they almost always do, that by compelling a wife to use her husband's name they are preserving family unity. "This Court," said Wisconsin Judge Podell, "feels very strongly that family unity . . . requires that all members bear the same legal name." "It seems to me," said Florida Judge Boyer, that permitting a wife to have a name different from her husband's "is but another step towards the destruction of the family, the basic unit in our society." "If all the members of a family did not have the same name," said Maine Chief Justice Dufresne, it "would so neutralize familial and marital ties as practically to deny the very concept of the family." But in a society in which ninety-nine percent of wives do take their husbands' names and in which, nevertheless, the annual number of divorces rose by eighty percent between 1960 and the early 1970s, it can hardly be said the family unit has been preserved by all members having the same name.

What these judges fundamentally fear, a fear some express, is that once custom is broken and wives do not take husbands' names, "the problem would also arise of what surname to give the children" (Application of Lawrence, 319

Atlantic Reporter 2d 793). A Virginia judge was willing to permit two married women to resume their maiden names in part because "they had agreed that any children born of their marriage would bear the husband's surname" (In re Strikwerda, 220 South Eastern Reporter 2d 245). So long as children take the father's name, men feel less threatened by wives who do not take their husband's name. They feel less threatened because only male names will continue to be handed down to posterity and men can go on believing what mankind believed for thousands of years, that men were the only begetters of children.

Only the father's name was handed down to posterity and women took their husband's name to signify that the husband, the male, was the sole progenitor of children that were merely borne by women. For most of history philosophers and scientists stoutly maintained that the female sex only nurtured new life, that the male sex alone generated new life. That the female as well as the male generated new life was not fully demonstrated until the late 1870s.

Judges, like the culture generally, are reluctant to face the new facts of life; they would like to go on living in a world in which the male sex, be it in name only, is still the One God of Creation. It is men's fear of losing that divine status that has made them so "hung up" on married women's names.

19

THE MOTHER OF US ALL

Male Mothers

That children for several centuries have been given only the father's surname, as if children were descended from the father alone, is merely one manifestation of the deep desire of men to be the mothers of mankind, a desire that from time to time still crudely surfaces:

BIRTHS

Born to:

ANDREWS, Norman . . . [address] . . . May 8, 1975, a daughter
BRUBAKER, Randall . . . [address] . . . May 26, 1975, a son . . .

The proverbial man from Mars who read these birth announcements in the August 14, 1975 *San Francisco Examiner* would have to conclude that Norman Andrews and the other men listed had recently had babies, that men on planet Earth were the sex that gave birth, a belief that would be confirmed when he consulted man's holy book, the Bible, where he would read in Genesis 2:21-24 an account of the first man's accouchement, of Adam put into a deep sleep while a rib is taken from his side and made into a new being. Afterwards, when Adam first looks at the life created from his own body, he, like a new mother, thinks with awe, this is "bone of my bones and flesh of my flesh," then he gives the new life a name, Woman, a name he says means "taken out of Man." In other words, just as men in 1975 give children their own surname to seal them as their own, so Adam in 700 BC (the probable date of Genesis 2) gave his offspring a name that meant it had come from his own body.

Adam was one of many male mothers. Indeed, in Genesis itself there was another male mother, for God alone was the progenitor of Adam, creating him out of dust in His own image, just as in Greek myth Prometheus created man out of earth in the image of the gods and Hephaestus created Pandora out of earth. Hephaestus also served as midwife for Zeus, splitting his head open with an ax to facilitate the delivery of Athena. Zeus had another baby: when Semele prematurely gave birth to Dionysus, Zeus snatched up the child and sewed him into his thigh and carried him to term.

Stories of men giving birth appear in all countries, so much so they deserve to be classified among the Jungian archetypes of the collective unconscious, especially since in almost all primitive societies men used to act out giving birth. When his wife was having a baby the husband took to his bed and groaned and cried out like a woman in labor. After delivery the baby was sometimes placed in his arms, and the man dressed in his wife's clothes was the one who received congratulations. The wife quickly went back to work, but the father remained in bed for days, fasting or undergoing other rituals to assure the child's welfare. Couvade, which is what this widespread custom is called, was by no means the only way in which men used to pretend they could give birth.

In most primitive societies boys had to undergo subincision or circumcision, whose purpose seems to have been to make male genitals more like female's. Subincision (slitting the penis the whole length of the urethra), which was universally practiced among the central tribes of Australia, makes the penis resemble the vulva, and the subincision wound was sometimes actually called a vagina or penis womb. Since boys with subincisions lose control of the flow of urine, they must like women squat when urinating. Moreover, the blood shed in circumcision was believed to be analogous either to the blood of defloration or to menstrual blood. Boys of the Arunta tribe regularly opened their subincision wounds and caused them to bleed again, an obvious imitation of monthly menstruation. The blood shed in circumcision was also believed to be analogous to menstrual blood, and in some tribes, like the Qatu of the New Hebrides, boys after circumcision were secluded the ways girls were at first menstruation, or, as in many East African tribes, were dressed in female clothes. Among the Azande of the Belgian Congo, the word for circumcision and midwife were the same and the prepuce and the umbilical cord were believed to have identical medicinal properties.

Circumcision and subincision were performed during initiation ceremonies that took place in houses sometimes called "wombs" or "birth enclosures" and whose exit resembled a gaping vagina, for as a result of initiation boys were believed to be reborn, and after initiation the adult males in charge treated the boys as if they had just been born, giving them new names and milk to drink, carrying them on their shoulders as if they could not walk and requiring the boys to be silent as if they did not as yet know how to speak. Paradoxically, these ceremonies were often called "man-making" ceremonies and initiated boys into adulthood. It was as if men were saying that although women gave birth to boys, only men could give birth to men, and by circumcising or subincising the boys so their genitals looked more like those of females, they enabled the boys in their turn to someday give birth to the next generation of men.

That men should have been willing to mutilate their penises so they resembled female genitalia, that they should have devised ceremonies and created myths in which they imagined themselves giving birth seem less perverse when one understands how envious men originally must have been of women's capacity to give birth, for men originally did not know they had any role in the creation of new life. Little boys who walk around with their bellies stuck out have to learn they cannot, like mama, have a baby, but eventually they do learn they are essential to reproduction. According to a 1964 Swedish study, children do not learn what the male's role is in reproduction until they are about eight years old when either friends, parents or books provide them with that knowledge. Without that knowledge, they would, like early man, think women had babies on their own without the help of men. A perfectly natural assumption since the function of semen is not obvious nor is the relationship between sex and conception, for the first signs of pregnancy do not occur until some time after conception and most acts of intercourse do not lead to conception.

E. S. Hartland in the two volumes of his *Primitive Paternity* (1909-10) collected a massive amount of evidence that indicates early man regarded impregnation not as the result of a sexual act but of a supernatural one. Impregnation was believed to occur at quickening, the moment when the woman feels the fetus move. It was thought that at that moment a spirit entered the woman, either from the wind, stars, water, moon (the father of albino children), trees, lizards, birds, food or whatever happened to be near the woman at quickening. Phyllis Kaberry, when she was studying Australian aborigines in the 1930s, discovered that the Kimberley tribe, despite thirty years contact with whites, were still totally and adamantly ignorant of physical paternity. They insisted on believing, in spite of all attempts to tell them the facts, that conception occurred when a spirit entered a woman. Two old men, who must have had some notion of the truth since they believed the rainbow serpent Kaleru had originally created spirits from his semen, nevertheless denied that "the semen of the living man had anything to do with conception." The Kimberleys explained a child's resemblance to its father in a variety of ways, as the result, for example, of paternal impression, the close proximity of the man to the woman when she was carrying the child. But the white skin of a half-caste was likely to be regarded as an effect of the white flour a woman ate when she was living with a white man, not on the proximity of the white man, nor of course on her having had intercourse with him. In most primitive societies every child was the Christ child in that children were believed to be created without intercourse, were believed to be the result of some extra-physical force, some supernatural Spirit entering a woman.

Long after the male role in procreation was understood, the belief women could be impregnated by a nonhuman force lingered on in most countries. The Greek myths in which gods descend from the sky in the form of a shower of gold or a bull and copulate with women who always conceive are remnants of the old belief in spiritual impregnation, as is the legend that Lao-Tze was conceived by a shooting star. In the sixteenth century Martin Luther actually believed a woman had given birth to a rat, conceived when she was frightened by one that ran across her path. According to Arthur W. Meyer in *The Rise of Embryology* (1930), "The idea that a woman might conceive through an influence of the stars in the sky . . . and the further idea that sperm is disseminated in the air and in the water, survived up to the days of Harvey (1578-1657) and Buffon (1707-1788)." The story that used to be told children—that the stork brings the baby—probably had its origins in the ancient belief in impregnation by a Spirit.

The persistence of such notions shows how ancient and deep was the belief women could procreate without men. Significantly, in most early cultures only the word mother means procreator, father meaning merely elder man or provider. The oldest Chinese clan names contain the determining sign "woman" and the modern character meaning "family name" also contains the sign "woman," but not the sign for "man" or "father." Jews still reckon descent solely through the mother, for in a mixed marriage if the mother is a Jew the child is regarded as Jewish, but if only the father is a Jew the child is not Jewish. In the very earliest myths the sole creators of the universe were female; among the Greeks, for example, it was Gaea, the earth goddess, who on her own gave birth to the heavens and created the world. The earliest religions were devoted to the worship of the Magna Mater, the great mother in whom the Spirit of Life chose to reside. According to E. O. James in *The Cult of the Mother-Goddess* (1959), "the earliest manifestation of the concept of the Deity" and "the most persistent feature in the archeological record of the ancient world" was the Mother Goddess.

Even when the male's role in procreation was understood, Mother Goddess religions continued to predominate and the male's role was perfunctory and ancillary. The Goddess would summon the male god to her couch as one would order a servant, and the male whom the Divine Mother chose to be her consort was necessary only to impregnate her, after which he was often killed, like the male bee who succeeds in impregnating the queen bee only at the cost of his own life. Male priests in Mother Goddess religions tried, quite literally, to assimilate themselves to Her by becoming sexually like Her. At the spring festival of the Goddess Astarte, Her priests, known as the Galli, castrated themselves and received in exchange for their testicles female clothes and ornaments. Just as circumcision or subincision was an almost universal part of primitive initiation ceremonies, so some form of male sexual mutilation was a recurrent feature in Mother Goddess religions, and its purpose was to make men capable of giving birth. At the festival of Ariadne in Cyprus the priests lay in bed imitating the groans of women in labor, like primitive men in couvade. But whereas primitive men could only preempt the baby after delivery, male shamans among the Yakut of Siberia were believed actually capable of having children.

The early Christians at first also tried to make themselves physically more like women. Thousands of them, like Origen, castrated themselves. Ostensibly they did so to save themselves from the lustful snares of women. But early Christians did not want to have sex with a woman because they wanted to negate woman as mother. The early Christians as much as possible ignored or belittled woman as mother. Unlike virtually all other societies and religions, they had no ceremonies associated with birth. The birth of a baby was not celebrated; it was ignored. Even the birth of Christ was originally ignored; the date of his birth was unknown; the 25th of December was later arbitrarily chosen as a way of Christianizing the pagan celebration of Saturnalia. Mark, the earliest of the Gospels, begins the story of Christ's life not with his birth but with his adult baptism, and until late in the fourth century only Christ's baptism on January 6, Epiphany, was celebrated. Christ's physical birth and that of all early Christians was ignored and only one's baptism was an occasion for celebration because one was not believed to be truly born until after baptism. Baptism, a ceremony originally only for adults, was what early Christians regarded as a person's true birth, his birth into eternal, immortal life.

"The birth of Christians is in baptism," said Cyprian in a letter written in 256. Baptismal water was the "Water of Life" not amniotic fluid. As Clement of Alexandria put it, "He [Christ] generated us from our mother—the water," by which he meant baptismal water (*The Stromata*, Book IV, ch. 25). After baptism one was called a "newborn babe," a "babe in Christ," "an infant," and often received a new name and drank milk and honey. In addition, the new babes in Christ, like boys after initiation ceremonies, were supposed to imitate children—according to Papias, to be as frank and guileless as a child; according to Clement, to be as simple, tender, joyous and sensually pure. The custom among early Christians of "speaking in tongues," uttering ecstatic gibberish, was also in part an imitation of an infant's babbling.

Early Christians were born by means of baptism not by means of mothers because the Church, the embodiment of Christ and God the Father, had taken over the procreative function of woman and become *Mater Ecclesia*, as the early Church was called. Woman was no longer our mother, our source of life, the Church was. In the Old Testament Eve, a woman, was "the mother of all living," but in the New Testament the Church, as Paul said in Galatians, was "the mother of us all," or as Tertullian put it, the Church was "the true mother of the living . . . the second Adam" (*De Anima*, ch. 43).

Not only did the Church, not woman, give us birth, but the Church, not woman, was our true nourisher. "The Lord Christ," said Clement, "did not pronounce the breasts of women blessed, nor selected them to give nourishment; but when the kind and loving Father had rained down the Word, Himself became spiritual nourishment." Clement compared seeking Christ to suckling: "for to those babes that suck the Word, the Father's breasts of love supply the milk" (*The Instructor*, Book I, ch. 6). In the eighth *Ode of Solomon* (anonymous Christian odes probably written in the second century) God says: "My own breasts I prepared for them, that they might drink my holy milk and live thereby." Or as Peter put it, Christians are fed not by mother's milk but by "the milk of the word."

The early Christians would have liked to reject the mother entirely. They loved to point out that Adam, a male, was created first and that Adam was the first mother, not a woman. "The man is not of the woman, but the woman of the man," said Paul in Corinthians. Some early Christians grieved that men after Adam had to be physically born of woman. To save Christ from this taint, a sect called the Docetes denied Christ was born of woman. Mary, as the mother of Christ, was ignored for two centuries and was not officially recognized as Theotakis (god-bearer) until the fourth century, and then only because she had been purified of physical motherhood, that is, honored as a Virgin, as one who became pregnant without sexual intercourse and who despite having had a child still bore the name of Virgin. Mary exists in the Church not as a Mother Goddess, a Fertility Goddess, a Giver of Life, but as a symbol of the Church's affectionate concern and love for its children.

The Christian church replaced a Mother Goddess with a Father God who was far more than the source of physical life; he was, as it were, the Fertility God of Immortal Life. Just as Greek gods flew down to earth as a shower of gold and impregnated mortal women, so God the Father as a Holy Spirit in the form of a dove impregnated the mortal Mary, and just as the offspring of pagan gods were immortal, so was the son of God the Father, Jesus Christ. Moreover, Christ in His turn, after many hours of physical suffering and after seeming to die in agony, was able to deliver the gift of immortal life to mankind. Mother religions had merely celebrated the mystery of natural life—the endless cycle of birth, death and rebirth—but the new father religion offered mankind a superior form of life—immortal life. Whereas women and Mother Goddesses could create only fleshly beings who would die, men—God the Father and Christ—could produce spiritual beings who need never die. But the early Christians' very exaltation of immortal life and their vituperative denunciations of fleshly life and the women who brought it into the world clearly reveal their unconscious envy of the sex who had the babies.

Most early societies and tribes, unlike the Christians, did not create a new religion from the new facts of life. Once men discovered that the Spirits of Life were not in a star or a bird or in food a woman ate but resided in their own semen, they set themselves up as the One God of life, the sole procreators and looked upon woman, not as a mysterious Mother Goddess, but as the mere receptacle of man's seeds of life. The transition from the old view to the new, from awe of woman as the creator of life to a new respect for fathers can be seen in Aeschylus' *The Eumenides* where when Orestes feels guilty because he murdered the mother who gave him life, Apollo frees him of guilt by explaining that the mother was not the "true life-begetter" but just a "nurse of live seed," that the father, "the sower of the seed alone begetteth." The ancient Egyptians and other early peoples felt free to use females captured in war as concubines because they believed the resulting offspring would have no taint of foreign blood since woman was merely the earth in which male seed was sown. The Pilagá of South America believed the male ejaculated a minuscule baby into the womb, the place where a baby stayed until it was big enough to come out. Or as an old Japanese proverb explained, "A woman's womb is a borrowed vessel to beget a child."

Early scientists and philosophers liked to think of men as generating life in the female the way Spirits used to or the way God the Father generated life in Mary. Aristotle, whose theory of generation predominated for centuries, thought of the male as the Master Creator, the female providing the raw material the male gave form to, that is, semen activated inert menstrual fluid just as milk coagulated when rennet was added to it. Or as Thomas Aquinas later expressed it, "The power of the female generative virtue provides the substance but the active male virtue makes it into the finished product." The seventeenth-century scientist Thomas Fienus called semen "the rational soul" that entered the uterus and gave the shapeless material it found there a form. Or as the eighteenth-century naturalist Buffon put it, "The male semen is the sculptor, the menstrual blood is the block of marble, and the foetus is the figure which is fashioned out of the combination." Semen was the creative principle, the Vital Spark, the First Cause, the Idea that turned the dead matter of the female into a living soul.

Buffon, like many other scientists, continued to believe in the magical action of semen even though spermatozoa had been discovered. When Leeuwenhoek in 1677 put semen under the powerful microscope he had developed and saw the wriggling "animalcules," he immediately thought he had discovered men's babies, for he believed sperm were homonculi, complete men and women in miniature (he thought he could distinguish the sex of the animalcules), which minute babies the male delivered into the female for nurturing. Leeuwenhoek believed he had discovered what the Pilagá of South America intuited—the minuscule babies in semen. Some of his followers, like Hartsoeker, actually drew pictures of the babies they fancied they saw:

"Homonculus in human sperm"
drawn by Hartsoeker,
originally published in
Essai de Diatropique (1694)

Leeuwenhoek's theory was not popular because the male's role in generation was too obviously like a woman giving birth. But whether semen was believed to eject a baby into the womb or ignite the Vital Spark of life, scientists were almost all certain the male was the essential giver of life, the female merely supplying the raw material or nourishment for that life. So eager were men to be the sole procreators that the fact that a woman could become pregnant when unconscious was regarded as solid evidence that women contributed nothing vital to the new being. A child's resemblance to its mother was explained as the effect on the seed of the soil it grows in or as an effect of maternal impression, that is, of the formative influence of the mother's emotions and experiences on the developing fetus, a theory similar to the belief in paternal impression of the Australian aborigines. From time to time one does find scientists, like Leonardo, Needham and Maupertuis, who reasoned that male and female must both contribute equally to the child's heredity, but such scientists were usually a minority and even they tended to give the male the more important, the vital role. Many scientists, for example, believed the embryo was formed by the mixture of male and female semen (vaginal secretions), but they assumed, like Hippocrates, that male seed was "stronger than female seed," or, like Avicenna, that male semen "by the command of God" gave form, whereas female semen took on form, or that male semen was the spiritual seed that activated, whereas female seed was the material seed that nourished. Others declared that semen produced the embryo, whereas the ovum merely produced the placenta. Even the ovists, scientists who believed the embryo was preformed in the ovum, regarded the embryo as inert until male semen, like God breathing into Adam's nostrils, transformed it into a living soul.

The ovists were not popular. Indeed, for many centuries the existence of ova in human females had been denied. Although Galen in the second century discovered "the female's testicles," so-called because he believed they manufactured female semen, his discovery was largely ignored for hundreds of years, and scientists, in spite of the knowledge of the existence of ova in other animals, denied their existence in mammals, that is, they denied their pre-existence: Harvey and most other seventeenth-century physiologists believed the ovum was created in the female after coitus by action of an "effluvium" of the sperm. It was not until 1672 that de Graaf discovered the ovarian follicles, and many scientists refused to believe they had anything to do with procreation; one scientist, Caspar Friedrich Hoffman, was certain they had no more functional value than the male's nipples. And de Graaf himself believed the follicles (which he mistook for the ovum) had a solely nutritive function and ruptured as a result of being fertilized by sperm.

The ovum is the largest cell in the human body and is, though just barely, visible to the unaided eye, but because of the almost universal belief that it was either formed or activated only as a consequence of coitus, it was not discovered for hundreds of years. Scientists were looking for it at the wrong time—after copulation, after semen had presumably given it life. It was not until 1827 that the mammalian ovum was discovered, and even its discoverer, von Baer, believed it was inert until activated by semen and that its role in generation was wholly nutritive. That the ovum was more than a source of nourishment for the embryo, that it was the female sex cell was not comprehended until 1861, and it was not until over a decade later, between the years 1875 and 1879, that the equal participation of the egg and sperm nuclei in fertilization was completely demonstrated. Mankind, then, did not acquire knowledge of the true facts of life until about one hundred years ago, and certainly one reason for the delay was the male sex's stubborn faith that He was the God of creation.

For most of history the male's role in generation was believed to be like that of Mary Shelley's Frankenstein, who "infuses a spark of being" into "lifeless" matter. Until well into the nineteenth century, the female was believed to affect the fetus only after creation by nutrition or some form of maternal impression. Dr Oliver Wendell Holmes in *Elsie Venner* (1861) accounted for Elsie's low forehead, hypnotic "diamond" eyes and her evil nature by her mother having been bitten by a snake two months before she was born. Even Francis Galton in his first paper on "Hereditary Talent and Character" (*Macmillan's Magazine*, 1865) wrote only of what the father, grandfather and great-grandfather transmitted to a child's heredity, making no mention of the mother's hereditary contributions. Mendel's discovery in the mid nineteenth century that each parent contributed one set of genes to the new offspring and, indeed, that the female was as likely as the male to contribute dominant genes, may well have remained unnoticed until 1900 because it was the final blow to the male ego that for most of recorded history had maintained that the male sex was the sole source of the life of the future individual, the female sex contributing inert matter. Nevertheless, Mendel's discovery did at long last signal the end of the reign of the male mothers.

Sole Progenitor

The belief the male sex was the mother of us all did far more than retard for centuries knowledge of the true facts of life or provide the unconscious motivation of the Christian religion. That belief was the origin of many social customs and laws and was the fundamental reason why women came to be regarded as inferior to men.

The belief the father was the sole progenitor of children was the reason why until less than a century ago in virtually all countries the father and the father only was the legal guardian of children. During marriage he had an absolute right to take the children away from his wife and give them to another to bring up, and in his will he could make someone else their legal guardian after his death. Upon divorce the father, not the mother, was routinely granted custody of the children, the mother having no legal right to them whatsoever. Not until 1886 in England could a woman get custody of the children, and then only if the father had been guilty of gross misconduct. In America in the 1890s all but five states in the Union made the father sole legal guardian. *The Woman's Journal* on September 3, 1892 recounted the case of an American woman married to a Chinese who, three days after the birth of their child, gave it to his brother to take to China. When the woman tried to get the baby back, the courts decided the father was within his rights, that as "the sole legal owner of the baby, he had the sole right to say what should be done with it." The father as sole progenitor had sacred rights.

In less civilized days, the father's sacred rights had included the right to kill his children at birth, for as the sole progenitor, the one who had given the child life, the father had the right to take that life away. We are most familiar with the right of Greek fathers to expose unwanted infants, but in many patriarchal primitive tribes there was a widespread ceremony called the "lifting up" in which the father either lifted up the infant and thereby acknowledged it as his own or did not lift it up, whereupon the child was either killed or suffered the life of an outcast. Almost identical was the ancient Roman custom of placing a newborn baby on the ground; only if the father raised it was it allowed to live, the phrase "to raise a child" deriving from that custom. The father had life and death rights over a newborn child not only because as sole progenitor the baby was solely his property to do with as he wished; the father's right to kill the baby or let it live was another way of asserting, and quite literally, that the father, the male, actually gave the baby its life.

The belief the male was the sole progenitor, the female functioning only as his womb, also explains the male's traditional prohibition of abortion. When women were believed to be impregnated by Spirits, they arranged their own abortions, but when men decided the Spirits dwelt in their semen, women lost that right. They lost the right because the unborn life was now believed to derive wholly from the father and a pregnant woman might be said to be only taking care of the father's baby until she could safely deliver it into his arms. When a woman from Miletus was executed for having an abortion, Cicero approved because the woman had robbed the father of his most precious property—the means of carrying on his life—and had also robbed the state of a citizen. Christians disapproved of abortion for the same reason, except that the real father of the child was God. As Lactantius in the fourth century explained in *Divine Institutes*, since it was God who had given the child life, only God could take that life away. For the same reason, Christians used to regard contraception as a sin since it prevented God from having his babies. Moreover, since Christians believed the child did not acquire real life, immortal life, until after baptism, to abort a fetus meant depriving God of a soul for eternity, which was also why Catholic doctors in a difficult birth saved the life of the un-baptised child, not the life of the already baptised mother.

A man had proprietary interest in assuring not only that his life was not destroyed by contraception or abortion but that his wife was carrying his seeds of life and not another man's. The sexual double standard, chastity for women only, came into existence so a man could be sure a woman was having his child. When the relationship between sex and conception was not understood, virgin-ity of course had no value. On the contrary, men valued women whom the Spirits had favored with children. During the Anglo-Saxon period women were not expected to be virgins before marriage or sexually faithful after mar-riage because the old belief that women were impregnated by Spirits still lingered on, finding expression in the cult of the hero, a semi-divine figure, the noblest male specimen whom Anglo-Saxon women, like fertility goddesses, were eager to sleep with. In a Provençal romance a wife who is reproached by her husband for sleeping with another man tells him he was not dishonored be-cause her lover was a hero, the mighty Roland. The husband was appeased because children born of such unions were held in high esteem; Clothwig, the founder of the Frankish kingdom, left the largest share of his land to the child his wife had by another man, not to his own sons, and precisely because that child was a bastard, that is, the son of a hero. The word bastard used to be an honorific; men boasted of being bastards. The man we now call William the Conqueror preferred to call himself William the Bastard, and Charlemagne and Roland were honored to have bastardy imputed to them. All the famous heroes in Irish myth were bastards, as were King Arthur and Gawain.

The Catholic Church in England had great difficulty in making bastardy a disgrace. The Anglo-Saxon synod in 786 decreed that "the son of a meretricious union shall be debarred from legally inheriting," but it took several centuries before the mysterious glamour of having an unknown father who might be a hero finally faded away. Only then did it become a disgrace to be a bastard, and only then was a bastard "debarred from legally inheriting." A bastard could not inherit because he had come to be regarded as *filius nullius*, to use the old Roman legal term meaning "not a son." A bastard was not a son be-cause his father was unknown, the law recognizing no physical relationship to the mother. In the light of the prevalent physiological beliefs, there was none since women were thought to be merely the conduits through which men had their children. Since a bastard had no known progenitor, he had no relations from whom he could inherit and had no accepted place in society. But bastards were social outcasts for a more fundamental reason; they were an insult to male motherhood. Being children with a mother only, they were reminiscent of the children who in ancient times had been created by women alone with no apparent need of men. For the same reason, an unmarried woman who had a baby also outraged male motherhood and had to suffer "social death." She had committed the unpardonable sin of having a baby on her own, as if she, like a Mother Goddess, had been the sole progenitor.

Once it became a sin for a woman to have a baby without a certified father, women were required to be virgins before marriage and sexually faithful after marriage; otherwise a woman might bear a child not her husband's and thus cheat him of his posterity. Since an adulterous wife might present her husband with adulterated, that is, spurious issue, adultery became the highest crime a wife could commit. No longer were romances written in which a wife glories in having a hero for a lover; in Elizabethan dramas a wife who is merely suspected of adultery must, like Desdemona, die. It is fitting that at the same time as European women were losing their sexual freedom, chastity belts came into use. According to Eric Dingwall's *The Girdle of Chastity*, they were introduced from the Orient about the second half of the twelfth century and continued to be used until the sixteenth or seventeenth century, probably more women being subjected to them than we would now like to imagine. But however many women were actually locked into chastity belts, an invisible chastity belt now imprisoned all women. In the interest of male motherhood, the sexual double standard had supervened, and to make sure no woman slipped her sexual leash, her social life was severely restricted. Women were chaperoned, duennaed and in certain periods not even allowed to go for a walk unescorted. They were also forbidden, except in minute quantities, to partake of alcohol, for as Ovid explained in *The Art of Love*, "In women full of wine there's no resistance," that is, an intoxicated woman might tumble into bed with any man and bring a bastard into the world.

Illegitimate children used to be called "nameless" children because the man who had given them life was unknown. Legitimate children, on the other hand, children whose father was known, bore his name, the name of their sole progenitor, the man whose seeds of life had been transmitted to them. For to the civilized as well as the primitive mind, names are coequal with a person's life. Most of us still feel an affinity with a person who has the same name we have, and primitive men felt the affinity so strongly they believed two people should not bear the same name simultaneously. Only when a person was no longer alive could his name be given to another. The Eskimos believed that after death a person's name left him and entered the body of a pregnant woman and was reborn, the baby inheriting the qualities of the person whose name he inherited. Children in the earliest societies would not inherit a living father's or a living mother's name. Records from the Hammurabi dynasty (ca. 1700 BC) reveal that children were never named after their parents, and children of Orthodox Jews are still not named after a living person. When children were believed to derive their life from Spirits, the mother would name the child after the place where she thought the Spirit had entered her, or after the place where the child was born, or after some event that occurred at childbirth. Although at first women did not give their own name to children, children did derive additional identification from the mother's name. An ancient Egyptian child would be described as "Anhor, born of Neb-onet [mother's name]" and Greek gods were described as "Apollo, son of Leto," "Dionysus, son of Semele." Eventually, in some cultures, as in ancient Lycia or Xanthia, mothers transmitted their own name to children. But whatever the custom, the mother named the child because she was the one who gave the child life. The father did not name the child because, so it was thought, he had nothing to do with giving the child life.

As woman was dethroned from her role as the Great Mother and as man became the One God of Life, fathers took over the naming of children. Hebrew manuscripts examined in chronological order reveal that in earliest times the mother almost always named the child but that slowly father naming increased. A naming custom of the Australian aborigines may reveal the transition from mother to father naming. Children were given two names: the first usually derived from the exact place where the child was born, as was the custom when women were believed to be impregnated by Spirits; but the second name was given to the child by the headman, a name that was a secret name never uttered in the presence of women, a custom that seems to show men in the process of preempting procreative power.

When men had totally preempted procreative power, fathers named children, and eventually fathers transmitted their own name to children as a way of signifying their life had been transmitted to the child. Surnames became male pedigree names, male "life lines," and men wanted children to carry on their name because they wanted pledges of immortality, children to carry on their life. Not children, sons.

Men preferred sons to daughters because only by means of a son could a man perpetuate himself. A father's seeds of life did of course generate daughters, but since a daughter had no seeds of life she could not pass them on; a daughter was a genetic dead end. If a man did not have a son, he did not have a descendant, for his seeds of life had not been transmitted to the sex who could in turn transmit them to the next generation. That was why kings needed male heirs to carry on their line and why men in many cultures were allowed to divorce a wife who produced no male children. For the same reason, the

Chinese would count as their children only their sons and felt free to kill female infants. That custom seems less cruel when one understands that females were not believed to be essential to the carrying on of life; they were only the receptacles in which men incubated their life, and any womb would do. When males were believed to be the sole progenitors, women were of much less biological value than men.

The fact that women did not have seeds of life not only made them biologically defective, it was the cause of their intellectual deficiencies. For semen was believed to be a "drop of the brain," as a Pythagorean put it; in other words, semen was thought to be generated in the head, whence it traveled down the spinal column to the testicles. It was therefore argued, as was discussed at length in Chapter Six, that since women did not have semen, they did not have any life in their heads either, for semen generated mental as well as physical life, was the source of new ideas and images as well as babies. The only sort of intelligence women were thought capable of was intuition, an insight gained without effort and seemingly all at once from some mysterious source, a belief analogous to the old theory that Spirits suddenly entered a woman to create new life. Male intelligence, on the other hand, was different; it was not the light that suddenly illuminated the darkness of the female mind, though occasionally a man might have an inspiration. Generally, however, male intelligence was like having a baby, the semen in men's brains conceiving an idea and after long gestation and hard labor, delivering it into the world. Men's heads were the mental wombs of the world, giving birth to books, paintings, music and all other artistic and intellectual creations. Thus did men preempt intellectual as well as physical motherhood.

It was because men became the sole progenitors that women became the inferior sex. After many hundreds of years, woman as Mother Goddess was toppled and man as Father God set himself up in her place. Or rather, in a higher place, for the Spirits had merely from time to time chosen to dwell in a woman and be reborn into human life, but the Spirits were constantly indwelling in man's semen, who was therefore like a God. "Man is the whole world, and the breath of God; woman the rib only and crooked piece of man," boasted Sir Thomas Browne in the seventeenth century, for after men discovered they were the sole progenitors they delighted in extolling themselves as the darlings of creation, the perfect sex, and disparaging women as "the weaker vessel," to cite the New Testament, or as "this fair defect of nature," to use Milton's words.

But when men set themselves up as the lords of creation, they could not put women down quite so low as men once had been; for when men had been the defective sex, they had seemed to be totally useless, the sex with no reason for being, since women appeared to create life without any need of men. But when men became the Gods of life, they could not dispense with women. It was, alas, woman's belly that grew big and delivered babies into the world. Faced with this conspicuous fact, men might have reasoned that since both sexes were equally necessary in the creation of new life, woman was not inferior to man. They did not, and in the light of their physiological beliefs they were right not to. On the principle that the mysterious power to generate life is greater than the mundane power to nurture it, that Spirit is more exalted than matter, men were indeed superior to women. At any rate, men decided woman's role in procreation was vastly inferior to man's, that her womb was merely the place where man's life was nurtured, that woman's fundamental reason for being was to serve as man's womb and, by extension, to serve man generally. Man came to regard himself as the primary existence and woman as ancillary to that existence. Just as mankind came to believe animals were created solely for the use of Homo sapiens, so men came to believe women were created solely for the use of men. Our Ford in *Brave New World* created Epsilons defective because they were meant to be the servants of higher beings. Similarly, God in Genesis created Woman not, like Adam, to exist in her own right, but "as a help meet for him"—to copulate with him and bear his children and in all other ways serve his physical needs. "A woman is a worthy wyght, She serveth a man both day and night" goes an anonymous fifteenth-century song, and that woman was man's servant did not make men feel guilty, just as we do not feel guilty when we set the handicapped to do simple menial tasks.

Woman's fall from a Mother Goddess to man's servant was recorded in myth, in myths that suggest, albeit symbolically, that woman's fall did result from the new knowledge of the role of the male sex in procreation. In Genesis 3 it was Woman who brought about her fall, and that women, not men, discovered copulation was essential for pregnancy seems probable since women would be far more likely than men to notice they did not get pregnant when they did not have sex; at any rate, according to Genesis it was a serpent (= penis) that led Woman to the new knowledge, which she transmitted to Adam. That the new knowledge was sexual knowledge explains why after Adam also ate fruit from the tree of knowledge they both became conscious for the first time that "they were naked" and immediately "sewed fig leaves together" to cover their sex organs, trying to conceal from God what they now knew—the reason for genitalia, knowledge of the source of life. Knowledge that made Woman subordinate to Adam, for after discovering the male's role in procreation, Woman no longer gloried in her capacity to create life; she now brought forth children "in sorrow," and since she now felt man was her superior, she had a desire to submit to her husband, who henceforth ruled over her. After becoming her ruler, Adam changed Woman's name to Eve, a name he said meant "the mother of all living." No children had been born in the Garden of Eden. Only after Woman came under the rule of Adam, only after children were no longer woman's but man's, did the author of Genesis permit Woman to become Eve, a mother.

According to a Greek myth, woman lost her high status because of a contest between a female and a male god. Athena and Poseidon, both wanting to be the patron of a city, offered the city gifts, Athena causing an olive tree to spring up and Poseidon a fountain of salt water. The citizens voted, all the women voting for the goddess and all the men voting for the god, and since there was one more woman than man, the goddess won. Athena became the patron of the city that was named Athens after her, just as at that time women gave their names to their children. But Poseidon, enraged that he had not prevailed, caused a great flood, a flood he agreed to stop only when women were punished. Athens continued to be called Athens, but women no longer gave their names to children, neither could they vote nor enjoy any other right of citizenship.

The myth looks back to the time when descent was traced through women, for only then did children (or cities) derive their names from women, a custom that changed, so says the myth, because of a male god's fountain of salt water, a gush that certainly could symbolize ejaculating semen. Moreover, the fact that Poseidon was a god of the sea could be another symbolic way of asserting life came from the water of a male god, just as early Christians insisted life (immortal life) came from the water of baptism, not from amniotic fluid. At any rate, the ascendancy of a male god broke the custom of tracing descent through women; after Poseidon's triumph descent was traced through men; fathers henceforth handed down their names to children. And when descent ceased to be traced through women, women lost their high status in society; they no longer had a say in their own government but came under the rule of men.

Absolute Sovereignty

In the myth of the contest between Athena and Poseidon we learn of women who could vote and were full citizens, and books like Robert Briffault's *The Mothers* prove in great detail that women once did have civic rights and were the superior sex. Women in different societies lost their high status at different times, depending upon when the role of men in procreation was fully understood, Greek women, for example, becoming the despised sex many centuries before Englishwomen, who at the beginning of the Anglo-Saxon period still had many rights. As Pollock and Maitland graphically imagined in their *History of English Law Before the Time of Edward I*, "On the extreme verge of our legal history we seem to see the wife of Aethelbert's day [late sixth century] leaving her husband of her own free will and carrying off her children and half the goods."

A wife could take the children because children still belonged to the mother. Women in the Anglo-Saxon period had not yet lost all the freedom of the Mother Goddess, which was why they were not expected to be virgins before marriage nor sexually faithful afterwards and why having a child outside of marriage or a child that was not the husband's was no disgrace for woman or child. Indeed, marriage at that time was as often as not a temporary arrangement; it was perfectly possible to contract to marry someone for one year and divorce by mutual consent was common. King Clothacar I, a Frankish king, had seven wives, the fifth of whom, Radegund, left him. As late as the tenth century Howel the Good passed an ordinance permitting seven year trial marriages (and one year trial marriages existed in Scotland until the Reformation). Under such a loose marital system, women did not assume the rank of their husbands; they retained their own rank (and name) and continued to owe allegiance to their own family, who in turn continued to be responsible for any crimes they might commit. They could also own property, incur debts and make wills and, as we have seen, if they left their husbands they could take half the property, and all the children and return to their own family.

During the Anglo-Saxon period marriage was not the only way a woman could maintain herself; she could choose to pursue a more honorable profession. Radegund, King Clothacar's fifth wife, disliking married life, left her husband and became a nun, which did not then mean becoming a praying recluse. Far otherwise, nuns were not cloistered, nor did they wear special clothing. Nuns were among the most learned people in the Anglo-Saxon world, for they studied Latin and both profane and sacred literature; many an English boy was educated by nuns. Furthermore, nuns could hope to become abbesses, a rank just below a bishop, and an abbess frequently ruled over a double monastery, one for men and one for women. Nuns not only pursued learning, they were also businessmen, being independent landowners and running the monastery and the farms attached to it. As late as the early thirteenth century, the author of the tract *Holy Maidenhood* could say that whereas wives were slaves, nuns were free women.

Lower class wives might have been slaves, but upper class wives in the thirteenth century had almost as much freedom as nuns. Just as nuns managed monasteries, so the lady of the manor managed her husband's estate. For her husband was often away at war or at court or on a pilgrimage or crusade, so that it was the wife's job to supervise the farm and all the household industries (like cloth spinning and meat preserving), to purchase whatever was not grown on the estate, to hire and fire servants, physic the sick, set broken bones and even fight lawsuits. Married women could and did appear and speak in court and a husband occasionally appointed his wife to act as his attorney. Wives could also convey land, execute deeds and make wills with their husband's consent, and a husband generally needed his wife's consent to convey land since to a large extent the property of husband and wife was treated as community property. Upper class wives had time to fight lawsuits and manage estates because child rearing was the least of their jobs. Babies were handed over to wet nurses and both male and female children at an early age were sent to other households to be brought up. Moreover, childhood officially did not extend beyond the twelfth year and children frequently married at the age of seven.

Being female did not debar a woman from such masculine jobs as waging war and ruling countries. Aethelfraed, King Alfred's sister, helped her brother put down the Danes, and in the early thirteenth century Blanche of Champagne, in order to protect the interests of her minor son, fought a war for fourteen years. Aethelflaed, Alfred's daughter, reigned alone over Mercia from 911 till her death in 918, and after Blanche of Castile's husband died in 1226 she, during Louis IX's boyhood, became the effective ruler of Capetian France and later again acted as ruler when Louis was away for six years on a crusade. Women also held other positions of authority. During the reign of King John, Nicoli Delabair served as High Sheriff of Lincolnshire. In addition, women practiced medicine. There were female physicians in England during the period of the Crusades, and a Cecilia of Oxford was said to have been appointed Court Surgeon by Queen Philippa, wife of Edward III. When the Guild of Surgeons was founded in 1389, it recognized a few women surgeons.

Women were also in business. It is true that many crafts were closed to them and that the law officially barred them from being in business except under the supervision of their husbands; nevertheless, a fair number of towns passed special ordinances giving wives permission to do business on their own, and so competent were medieval businesswomen that husbands frequently made their wives executors of their wills. Lower class women also had many and varied jobs; they were, for example, thatchers' assistants, sheep shearers, spinners of cloth, and the making of ale (the national drink) was largely the work of women—alewives. Moreover, a female serf could work a farm and render service to her lord the way a man could (though she earned only subsistence wages).

Of course, even in early Anglo-Saxon times women were not treated as the equals of men, but women then and for some time later had rights and freedoms they eventually lost. By the end of the medieval period their former freedom of action had been greatly reduced. Gone were the Anglo-Saxon women who fought campaigns, gone the medieval businesswomen, and gone too were the learned nuns who managed farms and other church property. Nuns had become praying recluses who often knew only enough Latin to understand the church services. Also gone were the women physicians; in 1421 the Surgeons' Guild petitioned Parliament that no woman should practice medicine under pain of long imprisonment. A woman's only vocation eventually became marriage.

Just as women were barred from practicing medicine, so around the tenth century they began to be barred from owning property. Whereas daughters had sometimes been able to inherit if there were no sons, during feudalism it became the rule, to which there were few exceptions, that females could not inherit, and in France after the passage of the Salic laws women could not succeed to family titles and offices. In addition, the civil law gradually abandoned the principle of community property between husband and wife, replacing it with the rule: "Whatsoever is the wife's is the husband's and the converse is not true," According to Pollock and Maitland's *History of English Law Before the Time of Edward I*, during the twelfth century wives could make wills, but slowly it came about that a wife had only such power to make a will as her husband gave her, then by the middle of the fourteenth century lawyers disputed whether or not a wife had a right to make a will even with her husband's permission.

Women were more and more losing control over their own lives and coming under the control of their husbands. "Feme covert" and "coverte de baron" are French legal terms that began to be used in English law in the late thirteenth century and that mean "covered woman" and "woman covered by her lord." The terms are now given a crude sexual interpretation, but feme covert more likely signified that when a woman married she was henceforth covered by her husband in the sense that he now stood for her, represented her. In *The Lawes Resolutions of Womens Rights* (1632) it was argued that women had no voice in Parliament and made no laws because they were understood to be actually or potentially married. In other words, women did not make laws because their husbands, their representatives, made laws for them, just as the residents of a district send a representative to Congress to make laws for them.

Women had come to be regarded not as under the jurisdiction of the state at large but under the jurisdiction of their husbands. The Treason Act, passed in 1351, illustrates the change. Before the Act a woman who killed her husband was simply guilty of murder, but after the Act she was guilty of petty treason, the new idea being that just as a man who killed his sovereign was guilty of the higher crime of treason, so was a wife who killed *her* sovereign, her husband. As Jean Bodin explained in *The Six Books of the Republic* (1576), the law of "commanding and obeying" prevailed in the universe, which meant that just as God commanded the universe, which must obey his laws, and a sovereign commanded men, who must obey his laws, so a husband commanded his wife, who must obey his laws. The husband was the sovereign in the separate state he ruled, which was why a husband who killed his adulterous wife or her lover was rarely punished by the state at large; he was not because a husband was the agent of the law in his domestic state and as such he had merely performed his job of punishing those who violated its chief law. In the story of Patient Griselda, when Griselda's husband Walter takes away her infant daughter, presumably to be killed, it does not cross her mind she should send for the sheriff to stop a murder; she regards herself as wholly under the law of her husband, an absolute sovereign.

Patient Griselda, one of the stories in Boccaccio's *Decameron* (1353), not only illustrates how totally women had come under the rule of husbands, but also the new psychology of masculinity and femininity that brought about the new order. For Griselda's abject submissiveness and Walter's will to dominate were not expressions of the eternal archetypes of female and male. One need only remember the many courtly knights in medieval romances who, perhaps still under the mystique of the Mother Goddess, used to swear eternal subjection, reverence and obedience to their lady love and promise to remain her humble vassal no matter how badly she treated them. Griselda is in many ways a female courtly knight when she swears total obedience to Walter and promises never to say No when he says Yes and never to be angry whatever he does. And she, like a courtly knight, feels no anger, only greater love and humility, the more cruelly Walter treats her—when he takes away her daughter, then her son, then informs her he is divorcing her and orders her to prepare the castle for his new wife. Walter, in turn, when he makes his ever more harsh demands on Griselda, seems very much like a medieval court lady exerting more and more mastery over the man who loves her. For in the Renaissance the sexual stereotypes changed, at least women were no longer supposed to be masterful; they had to give up the assertive characteristics that had made them abbesses and managers of estates and able to fight lawsuits and face the world on their own. Instead, they were to be dependent and submissive, which is why Walter calls his assertion of mastery over Griselda a "trial of her womanhood," an absurd trial since Griselda is wholly submissive from the very first. It is Walter who must prove his manhood by demonstrating again and again and more and more cruelly his ability to dominate Griselda, just as men in 1970s sex movies prove their manhood by forcing women to submit to more and more humiliating forms of copulation.

Petruchio in Shakespeare's *The Taming of the Shrew* demonstrates his manhood far better than Walter because the woman he masters is not docile. In Kate we see the aggressive independent woman of the old era being transformed into the new submissive woman. For the trouble with Kate is she is very much like a man, like Petruchio himself—outspoken, intelligent, knowing her own mind, independent, cruel. But what is admirable in a man is no longer admirable in a woman, and Petruchio proceeds to transform Kate into the new ideal woman by making her meek, obedient, silent unless spoken to, with no mind of her own and a will wholly controlled by her husband. By the end of the play she has been so transformed she sermonizes on a wife's duty to obey her sovereign:

> Thy husband is thy lord, thy life, thy keeper,
> Thy head, thy sovereign . . .
> Such duty as the subject owes the prince,
> Even such a woman oweth to her husband;
> And when she is froward, peevish, sullen, sour,
> And not obedient to his honest will,
> What is she but a foul contending rebel
> And graceless traitor to her loving lord?

Shakespeare was writing these lines at a time when the idea of nationalism was in the ascendant, when men were abandoning the medieval ideal of a united Christendom under one Pope and were dividing into individual nations, each ruled by a king with absolute power. And within each nation, husbands, like kings, were becoming absolute sovereigns in the domestic state.

In the state at large men early began to rebel against the idea of absolute authority; in 1215 feudal barons forced King John to sign the Magna Carta, which greatly restricted his authority and gave the barons more rights. During the Renaissance and Reformation men lost their respect for civil and religious authority and came to believe that men ought to resist tyranny, that men were created with free will and therefore ought to have the right to use their abilities freely and exert their own power. Concomitantly, men freed themselves from the intellectual blinders imposed by the church and rediscovered classical learning and began to make scientific discoveries. They also freed themselves from the early Christian idea that sex was evil and began to celebrate the body.

But such freedoms—sexual, intellectual and political—were for men only.

A Renaissance man might believe a sovereign no longer had the right to seize his subjects' property but nevertheless believe a husband had the right to seize "the profit of all the lands and goods" of his wife, to cite Jean Bodin. A Renaissance man might respect, even worship, learning, but not in women, who continued to be ignorant. An occasional upper class woman, like Queen Elizabeth and Lady Jane Grey, was allowed to become learned, and Protestants did teach girls as well as boys to read the Bible, but the general belief women needed no education prevailed. And whereas a Renaissance man might write an ode to sensuality, he would see nothing contradictory in locking his wife into a chastity belt, and though he spoke up against the church and state, if his wife talked back to him he was capable of locking her into the iron head cage called the brank. The Renaissance was for men only. Men, like Milton, rebelled against the King's authority and yet were kings themselves at home. In the state of marriage feudalism continued; when a woman married she became a serf, ruled by an absolute authority it was treason to resist, with little free will or individual freedom and no power, taught to believe she had no rights, only duties. Women remained encapsulated in feudalism.

A woman at marriage now had to swear to obey her husband, not God, utterly. For "obey" was added to the marriage service during the Reformation, the church obligingly, if sacrilegiously, accommodating itself to the new secular view of woman. The church obliged because it was then losing its power in the state, and in regard to marriage it had long had difficulties imposing its views on a people who had the custom of one year marriages, trial marriages, who divorced by mutual consent and who saw no disgrace in being a bastard. The English had regarded marriage as a private contract made or dissolved by the man and woman without interference of the state or church. Not until 1164 was marriage incorporated into the list of the sacraments, and as R. H. Helmholz illustrated in his *Marriage Litigation in Medieval England* (1974), only slowly and over 300 years did the church succeed in changing marriage from a private contract to a divine one. The sacramental nature of marriage had to be reaffirmed in 1439 and it was not until 1563 that the Council of Trent succeeded in establishing that no marriage was valid unless performed by a priest and according to the rites of the church.

One reason why the church managed to gain full control over marriage at a time when it had lost its power in every other area was its willingness to think of women the way laymen now did. Not only did the church decide to permit a woman to swear her primary allegiance to her husband, not God, but the church, like the state, now professed that a woman's only vocation was marriage. The church had used to honor virginity and had encouraged married women to leave their husbands and enter a nunnery. But in the sixteenth century the Catholic church stopped urging women to be nuns. Officially, Catholics retained their former position, the Council of Trent decreeing that anyone who said marriage was superior to virginity "let him be anathema"; nevertheless, the church began to promulgate the view that a woman's highest vocation was to be found in the home. The Virgin Mary was no longer honored because she was a virgin but because she was a mother, because she "conceived and bare Christ in her womb," to quote a sixteenth-century sermon. And the Protestants honored Mary as mother as much as the Catholics.

The Protestants did destroy images and statues of Mary, but they swept her off the pedestal to set her up in every man's home. In June 1525 Martin Luther, a former priest, married Katharina von Bora, a former nun, and proceeded to turn her into the ideal wife—a household drudge. Within eight years she had six children and besides taking care of them she took care of a small farm, an orchard, a fishpond and Martin himself during his many bouts of illness; and Katharina, unlike upper class medieval wives, did most of the physical work herself. Luther viewed her transformation from a nun into a wife and mother with satisfaction, for as he wrote in 1524 to three nuns who were considering leaving the cloister, God fashioned woman's "body so that she should be with a man, to have and to bear children." Luther, like Freud, believed anatomy was destiny, that man and woman's different roles in society were an inevitable consequence of their different physiques. In 1531 he remarked: "Men have broad shoulders and narrow hips, and accordingly they possess intelligence. Women have narrow shoulders and broad hips and a wide fundament to sit upon, keep house and bear and raise children," a view of woman that was to prevail for the next 400 years. A woman's sphere of action had been reduced to the circle of her hips.

The fairly independent woman of the Anglo-Saxon period had finally been reduced to her reproductive parts by having been economically, mentally and physically stunted. Economically she had been crippled by having all jobs by which one could earn a decent wage closed to her. Mentally she had been dwarfed by being deprived of all but an elementary education. Physically she had been maimed by having her legs confined in cages (farthingales and hoops) or encumbered by long heavy skirts, and by having her waist compressed in some sort of vise. Moreover, young girls were discouraged from participating in muscle-building sports, and, as the centuries passed, only poor women were allowed to perform hard physical labor outside the home; middle class women labored physically only in and around the home, and upper class women did no physical labor at all. Consequently, women developed little strength in their arms and legs. All a woman was permitted to develop was her belly, her ability to have babies. There is a grotesque truth in seeing woman as having become a large womb with rudimentary limbs, attached to a man below his head.

The Conjugal Centaur

Shortly before Luther married, he remarked to a friend that since he was writing so much about marriage and having so much to do with women (he was arranging marriages for nuns), it would be surprising if "I do not turn into a woman." And after marriage made him the head of Katharina von Bora's body, he who had been a lean ascetic acquired "the appearance of a buxom *hausfrau*," to use V. H. H. Green's description. More will be said later of Luther's unconscious belief he had turned into a woman, but the most fundamental reason why the church was able to gain full control over marriage during the Reformation was that the Christian concept of marriage allowed men to give symbolic expression to the unconscious male desire to acquire a female body, a desire clearly expressed by Paul in his Letter to the Ephesians. There Paul had said that just as Christ is the head of the church that he loves as his own body, so husbands are the head of their wives whom they love "as their own bodies."

Paul described Christian marriage, the acquisition by a man of a woman's body, as "a great mystery," but if it were a mystery it was not a Christian one; it was as old as man, Zeus participating in the same mystery when, observing that his first wife Metis was pregnant, he swallowed her and carried the baby to term himself, giving birth to Athena through the male creative organ, the head. Early man, like Zeus, felt the same desire to make woman part of himself and used to feel deficient until he had in one way or another assimilated woman. Boys in primitive tribes were called "incomplete beings" until after the initiation ceremonies that symbolically feminized them. In the Eleusinian mysteries and other early Greek religions the male initiate was required to undergo a ritual that made him one with Demeter or some other goddess of fertility. "While being male one should cleave to the female," advised Lao-Tze in the *Tao Te Ching*, for a man thus becomes "possessed of a power" he can get no other way. In India during the Vedic period (4000-300 BC) religious sacrifices and ceremonies could not be performed by a man alone because he was believed to be spiritually incomplete; the presence of his wife was essential. In Genesis 2 as soon as Adam gives birth to Woman he immediately reassimilates her—he cleaves to her and they become one flesh, a passage that according to the Midrashim, Jewish commentaries on the Scriptures, means that "He who is not married is hardly a (complete) man." Paul's description in Ephesians of the conjugal centaur, the man with a woman's body, was merely the Christian version of man completing himself by becoming one with woman.

In December 1677 John Wilmot, Lord Rochester was informed he had "a daughter borne by the body of Mrs Barry." Mrs Barry was Rochester's mistress, and if men had been content to be the sole progenitors, they would simply have copulated with many women, filling the wombs of the world with their progeny. But they were not content until they had succeeded almost as completely as Zeus in incorporating woman's capacity to give birth by creating a society in which women virtually could not exist unless they attached themselves to a man and served as his womb. Men were not content until they had made the whole reproductive process their own.

The male compulsion to become an androgyne, to be like certain flatworms that have both testes and a uterus and can reproduce offspring on their own, made woman a parasite, a dependent, one who literally had to hang on to man for her very life and only thus give birth to man's life. The male compulsion to make woman's womb belong to him created a society in which woman's sphere came to be wholly within man's and wholly controlled by man. The actualization in history of the conjugal centaur—a man's head on a woman's body—deprived woman of her rights because it deprived her of the attributes of a complete person and made her part of a man.

It was when woman was losing her status as a complete person and becoming part of a man that the concept developed that husband and wife were one and the one was the husband, a concept that if understood as an actual physical merger makes the development of various customs, legal practices and mental sets more comprehensible.

Only when woman had become part of man did easy divorce by mutual consent become impossible and the Christian view of the indissolubility of marriage take hold. For if a wife is regarded as having been physically merged with a man, how can what has thus been joined together, ever be separated? Or as Henry Cornelius Agrippa explained in *The Commendation of Matrimony* (1545), divorce was not lawful for any cause because no man can "departe from him selfe," woman being "made of mannes ribbe, of fleshe, the same fleshe, and the same bone of bones." Not only can a man not part from himself while alive, how can that which is part of him live on after he is dead? The Indian custom of suttee, of the wife immolating herself on her husband's funeral pyre, was a way of demonstrating that a wife could not continue to live after her husband's death, just as parasites must die when their host dies. In Western countries wives were not required literally to die when their husbands did, but they were required to wear symbols of death, the heaviest, blackest clothing and a long black veil that made them resemble walking sepulchres.

A husband when his wife died wore only a black armband because he had been deprived merely of a replaceable part, a part a man used to feel he had the right to divorce from him if it proved to be incapable of performing its function, which was why Henry VIII kept replacing one "womban" with another in his quest for a son. A husband could also separate himself from his "womban" if it was contaminated with another man's seed, wifely fornication being the unpardonable sin, but perhaps not just because it could produce children not the husband's. Perhaps when a man unconsciously regarded his wife's womb as his womb, he unconsciously reacted to her fornicating with another man as if his own body had been sexually violated, homosexually violated. A man's unconscious belief his wife's body was himself may also explain why men have often treated sexual intercourse as a form of autoeroticism and preferred women to seem like the life-size rubber dolls sold in sex shops and were genuinely puzzled by complaints of sexual dissatisfaction.

But to return to less disputable effects of merger. A wife lost her name and took her husband's only after she came to be regarded as part of her husband, for only then did it make sense for a woman to assume the identity of the man she merged with. Similarly, only when women were losing their right to live independently in society and were becoming forced to depend wholly on husbands did the legal fiction develop that upon marriage a woman was "incorporated and consolidated" into her husband, to use Blackstone's words, and that legal fiction, if considered as literal fact, makes the legal disabilities of wives more understandable. For if a wife is a physical part of her husband, how can she buy property or sue and be sued or run a business or hold public office? Having been, as it were, grafted onto her husband, how can a wife act on her own? As the Governor of Louisiana explained in 1885 when feminists were demanding that women be appointed to the school board, if a married woman were to be appointed to a public office, "her husband would share it with her; would, in fact, be the officer." Until 1887 the Government Land Office did not let married women buy land because "the law did not contemplate married women as separate from their husbands," a merger that was meant more literally than we can now imagine.

By imagining a wife as having become physically a part of her husband, we can also better understand why the wife took the status of her husband and not vice versa, why a housemaid who married a Lord became My Lady, but a Lady who married a footman became Mrs Footman. "A man raises a woman to his own standard, but a woman must take that of the man she marries," explained

Trollope in *Dr Thorne* (1858), and that was so because marriage was the male incorporation of the female, which was also why women who married foreigners used to lose their citizenship and automatically acquired their husband's, and why on old passports only the name, date of birth, description and signature of the husband were required, the wife's presence being acknowledged only in a note that said she was accompanying her husband.

The male incorporation of the female also explains why it used to make sense to men that if women were to be allowed to vote, only single women should do so. "I am not disposed to proceed any further than to give the vote to women householders who are spinsters," said Lord Denman in a debate in the House of Lords on June 24, 1892. A single woman, a woman who had not become part of a man, might perhaps be permitted to vote, but once a woman had been merged with a husband, to give her the vote would be like giving her husband two votes. The tendency to regard wives as inseparable from husbands was also why, even after women got the vote, most men used to feel a wife would vote just like her husband or, if she did not, that her vote would cancel out his, a complaint of Alistair Cooke's father whenever his wife voted differently from him. Strange reasoning, that made sense to men because they thought of a wife as fused with her husband. For if a cousin who lived in the same house voted the same way as or differently from the husband, his vote would not be thought to double or negate the husband's because the cousin would be regarded as a separate person.

It was because men unconsciously regarded wives as part of themselves that they so guiltlessly appropriated work done by their wives and at best gave them only token credit. In 1715 Thomas Masters received the first patent issued to an American colonist for a new method of grinding corn; one has to read the patent carefully to discover the inventor was really his wife Sybilla. Thomas may not have wanted to seem to get credit for what he did not invent, but the law then did not permit a married woman to get a patent in her own name; it had to be in her husband's name, the law actualizing the belief that since husband and wife were one person and that person was the husband, he in fact was the inventor. The cultural assumption that in a marriage a wife became an adjunct of her husband's head was why Peter Zenger alone was regarded as the father of the freedom of the press, even though Anna Zenger also edited the *New-York Weekly Journal* and when her husband was arrested for criticizing the royal governor of New York kept the newspaper going and wrote some of the columns herself. Whenever a man worked with a woman, even when she was not his wife, he tended to regard her as an extension of himself, which was at least one reason why although more than half the work for Thomas Bowdler's expurgated *Family Shakespeare* (1818) was done by his sister Harriet, he put only his own name on the title page, or why Heywood Broun signed his newspaper columns with his name alone, although he admitted Ruth Hale wrote a " considerable percentage," or why only Edwin Newman's name was on the title page of *Strictly Speaking* (1974), although he acknowledged there would have been "no book" without his wife's contributions.

But we tend not to take such acknowledgments seriously; we think of them as male gallantry—a chivalrous husband giving the little woman more credit than she deserves. For we take it for granted that the man must have done the real thinking, the woman the routine research or typing, that the woman merely listened while the man expounded his ideas, or that the woman's help consisted in keeping the man's mind alert with cups of coffee, his strength up with regular meals and his self-confidence high with much praise. We assume that men produce the brainchildren and that women are their midwives. Men have so often taken total credit for what was often a real collaboration for the same reason a writer would not think of giving credit for writing a book to his hand.

Of course, another reason why men did not give their wives credit was that their wives did not object, woman having been taught to "so infuse herself" into her husband, to use Charlotte Yonge's words in her essay on "Wives," that she did not think of herself as separate from him. For a woman love meant absorption into a man. For despite protestations like "I am what you are, and you are what I am," which the husband still recites in Vedic marriage ceremonies, after the ceremony it was the wife who became subordinate to her husband and one with his interests. In 1834 William Lloyd Garrison, in the ecstasy of love, wrote to his beloved: "I am no longer William Lloyd Garrison but Helen Eliza Benson. There is such a fine and perfect affinity between us, that I have lost my identity, and am now completely engrossed in your person." But after they were married, Helen Eliza Benson became completely engrossed in William Lloyd Garrison. "I want it to be not you and me, but us, one being not two," wrote Eugene O'Neill to his second wife Agnes Boulton, by which Agnes understood, as is clear in her *Part of a Long Story* (1958), that she should become part of his life and serve his needs. That Eugene might become part of her life and serve her needs did not cross either of their minds. It was men who, like Zeus, swallowed their wives.

But the women as well as the men longed for the union, wanted "it to be not you and me, but us, one being not two." "I feel, my Theodore, that we are the two halves of one whole, a twain one, two bodies animated by one soul and that the Lord has given us to each other," wrote Angelina Grimké to Theodore Weld in 1838 shortly before their marriage. That feeling, commonly called love, Plato tried to account for by the myth of the androgyne, the creature half man and half woman who, because it attacked the gods, was split in two, for which reason each half now tries to unite with its other half, and for which reason each sex is felt to be incomplete without the other. "An unmarried man or woman, standing alone in the world, is but half of the perfect being God designed in his creation of humanity," said Louisa Greene Richards in a speech in 1895 at the National Women's Council in Washington DC.

The common feeling that each sex is incomplete without the other need not be explained by Plato's myth of the androgyne or by God's design for a perfect being. The feeling is generated in each generation as a result of the male incorporation of the female, an incorporation that, once completed, required men and women to behave as if they were two different species with totally different characteristics.

The yin-yang, the ancient Chinese symbol of "the supreme ultimate," was a circle divided into two intertwining dark and light areas symbolizing the two basic principles of life—the female and the male, the passive and the active. Almost all other cultures have also described males and females as having opposite characteristics—the male active, brutal, strong, the female passive, timid, weak; the male rational, intelligent, controlled, the female emotional, stupid, hysterical; the male a selfish determined leader, the female a self-sacrificing chameleon-like follower; the male boastful and competitive, the female modest and retiring; the male impatient, the female patient; the male commanding, the female submissive; the male dispassionate, the female compassionate, and so on and so on.

It has been customary to explain the male-female characteristics as either innate or as having originated because women had the babies and nursed them, which biological function weakened them and limited their activities, thus producing the male-female division of labor, women staying at home tending children and men adventuring out to hunt and make war. But in primitive societies women did not have a baby every year and they were little incapacitated by pregnancy, usually working till term and going back to work shortly after childbirth with their new baby on their back. Women then were strong and were in fact the beasts of burden, so that in most early societies there is little difference in physical strength between the sexes. Women in civilized societies, however, were eventually not permitted to develop physical strength, and they were also intellectually and economically crippled, being only allowed to have babies and keep house.

The reduction of woman to a womb produced the male-female stereotypes. For the so-called male characteristics were an effect of men being free to use their brains and strength, and the female characteristics an effect of women being free only to use their womb. It is true that the Y, the male sex chromosome, is linked with more physically aggressive behavior, but this natural difference between the sexes was grossly exaggerated because woman's power to be aggressive was severely crippled by her not being permitted to develop her strength or intelligence. Men, on the other hand, were encouraged to become strong and to use their intelligence, and not surprisingly they became self-confident, forceful, domineering, daring, brave. And also not surprisingly women became meek; having become wombs under a husband's head, they developed the characteristics of subordinates. Subordinate literally means to order under and women developed the characteristics of underlings—submissiveness, obedience, compliance, modesty, patience, humility, deviousness, coyness, willingness to do humble tasks and an eagerness to please. The only positive characteristics women were allowed to cultivate were those associated with the womb—nurturance, tenderness, caring. The allegedly innate male-female characteristics resulted from the incorporation of women by men, men becoming the head and limbs of society, women the womb.

The Male Maternal Instinct

Although women became the wombs of society and were idealized in religion and popular sentiment as Madonnas and credited with the virtues of nurturance that presumably flowed like milk from their built-in maternal instinct, women in real life rarely conformed to the maternal ideal. Indeed, history reveals that, if either sex has a maternal instinct, men had far more of it than women.

Woman's maternal instinct did not keep women from killing their illegitimate babies. The sewers and rivers in medieval Rome used to be clogged with their bodies. An act was passed in England in 1633 "to prevent the Destroying and Murthering of Bastard Children," apparently to no effect. Joseph Addison in 1713 noted that "there is scarce an assizes where some unhappy wretch is not executed for the murder of a child." Frederick the Great wrote to Voltaire in 1777 that the largest number of executions occurring in Germany were of girls who had killed their illegitimate infants.

When society condemned a woman to social death for having a child out of wedlock, it was natural that many women would try to get rid of the evidence; fear of ostracism was far stronger than the maternal instinct. But, as a result, the infant victims of the fate a male society imposed upon them were able to be saved by male compassion. In 787 Archbishop Datheus of Milan opened a foundling hospital where women could secretly leave their illegitimate children instead of throwing them into the sewers and rivers. Similarly, in 1204 Innocent III, appalled by the number of dead infants fishermen found in their nets, opened a section of the hospital at Rome for illegitimate children. Again, in 1720 Thomas Coram, upset in his frequent walks to London by seeing infants abandoned on dunghills or on the sides of the road, "sometimes alive, sometimes dead, and sometimes dying," conceived the idea of a foundling hospital, a place where fallen women could have an alternative to killing or abandoning their infants.

Not only did women's allegedly innate tenderness not keep them from tossing illegitimate babies onto dunghills, their maternal instinct did not protect legitimate babies. Many an infant was done to death by having been inadvertently overdosed with opium or alcohol. The use of opiates to quiet infants can be dated as far back as ancient Egypt, and they continued to be used throughout the nineteenth century. In Hogarth's *March to Finchley* we see infants sucking on gin bottles. The use of alcohol to calm infants was so common in England and so accepted that when Coram's Foundling Hospital was finally established, the Board of Governors wrote to the College of Physicians to ask if the infants in the hospital should be given alcohol as a pacifier. The maternal instinct also taught women to feed newborn infants such foods as butter, black cherry water and roast pig. Babies were then dipped in cold water and wound tightly in swaddling bands, which were not changed more than once a day (if that often), for mothers believed changing and washing babies "robbed them of their nourishing juices." The maternal instinct also did not incline women to breast-feed their babies. In Greek and Roman times among the upper classes, it was not fashionable to suckle one's infants; slaves were wet nurses. But not only the rich were reluctant. It is estimated that in eighteenth-century England only 3 percent of children in towns were nursed by their own mothers; poor mothers regularly hired wet nurses because they were obliged to work. And to put a baby out to nurse, which generally meant sending it to a woman in the country, was virtually to sentence it to death, for these baby farms, as they came to be called, were notorious for neglecting babies to death. In mid eighteenth-century England 74.5 percent of children died before they were five years old. They had always died in such great numbers and disease was not the chief killer; it was maternal callousness, ignorance and neglect. The maternal instinct women were presumably supplied with had not taught them how to care for infants.

It should be said in exoneration of women that a sex inculcated with the belief it was stupid and that remained largely uneducated was not likely to have the self-confidence to observe babies objectively and thus discover what was good or bad for them; women would feel safer following custom. Moreover, since women were taught to think of themselves as incompetent, helpless and second-rate, they would despise babies for the same reason they despised themselves—because babies too are incompetent and helpless. It may be that for much of history childhood was despised as a period of inferiority and deficiency and childhood was nasty, brutish and short because the women who brought children up despised themselves. Furthermore, women must have disliked having babies since pregnancy was not admired as an important and awesome creative act; rather, women's big bellies were laughed at, and childbirth was considered shameful, obscene and disgusting. Nevertheless, women were forced to undergo pregnancy and childbirth yearly in order, moreover, to have babies that science, religion and the law told them belonged wholly to their husbands. Whatever compassion for infants women did manifest was a triumph over nurture.

Interest in childhood and in methods of child rearing did not begin to flourish in civilized society until the mid eighteenth century, and it was not women who began to show an increased concern for children. Our cultural maternal instinct was first manifested in men. Appalled by the high mortality rate of infants, men began to teach women how to care for babies. Dr William Cadogan in 1748 wrote a pamphlet on the *Nursing and Management of Children from Their Birth to Three Years of Age*, a pamphlet that, Dr Cadogan said, was based on his own "observations and experience," which had taught him that infants ought not to be wrapped in swaddling clothes, ought not to lie unwashed, ought not to be fed roast pork at birth. His pamphlet became the bible of Coram's Foundling Hospital, the nurses being required to follow his recommendations, which were also followed by many mothers and physicians, this eighteenth-century "Dr Spock" going through ten editions.

In that and the next century men continued their efforts to supply women with a maternal instinct. Physicians like Cadogan established pediatrics as a special branch of medicine and taught women how to take better physical care of their children. Male philosphers and child psychologists also taught women what they now know about child rearing and child development. Locke in 1690 wrote a book about education in which he advised parents to play their children into learning; Rousseau urged mothers to breast-feed their children and let them run about freely; learned men like Thomas Reid and Joseph Priestley had a heated controversy (based, they said, on the careful observation of both) over whether sucking was instinctive or learned; Richard Edgeworth devoted most of his life to supervising the education of his children (he had twenty-two) in order to try to understand how the minds of children operate; and Bronson Alcott (the father of Louisa May Alcott) in the 1830s devoted several years to observing the minutiae in the daily lives of his children and making voluminous notes. Because of these early child psychologists and their followers—G. Stanley Hall, Freud, Piaget, Gesell, all of whom studied children intensively— mothers know more about how to bring up their children. Today the new mother acquires a maternal instinct by buying a copy of the chief repository of the maternal instinct in the twentieth century—Dr Spock's *Baby and Child Care*. Moreover, even before she has the baby, the mother-to-be learns how to give birth, naturally, from men—Drs Grantly Dick Read, Fernand Lamaze, and recently Dr Frederick Leboyer.

If the maternal instinct is defined as an urge to want, love, cherish, protect and be interested in children, then down through the centuries men have manifested more of a maternal instinct than women. For who tossed illegitimate babies into sewers? Who fed them roast pork at birth? Who doped infants with opium and gin? Who refused to breast-feed babies and whenever possible hired servants to take them off their hands? Whose ignorance and neglect caused most babies to die? Who in the early years of this century were agitating for birth control and who are now clamoring for abortions and child care centers? Women. Who, on the other hand, recorded in the Bible a man was the first mother? Whose desire to be a mother created the custom of couvade and scientific theories that the male sex was the sole progenitor of babies? Who established foundling hospitals for unwanted children? Who studied the psychology of infancy and childhood? Who taught women how to take care of babies and even how to give birth to them? Who studied the medical problems of babies so that now most of them live and who made contraception and abortion a crime? Men. It is not too much to say that we would not be living in a world overflowing with babies if it had not been for the male maternal instinct.

But the obsessive male drive to be the mother of mankind remains largely unrecognized. All evidence to the contrary notwithstanding, men maintain and have always maintained that women are the sex with the maternal instinct, a belief they continue to hold despite modern studies that demonstrate a maternal instinct does not exist even in female primates. Monkeys brought up without a mother want nothing to do with their own babies; they refuse to look at them; they flick the baby off their back as if it were a bothersome fly. Such were the observations of Harry Harlow, and George Schaller similarly observed that zoo apes that have never seen another female handling an infant ignore their own newborn babies or are afraid of them. Even when monkeys grow up in monkey society watching mothers tending children, experience is important; Phillis Jay observed that female langurs take much better care of their second child than they do of their first. Yet though it is now conceded that female primates do not innately know how to take care of their infants, female human beings are still believed to have such instinctive knowledge. Girls are not required to take courses in child care, and Dr Benjamin Spock's first piece of advice to mothers in the first edition of *Baby and Child Care* (1946) was to trust their instincts; what they instinctively felt like doing for their babies, he said, was usually best. Most men and women believe that merely by virtue of being female a woman will know how to take care of a baby.

Female human beings, moreover, are also believed to be endowed with an instinctive desire to want to have babies, an instinct female primates have never been accused of. Scientists never thought a female chimpanzee making overtures to a male did so because she knew copulation would give her the baby her heart desired. Scientists understood it was only necessary for animals to have a sex drive for babies to be produced. But not so with women who, unlike all lower animals, are believed to be programmed not by culture but by biology to want babies more than anything else in life. "The maternal instinct is, with the average woman, the ruling instinct of her whole nature," asserted an anonymous writer in the 1899 *Westminster Review*, and Erik Erikson in the spring 1964 *Daedalus* similarly asserted that woman's "somatic design," her "inner space" made the fulfillment of children a biological and psychological necessity of her nature. Or as Dr Benjamin Spock put it in the March 1969 *Redbook*, "Biologically and temperamentally . . . women were made to be concerned first and foremost with child care."

It cannot be denied that throughout the centuries most women have desired to have babies above all else. Yet why shouldn't that have been their chief desire since they could survive and have status in society only by marrying and having babies? The deep desire of women to have babies may also have been a conditioned response—women, having been taught it was their first duty to live for and through others, dutifully desired to have a child and live through it. Perhaps literally. For although babies were believed to be the fruit of men's seed, women could not have helped feeling that the new being that developed in them and came out of their body was a splitting off from them, a reduplication of themselves, themselves reborn. The deep desire of women to have babies may therefore have been the yearning of inferior beings for another chance at life, the yearning to be born again and at least relive the time when they did not yet know they were the despised sex. And if they were lucky, they might be reborn and live again as one of the superior sex, which may be why women have so favored and doted on sons, sons whom many of them almost consciously regarded as themselves reborn male. The deep yearning of women to have babies may be the yearning of an oppressed class to be reborn into a better life.

But men never analyze why women want babies; they unquestioningly believe women are driven by instinct, forgetting that in another part of their mind they know that even female monkeys have no such maternal instinct. Men also never seem to be aware of their own maternal drive. Dr Spock, our contemporary Madonna, forever associated in our minds with a child, manages to maintain that "women were made to be concerned first and foremost with child care" without asking whence came his own lifelong concern with child care? And Erik Erikson has apparently never asked why, though he lacked the female's inner space, he filled many years of his life studying children?

The male obsession to be the mother of mankind remains largely unrecognized. Men manage to be blind to the most obvious evidence of the maternal drive even in other men. Couvade is a case in point. Male anthropologists, confronted by men taking to their beds and groaning when their wives were in labor, could not see what was in front of their eyes—that the men were acting out their desire to give birth to a baby. Instead, they were puzzled and contrived subtle abstract theories to explain the mystery. Some reasoned that couvade signified the beginning of a patriarchal culture, the man thus symbolically establishing his fatherhood. Others argued that the man was signifying his obligations to the child, or was warding off malevolent spirits either from the child or the wife, or that the man was expressing sympathy for the wife's pain by empathizing with her. Claude Lévi-Strauss in *The Savage Mind* (1962) insisted that the father was not playing "the part of the mother"; rather, the father, because he feels the child is himself reduplicated, "plays the part of the child." As late as the early 1970s men found it difficult to take the blindfold off their eyes. Dr W. H. Trethowan, a British psychiatrist, writing in the November 1972 *Sexual Behavior*, discussed at length "Pregnancy Symptoms in Men," pointing out that at least one man in seven when his wife is pregnant suffers from nausea, vomiting, loss of appetite, craving for a particular food, abdominal swelling and, the most common symptom of all, toothache. Dr Trethowan found this last symptom impossible to explain, but it may be that the pain of toothache and the deliverance from pain of an extraction is an oral reenactment of childbirth. Be that as it may, Trethowan summed up recent explanations for the abdominal symptoms offered by his colleagues. According to one theory, pregnant women give off large quantities of hormones which make their husbands, as it were, radioactively sick to their stomachs. According to another theory, pregnant women, because they feel unwell, neglect their domestic duties and serve badly cooked meals to their husbands, who as a consequence suffer from indigestion. His own theory is that some men feel hostile towards their wives and since it is especially taboo to feel hostile towards a pregnant wife, they feel instead anxious, anxiety commonly producing nausea, vomiting, and abdominal pains. Such husbands may also ward off their guilty hostility by sharing their wife's suffering. Trethowan could not bring himself to offer the far simpler explanation that many men are apparently so envious of woman's ability to give birth that when their wives are pregnant they act as if they too were pregnant.

Not only do many men in the twentieth century have pregnancy symptoms they find inexplicable, scientists are now spending vast amounts of money and energy trying to become "the mother of us all"and seem to have no understanding of the real drive behind their endeavors. Just as Aldous Huxley predicted in *Brave New World* (1932), men are now trying to replace natural conception, pregnancy and childbirth with man-made contrivances. *Utopian Motherhood*, as Robert T. Francoeur called it in a 1970 book, would mean that artificial ovulation, artificial insemination and artificial wombs would become the surrogates for human mothers. The genetic engineers believe artificial reproduction would be far superior to natural motherhood because the sex of the child could be predetermined, genetic defects eliminated, the brain size of the child increased and thousands of superior children produced by cloning. Just as the early Christians believed they could create a form of life superior to the life women could create—immortal life, so the genetic engineers believe they can outdo women by creating perfect human beings. And just as the early Christians believed Christ came down from heaven to share with man God's supernatural power to live forever, so the genetic engineers are convinced that, to quote Francoeur, "the Creator has somehow shared with us his omnipotence." The life-without-birthers without any embarrassment compare themselves to God but would blush to compare themselves to women.

Our understanding of male psychology has been seriously held back because of men's inability to face the fact that men have a powerful unconscious desire to give birth. Freud erected a huge totem pole to penis envy but could not see that men might be equally envious of the magic cauldron of the womb. Most of Freud's followers have echoed the master, being convinced that women are eaten up with penis envy but that womb envy is an insignificant fantasy of little boys or the isolated neurosis of an odd man. When in 1930 Felix Boehm in the *International Journal of Psychoanalysis* discussed "The Femininity Complex in Man," a paper in which he coined the phrase "parturition envy," and when at about the same time Karen Horney discussed the prevalence of the desire to become pregnant in her male patients, the psychoanalytic profession dismissed their arguments as "not very convincing," to quote Otto Fenichel, who in *The Psychoanalytic Theory of Neurosis* (1945) said that Boehm was wrong because although boys as well as girls "may have a passionate wish to give birth to babies," "little girls cannot have babies either." Fenichel apparently forgot there are many things children learn they cannot do until they grow up and that boys, unlike girls, have to learn they can never have a baby. It is amusing that Fenichel felt he had clinched his argument when, after saying that, "little girls cannot have babies either," he added, "but little boys can actually get pleasure from their penis." A strange non sequitur. For the female equivalent of the penis, the organ little girls actually do get pleasure from, is the clitoris. But what Fenichel implicitly compares to the pleasure boys get from their penis is having babies, as if having a baby was a comparable "pleasure." And Fenichel thought he was proving men were without womb envy! Psychiatrists still compare penis envy with womb (not clitoris) envy, thus unconsciously revealing they think having a penis is comparable to, is as enviable as, having a womb.

The Freudians inability to recognize male womb envy makes their analyses of men one-sided. In *Young Man Luther* (1958) Erik Erikson studied Martin Luther's identity crisis solely in terms of his father complex. He did admit Luther was "torn between his masculine and feminine sides" and at one time must have felt "he was like his mother," but Erikson was convinced Luther's fundamental development was "an almost exclusively masculine story," the story of his coming to terms with his father.

Erikson found little or no significance in the considerable amount of evidence that might lead one to conclude Luther was a man who very much wanted to give birth and who resolved his psychological and religious problems by unconsciously coming to believe he was a pregnant woman. Erikson, for example, does little more than mention Luther's lifelong constipation, a condition that seems to have been symptomatic of Luther's womb envy. For Luther apparently retained the childish belief in birth through the rectum; he once ordered a woodcut made that portrayed the Church as a whore giving rectal birth to devils. Luther may well have had difficulty defecating because for him it was the act of giving birth he both feared and longed for. Eating is another way children and primitive men believe one can become pregnant and when Luther was depressed he characteristically felt empty and ate enormously so his belly became distended (and so he produced, hopefully, many fecal babies). Luther, in addition, suffered from kidney stones that also made him swell up and when he was passing one he liked to say he was "in labor." Luther was also fond of saying a man should "keep his belly as full as his head," which may have been an unconscious way of saying a man should be an androgyne, that is, not only keep his head full, as a man should but his belly as well, like a pregnant woman.

Luther's great revelation, the revelation that stopped his religious torments, came to him during a bout of constipation when he was at stool (that is, when he was symbolically trying to give birth). The great truth then revealed to him was that in order to be saved, works, one's actual deeds, were not essential.

All that was necessary was faith. By faith Luther did not merely mean an unquestioning belief that does not require proof. He had an allegorical definition of faith; faith was the symbolic marriage of a man with Christ. In *On Christian Liberty* he said faith "unites the soul with Christ as a bride is united with her bridegroom . . . Christ and the soul become one flesh," which was why once a soul had faith he could do no wrong since he was one flesh with Christ. Luther's definition of faith was of course the same as St Paul's definition of marriage in his Letter to the Ephesians—the uniting of a man with a woman so they become one flesh, the woman becoming her husband's body. It would seem then that Luther resolved his religious torments by acquiring faith, by imagining he had become the bride of Christ, that like a woman united to her husband, he had become Christ's womanly body.

After Luther married, he often jokingly called his wife "My Lord," as if he were indeed a bride married to My Lord Jesus Christ, and all his abdominal symptoms increased (undoubtedly most severely when his wife was pregnant). Also after his marriage, he often spoke of how necessary it was for ministers to have an attitude of womanly conception, and in his sermons he would say he was feeding his audience like a mother suckling her child. His best sermons were on the nativity in which he empathized with Mary's sufferings when she was giving birth. Moreover, Luther's patron saint was a woman, a woman who was a saint only because she was a mother, Saint Anne, the mother of the Virgin Mary.

Much else in Luther's life makes sense when one views him as a man who unconsciously wanted to give birth, but so taboo is that desire in our male culture that a mountain of womb envy is seen, if it is seen at all, as a molehill.

Why is it that intelligent men like Erikson or Freud or the genetic engineers cannot recognize a maternal drive in themselves or in other men? Of course, those who study children or who try to manufacture them in test tubes would insist their interest in children is not maternal, that it is scientific. But the scientific interest in children is a sublimation of the originally conscious desire of men to have woman's capacity to give birth. Men in primitive societies go to bed and groan when their wives are in labor, but men of science create babies by intellectual labor, by thinking, the traditional male compensatory device. Since the time of the early Christians men have transmuted their desire to have babies from the physical to the mental. For the early Christians "the Word was God" because by means of words they managed to believe God the Father, not women, created real, that is, immortal life. By abstract reasoning early philosophers and scientists convinced themselves semen was the Vital Spark that created life in the dead matter of the female; modern chemists and biologists actually try to generate the spark of life in test tubes. Child psychologists abstract concepts out of the babies they observe in laboratories; they do not diaper babies, they think about them; they are intellectual midwives who, by studying babies, have extended male control over child rearing, not unlike obstetricians who, having displaced midwives, arrogated to men full power over giving birth.

Child psychologists perhaps have a more intense maternal drive than the average man, who can satisfy his desire to be a mother merely by being conventional, by following the customs of a society that evolved in response to man's desire to make woman's womb his own. Little boys in every generation have a natural and conscious desire to have babies, a desire they are told is unmanly and which they repress. Yet they grow up in a society in which they are also told that girls were specially created to function as men's wombs, that by the magic ceremony of marriage a man can make a woman part of himself, an incorporation the woman acknowledges by assuming the man's identity. That the woman becomes the man's womb is signified by the fact that the children born from that womb are named after the man, as if he alone gave them life, and by the fact that the law, until recently, regarded children as belonging solely to the man. Thus, merely by marrying and having children a man acquires a womb and becomes a mother, and he can act out his maternal drive without being conscious of it because the mechanisms of projection have been built into the culture.

Men have projected their maternal drive onto women, who have been permitted to exist and acquire status in society only by attaching themselves to a man and functioning as that part of him where he keeps securely in its place his own maternal drive, which is why men fiercely resist women's efforts to detach themselves from men and become independent and why, despite all biological and historical evidence to the contrary, men continue to believe in the existence of a maternal instinct. It does exist—in men's minds, the manifestation of their own longings for maternity.

The man in the street, however, feels certain he has no longings for maternity because pregnant bellies make him titter or fill him with secret horror. And yet most newspapers, when they do not announce that John Jones gave birth to a daughter or son, announce that Mr and Mrs John Jones had a baby, thus suggesting Mr Jones has also somehow given birth. Moreover, the average man, despite our present knowledge of the true facts of life, still clings to the fantasy that babies wholly belong to men. Husbands continue to refer to their wives as "the mother of *my* children," and wives obediently echo, "I bore *his* children." The DeBeers company in a 1969 ad said that when a man gives his fiancée a diamond ring it means, "Marry me, bear my babies," and Paul Anka's 1974 song "(You're) Having My Baby" sold over a million records.

It is not only the masses who continue to speak as if women had men's babies; so do the learned. Erik Erikson said woman's inner space was destined to bear "the offspring of chosen men," as if the offspring were wholly the men's. In Frederick Leboyer's *Birth without Violence* (1974), he imagined a father looking at his newborn son and thinking contentedly that the baby would "grow up to reproduce, trait for trait, the father's perfections," as if the mother contributed no traits to the child.

Our ways of thinking perpetuate the old biology, that is, we continue to speak as if we still believed men were the sole progenitors. To father a child still means to beget a child and to mother a child still means to nurture it. The dictionary definitions of male, female and fertilize also imply that the male sex is the only begetter. The 1970 edition of *Webster's New World Dictionary of the American Language* defines male as "the sex that fertilizes the ovum of the female and begets offspring," female as "the sex that produces ova and bears offspring" and fertilize as "to make (the female reproductive cell or female individual) fruitful by introducing the male germ cell," definitions that not only suggest that the male alone begets, but that the male germ cell does not need fertilization as much as the female germ cell. A dictionary that had assimilated our new knowledge of the female's role in reproduction would define male as the sex that produces sperm that in union with the ovum begets offspring, female as the sex that produces ova that in union with sperm begets offspring and that also bears offspring, and fertilize as the union of the male and female germ cells that produces new life. Both sexes beget; the female additionally bears.

That language lags behind our present knowledge should not surprise us. The equal participation of the egg and sperm nuclei in fertilization was not completely demonstrated until the late 1870s, less than one hundred years ago, a short time considering it was often many hundreds of years after a tribe or country discovered semen was the sine qua non of babies that that knowledge toppled Mother Goddesses and set up the Father God as the one god of creation. In the twentieth century when knowledge is rapidly disseminated, it ought not to take so long for the Father God to be toppled and for both sexes to achieve equal power and status. But since there never has been a time when men and women were treated as equals, equality will not be achieved quickly, involving as it must remaking the psychological structure of society. Sexual equality ought to be achieved slowly, for, as Elizabeth Cady Stanton realized, it will be "the greatest revolution the world has ever known."

Eventually, though, the new knowledge of woman's equal role in the creation of life will destroy the long reign of the Lords of Creation. Women will stop regarding themselves as the inferior sex created to be "a help meet for" men and will stop vying with each other to become some man's womb but will remain independent beings. And men, as their wombs are taken away from them, will be forced to become conscious of their desire to be mothers. However, by becoming conscious of it, they will become able to accept it, will stop being possessed by it, for our unconscious desires drive us only until we become conscious of them.

And men do seem to be beginning to more frankly confront their desire to have babies. Psychiatrists, even male ones, are discussing womb envy with more seriousness, though most of them still confuse womb envy with woman envy, insisting that men envy only woman's easier life, her not having to compete in the harsh competitive world. But that raw womb envy is obtruding into male consciousness may be indicated by the appearance in 1973 of the movie *The Most Important Event Since Man Walked on the Moon*, the most important event proving to be a man who became pregnant, and the "mother" was acted by no other than Marcello Mastroianni, a male sex god, who shamelessly thrust his huge belly across the superscreen.

20

BEYOND WIFEHOOD

No Less Perfect than Man

"Woman is a most arrogant and extremely intractable animal; and she would be worse if she came to realize that she is no less perfect and no less fit to wear breeches than man." That was why, explained the sixteenth-century Italian anatomist Borgarucci, nature "placed the female testicles internally." For if woman knew she was endowed with "what is necessary for our procreation," her "continual desire to dominate" would be unbridled; therefore, a wise nature "arranged things so that every time she thinks of her supposed lack, she may be humbled and shamed." Similarly, another sixteenth-century anatomist, de Valverde, in a book on the structure of the human body, said he would have preferred to omit the chapter on the female testicles "that women might not become all the more arrogant by knowing that they also, like men, have testicles, and that they . . . too put something of their own into it [the child]."

What these anatomists thought women put "of their own" into the child was far inferior to what men contributed, but they did not like to think women contributed anything at all. After de Graaf discovered the ovarian follicles, one scientist insisted they were of no more functional value than men's nipples. Men wanted to go on believing woman conceived the way Catholics imagined Mary had, as the result, as it were, of an electric discharge from a superman's dynamo, woman herself containing no life-generating power. Men were terrified that if women should prove to be equally important in the creation of new life, they would cease to feel "humbled and shamed," would think themselves just as important as men and would become just as arrogant. No wonder it was not until 1827 that von Baer discovered the ovum.

It may well be that a man was finally able to see the ovum, the largest cell in the human body and visible to the naked eye, because men had been forced to see women in a different way. Starting in the late eighteenth century, women began to reason that the female sex must have been created no less perfect than the male sex, and women became more arrogant, loudly asserting woman's equality with man. Constrained to look upon women in a new aggressive light, scientists may at last have been able to see the ovum playing an active part in procreation. Be that as it may, the scientific discovery that women were equally necessary in the generation of new life went hand in hand with women's self-discovery that they were "no less perfect and no less fit to wear breeches than" men.

For hundreds of years men and women had believed that God or nature had created the female sex defective, that women could not generate physical life in their wombs, that they could barely generate mental life in their heads, and that they were as weak in body as in mind. Men and women therefore believed women were created to serve the perfect sex, to function as the womb for men's babies, a belief that succeeded in turning women into cripples, creatures with overdeveloped wombs and breasts, with tiny heads and rudimentary arms and legs that needed the support of man's strong mind and body in order to survive. The aim of the feminist movement, at its simplest and most fundamental, was to give woman back her head and strong limbs and to detach her body and womb from man so she need not cling like a swollen leech to a husband.

During the nineteenth and twentieth centuries feminists have been demonstrating that women are complete human beings who can stand on their own feet. Women proved that the head on their shoulders was not a dummy, establishing in virtually all fields woman's intellectual equality with man. Women also forced men to accept the fact that women are bifurcated creatures, that they too have those instruments of strength and assertion alleged to be distinctively male, which was why when feminists in the early 1850s put on Bloomers they shocked the world, a shock still reverberating in 1969 when Representative Charlotte Reid's wearing a pantsuit into the House made the front pages of newspapers throughout the country. Reid would not have shocked her colleagues if she had worn the then fashionable miniskirt, which exposed women's legs almost to the crotch. For women were eventually permitted to reveal their legs when they displayed them as decorative sexual props as unlike men's as possible, which was why women's legs had to be shaved of hair, covered with sheer fabrics and were admired for being slim. Not until the late 1960s did a few women dare to stop artificially feminizing their legs by leaving them as hairy as nature made them, by covering them with trousers most of the time and by not fearing to develop the muscles in their calves and thighs by exercise. Female athletes in the 1970s finally got over their fear of having "masculine" biceps and, like men, began to use weights to develop their muscles. Such athletes and the college women who now participate in almost as many sports as men are the heirs of the bold young women in the 1890s who dared take up bicycle riding and the other nineteenth-century sportswomen who began the process of demonstrating that women were not fragile flowers but could be almost as strong as men.

At the same time as women were strengthening their bodies and, by demonstrating their intellectual competence, proving they need not be helpless creatures dependent upon some man, they were also detaching themselves from husbands. Not only did it become much easier for wives to permanently separate themselves from husbands by divorce, but within marriage wives succeeded to a large extent in being treated as separate entities, as persons who could act independently by buying property on their own and by suing and being sued on their own. The process of political separation also began, its aim being to treat women as citizens in their own right, not as potentially or actually merged in the husbands who represented them in the public forum. In other words, women in certain states and for certain purposes won the right to vote, a right fully won in the twentieth century, when women also succeeded in making their wombs their own. In the 1920s women in large numbers began to learn how by various contraceptive devices they themselves could limit the number of babies they had, and in the 1960s and 70s the contraceptive pill made pregnancy a matter of choice determined by the woman alone. And should contraception fail, 1970s court decisions have given the wife the right to have an abortion. The United States Supreme Court held in 1973 that because of a person's right to privacy the decision to have an abortion rested solely with the woman and her physician (Roe v. Wade and Doe v. Bolton, 401 United States Reports 113, 179), a decision interpreted as meaning a wife may have an abortion or be sterilized without her husband's consent. The Oklahoma Court of Appeals, for example, decided in 1974 that a wife had the right to be sterilized in spite of her husband's objections, the judges asserting that "the right of a person . . . to control his own body is paramount" (Murray v. Vandevander, 522 Pacific Reporter 2d 302). Missouri and other states did pass laws making the husband's consent necessary for an abortion, but in another decision rendered in 1976 the Supreme Court declared such laws unconstitutional (Planned Parenthood of Central Missouri v. Danforth, 96 Supreme Court Reports 2831).

No court would have or could have decided a wife had the right to have an abortion over her husband's objections if men were still believed to be the sole progenitors and women the wombs in which men's seed was brought to fruition. No court would have or could have decided a wife had paramount control over her own body if it had not been discovered that women contributed as much as men to the generation of new life, that women were the procreative equals of men.

Liberation Names

When women were believed to be merely the conduit pipes through which men reproduced, it made sense that children were given the surname of their only begetter. Recognition of woman's procreative equality with men will mean, therefore, that the custom of giving children the father's surname will break down and, in fact, the tradition of handing down only male names to posterity has already begun to be seriously challenged and defied.

Even in the late nineteenth century one can find occasional rebellions against the male naming tradition among feminists and women outside conventional society. In the 1880s the feminist Alice Chenoweth Smart, instead of merely divesting herself of her husband's surname and using again the name her father conferred on her mother, chose a new, non-hereditary name for herself—Helen Hamilton Gardener. In 1887 the actress Ellen Terry had the surname of her two natural children by Edwin Godwin changed to Craig, a name chosen because on a trip to Scotland she had been struck by the beautiful name of a rock called Ailsa Craig. During the first sixty years of the twentieth century dissatisfaction with the male naming tradition began to increase. In Charlotte Perkins Gilman's 1911 novel *Moving the Mountain* the members of a Utopian community in which men and women were equal gave male children the father's surname and females the mother's, but then the community began to feel that naming system was unsatisfactory: "There's a strong movement on foot to drop hereditary names altogether." Gilman, as usual, was ahead of her times. During the next several decades a few women, like Margaret Bourke-White in the 1920s, Flanders Dunbar in the 1940s, or Dr Judianne Densen-Gerber in the 1950s, made their mother's maiden surname part of their own name. Rare women, like Dr May Wilson and Dr Edith Summerskill, gave their children their own surname, and a handful, like Dr Marie Stopes, Elsie Hill and Flanders Dunbar, gave their children the combined surname of both parents. But not until the late 1960s did there begin to occur a strong movement to break away from the solid dynasty of male names.

At the March 1970 convention of the National Organization for Women, the resolution advocating that married women keep their own names also suggested that a husband and wife might choose "a neutral second name to be used also by the children" or that the children "use both the wife's and husband's name." During the next few years, in addition to the thousands of women who decided to retain or resume their own name after marriage, a few hundred chose to give themselves or their children a non-traditional name, either a hyphenated or combined surname that recognized woman's contribution to heredity, a mother's maiden surname or first name converted to a surname, or a totally non-hereditary name.

In a 1971 pamphlet a Washington woman informed her parents "Why I Added Legally My Mother's Maiden Name to My Father's Surname." The former Joy Conrad had become Conrad-Rice, adding her mother's maiden name to her father's in order "to declare more accurately my genetic composition." Conrad-Rice's desire to have her surname reflect her ancestry on her mother's as well as her father's side was shared by many couples who gave their children hyphenated surnames. For example, in 1973 Diana Altman and Richard Siegal of Massachusetts named their daughter Claudia Altman-Siegal and in 1974 Janice Abarbanel and Marshall Wolff of Connecticut named their son Benjamin Abarbanel-Wolff. An Arizona Appeals Court in 1975 had to deal with what the court thought was the first reported case "where the mother has attempted to add her maiden name to the given surname" of her children. A divorced woman, Nancy Eliot Laks, had wanted to change the name of her three children from Laks to Eliot-Laks as "an appropriate recognition of the interests of both parents in a child's name" (Laks v. Laks, 540 Pacific Reporter 2d 1277). Since her ex-husband objected, the court refused her request, but so long as a father did not object, there was no legal obstacle to giving a child a hyphenated surname. There was, rather, the pyramiding obstacle. For should Claudia Altman-Siegal marry Benjamin Abarbanel-Wolff, would their children bear the surname Altman-Siegal-Abarbanel-Wolff? And in the next generation would a husband and wife who each had four surnames give their children eight surnames? Conrad-Rice felt that such a naming system was the only accurate one and that some of the surnames could be abbreviated for most purposes. Other women felt that husband and wife could choose two surnames from the pair each had or that, instead of a hyphenating system, female children could be given the mother's surname and male ones the father's, a naming system advocated by Lucia Lane in her 1974 pamphlet *Equal Names for Equal Sexes*. A few couples obviated the problem by combining their surnames into a single name. Thus in 1975 the former Johanna Boswell and James Hagelin of California had their names legally changed to Boslin.

Other feminists broke with the solid dynasty of male names by changing their surname to their mother's maiden name. A bill introduced into the California legislature in 1971 would have given any person over the age of twenty-one the right to change his or her name to the mother's maiden one. A Massachusetts woman, who in 1973 could not get her own surname recorded as the surname of her child on its birth certificate, demanded that the Attorney General research the law and in January 1974 he issued the opinion that under Massachusetts law a child need not bear its father's surname, that it was only a custom, a custom he felt was likely to change now women were recognized as legal entities and many wives were keeping their own identity after marriage.

Other women, feeling their mother's maiden name was just another male name handed down to posterity, adopted as a surname their mother's first name to which they added the suffix "child" or (much less often) "daughter." Pinny Lauerman in 1971 petitioned an Arizona court to have her surname changed to Debrachild, Debra being her mother's given name. Similarly, the former Kathie Amatniek, a New York radical feminist, changed her surname to Sarachild.

Other women and men broke with tradition by adopting for themselves and/or their children a name that had no connection with their mother's or their father's. In 1971 the former Mrs Ron Szymalak of New York, whose maiden name had been Nola Claire Dorries, dropped both her husband's and father's name and had her name legally changed to Nola Claire. In 1972 Susan Sadoff-Lorenzi and Henry Lorenzi of Washington DC, upon the birth of a child, adopted Sojourner as a family surname, a name chosen to honor Sojourner Truth, the nineteenth-century black woman who preached against slavery and for women's rights, a name that also appealed to them because of the meaning of sojourn—a brief resting place in "the long journey which is life for us all." In 1973 before Ann Gelb and Arnelle Pope of San Francisco married, they had their surnames legally changed to Sebastian, a name chosen from Sebastian Dangerfield in J. P. Donleavy's *The Ginger Man*, a character whose confusion and indecisiveness they empathized with. Starting about 1969 a fair number of feminists decided to change their surname or whole name to one symbolic of woman's struggle for equality, among them Ann Forfreedom, Varda One, Ann Pride, Una Stannard, Dair Struggle, Laura X, names Varda One dubbed "liberation names."

A few women and couples decided to give their children a surname different from their own or their spouse's. When the rock star Grace Slick had a daughter in 1971 she said she was not going to give her the name of her husband Jerry Slick or of the child's father Paul Kantner. As she told a *Newsweek* reporter, "Some one else is already using these names." When the actress Jane Fonda and Tom Hayden had a son in 1973 they chose to give him the name Troy O'Donovan Garity.

Fola La Follette in her 1914 speech on a woman's right to keep her name had suggested that parents might "pick the last name for the child the same way they select the first name," and in the future parents might think it as absurd to give each of their children the same surname as we would now think it absurd to give each child the same first name. If each child in a family were given its own surname, that naming system, though it would drive genealogists wild, would not be at odds with the new facts of heredity. A child does get its genes from both parents, but it is no simple amalgam of their traits since it gets only half of each parent's genes, genes, moreover, that are variously recessive and dominant and may give it traits not manifest in the parents but in grandparents or earlier ancestors, all of which variables insure that no person (except for identical twins) is like any other. Since, therefore, every child is unique, it would be biologically accurate to give each child a unique name.

Whatever naming system prevails in the future, the era when children were given only the father's surname is ending because the era when women were believed to be the wombs in which their husbands' progeny was nurtured is also ending.

No Longer Destined for the Home

Now that women have begun to understand they are "no less perfect" than men, that they are neither mentally, physically nor procreatively defective, women are ceasing to believe they were created to be a man's womb and body servant, that is, a wife. Marriage is ceasing to be the one object of their lives; they are working at as many different types of jobs as men and becoming independent, which is why society is now radically changing and a world is being created in which the role of wife as it was known for thousands of years is ceasing to exist, a world in which more and more women after marriage do not assume the label "wife of," a world in which being known as Mrs Someman will become more and more uncommon because it will prove to be increasingly inconvenient, impractical and, finally, meaningless.

The simplest reason why many women in the future will not take their husband's name is that women in increasing numbers will choose not to marry. Because of reliable contraceptive devices and the acceptance of female sexuality, women in the 1970s no longer have to have a husband in order to have both a sex life and respectability. Girls used to marry young because that was the only way they could lose their virginity without losing their reputation. Now that the culture permits them without condemnation to express their sexual feelings outside of marriage, they are marrying later or not marrying at all. The image of the unmarried woman is no longer that of a frustrated old maid but of a free spirit who prefers a variety of men to being tied down by a husband and children. It has become acceptable, even glamourous, to be single, and a single woman, with no loss of respectability, may have affairs and live openly with a man without being married to him. In the mid 1960s college students called such arrangements "super going steady" and the custom has become increasingly popular for some ten years. Most girls of seventeen and up will live with a series of men and not be ashamed of having two names on the mailbox. After actress Michelle Triola began to live with actor Lee Marvin in 1964, she had her name legally changed to Marvin; if she had begun to live with him in 1974, she would not have tried to assuage her sense of shame by assuming the name of the man she was living with. Whereas in the 1920s married couples who registered at hotels under separate names shocked the management, in the 1970s unmarried couples who boldly register as Mr and Miss are, according to the July 18, 1974 *New York Times*, being accepted by more and more hotels.

Single women are not only openly living with men, they are also becoming mothers without being wives. In the nineteenth century single women who wanted the experience of motherhood had to adopt a child, as did Dr Elizabeth Blackwell in 1854. Notable exceptions were those first liberated women, actresses, who, like Ellen Terry, were able to have illegitimate children and nevertheless continue to be famous and make money. Ellen Terry had to be discreet, but modern actresses, like Vanessa Redgrave, announce "with great joy" the birth of an illegitimate child in the personal columns of the newspaper. Ordinary women eventually follow the lead of actresses and a larger and larger number of women are shamelessly having babies out of wedlock. Victoria, the daughter of Lord and Lady Harlech, lived with a man and had a baby in 1973, not deciding to marry until the baby was one month old. She was not ostracized from society, nor are women who have babies and do not ultimately marry the father. Francoise Giroud, appointed in 1974 French State Secretary on the Condition of Women, freely admitted to having had an illegitimate child and was regarded as courageous not immoral. In a world in which women are free to have babies without benefit of a husband, the concept of the illegitimate child will again disappear. A child will no longer need a father "to give it a name," or to put it another way, women will no longer need a husband's name to give their children society's seal of approval.

In the future not only will many women remain single or have unmarried unions, there will be other forms of marriage. Books are being written called *Open Marriage, The Death of the Family, Beyond Monogamy* that advocate a looser form of marriage or predict the end of the nuclear family. Monogamy is ceasing to be regarded as an unalterable law of nature, and men and women at the present time are experimenting with varieties of group marriage. Although one group may choose to have a common name, as in Robert H. Rimmer's *Proposition 31* (1968), women in a collective will not have husbands as such whose names they will assume.

Women who do decide to enter conventional unions will no longer regard them as "until death do us part." Many couples are now omitting that phrase from the marriage service and substituting "until we no longer love each other". Few women who marry in the 1970s are certain their marriage will last "forever"; most are very much aware that if the present divorce rate continues they will marry at least twice, and if Alvin Toffler's prediction in *Future Shock* (1970) is right, they will marry four or five times. Women who marry fully aware their marriage will probably not be permanent are less likely to submit to the inconvenience of changing their name to one they know they will have to change again and again. Moreover, these women will very likely find themselves in a second or third marriage living with a new husband and children from a previous marriage, children whose surname will be different from the husband's. The increase in the number of families without a common surname will make women who retain their own name less conspicuous and therefore more acceptable.

One reason why young women are now capable of accepting the probability their marriage will not be permanent is that they are tending to marry for the first time when they are older, in their mid or late twenties, when they have lost the happily-ever-after romanticism of the teen-ager. More important, they have, and in increasing numbers will have, a job they do not regard as a stopgap till marriage but as their lifework. A young lawyer, teacher, copy-editor, social worker, programmer, buyer will be less likely to give up the name she had begun to make for herself, especially now when women are being allowed to work their way to the top or quite close to it, to become heads of firms, full professors, vice-presidents of banks, managing editors of newspapers, general managers of hotels, directors of government offices. When women know they can fully realize their ambitions, they will want to find their identity in work, not in the men they marry. As it becomes easier for a woman's own name to have status, fewer women will want to take a man's name in order to share whatever status he may have. It is fitting that the three-volume *Notable American Women* was published in 1971 when large numbers of women were repudiating "the quiet name of wife" and becoming eager to be notable in many fields.

In a world in which wives as well as husbands have jobs they regard as their life work, husbands will encourage wives to keep their own name. For men in the past suffered a good deal when wives appropriated their names for their own purposes, and such double identity problems continue to occur. In 1963 in Louisiana Vernon J. Wilty Jr had to go to court to stop his wife from running against him for the office of Assessor under the name Mrs Vernon J. Wilty Jr. In 1970 in France the electoral commission of the Loire refused to let Mme Irène Durafour, wife of the deputy-mayor of Saint-Etienne, run under the name Durafour, requiring her to have new circulars printed and to take out new voting papers under her maiden name of Irène Blomer, the tribunal feeling that a husband had the right to stop his wife from using his name in literary, artistic, commercial and political fields. From the man's point of view, it is unfair when his name, the name associated with his career, is appropriated by his wife for her own career. But from the woman's point of view, it is also unfair to have to stop using the name by which she has been commonly known for years. To obviate such problems, a growing number of husbands and wives will find it more practical to have different surnames.

As work comes to mean as much to a woman as marriage, marriage will stop being regarded as the most important event in a woman's life. Marriage used to be thought of such monumental importance it was one of the three occasions (the others being birth and death) when a woman's name might, with propriety, appear in the newspaper. Now, however, wedding announcements are disappearing from many newspapers. The two papers in Houston, Texas stopped printing them about 1969; *The Los Angeles Times* now uses them only as fillers, and a good many other newspapers have de-emphasized them. They have in part because as the population increased the number of announcements was taking up too much space, but another reason is that becoming a wife has begun to mean no more to a woman than becoming a husband means to a man. That is why a great many women are not only not announcing their marriages in their local newspapers but are also objecting to marriage services that pronounce a couple "man and wife" and are either changing the phrase to "husband and wife" or are omitting it and having the minister or judge say instead, "I now pronounce you, Mary and John, married." In a world in which marriage means no more to women than men and in which work is as important to women as marriage, women will no longer want to be classified as wives because their role in life will not be keeping a husband's house and rearing children.

Those traditional jobs are even now ceasing to be women's work. In many homes wives are no longer assumed to be solely responsible for housework. Until recently the wife who worked had a double job. In "Why Get Married?" in the March 1938 *American Mercury* "A Wife" complained that although she earned as much as her husband, she was the one who had to fix breakfast, wash dishes, market, cook, clean and take care of the laundry. An occasional feminist in the past did manage to get her husband to do his share. The grandmother of Robert Frost, Judith Colcord Frost, an active suffragist in the mid nineteenth century in Lawrence, Massachusetts, convinced her husband wives should not be enslaved to housework and got him to do his share of dishwashing, bedmaking, cooking and cleaning. But the usual solution to the problem was to hire a maid or to advocate, as did Charlotte Perkins Gilman, cooperative kitchens. Women in the present feminist movement have favored the solution of Judith Frost and have protested vigorously against the male assumption woman was created with a special propensity for housework, a task that early got the name shitwork. One of the most popular posters in the women's liberation movement shouted "Fuck Housework!" and even conventional wives put on aprons that asked, "Did I Go To College Four Years For This?" Young and middle-aged wives began to demand that their husbands share the housework, and in many homes where husband and wife both work, both cook, clean, wash dishes and feel responsible for running the household. In a few homes where the wife works and the husband does not, the husband does most of the housework.

The job of wife is also changing because attitudes towards women as mothers are changing. The myth of the maternal instinct was exploded by articles like Una Stannard's "The Male Maternal Instinct" (*Trans-action*, 1970), books like Ann Oakley's *Sex, Gender and Society* (1972), and confessions like Jane Lazarre's in *The Mother Knot* (1976) of the anger, frustration and resentment motherhood produced in her. Studies of the way women bring up children are also making clear that women are not by nature more nurturant, loving and giving than men and that mothers, more often than not, psychically damage their children. As a consequence more and more women have stopped thinking that having children is their natural vocation and feel justified in fulfilling themselves in other ways. Books like Anna and Arnold Silverman's *The Case against Having Children* (1971) and Ellen Peck's *The Baby Trap* (1971) advised women not to have children, telling them that most women have them because they have nothing else to do or feel safer living through children than developing themselves, that women are pressured to have children by parents who long to be grandparents and by religion and the mass media, which glorify motherhood to keep women in their god-ordained place or to keep the manufacturers of baby goods in business. An increasing number of young women, either because they feel dedicated to their careers or because they feel the threat of world overpopulation, decide to have no children and a few take the irrevocable step of being surgically sterilized. Most women, however, decide to have one or two children and when that decision is made more and more husbands are choosing to become equally involved. No man can have a baby, but a 1974 book, *Birth* by Caterine Milinaire, was advertised as containing the "varied and illuminating experiences of childbirth" of "sixteen mothers and twelve fathers." Men participate by accompanying their wives to natural childbirth classes and by being with them in the delivery room where they help them breathe correctly during labor, give them emotional support and witness the birth of the child. A few fathers deliver their babies at home or are permitted to do so in certain hospitals, like Nesbitt Memorial in Pennsylvania.

Fathers are now also feeding, diapering and comforting babies, and not because mother is tired but because child rearing is becoming a shared responsibility, so much so the word "parenting" has been invented to describe the new non-sexist concept of mothering. The 1976 edition of Dr Benjamin Spock's *Baby and Child Care* insisted that child care was as much the responsibility of the father as the mother and had pictures of fathers feeding and bathing babies. The phenomenon of the "househusband" has also emerged, the man who chooses to stay home and bring up the children while his wife works. In addition, more and more fathers, upon divorce, are demanding custody of the children and are being granted it. That bringing up children is ceasing to be thought of as solely woman's work but as also the responsibility of men and the state is indicated by the great increase in the number of child care centers and the demand for many more, in which centers the child care counselors are often men.

In a world in which men will feel as free as women to have a career that involves tending children or in which men may choose to perform the main parenting job while their wives pursue careers or in which both husband and wife or the husband as readily as the wife will take on the job of running the home, the job of wife will have ceased to be the special job of women. In such a world it will become an anachronism for a woman when she marries to become Mrs Herhusband, as if her job were still that of wife.

That the job of wife is ceasing to exist is also attested to by the appearance of a new title for women. New titles are rarely invented; it is therefore of great significance that a new one has come into existence for women, one that, like Mr, indicates only sex not whether or not a woman is a wife. Ms is supposed to have originated with the wide use of the computer, which was programmed to print out Ms when it had not been told if a woman were Miss or Mrs. Whatever its origin, the title appealed to feminists who, like feminists in the past, thought it was none of society's business to know whether or not a woman was married. In March 1970 at the annual conference of the National Organization for Women, a resolution was adopted advocating the use of Ms, and the next month Representative Jonathan B. Bingham of New York in a speech in the House informed his colleagues that "an increasing number of American women . . . do not wish to be identified as Miss or Mrs," preferring the title

Ms. He and later Representative Bella Abzug introduced bills that would prevent states from requiring women to declare their marital status as a condition for voting in Federal elections and that would stop the Federal government from using "any title which indicates marital status."

Just as there were women who refused to vote in their husband's name, there were women who refused to write down Miss or Mrs in order to vote. For example, in 1971 Merna Ellentuck of Roosevelt, New Jersey was refused the right to vote because she would not sign "Mrs" before her name on the voter registration rolls. In 1972 both Nancy Allyn of California and Donna Brogan of Georgia were not allowed to register to vote when they insisted their title was Ms, not Miss or Mrs. Some of these women, like the women who wanted to use their own name for voting, were willing to go to court for the right to use a title that did not tell the world whether or not they had a husband. Nancy Allyn lost her case and was appealing it when in 1974 California passed a law permitting women to register as Ms. Other states, like New Jersey in 1972, passed laws eliminating the Miss/Mrs requirement for female voters.

The Federal government has also made some concessions to the new desire of women not to be classified as married or unmarried. In late 1972 the Treasury Department dropped its rule that the names of female purchasers of United States Savings Bonds had to be prefixed by Miss or Mrs, and in February 1973 the Government Printing Office in a revision of its manual of style listed Ms as an acceptable "optional prefix." The new title is also used by many businesses, which find it convenient to have one title for women. Some application and subscription forms have added a Ms box to those of Miss, Mrs and Mr. Many newspapers and magazines also use Ms, although most use it only when the woman named is a feminist.

But whether or not the title is Ms, it seems likely that women in the future will stop having a title that indicates their marital status. Europe at present seems to favor using Mrs for all mature women. France has long had the custom of calling adult women Madame, and as early as 1964 Sweden adopted the title Fru for women past a young age. Similarly, in 1970 the Austrian government decided to address all female employees as Frau. America, on the other hand, has a long tradition of calling female actors and writers Miss. But Miss, since it generally means a woman is single, will not appeal to the great many women who still feel there is a stigma in not being married. Ms, on the other hand, has the advantage of being ambiguous. Moreover, the new title is being widely impressed on the public's mind because in 1971 when Gloria Steinem conceived the idea of a national feminist magazine for the average American woman, she chose *Ms* as its title. The overwhelming success of *Ms* may well lead to the acceptance of Ms as a general title for women. At any rate, the hundreds of thousands of readers of *Ms* are being taught to think of themselves as female human beings who can do whatever they set their minds to, not as Miss or Mrs, that is, "not a wife" or "wife of." Whether or not Ms prevails, there will be only one title for women, not two that separate wives from non-wives; Miss or Mrs will come to mean simply woman. No title meaning wife will be needed in a world in which the role of wife will have ceased to exist.

In 1960 when the Radcliffe Institute was founded it was meant to be a place where talented women (usually with PhDs) who had married young, moved to suburbia and had several children could find a quiet place away from home where they could begin to take up the careers they had put aside in order to be wives. In 1975 in the June *Radcliffe Quarterly* Dean Patricia Graham announced the Institute was taking a new direction because women's lives had changed. Many women were remaining single, marrying later, divorcing in greater numbers and having no or few children, children whom they were not taking time out from their careers to raise because they had committed themselves to work as wholeheartedly as men. The Institute consequently decided to cater to the new professional women in order to help them move into the top positions in their fields, for which purpose the Institute, renamed the Radcliffe Institute Research and Resource Center, is doing research in men's as well as women's roles in order to help create a world in which men as well as women can achieve "a better balance between home and job."

The change in the Radcliffe Institute is a witness to how radically women's role in society has changed in the short span of fifteen years, a change also reflected in decisions of the United States Supreme Court. In 1961 when the court ruled that a Florida statute exempting women from jury duty was constitutional, it said that "woman is still regarded as the center of home and family life" (Hoyt v. Florida, 368 United States Reports 57). The court's opinion was not at all different from what it had been in 1872 when it decided Illinois had the right to forbid Myra Bradwell from practicing law because "the paramount destiny and mission of woman are to fulfill the noble and benign office of wife and mother." The Supreme Court in 1872 was certain that was the unalterable "law of the Creator," and almost everyone in the nineteenth century, whether feminist or anti-feminist, believed "women will always be wives and mothers, above all things else," to quote John Hooker, writing in favor of woman suffrage in the January 17, 1871 *Connecticut Evening Post*. But one hundred years later that immutable "law of the Creator" has been found to be mutable; women no longer are regarded as wives and mothers "above all things else," an opinion the conservative United States Supreme Court has come to share. In April 1975 the court decided a father must pay child support up to the age of twenty-one for girls as well as boys because girls need as much education as boys. "Women's activities and responsibilities are increasing and expanding," said Justice Blackmun. Women are "in business, in the professions, in government, and, indeed, in all walks of life." "No longer is the female destined solely for the home and the rearing of the family, and only the male for the market place and the world of ideas" (Stanton v. Stanton, 421 United States Reports 7).

Over 80 percent of the freshmen women who entered college in 1975 agreed with Justice Blackmun. In a survey sponsored by the American Council on Education, only slightly over 18 percent of the women thought "the activities of married women are best confined to the home and family," and almost 17 percent were already planning careers in business, engineering, law or medicine.

If the freshmen of 1975 prove to be like their sisters in recent years, few of them after graduation will rush into wifehood and motherhood. The June 1976 *Radcliffe Quarterly* revealed that an astonishing 86 percent of the class of 1969 were in 1974 still childless. That issue, devoted to the liberated lifestyles of recent alumnae, also revealed that many Radcliffe women were planning to remain childless or to have one or at most two children, a few women without first acquiring a husband and a few while living in a collective. Most women were strongly committed to a career, continuing to work after marriage and the birth of a child, and had husbands who as a matter of course did their share of housekeeping and child care chores. As Avarita L. Hanson, class of '75, said of her marriage, it is "a 100:100 percent relationship, not 50:50," which expresses well the emerging idea that husband and wife are not halves of a complete human being, but that men and women are in themselves complete human beings.

Avarita Hanson, a law student, kept her own name after marriage, as did another of the four young married women who wrote about their liberated lifestyles, Mary Procter, a management consultant and a member of the Harvard Board of Overseers, who, moreover, gave her daughter her husband's surname chiefly because it was "more interesting" than her own surname. Since 1970 the number of Radcliffe alumnae who in the Class Notes announce they are retaining their own name after marriage or that their child has been given the combined surname of both parents has slowly increased. In the 1920s the United States Senator Clarence Dill married a Lucy Stoner; in the 1970s there was a Lucy Stoner in the House: Representative Martha Keys in December 1975 announced that after her forthcoming marriage to Representative Andrew Jacobs Jr, they would be maintaining their individual names. Late in 1976 the famous Dr Spock took a second wife who chose not to share his famous name and to use instead not her first husband's name nor her father's but her own first name and middle surname and become Mary Morgan. At present only a tiny percentage of married women keep their own name or take a non-traditional name or name their children non-traditionally, but they are the women of the future. In the nineteenth century a few women, ahead of their time, wore trousers, or Bloomers as they were then called. And these women were by no means only professional feminists like Susan B. Anthony and Lucy Stone; plain housewives wore them. The grandmother of the playwright Howard Lindsay, who lived in Aroostook, Maine, wore Bloomers for a couple of years, but when her neighbors did not do likewise, she gave them up. Ultimately, however, women were free to stop wearing skirts. And so it will be with husbands' names.

A Dying Breed

The era when all women will be Lucy Stoners is still many decades away. The majority of women have not as yet advanced beyond Richardson's eighteenth-century maidservant Pamela "glorying in my change of name!" when she succeeds in marrying Mr B. Even most career women still seem to take pleasure in wearing the wifely feather in their domestic cap. America's leading advertising executive humbly proclaimed in the October 22, 1971 *New York Times*: "I'm much prouder of being Mrs Harding Lawrence than I was of being Miss Mary Wells."

Suspecting that most women, despite the women's liberation movement, wanted to go on being wives, the Republicans at their 1972 presidential convention honored women chiefly for their "great contributions . . . as homemakers and mothers" and a pageant of Women of Achievement consisted mainly of wives of presidents. The Republicans took the pulse of American womanhood accurately. In the 1974 *Good Housekeeping* poll of the most admired women, six of the top ten were wives of (or in one case the daughter of) famous men, mostly presidents. The average woman could not bring herself to admire women who had achieved fame because of their own accomplishments; she felt safer admiring women who shared a husband's fame.

So opposed were most women to the idea of liberation that the new feminist movement immediately produced a backlash of housewives shamelessly defending the virtues of subservience. A Pussycat League was actually founded in 1969 to promulgate the old view that women's "major responsibilities" were "looking, cooking and smelling good for men." A book written in 1965 that told women they were happiest satisfying their husbands' needs picked up sales after the women's liberation movement was under way, and by 1975 Helen B. Andelin's *Fascinating Womanhood* had sold 400,000 copies. A similar book, one that advised "gals," as the author called women, to obey their husbands, praise them for their strong muscles and great accomplishments and keep them sexually aroused by, for example, meeting them at the door in black mesh stockings, high heels, an apron and nothing else, was, according to *Publishers Weekly*, the top bestseller in the United States in 1974. The book was Marabel Morgan's *The Total Woman*, the title a Nixonism since it said the opposite of what Mrs Morgan advocated, for she did not want women to become complete human beings but remain stunted freaks, women with minuscule heads and bodies that clung to the husband who supported them. Mrs Morgan and the Pussycats wanted women to continue thinking of themselves as secondary creations, the sex "created for the comfort of men," to use the words of William Dean Howells.

Various organizations were founded whose purpose was also to keep women in their old unequal place. After the 1973 Supreme Court decision legalizing abortion, the Right-to-Lifers organized to fight for the inalienable right of every embryo to live and they became sufficiently popular so that a woman, Ellen McCormack, ran in the 1976 presidential primaries on an anti-abortion ticket. The Right-to-Lifers, who use arguments substantially identical to those once used against contraception, want women's wombs to continue to be controlled by men and the state, want women's lives to continue to be subordinated to the chief duty of being fruitful and multiplying. Similarly, after the Equal Rights Amendment was passed in 1972, Leagues of Housewives organized to oppose it and in 1975 succeeded in getting the Amendment rejected in sixteen state legislatures and Equal Rights Statutes defeated in New York and New Jersey. They succeeded by appealing to the average woman's fear of losing her old role, by telling her, erroneously, that as soon as the Equal Rights Amendment was ratified husbands would forthwith stop supporting their wives and children, young women would be drafted into the armed forces and college girls forced to play football and wrestle with men.

The Leagues of Housewives and the Right-to-Lifers are very much like the anti-suffrage women in the nineteenth century who wanted women to remain "tenderly anchored . . . in the peaceful, blessed haven of home," to quote from Augusta Jane Evans' 1866 bestseller *St Elmo*, where she predicted that if women were to leave the "blessed haven" to vote, the race would be consigned "to a night of degradation and horror infinitely more appalling than a return to primeval barbarism." Phyllis Schlafly and other twentieth-century Augusta Janes are also terrified of a world in which women would no longer be delicate creatures, eternal mothers, protected in the home by strong fighting men.

Schlafly and Morgan are middle-aged, but there are women who were in their teens at the height of the women's liberation movement and who became feminists who are now wondering if old-fashioned wifehood and motherhood are not, after all, best. Anne Taylor Fleming, in a column in the August 11, 1975 *Newsweek*, said she and other feminists were secretly yearning to trade back their "full heads and empty wombs for empty heads and full wombs," but were afraid, like nineteenth-century men, that their full heads had unloosed a screw in their baby-making machinery. Mrs Fleming, having started a career and probably not found total fulfillment in making her way in the rough competitive world, probably now imagines the grass is greener in Motherland and yearns for the haven of the vine-covered cottage and the patter of little feet. There are certain to be many more Mrs Flemings.

Women have been wives and mothers for thousands of years and will naturally find it difficult to stop believing female happiness is achieved by having babies and serving men. Moreover, since the majority of women are wives and mothers, they want to feel justified in doing what society forced them to and therefore are hostile to a movement that says women are endowed by their Creator with the capacity to pursue happiness in a large variety of ways. Freedom is choosing, and most people find it easier to live in a world in which they have little or no choice. Especially women, who in return for giving up their freedom get substantial benefits—free food, clothing and shelter and often material comforts and luxuries, a halo of sanctity conferred for the mere physical production of a baby, the glory of sharing the limelight of whatever status their husband achieves, immunity from having to compete in the market place and learn one's limitations, instead unlimited power over little children and the safety of living through a husband and children while dreaming of how successful one might have been if . . .

"It is maintenance that women want who 'don't want to vote'," said Tennie C. Claflin in 1871 in *Constitutional Equality*. Most women, she said, "prefer to remain under the dominion and support of man rather than to take on themselves the responsibilities and duties of freedom and a noble independence and self-reliance," a statement that over one hundred years later is, alas, still true of the majority of women.

Not only do most housewives still prefer the slavery of maintenance to freedom, most feminists still dress like slaves in a crowded harem trying to capture the attention of the Sultan by wearing make up, low cut necklines, excessively short skirts, tight pants or whatever form of undress fashion dictates. Feminists, perhaps, still need to reassure themselves of their femininity by wearing the stigmata of beauty. They may also continue to falsify or exaggerate women's physical differences from men because women are going through a stage all oppressed groups go through as they gain self-confidence, the stage of emphasizing the characteristic for which society discriminated against them. Just as Jews used to say "I'm proud of being Jewish" and blacks that "Black is beautiful," so feminists obtrude the fact of their femaleness everywhere, and not only in dress.

They also force their femaleness into language, insisting a female representative to Congress must be called a Congresswoman, a female head of a committee a chairwoman, even a female orchestra conductor a maestra. At feminist functions there are no-hostess bars and mistresses of ceremonies, and feminists themselves have resurrected the feminine suffix, deliberately using poetess, aviatrix, murderess. Their rationale is that women must be verbally integrated into the English language, just as they must be integrated into the male workaday world. They therefore refuse to use the combining form -man and think it a slur to call a woman a spokesman, chairman or newsman, and even find discriminatory such a word as manpower (human as distinct from horsepower). They have instead invented the neutral forms -one and -person, as in chairone and spokesperson. They seem afraid to call themselves men, afraid probably of being thought of as lesbians, the twentieth-century equivalent of the nineteenth-century smear word "hermaphrodite." They do not as yet have the courage of the classicist Jane Ellen Harrison, who in an essay written about 1908 boldly asserted, "Homo Sum," I am a man, a human being, and only incidentally a female. But women will have to acquire the self-confidence to present themselves to the public primarily as human beings, not as females, so that the Barbara Walters of the future will use no more beauty aids than do the Walter Cronkites, and so that Congressman Smith will mean either a female or male representative and no one will think it of first importance to know if Congressman Smith is female or male.

Of course, not only women are afraid of a world in which there would be little sexual differentiation; the majority of men are also afraid, which is why many male legislators feel it their duty to vote against ratifying the Equal Rights Amendment and are opposed to abortion and all legislation that would give women as much freedom and power as men. Out of the same fear, newspapers, magazines and television give little space to feminists and headline the Pussycats and Total Women. Male anger at the women's liberation movement has also been repeatedly vented in the spate of movies in which a pair of male friends, who are all in all to each other, shoot and fight their way to glory or a glorious death, using women only for an occasional punching bag or rape. Twentieth-century men obviously feel their psychological welfare depends upon women remaining subservient, just as in ancient Greece the upper class believed civilized society could not exist without a slave class, or just as in eighteenth-century England the rich believed a well-ordered society depended upon the poor staying in their place, or just as in nineteenth-century America slave-holders believed God created blacks to be the workhorses of whites.

Men will find it difficult to stop believing they were created to be the master sex, just as women will find it difficult to stop believing they were created to be the servants of men. But however slowly and reluctantly, men and women will finally stop playing master and slave and will learn to live with each other as equals, and when men and women stop believing women are a sub-species specially designed to serve men and bear their children, no woman will change her name to her husband's because women will no longer be a despised group.

In "Name-changing," an essay in *The Liberation of the Jew* (1966), Albert Memmi said Jews used to change their names to Christian ones because their own names revealed they were a member of a despised minority. The Christian name they adopted was a camouflage, a mask that made them seem to be one of the accepted majority. Jews, an oppressed group, put on the guise of Chris-tians in order to live more easily in a hostile world. But they also put on the guise of Christians because oppressed groups tend to identify with their oppres-sors, long to be like the superior group, so that the price the Jews paid for their security was the destruction of their own identity. Changing their names was a form of self-rejection.

Women have changed their names to their husbands' for the same reasons. They too were a despised and oppressed group who wanted to take the name of their oppressors in order to pass into the world of the accepted majority. They too changed their names in order to live more easily in a world hostile to them. And they too identified with their oppressors, not only by becoming one with them in name but by adopting the values of their oppressors. Like the Jews, they too paid for their security with the sacrifice of their own identity. Chang-ing their names was also a form of self-rejection.

Men have no difficulty understanding the importance of names to men's sense of their identity. Albert Memmi understood the self-rejecting psychology of the Jew who changes his name. Henry James was certain his having the same name as his father made it difficult for him to find his own separate identity. A reviewer of John Berryman's poetry in the February 23, 1973 *Times Literary Supplement* suggested that Berryman's acute sense of the gap between his private and social self was in part caused by his name having been changed when he was a boy. In *The Story of Our Names* (1950) Elsdon C. Smith waxed lyrical when he wrote of names and self-identity. A man's name remains, he said, "when everything else is lost; it is owned by those who possess nothing else . . . when one dies it is the only part that lives on in the world." Smith, of course, was speaking only of men; he thought Lucy Stoners were neurotic. Men seem incapable of understanding that women too have a sense of identity it is important for them to preserve.

Occasionally a woman understands. Jessamyn West in *Hide and Seek* (1973) recalled that when she was about fourteen and was walking home one night, she suddenly felt transformed and said out loud, "You are M. J. West" (her full name was Mary Jessamyn West), a declaration of identity that seemed to her "a great piece of good news," the news that she, a unique being, was alive in the world. So strong was her feeling of the "I within my written name" that although she is known legally and socially as Mrs H. M. McPherson, she can never sign any other name but Jessamyn West "to anything that is part of myself."

When women and men finally understand that women are "primary existences," to quote Emma Willard, "the companions not the satellites of men," women will stop offering up their identity to men. There will be no more Elizabeth Griscom Ross Ashburn Claypooles. No more Mrs President Tylers and Mrs Stuyvesant Fishes. No more women who make a career of marriage and whose husbands' names trail after them like a string of railroad cars— no more Betty Brook Phipps Reeves McLean Blake Guibersons or Barbara Hutton Mdivani Reventlow Grant Troubetzkoy Rubirosa Von Cramm Champassaks. No more women like Mrs Edward B. Close, Mrs Edward F. Hutton, Mrs Joseph E. Davies, Mrs Herbert A. May, intermittently known as Marjorie Merriweather Post. No more writers like Mary McCarthy, privately known as Mrs Johnsrud, then Mrs Wilson, then Mrs Broadwater, then Mrs West. No more lawyers like Belva Ann Bennett McNall Lockwood or Yvonne Watson Brathwaite Burke, changing their names again and again in mid career. No more famous women like Mary Wells, proud to take on the identity of a second husband. At long last, no more women will manage to convince themselves they become more womanly when they assume the colors of their male host, and, when that time comes, the chameleons of the human species will have faded into history.

The establishing of woman on her rightful throne
is the greatest revolution
the world has ever known
or ever will know.

Elizabeth Cady Stanton
December 28, 1869

SOURCES

Discovering the names married women actually used is difficult. Collections of letters often omit signatures, and biographers generally do not pay attention to wives' names, so that a Colonial wife will be called Mrs George Washington, although that style was not used in the Colonial period, or a couple will be called "the Smiths" even though the wife used her own name professionally or a hyphenated name for all purposes, or a woman who married two or three times will always be called Mrs Her-Last-Husband and thus her name changes will not be graphed, nor, perhaps, that she used her own or a previous husband's name for professional purposes. In addition, the Library of Congress almost always catalogued women who published under their own name under their husband's name, and *Who's Who*s will list a woman as "Mary Smith (Mrs John Jones)" although the woman herself never used her husband's name.

The tendency not to pay attention to the names married women actually used and to call them Mrs Theirhusband is, of course, the theme of *Mrs Man*— woman's absorption into her husband. But though women were in nominal purdah, their nominal history can be reconstructed—a fact here and a fact there—by consulting a great variety of sources, among them:

WHO'S WHOS AND BIOGRAPHICAL DICTIONARIES:

British Museum General Catalogue of Printed Books, Contemporary Authors, Current Biography, Dictionary of American Biography, Dictionary of National Biography, National Cyclopaedia of American Biography, National Union Catalog [Library of Congress catalog], *New Century Cyclopedia of Names, Who's Who, Who's Who in America, Who Was Who in America*, and in the following that list women only:

Woman's Record, comp. Sarah J. Hale (1853)

A Woman of the Century, eds. Frances E. Willard and Mary A. Livermore (1893)

Woman's Who's Who of America, 1914-15, ed. John Leonard

Biographical Cyclopaedia of American Women, ed. Mabel W. Cameron et al., 3 vols. (1924-28)

American Women, ed. Durward Howes (1935-39)

Who's Who of American Women (1958-   )
Notable American Women, eds. Edward T. James, Janet W. James and
    Paul S. Boyer, 3 vols. (1971)

GENERAL:

Mary S. Benson, *Women in Eighteenth-Century America* (1935)
Nelson M. Blake, *The Road to Reno, A History of Divorce in the United
    States* (1962)
Arthur W. Calhoun, *A Social History of the American Family*, 3 vols. (1919)
Carroll Camden, *The Elizabethan Woman* (1952)
Mary R. Coolidge, *Why Women Are So* (1912)
Abbie Graham, *Ladies in Revolt* (1934)
Ida H. Harper, *The Life and Works of Susan B. Anthony,* 3 vols. (1898-1908)
Inez H. Irwin, *Angels and Amazons* (1933)
John C. Jeaffreson, *Brides and Bridals,* 2 vols. (1873)
Aileen S. Kraditor, ed. *Up from the Pedestal* (1968)
Edythe Lutzker, *Women Gain a Place in Medicine* (1969)
Mabel Newcomer, *A Century of Higher Education for American Women*
    (1959)
Julia O'Faolain and Lauro Martines, eds., *Not in God's Image* (1973)
I. B. O'Malley, *Women in Subjection* (1933)
Ishbel Ross, *Ladies of the Press* (1936)
Andrew Sinclair, *The Better Half* (1965)
Elizabeth C. Stanton et al., *History of Woman Suffrage*, 6 vols. (1881-1922)
Margaret F. Thorp, *Female Persuasion* (1949)
Mary O. Whitton, *These Were the Women* (1954)
Helen B. Woodward, *The Bold Women* (1953)

In addition to the sources cited in the text, see also:

1   WIFE OF

E. E. Evans-Pritchard, *The Position of Women in Primitive Societies* (1965)
Thomas J. Pettigrew, *Chronicles of the Tombs* (1902)
Edward J. Wood, *The Wedding Day in All Ages and Countries*, 2 vols. (1869)
On surnames, see sources for Chapter Eleven

2   MRS GEORGE WASHINGTON JONES

Letters of Mrs Adams, ed. Charles F. Adams (1848)
Isabel Burton, *The Romance of Isabel Lady Burton* (1897)

Jean Burton, *Sir Richard Burton's Wife* (1941)

Gerald Carson, *The Polite Americans* (1966)

Elisabeth A. Dexter, *Career Women of America 1776-1840* (1950); *Colonial Women of Affairs* (1924)

Bess Furman, *White House Profile* (1951)

Alma Lutz, *Created Equal: A Biography of Elizabeth Cady Stanton* (1940)

Ralph G. Martin, *Jennie, The Life of Lady Randolph Churchill*, I (1969)

Harriet Martineau, *Autobiography*, ed. Maria W. Chapman, 2 vols. (1877)

Myra Reynolds, *The Learned Lady in England 1650-1760* (1920)

Arthur M. Schlesinger, *Learning How to Behave* (1946)

Margaret B. Smith, *The First Forty Years of Washington Society*, ed. Gaillard Hunt (1906)

Theodore Stanton and Harriot S. Blatch, eds., *Elizabeth Cady Stanton, As Revealed in Her Letters*, 2 vols. (1922)

Ada Wallas, *Before the Bluestockings* (1929)

The Diaries of George Washington, ed. John C. Fitzpatrick, 4 vols. (1925)

3   MRS ASTOR'S PROFESSION

Elizabeth Eliot, *Heiresses and Coronets* (1959)

Lucy Kavaler, *The Astors* (1966)

Ward McAllister, *Society As I Have Found It* (1890)

Marianne Means, *The Woman in the White House* (1963)

Joanna Richardson, *The Courtesans* (1967)

Ishbel Ross, *Silhouette in Diamonds, The Life of Mrs Potter Palmer* (1960)

Madeleine B. Stern, *Purple Passage, The Life of Mrs Frank Leslie* (1953)

Louise H. Thorp, *Mrs Jack* (1965)

Cornelius Vanderbilt Jr, *Queen of the Golden Age* (1956)

Horace Wyndham, *The Magnificent Montez* (1935)

4   THE SECOND OLDEST PROFESSION

Mary Clemmer [Ames], *Men, Women, and Things* (1886)

Archie Binns, *Mrs Fiske and the American Theatre* (1955)

Joan Bulman, *Jenny Lind* (1956)

Edward G. Craig, *Ellen Terry and Her Secret Self* (1932)

Mrs John Drew, *Autobiographical Sketch* (1900)

Janet Dunbar, *Peg Woffington and Her World* (1968)

Rosamond Gilder, *Enter the Actress, The First Women in the Theatre* (1931)

The Lost Letters of Jenny Lind, tr. W. Porter Ware and T. C. Lockard Jr (1966)

Roger Manvell, *Ellen Terry* (1968)

The Life of Charles James Mathews, Chiefly Autobiographical, ed. Charles
     Dickens (1879)

Charles E. Pearce, *Madame Vestris and Her Times* (n.d.)

Charles E. Russell, *Julia Marlowe, Her Life and Art* (1926)

Esther K. Sheldon, *Thomas Sheridan of Smock-Alley* (1967)

Gladys D. Schultz, *Jenny Lind, The Swedish Nightingale* (1962)

Harold Simpson and Mrs Charles Braun, *A Century of Famous Actresses*
     1750-1850 (n.d.)

Cornelia O. Skinner, *Madame Sarah* (1967)

E. H. Sothern, *Julia Marlowe's Story,* ed. Fairfax Downey (1954)

Arthur P. Stanley, *Historical Memorials of Westminster Abbey* (1896)

Edward Wagenknecht, *Seven Daughters of the Theater* (1964)

5   THE VEILED LADIES

Eric W. Barnes, *The Lady of Fashion, The Life and the Theatre of Anna Cora
     Mowatt* (1954)

Katherine D. Blake and Margaret L. Wallace, *Champion of Women, The Life
     of Lillie Devereux Blake* (1953)

Janet E. Courtney, *The Adventurous Thirties* (1933)

William P. Courtney, *The Secrets of Our National Literature* (1908)

Charlotte P. Gilman, *The Living of Charlotte Perkins Gilman* (1935)

John S. Hart, *The Female Prose Writers of America* (1852)

Annie R. Marble, *Pen Names and Personalities* (1930)

6   GETTING A HEAD

Thomas Allsop, *Letters, Conversations and Recollections of S. T. Coleridge*
     (1836) [on Lamb]

William Andrews, *Bygone Punishments* (1899)

Samuel Edwards, *The Divine Mistress* (1970) [on Emilie du Châtelet]

The George Eliot Letters, ed. Gordon S. Haight (1954)

Milton E. Flower, *James Parton* (1951) [on Fanny Fern]

Jan Fortune and Jean Burton, *Elisabet Ney* (1943)

Roger Fulford, "Ruskin's Notes on Carlyle," *Times Literary Supplement,*
     April 16, 1971, p. 453

Jane E. Harrison, *Alpha and Omega* (1915)

Thomas W. Higginson, *Women and the Alphabet* (1881)

Frances J. Hosford, *Father Shipherd's Magna Charta, A Century of Coeducation in Oberlin College* (1937)

Caroline Howard, "Autobiography," John S. Hart, *The Female Prose Writers of America* (1852)

Heinrich E. Jacob, *Felix Mendelssohn and His Times*, tr. Richard and Clara Winston (1963)

Elaine Kaye, *A History of Queen's College, London, 1848-1972* (1972)

George S. Layard, *Mrs Lynn Linton, Her Life, Letters, and Opinions* (1901)

Gerda Lerner, *The Grimké Sisters from South Carolina* (1967)

Alma Lutz, *Emma Willard* (1964)

André Maurois, *Lélia, The Life of George Sand* (1954)

Samuel J. May, *Some Recollections of Our Antislavery Conflict* (1869)

Richard B. Onians, *The Origins of European Thought about The Body, The Mind, The Soul, The World, Time, and Fate* (1951)

Edd W. Parks, *Charles Egbert Craddock (Mary Noailles Murfree)* (1941)

Peter G. Patmore, *My Friends and Acquaintances* (1855) [on Lamb]

Mary Somerville, *Personal Recollections* (1873)

Madeleine B. Stern, *Heads & Headlines: The Phrenological Fowlers* (1971)

Lionel Stevenson, *The Wild Irish Girl, The Life of Sydney Owenson, Lady Morgan* (1936)

Margaret F. Thorp, *Female Persuasion* (1949)

7   THE QUIET NAME OF WIFE

Margaret Armstrong, *Fanny Kemble* (1938)

Dr Elizabeth Blackwell, *Pioneer Work for Women* (1914)

Leota S. Driver, *Fanny Kemble* (1933)

The Letters of Mrs Gaskell, eds. J. A. V. Chapple and Arthur Pollard (1967)

Gordon S. Haight, *Mrs Sigourney, The Sweet Singer of Hartford* (1930)

Bertita Harding, *Concerto, The Glowing Story of Clara Schumann* (1961)

Vinnie Ream Hoxie, "Lincoln and Farragut," *The Congress of Women*, ed. Mary K. O. Eagle (1894)

Berthold Litzmann, *Clara Schumann*, tr. Grace Hadow, 2 vols. (1913)

Frances Winwar, *The Immortal Lovers, Elizabeth Barrett and Robert Browning* (1950)

8   NOMINAL POLYANDRY

William D. Orcutt, *Mary Baker Eddy and Her Books* (1950)

Edwin S. Parry, *Betsy Ross* (1930)

Robert Peel, *Mary Baker Eddy; The Years of Discovery (1966); Mary Baker Eddy; The Years of Trial* (1971)
Ishbel Ross, *Charmers and Cranks* (1965)
Madeleine B. Stern, *We the Women, Career Firsts of Nineteenth-Century America* (1963)
Charles L. Wallis, *Stories on Stone, A Book of American Epitaphs* (1954)

9   DOUBLE IDENTITIES

Louisa G. Anderson, *Elizabeth Garrett Anderson 1836-1917* (1939)
D. C. Bloomer, *Life and Writings of Amelia Bloomer* (1895)
Dorothy R. Blumberg, *Florence Kelley* (1966)
Sigmund Freud and Lou Andreas-Salomé, Letters, ed. Ernest Pfeiffer (1973)
Anna E. Klumpke, *Memoirs of An Artist,* ed. Lilian Whiting (1940) [on Rosa Bonheur]
Allen Lesser, *Enchanting Rebel* (1947) [on Adah Isaacs Menken]
Paul Lewis, *Queen of the Plaza, A Biography of Adah Isaacs Menken* (1964)
Alma Lutz, *Created Equal, A Biography of Elizabeth Cady Stanton* (1940)
Jo Manton, *Elizabeth Garrett Anderson* (1965)
Marta Milinowski, *Teresa Carreño* (1940)
The Correspondence of Berthe Morisot, ed. Denis Rouart, tr. Betty Hubbard (1957)
Arthur H. Nethercot, *The First Five Lives of Annie Besant* (1960)
Louis A. Sigaud, *Belle Boyd, Confederate Spy* (1944)
Rhoda Truax, *The Doctors Jacobi* (1952)
Anne H. Wharton, *Heirlooms in Miniatures* (1897) [on Anna Peale]
Mary A. Wyman, *Two American Pioneers, Seba Smith and Elizabeth Oakes Smith* (1927)

10   LUCY STONE (ONLY)

Alice S. Blackwell, *Lucy Stone, Pioneer of Woman's Rights* (1930)
Olympia Brown, *Acquaintances, Old and New, Among Reformers* (1911)
Ida H. Harper, *The Life and Works of Susan B. Anthony,* I (1898)
Elinor R. Hays, *Morning Star, A Biography of Lucy Stone* (1961)
Alma Lutz, *Susan B. Anthony* (1959); *Created Equal, A Biography of Elizabeth Cady Stanton* (1940)
Louise R. Noun, *Strong-Minded Women, The Emergence of The Woman-Suffrage Movement in Iowa* (1969) [on Amelia Bloomer]
Elizabeth C. Stanton et al., *History of Woman Suffrage,* I & II (1881, 1887)

11   LUCY STONE v. THE STATUS QUO

Charles W. Bardsley, *English Surnames* (1875)

Catherine D. Bowen, *The Lion and the Throne, The Life and Times of Sir Edward Coke* (1956)

William W. Comfort, "Quaker Marriage Certificates," *Bulletin of the Friends Historical Association*, XL (1951), 67-80

George Denoon, "Married Women's Surnames," *South African Law Journal*, LXIII (1946), 53-64

C. L'Estrange Ewen, *A History of Surnames of the British Isles* (1931)

A. C. and C. B. Fox-Davies, *A Treatise on the Law Concerning Names and Changes of Name* (1906)

Virgil M. Harris, *Ancient Curious and Famous Wills* (1912)

R. H. Helmholz, *Marriage Litigation in Medieval England* (1974)

Anthony Linell, *The Law of Names* (1938)

Harry A. Long, *Personal and Family Names* (1883)

Mark A. Lower, *English Surnames*, 2 vols. (1849)

C. M. Matthews, *English Surnames* (1967)

Helena Normanton, "England Admits Choice of Name," *Equal Rights*, XI (November 29, 1924), 333; "The Institution of the Surname," *Equal Rights*, XII (March 7, 1925), 30-31

Notes & Queries, various notes on married women's surnames: December 23, 1865; August 13, September 10, October 8, 1887; February 25, May 12, June 9, December 8, 1888; August 17, September 21, 1889

W. P. W. Phillimore, *An Index to Changes of Name 1760-1901* (1905)

L. G. Pine, *The Story of Surnames* (1966)

P. H. Reaney, *The Origin of English Surnames* (1967)

Eusebius Salverte, *History of the Names of Men* . . . , 2 vols. (1862)

Elsdon C. Smith, *The Story of Our Names* (1950); *Treasury of Name Lore* (1967)

Matteo Spalletta, "Divorce in Colonial New York," *New York Historical Society Quarterly Bulletin*, XXXIX (October, 1955), 422-440

E. G. Withycombe, *The Oxford Dictionary of English Christian Names* (1969)

12   A NAME OF THEIR OWN

Olympia Brown

Olympia Brown, *Acquaintances, Old and New, Among Reformers* (1911)

Charles E. Neu, "Olympia Brown and the Woman's Suffrage Movement," *Wisconsin Magazine of History*, XLIII (Summer 1960), 277-287

Letters in the Schlesinger Library, Radcliffe College
Carrie Lane Chapman
    Alice S. Blackwell, *Lucy Stone* (1930)
    Louise R. Noun, *Strong-Minded Women, The Emergence of the Woman-Suffrage Movement in Iowa* (1969)
    Mary G. Peck, *Carrie Chapman Catt* (1944)
    The Woman's Journal 1890-1896 passim
Annie and Thomas James Cobden-Sanderson
    The Journals of Thomas James Cobden-Sanderson, I & II (1926)
Lydia Kingsmill Commander
    Who's Who in America, 1908-1917
    Isaac Broome, *The Last Days of the Ruskin Co-operative Association* (1902)
Florence Fenwick Miller
    Helena Normanton, "England Admits Choice of Name," *Equal Rights*, XI (November 29, 1924), 333
    Who's Who 1927
    Woman's Journal, January 1902, p. 1
Helen Hamilton Gardener
    Dictionary of American Biography, Notable American Women, letters in the Schlesinger Library, Radcliffe College
Lillian Harman
    The State v. Walker, 36 Kansas State Reports 297
    Memorial of Moses Harman, pbd. L. Harman (1910)
Dr Aletta Jacobs
    Information from Sacha Vries-van Poorten, International Woman's Foundation, Amsterdam, The Netherlands
Ida Lewis
    J. Earl Clausen, "A Half-Forgotten Heroine," *Putnam's Magazine* (February 7, 1910)
Olive Logan
    Notable American Women
Charlotte and Thomas Garrigue Masaryk
    President Masaryk Tells His Story, recounted by Karel Capek (1934)
    Paul Selver, *Masaryk* (1940)
Elisabet Ney
    Jan Fortune and Jean Burton, *Elisabet Ney* (1943)
    Vernon Loggins, *Two Romantics* (1946)
Olive Schreiner
    Vera Buchanan-Gould, *Not Without Honour* (1948)
    S. C. Cronwright-Schreiner, *The Life of Olive Schreiner* (1924)

D. L. Hobman, *Olive Schreiner* (1955)
Information in unpublished letters in the University of Capetown Library
supplied by C. P. Ravilious, Sussex, England
Martha Strickland
  Willard and Livermore, *A Woman of the Century* (1893)
Dr Mary Walker
  Charles McCool Snyder, *Dr Mary Walker* (1962)
Victoria Woodhull
  M. M. Marberry, *Vicky* (1967)
  Emanie Sachs, *"The Terrible Siren" Victoria Woodhull* (1928)

See also: St John Ervine, *God's Soldier: General William Booth*, 2 vols.
(1935); Mary M. Phelps, *Kate Chase* (1935); Dorothy R. Blumberg, *Florence
Kelley* (1966); Elizabeth G. Speare, "Abby, Julia, and the Cows," *American
Heritage*, VIII (June 1957), 54-7, 96 [on Julia Smith]; Alma Lutz, *Emma
Willard* (1964). Information about Sarah Lowe Twiggs, Corresta T. Canfield
and Mary Barr Clay from *A Woman of the Century*; about Harriet McConkey
and Zelia Nuttall from *Notable American Women*; about Eliza Farnham
from Gladys Tilden, Berkeley, California and Professor W. David Lewis,
Auburn University, Alabama.

13   THE MINOR POINT OF A NAME

Thomas W. Higginson, "On the Desire of Women to Be Individuals," *Concerning All of Us* (1893)
Richard Stiller, *Queen of Populists; The Story of Mary Elizabeth Lease* (1970)

14   TWO NAMES ON A GREENWICH VILLAGE DOOR

Keith Briant, *Passionate Paradox, The Life of Marie Stopes* (1962)
Vera Brittain, *Pethick-Lawrence* (1963)
William E. Carson, *The Marriage Revolt* (1915)
Allen Churchill, *The Improper Bohemians . . . Greenwich Village in its Hey-
day* (1959)
Margaret Cole, "Mary Macarthur," *Women of To-Day* (1938)
Floyd Dell, *Homecoming* (1933); *Love in Greenwich Village* (1926)
Max Eastman, *The Enjoyment of Living* (1948)
Barbara Gelb, *So Short a Time, A Biography of John Reed and Louise Bryant*
(1973)
Jane Grant, "Confessions of a Feminist," *American Mercury*, LVII (December
1943) 684-692; *Ross, The New Yorker and Me* (1968)

Francis Hackett, *I Chose Denmark* (1941)

The World of Haldeman-Julius, comp. Albert Mordell (1960)

Ruth Hale,*The First Five Years of the Lucy Stone League* (n.d. [1925?])

Mary A. Hamilton, *Mary Macarthur* (1925)

Fannie Hurst, *Anatomy of Me* (1958)

John Keats, *You Might as Well Live, The Life and Times of Dorothy Parker* (1970)

Dale Kramer, *Heywood Broun* (1949)

James R. McGovern, "The American Woman's Pre-World War I Freedom in Manners and Morals," *Journal of American History*, LV (September 1968), 315-333

George Martin, *Madam Secretary, Frances Perkins* (1976)

Ralph G. Martin, *Jennie, The Life of Lady Randolph Churchill*, II (1971)

Aylmer Maude, *Marie Stopes* (1933)

George Middleton, *These Things Are Mine* (1947)

Richard O'Connor, *Heywood Broun* (1975)

Richard O'Connor and Dale Walker, *The Lost Revolutionary, A Biography of John Reed* (1967)

George Oppenheimer, *The View from the Sixties* (1966)

Albert Parry, *Garrets and Pretenders, A History of Bohemianism in America* (1960)

Emmeline Pethick-Lawrence, *My Part in a Changing World* (1938)

Mark Schorer, *Sinclair Lewis* (1961)

June Sochen, *The New Woman, Feminism in Greenwich Village, 1910-1920* (1972)

The Autobiography of Lincoln Steffens (1931)

Raymond Swing, *"Good Evening!"* (1964)

Robert Windeler, *Sweetheart, The Story of Mary Pickford* (1973)

Alexander Woollcott, "Profile of Haldeman-Julius," *The New Yorker*, June 20, 1925

The Letters of Alexander Woollcott, ed. Beatrice Kaufman and Joseph Hennessy (1944)

Information on Dr May Wilson supplied by her niece Helen H. Harris; on Fola La Follette by her sister Mary La Follette; on Marie Washburn by her son Loron Washburn; on Phyllis Greenacre from a personal communication.

15   THE LUCY STONE LEAGUE

John Baragwanath, *A Good Time Was Had* (1962) [on Neysa McMein]

Edward L. Bernays, *Biography of an Idea* (1965)

Collected Edition of Heywood Broun, comp. Heywood Hale Broun (1941)

August Derleth, *Still Small Voice, The Biography of Zona Gale* (1940)

Doris E. Fleischman, "Notes of a Retiring Feminist," *American Mercury*, LXVIII (February, 1949), 161-8

Jean Gould, *The Poet and Her Book, A Biography of Edna St Vincent Millay* (1969)

Jane Grant, see sources Chapter 14

Ruth Hale, see sources Chapter 14

Margaret C. Harriman, *The Vicious Circle, The Story of the Algonquin Round Table* (1951)

David M. Kennedy, *Birth Control in America, The Career of Margaret Sanger* (1970)

Margaret Mead, *Blackberry Winter* (1972)

Mabel Newcomer, *A Century of Higher Education for American Women* (1959)

George P. Putnam, *Soaring Wings, A Biography of Amelia Earhart* (1939)

Ishbel Ross, *Ladies of the Press* (1936)

Victor Seroff, *The Real Isadora* (1971)

The Letters of Lincoln Steffens, ed. Ella Winter and Granville Hicks (1938)

Michael Strange, *Who Tells Me True* (1940)

Edith Summerskill, *A Woman's World* (1967)

Personal communications from Clara Eliot Raup, Margaret Good Myers and Dr Dorothy V. Whipple

16   DWINDLING INTO A WIFE

Franklin P. Adams, *The Diary of Our Own Samuel Pepys*, 2 vols. (1935)

Richard S. Aldrich, *Gertrude Lawrence as Mrs A* (1954)

Doris F. Bernays, *A Wife Is Many Women* (1955), see also under Fleischman, sources Chapter 15

Edward L. Bernays, *Biography of an Idea* (1965)

Clare Boothe, *Europe in the Spring* (1940)

Vera Brittain, "Surnames of Married Women," *Equal Rights*, XII (November 14, 1925), 317-18; *Testament of Experience* (1957)

Margaret H. Carpenter, *Sara Teasdale* (1960)

Theodore F. Harris, *Pearl S. Buck* (1969)

Beatrice Hinkle, "Marriage in the New World," *The Book of Marriage*, ed. Count Hermann Keyserling (1926)

Dale Kramer, *Heywood Broun* (1949)

Anita Loos, *A Girl Like I* (1966); *Kiss Hollywood Good-By* (1974)

George Martin, *Madam Secretary, Frances Perkins* (1976)
Aylmer Maude, *Marie Stopes* (1933)
Letters of Edna St Vincent Millay, ed. Allan R. Macdougall (1952)
Oliver Pilat, Pegler, Angry Man of the Press (1963)
Lorine Pruette, "Why Women Fail," *Woman's Coming of Age*, ed. S. D.
   Schmalhausen and V. F. Calverton (1931)
Marion K. Sanders, *Dorothy Thompson* (1973)
Mark Schorer, *Sinclair Lewis* (1961)
Stephen Shadegg, *Clare Boothe Luce* (1970)
Vincent Sheean, *Dorothy and Red* (1963)
Edith Summerskill, *A Woman's World* (1967)
Raymond Swing, *"Good Evening!"* (1964)
Florence E. Wall, "In Memoriam Calm Morrison Hoke," *The Chemist*
   (October 1952), 501-504
Elizabeth Yates, *Pebble in a Pool, The Widening Circles of Dorothy Canfield
   Fisher's Life* (1958)

Personal communications from Ruth Aryes, Elizabeth Brandeis, Dr Charlotte
McCarthy, Margaret Good Myers, Alice Mendham Powell, Lorine Pruette,
Clara Eliot Raup, Cornelia B. Rose Jr, Florence E. Wall, Caroline F. Ware,
Dr Dorothy V. Whipple

18   MANNERS MAKE LAWS

National Organization for Women Newsletters: a collection from various
chapters were on file at the International Women's History Archives, Berkeley,
California.

Also at the Archives (but now at the University of Wyoming) were newspaper
and magazine clippings about women keeping their name, among them:
   Barbara Aiello and Kathryn Scott, *Washington Post*, July 15, 1972
   Marcia Greenwold, *Glamour*, December 1972
   The Hambrick-Stowes, *The New York Times*, September 12, 1971
   Carol Joiner, *The Evening Star* (Washington DC), June 13, 1972
   Francia Leussen, *San Francisco Chronicle*, December 11, 1970
   The Littleton-Taylors, *Maine Freewoman's Herald*, June-July 1974
   Deonne Parker, *The Minneapolis Star*, December 17, 1971
   Karla Simone and Nancy Hermann, *Miami Herald*, November 6, 1971
   Mary E. Stuart, *Washington Post*, May 15, 16, 1972
   Terri Tepper, *Chicago Tribune*, June 29, 1972

For information about other women who kept their name, see *Booklet for Women Who Wish to Determine Their Own Names after Marriage*, comp. Center for a Woman's Own Name, Barrington, Illinois (1974) and its 1975 Supplement.

Personal communications from Anne Siefert-Hoyt, Kathy Sheley, Gail Griffin, Robey Lyle, Dr Barbara Moulton, Dr Patricia K. Putman [on Hawaii legislature].

Dennis L. Albrecht, "How to Avoid Forbush," unpbd. paper, George Washington University

Edward J. Bander, *Change of Name and Law of Names* (1973)

"Case Summaries: Names," *Women's Rights Law Reporter*, I (Spring 1972), 26-8

Pauline Kael, "Replying to Listeners," *I Lost It at the Movies* (1965)

19   THE MOTHER OF US ALL

The Ante-Nicene Fathers, ed. Alexander Roberts, 9 vols. (1913)

G. R. Beasley-Murray, *Baptism in the New Testament* (1962)

Bruno Bettelheim, *Symbolic Wounds* (1954)

Robert Briffault, *The Mothers*, 3 vols. (1927)

Ernest Caulfield, *The Infant Welfare Movement in the Eighteenth Century* (1931)

Claude Chavasse, *The Bride of Christ* (1940)

F. J. Cole, *Early Theories of Sexual Generation* (1930)

F. Cornwallis Conybeare, *Myth, Magic, and Morals, A Study of Christian Origins* (1910)

Eric J. Dingwall, *The Girdle of Chastity* (1959)

Sophie H. Drinker, "Women in American History," address delivered April 9, 1959 at the House of Detention for Women, New York City. On file at the Lucy Stone League. [on Sybilla Masters]

Lina Eckenstein, *Woman under Monasticism* (1896)

Erik Erikson, "Inner and Outer Space: Reflections on Womanhood," *Daedalus*, XCIII (Spring 1964), 582-606; *Young Man Luther* (1958)

Robert H. Fife, *The Revolt of Martin Luther* (1957)

V. H. H. Green, *Luther and the Reformation* (1964)

Harry Harlow, "Basic Social Capacity of Primates," *The Evolution of Man's Capacity for Culture*, ed. J. N. Spuhler (1959)

Edwin S. Hartland, *Primitive Paternity, The Myth of Supernatural Birth in Relation to the History of the Family*, 2 vols. (1909-10)

Stephanus Hilpisch, *History of Benedictine Nuns* (1958)

E. O. James, *The Cult of the Mother-Goddess* (1959)

Phillis C. Jay, "The Female Primate," *The Potential of Woman,* ed. S. M. Farber and R. H. L. Wilson (1963)

Phyllis M. Kaberry, *Aboriginal Woman Sacred and Profane* (1939)

Birgitta Linnér, *Sex and Society in Sweden* (1967)

Margaret Mead, *Sex and Temperament* (1935)

Arthur W. Meyer, *The Rise of Embryology* (1930)

Joseph Needham and Arthur Hughes, *A History of Embryology* (1959)

Erich Neuman, *The Great Mother* (1955)

Joseph C. Plumpe, *Mater Ecclesia, An Inquiry into the Concept of the Church as Mother in Early Christianity* (1943)

Sir Frederick Pollock and Frederic W. Maitland, *The History of English Law Before the Time of Edward I,* 2 vols. (1898)

Eileen Power, "The Position of Women," *The Legacy of the Middle Ages,* ed. G. C. Crump and E. F. Jacob (1926)

J. Rendle-Short, "Infant Management in the 18th Century," *Bulletin of the History of Medicine,* XXXIV (1960), 97-122

George B. Schaller, *The Year of the Gorilla* (1964)

G. Rattray Taylor, *Sex in History* (1954)

Conway Zirkle, "The Early History of the Idea of the Inheritance of Acquired Characters and of Pangenesis," *Transactions of the American Philosophical Society* , XXXV (1946), 91-151

CASE INDEX

Cases cited dealing with married women's names (in chronological order)

1823   The King v. Inhabitants of St Faith's (3 Dow. & Ryl. [England] 348), 115, 119-20

1833   Scanlan v. Wright (13 Pick. [Mass.] 523), 120

1856   Converse v. Converse (9 Rich. Eq. [South Carolina] 535), 115, 119

1860   Bell v. The State (25 Texas 574), 4-5, 120, 129

1871   St Johnsbury v. Goodenough (44 Vermont 662), 115, 120

1872   Martin v. Robson (65 Illinois 129), 105-6, 120

1873   Warren v. Quill (8 Nevada 218), 120

1878   Clark v. Clark (19 Kansas 522), 115, 120

1880   Elberson v. Richards (42 New Jersey 69), 126

1881   Chapman v. Phoenix National Bank (85 New York 437), 124-6, 127, 128, 130, 242-3, 245, 250, 257, 278

1886   State v. Walker (36 Kansas 297), 139

1889   Rich v. Mayer (26 New York State 107), 128, 242
      Lane v. Duchac (73 Wisconsin 646), 128, 242

1890   Freeman v. Hawkins (77 Texas 498), 127, 128, 242
      Wilkerson v. Schoonmaker (77 Texas 498), 127

1897   Blanc v. Blanc (21 New York Misc. 268), 127, 129-30, 242
      Rice v. The State (37 Texas Crim. 36), 129

1898   Carrall v. The State (53 Nebraska 431), 126-7

1901   Cowley v. Cowley (A. C. [England] 450), 164, 187, 278

1906   Uihlein v. Gladieux (74 Ohio 232), 242

1908   Emery v. Kipp (154 California 83), 127

1923   State ex rel. Thompson (179 Wisconsin 284), 241

1924   Brown v. Reinke (159 Minnesota 458), 241, 254

1926   Bacon v. Boston Elevated Ry. (256 Massachusetts 30), 243-5, 253

1930   Carlton v. Phelan (100 Florida 1164), 254

1931   Succession of Kniepp (172 Louisiana 411), 254-5, 257

1934   In re Kayaloff (9 Fed. Sup. [New York] 176), 218, 245-6

1937   Roberts v. Grayson (233 Alabama 658), 254

1938   Hanson's Appeal (330 Pennsylvania 390), 246
        Appeal of Egerter (52 York [Penn.] 40), 246
1941   State ex rel. Bucher v. Brower (21 Ohio Op. 208), 257-8, 260, 278
1945   Rago v. Lipsky (327 Illinois App. 63), 247-8, 251-2, 277-8, 279
        In re Fry (1 Chanc. Div. [England] 348), 251, 278
1957   Kelle v. Crab Orchard Fire Dist. (164 Nebraska 593), 254
1961   State ex rel. Krupa v. Green (19 Ohio Op.2d 341), 258-9, 278
1963   Wilty v. Jefferson Parish (245 Louisiana 145), 255-6, 257
1971   Forbush v. Wallace (341 Fed. Sup. [Alabama] 217), 269, 272,
           276-7, 277, 282, 286

1972
10/9   Stuart v. Board of Elections (266 Maryland 440), 269, 272-3, 277-8,
           278-9, 279-80
11/2   Gallop v. Shanahan (No. 120-456 Shawnee County Kansas), 280

1973
4/18   In Petition of Hauptly (294 NE2d [Indiana] 833), 285
11/27   Application of Halligan (350 New York State 2d 63), 274, 283

1974
1/29   Custer v. Bonaides (30 Connecticut Sup. 387), 273, 280, 284
6/25   Petition of Hauptly (312 NE2d [Indiana] 857), 269, 273, 281, 285
10/15   Marshall v. The State (301 So2d [Florida] 477), 274, 281, 287
10/24   In re Marriage of Banks (42 Cal. App.3d 631), 281, 284
12/5   Application of Halligan (361 New York State 2d 458), 281

1975
2/21   Cragun and Spiller v. Hawaii (Civil Judg. 43175), 283
3/6   Kruzel v. Podell (266 NW2d [Wisconsin] 458), 269, 273-4, 281
4/2   Application of Lawrence (337 A2d [New Jersey] 49), 274, 281,
           287-8
4/7   Dunn v. Palermo (522 SW2d [Tennessee] 679), 280
7/18   In re Reben (342 A2d [Maine] 688), 274, 281, 287
7/29   In re Montage (527 SW2d [Missouri] 402), 274, 281
10/8   Laks v. Laks (25 Arizona App. 58), 335
12/1   In re Strikwerda (220 SE2d [Virginia] 245), 274, 281, 288

1976
1/9   Weathers v. Sup. Ct. of Los Angeles, App. (126 Cal. Rptr 547), 282
2/3   Davis v. Roos (326 So2d [Florida] 226), 280
7/23   Whitlow v. Hodges (539 Fed.2d 582), 282

INDEX

Abarbanel, Janice, 335
abortion, 225, 299-300, 322, 333-4, 347, 349
Abraham, May, 66
Abzug, Bella, 343
Acheson, Lila Bell, 228
Ackerman, Phyllis, 196-7
actresses, 33, Ch. 2 (34-9), 46, 47, 61, 64, 92, 103, 163, 170, 174, 192-3, 197, 200, 227-8, 299, 334, 336, 338
    changing name at marriage, 35-9
Adam, 50, 289, 294, 297, 304, 305, 313
Adams, Abigail, 6, 14
Adams, Evangeline Smith, 198
Adams, Franklin Pierce, 207, 209, 224
Adams, Hannah, 48
Adams, John, 6, 14, 53, 54
Adams, Mary Mathews Smith Barnes, 75
Addison, Joseph, 319
adultery, 300-1, 301, 306, 309, 315
Aeschylus, 295
Aethelflaed, 307
aggression, female, 25-6, 29, 42, 166, 184, 332-3
    see also sexual stereotypes, strength
Agrippa, Henry C., 314
Aiello, Barbara Ann Osterman, 273, 275
Alcott, Bronson, 321-2
Aldrich, Richard Stoddard, 227-8
Allen, Elizabeth Chase Taylor Akers, 75
Allyn, Nancy, 343
Altman, Diana, 335
American Civil Liberties Union, 271, 277, 278, 283
American Jurisprudence, 259
American Law Reports, 212, 240-1, 243, 244, 245, 257, 259
Ames, Mary Clemmer, 24-5, 32, 35
Anacreon, 52
Andelin, Helen B., 346-7
Anderson, James, see Garrett Anderson
Andreas-Salomé, Lou, 88
androgyne, 314, 317-18
    see also conjugal centaur, sexual identity
Anglo-Saxon period, women in, 300, 306, 307, 308, 311
Anka, Paul, 328
Anthony, Susan B., 58, 59, 65, 66, 97, 98, 99, 101, 104, 110, 135, 136, 346

Antigny, Blanche d', 23
Aquinas, Thomas, 295
Arisian, Khoren, 270
Aristotle, 51, 295
Armstrong-Hopkins, Dr Salini, 86n.
Ashton-Johnson, Carrie, 86n.
Astell, Mary, 40
Astor, Mrs, see Millionaire, Mrs Richman
Athena, 305, 313
Attorney General Opinions, 162, 178, 200, 210, 215, 243, 245, 248-50, 251, 252, 279, 280, 282, 286
Austen, Jane, 5, 41, 49
authors
    use of anonyms, 40-1; male pseudo-
        nyms, 42; pseudonyms, 41-3, 105
    changing publishing name, 43-6, 225-6, 288, 229-30
    keeping constant name, 45-6
autoeroticism, male, 315
automobile registration in own name, 243-5, 253, 266, 272, 273, 274-5, 276-7, 280, 282
Avery, Rachel Foster, 65, 83
Avicenna, 297

Bacon, Francis, 51
Baer, Karl Ernst von, 14, 297-8, 331
Balzac, Honoré de, 55
Bancroft-Robinson, Jane, 86n.
Barbauld, Anna Aikin, 48-9
baptism, 293-4, 300
Barrett, Elizabeth, 41, 43-4
    see also Browning, E.B.
Barrows, Isabel Hayes Chapin, 75
Barucci, La, 23
bastards, 300, 301, 319-20, 338
Bayh, Birch, 285, 286
beauty, 22, 23, 26, 29, 34-5, 38-9, 46, 52, 56, 61, 185, 348-9
Beecher, Catharine, 57
Behn, Aphra, 55
Belasco, David, 196
Bell, Currer, 42
    see also Brontë
Belleville-Brown, May, 86
Benson, Helen Eliza, 317
Bernays, Edward, 193, 196, 209, 222, 224, 232, 238

Bernhardt, Sarah, 38, 70
Bernstein, Oscar, 191, 192
Berryman, John, 350
Besant, Annie, 89-90
Bethune, Mr and Mrs, 91
Bieber-Bohn, Hanna, 86n.
Billington-Grieg, Teresa, 166
birth certificates, mother's name on, 234, 336
Bishop, Harriet, 148
Bishop, Joel P., 124, 129
Black, Ruby A., 196, 206, 207, 233
Black, Shirley Temple, 229
Black, Winifred, 163
Blackstone, *Commentaries on Laws of England*, 9, 315
Blackwell, Alice Stone, 101, 159-60, 189
Blackwell, Rev. Antoinette Brown, 76, 83, 97, 100, 154
see also, Brown, Antoinette
Blackwell, Dr Elizabeth, 14, 66-7, 338
Blackwell, Henry B. (husband of Lucy Stone), 96-8, 100-1, 102, 105-9, 110, 136-7, 145, 164, 167, 213
Blake, Lillie Devereux, 74
see also Umsted
Blanchard, Phyllis, 209
Blanche of Castile, 307
Blatch, Harriot Stanton, 200-1, 209
Blomer, Irène, 340
Bloomer, Amelia, 91, 104
Bly, Nellie, 41
Boardman, Dr Irene, 215
Boccaccio, 309
Bodin, Jean, 309, 311
Boehm, Felix, 325
Boissevain, Eugen, *see* Milholland, Millay
Bonheur, Rosa, 80, 86n.
Bonner, Sherwood, 42
Bontecou, Josephine, 175
Booth, Agnes, 35
see also Schoeffel
Booth-Clibborn,-Hellberg, -Tucker, 142
Boothe, Clare, *see* Brokaw
Bora, Katharina von, 312, 313, 327
Bordeau-Sisco, Dr Patience, 166
Borgarucci, P., 331
Boslin, Johanna and James, 335
Boulton, Agnes, 317
Bourke-White, Margaret, 233, 334
Bowdler, Harriet, 317-17
Boyce, Neith, 176
Boyd, Belle, 80-1

Bowen, Betsy, *see* Burr, Mrs Aaron
Bracegirdle, Anne, 35
Braddon, Mary E., 41, 42
Bradlaugh-Bonner, Hypatia, 86
Bradstreet, Martha, 119
Bradwell, Myra, 102, 110, 122, 123, 344
Branch, Julia, 102-4
Brandegee, Mary Layne Curran, 74, 75
brank, 53, 311
breastfeeding, 320, 321
Brereton, Mrs, *see* Kemble, Mrs,
Bres, Rose Falls, 189, 192, 202, 218
Bridewell, Alma, 11-12
Briffault, Robert, 305
Brittain, Vera, 209-10, 212, 231, 232-3
Brokaw, Clare, *see* Luce
Bromley, Dorothy Dunbar, 216-17, 266
Brontë, Charlotte, 42, 56, 69-70
Brook, Betty, *see* Phipps
Brooks, Martha N., 217-18
Broun, Heywood (husband of Ruth Hale), 180-1, 188, 189, 191, 192, 193, 195, 200, 209, 215, 220-2, 317
Broun, Mrs Heywood
  Broun's mother, 180
  Broun's second wife, 221
  Ruth Hale's cat, 180-1
Broun, Heywood Hale, 200
Brown, Rev. Antoinette, 14, 76, 93
  see also Blackwell, Antoinette Brown
Brown, Helen Gurley, 31
Brown, Rev. Olympia, 106, 135-6, 156, 170, 173, 213
Browne, Sir Thomas, 303
Browning, Elizabeth Barrett, 43-4, 71
Browning, Robert, *see* Browning, E. B.
Brownsen, Orestes, 81
Brunton, Ann, *see* Merry, Mrs
Bryant, Louise, 176, 182
Bucher, Gertrude A., 258, 259, 260, 265
Buck, Naomi, 215
Buck, Pearl, 227
Buckel, Dr Cloe, 82
Buffon, Georges L., 292
Bullock Workman, Fanny, 85-6, 88, 159
Bullowa, Emilie, 209
Burdett-Coutts, Baroness, 142
Burke, Col. Kathleen, 179
Burke, Yvonne Watson Brathwaite, 351
Burnet, Elizabeth, 40
Burnett, Frances Hodgson, 82
Burney, Fanny, 40
Burr, Mrs Aaron, 73
Burton, Isabel, 11, 18-19

Busse-Smith, Florence, 215
Butler, Fanny Kemble, 62, 68-9
   see also Kemble, Fanny
Butler, Pierce, *see* Butler, Fanny Kemble
Byron, 10

Cable Act, 219
Cadogan, Dr William, 321
Callanan, Carolyn Williams, 265-6
Canfield, Dr Corresta T., 147
Canfield, Dorothy, 165
   see also Fisher
Cannon, Jane Grey, 10, 19
Carlton, Doris, 247
Carlsson, Kathleen, 271
Carlyle, Jane, 47
Carpenter, Edward, 172-3
Carreño, Teresa, 84, 87
Carruthers, Roy, 191
Carter, Mrs Leslie, 90
Casson, Herbert N.,
   see Commander
castration, 293
Catt, Carrie Chapman, 146-7, 181-2
   see also Chapman, Carrie Lane
Cecilia of Oxford, 307
Census Bureau and women's names, 262
Center for Woman's Own Name, 271
Chambers, Rev. John, *see under* whiskey
Champassak, Barbara, *see* Hutton
change of name laws, 119, 124, 253,
   280-1
changing name by court order, 183, 179,
   264, 266, 269-70, 273-4, 275, 281, 335,
   336
changing name, Jews cf. women, 350
Chapman, Carrie Lane, 31, 83, 146
   see also Catt
Charlemagne, 300
Chase, Kate, 148
Chase, Salmon P., 66, 98, 116, 118, 189,
   264
chastity belts, 301, 311
Châtelet, Emilie du, 54, 55
Chenoweth, Alice, *see* Gardener, H.H.
Chesterfield, Lord, 52
Child, Lydia Maria, 57, 70
   see also Francis
childbirth, men participating in, 341-2
   see also couvade
childbirth, natural, 322, 342
childbirth, as rebirth, 323
child murder and women, 319-20

child rearing
   father sharing, 220, 342, 345
   as woman's work, 22, 66, 186, 238, 345
   see also housework, infant care
children, custody of, 139, 298-9
children, names of, 98, 101, 134, 137,
   148, 194, 195-6, 200-1, 209, 225, 249,
   287-8, 289, 301-2, 305, 328, 334-7, 339
   given combined surname of parents,
   134, 137, 144, 179, 194, 200, 234,
   335, 345
   see also mother's first name as surname,
      non-hereditary names, surname
      (mother's)
children, women having fewer, 341, 345
Christensen, Janice, 284
Christianity, 152, 154-5, 293-5, 298,
   311-12, 313-14, 325, 327, 331
Churchill, Lady Randolph, 10, 178-9
   see also Jerome
Cibber, Susannah, 35
Cicero, 299
circumcision, *see* initiation ceremonies
civil law and names, 254-5
Claflin, Tennessee, 134, 348
Claire, Nola, 336
Clark-Shea, Susannah, 86n.
Clarke, Dr Edward, 51-2
Clay, Mary Barr, 148
Clay-Clopton, Virginia, 86, 87
Claypoole, Elizabeth Griscom Ross
   Ashburn, *see* Ross, Betsy
Clement of Alexandria, 293, 294
Clement, Clara, 45, 91
Cleveland, Mrs Grover, 17
clitoris, 290, 326
Clothacar I, 306
clothing, 12-13, 15, 18, 29, 55, 185, 217,
   312, 348-9
   see also beauty, trousers
Clothwig, 300
Cobbe, Frances Power, 41
Cobden-Sanderson, Annie and James,
   144-5
Cobden Unwin, Mrs, 86n.
Cochran, Jacqueline, 265
Cohn, Felice, 189
Cohen, Bella, 196
Coke, Chief Justice, 112, 113
Colby, Bainbridge, 190
Collins, Mrs E. Burke, 45
Commander, Lydia Kingsmill, 140-1,
   173

common law and names, 112-13, 114-16, 120-1, 130-1, 205, 208, 240, 245-6, 248-51, 258-9, 277-84
see also law and married women's names
Comstock, Elizabeth Rous Wright, 75
conjugal centaur, 313-19
Conrad-Rice, Joy, 335
Constantia, *see* Murray, Judith Sargent
contraception, 13, 104, 220, 299, 322, 333, 337, 341, 347
Cook, George Cram, *see* Glaspell, Susan
Cooke, T., *see* profundity, lack of
Coolidge, President Calvin, 206, 207, 208
Coppin, Fanny Jackson, 74
copyright in own name, 211-12
Coram, Thomas, 320
Corea, Gena, 270
Corpening-Kornegay, Dr Cora, 179
Corpus Juris, 249, 256, 259
Corpus Juris Secundum, 256-7, 259, 260, 278
Coryière, E. Miriam, 81
Cotes, Mrs Everard, 165
courtesans, 22-4
couvade, 290, 293, 324, 327
Cowper, William, 48
Craddock, Charles, E., 42, 49, 55
Cramm, Barbara Von, *see* Champassak
Crandall, Prudence, *see* Philleo
Crawford, Dr Mary M., 178
Crocker, Hannah Mather, 13, 83
Cronkite, Walter, 349
Cronwright-Schreiner, Samuel C., *see* Schreiner, Olive
Crosby, Fanny, 44
Cross, John Walter, 71
Culpeper, Frances, 73
Curie, Marie, 174
Curzon, George, wife of, 12
Custer, Margo, 273, 280
Cutler, Hannah Conant Tracy, 74, 75
Cyprian, 293

Datheus, Archbishop, 319
Davis, Florence, *see* title mania
Davis, Paulina Kellogg Wright, 74, 84
Dean, Rebecca Pennell, 76
Debrachild, Pinny, 336
Decker, Sarah Chase Harris Platt, 75
DeForest, Nora Blatch, 166
Déjerine, Augusta Klumpke, 76

Delabair, Nicoli, 307
Deland, Margaret, 167
Dell, Floyd, 175, 183-4, 184-5
Dembitz, Judge Nanette, 265, 266
Demont-Breton, Virginie, 86n.
Densen-Gerber, Dr Judianne, 266, 334
Dexter, Elisabeth, 5
Dickerhoff, Elsie, 241
dicta, legal, 126, 218, 243, 278
see also Chapman v. Phoenix Bank (case index)
Dill, Senator Clarence C., *see* Jones, Rosalie G.
Dillon, Mary Elizabeth, 198
Dingwall, Eric, 301
divorce
frequency of, 73, 167, 220, 287, 306, 314, 339
name after, 118, 119, 127, 128, 129-30, 148, 240, 244, 280-1, 282, 284
Docetes, 294
Donaldson, Lois, 215
Dorris, Nancy, 214
double standard, sexual, 300, 301, 337-8
Douglas, Helen Gahagan, 230
Douglas, William O., *see under* Heffernan, Cathleen
Drew, Mrs John, 35
drinking, taboo for women, 301
driver's license in own name, *see* automobile registration
Drucker, Rebecca, 191, 192, 193
Duffie-Boylan, Grace, 86n.
Dunbar, Flanders, 234, 266, 334
Duncan, Isadora, 167, 197
Dunham-Wilson, Louisa, 86
Duplessis, Marie, 23
Dyke, Mary Ann, 64

Eames, Emma, 174
Earhart, Amelia, 215
Eastman, Rev. Annis, 91
Eastman, Crystal, 169, 182, 192, 217
Eastman, Max, 168-9, 231
Eastman, Rev. Samuel, 91, 169
Eddy, Mary Baker Glover Patterson, 44-5, 76-9, 84
Edgeworth, Maria, 40
Edgeworth, Richard, 321
education of women, 13-14, 16, 26, 166, 217
see also Ch. 6 (47-62) passim
Edward, Prince, *see under* courtesans

Egerton, George, *see* Goldring-Bright, Mary
Eisenhower, Mrs Dwight D., 32
Eliot, Clara, 199
Eliot, George, 42, 43, 48, 51, 52, 55-6, 71
Elizabeth, Queen, 158, 311
Ellentuck, Merna, 343
Ellis, Havelock, 143
Elsie Venner, 298
Elstob, Elizabeth, 4, 6
Elston, Dorothy Andrews, *see* Kabis
Emerson, John, 196, 209, 222-3, 224
Equal Rights Amendment, 195, 204, 210, 263, 275, 277, 282-3, 285, 347, 349
Erikson, Erik, 323, 324, 326, 327, 329
Ervin, Sam, 285, 286
Ervine, St John, 194
etiquette as law, 239
Euripides, 47, 53
Evans, Augusta Jane, 347
Evans, Mary Elizabeth, 179
Ex-Feminist, Confessions of, 212-13, 223-4
Eyster, Rebecca, 3

Fairbanks, Mrs Douglas, 183
Fairchild, Mary Cutler, 74-5
fame, a name and
  and marriage, Ch. 7 (63-71) passim, 91, 134, 135, 137, 138, 227-30, 339
  not for women, 18-21, Ch. 5 (40-6) passim, 49, 57-8, 69-71, 189, 216, 222-3, 226, 227
  sharing husband's, 17-18, 198, 225-6, 346
  and society ladies, 20-1, 26
  women achieving, 32-3, 35-6, 39, 40, 162, 178-9, 339
  see also identity (loss of professional), male appropriation of credit, tombstones
Farley, Harriet, 64
Farnham, Eliza, 147-8, 260
father, meaning of
  contemporary, 383
  original, 292
feme covert, 308
feminine suffixes, 349
Fenichel, Otto, 325-6
Fenwick Miller, Florence, 131, 132, 137
Ferguson, Elsie, 192, 209
Fern, Fanny, 41, 43, 48

Fichte, Johann G., 9, 12
Fienus, Thomas, 295
Filsinger, Sara Teasdale, 228
Finch, Anne, Countess of Winchilsea, 41
Finch School of Design, 183
Finney, Ruth, 215
first lady, 24-5
first name, husband's, wife's use of, *see under* surname
first names, women's, 105, 152, 156
Fish, Stuyvesant, 90
Fisher, Dorothy Canfield, 228
Fiske, Minnie Maddern, 38
Fitzgerald, F. Scott, 185
Fitz-Gibbon, Bernice, 209
Fitzhenry, Mrs, *see* Gregory, Mrs
Flanner, Janet, 192, 193
Fleeson, Doris, 215
Fleischman, Doris E., 180, 193, 196, 200, 208, 222, 224, 231, 233, 234, 237, 238, 262, 264
Fleming, Anne Taylor, 348
Fonda, Jane, 336
Forbush, Wendy, 269, 272, 276-7, 277 282
Forerunner, The, 171
Forfreedom, Ann, 336
Foster, Abigail Kelley, 74
Foster, Hannah Webster, 41
Fourteenth Amendment, 110, 116, 122, 246, 248, 263, 276-7, 278, 282
Fowler, Orson, 60
Fowler-Lunn, Katharine, 215
Francis, Lydia Maria, 48
  see also Child, L. M.
Francoeur, Robert T., 325
Frankenstein, 48, 298
fraud, male fear of, 277, 286-7
Frederick the Great, 319
free love, 13, 14, 100, 103, 104, 122, 134, 137, 139-40, 154, 167, 168-9, 172-3, 175-6, 183, 201, 220, 225, 338
  see also hotel registration
Freeman, Alice, *see* Palmer, A. F.
Freeman, Mary Wilkins, 165
Freeman, Ruth Benson, 214
French-Sheldon, M., 86n., 88
Freud, Sigmund
  see Andreas-Salomé, penis (male pride in)
  and Luther, 312
Friedan, Betty, 267
Frost, Judith Colcord, 341
Fuller, Margaret, 14, 51

Fuller, Minnie Oliver Rutherford, 75, 90
Furman, Bess, 215

Gaea, 292
Gage, Matilda Joslyn, 154-5
Gale, Zona, 192, 215
Galen, 297
Galton, Francis, 298
Gardener, Helen Hamilton, 59, 137-8, 173, 334
Gardner, Mrs Jack, 27, 29, 30, 31
Garrett Anderson, Dr Elizabeth, 19, 82, 85, 88
Garrison, Wendell P., 156
Garrison, William Lloyd, 317
Gaskell, Elizabeth, 69
Gates, Eleanor, 163
Gawain, 300
Gellhorn, Martha, 228
Gerritsen, Cornelis V., *see* Jacobs, Dr Aletta
Gibson-Richard, Frances, 86n.
Gilman, Charlotte Perkins, 45, 161, 164-5, 171-2, 183, 192, 209, 334, 341 *see also* Stetson
Giroud, Francoise, 338
Glaspell, Susan, 176, 192, 197
Glass, Constance, 198
Godey's Lady's Book, 5, 41
Godwin, William, *see* Wollstonecraft
Goff, Regina, 266
Golden, Nora, 200
Goldman, Emma, 62, 167, 173
Goldring-Bright, Mary, 91
Goldsmith, Lucy A., 198
Goodrich, Sara Knox, 83
Gorki, Maxim, 226
Gouges, Olympe des, 14
Graaf, Reinier de, 297, 331
Graham, Ennis, 42
Graham, Patricia, 344
Grant, Barbara, *see* Troubetzkoy
Grant, Jane, 181, 187, 188, 192, 193, 195, 199, 209, 233, 234-5, 256, 262-3, 265
Graubert, Ella, 214, 246
Greenwich Village, 168-70, 176-6, 268
Gregory, Mrs, 35
Greeley, Horace, 89-90, 96
Greeley, Mary Cheney, 89-90
Green, Hetty, 56
Greenacre, Dr Phyllis, 183
Greene, Anna Katharine, 45

Greene, Belle da Costa, 196
Greenwold, Marcia, 269-70
Greenwood, Grace, 20, 41, 43
Grey, Lady Jane, 311
Griffin, Frances A., 61
Griffin, Gale, 274
Grimké, Angelina, 14, 57, 317
Grimké, Sarah, 14, 57
Griselda, 309-10
Guiberson, Betty, *see* Brook
Gurney Sawyer, Minnie, 145
Gwyn, Nell, 35

Hackett, Alice, 215
Hackett, Francis, 178, 192, 193
Hahn-Hahn, Countess Ida von, 85, 132
Haldeman-Julius, Emmanuel, 179, 231
Haldeman-Julius, Marcet, 179
Hale, Ruth, 180-1, 182, Ch. 15 (188-218) passim, 220-2, 317
Hale, Sarah Josepha, 41, 60
Hall, Helen, 265
Hambrick-Stowes, 269
Hamilton, Cicely, 167
Hamm, Margherita, 45
Hammond, William, 59
Hancock, Dorothy, 53, 73
handwriting, women's, 49
Hanson, Avarita L., 345
Hanson, Marjorie, 246, 247, 265
Harbert, Elizabeth Boynton, 83
Hardenbroeck, Margaret, 113-14
Harlow, Harry, 322
Harman, Lillian, 138-9
Harman, Moses, 138-9
Harney, Kathleen, 269, 274, 281
Harper, Ida Husted, 49
Harpman, Julie, 223
Harriman, Margaret Case, 233
Harrison, Jane Ellen, 60, 349
Harte Bret, 56
Hartland, E. S., 291
Hartsoeker, Nicolaus, 296
Hartwick-Thorpe, Rose, 86n.
Harvey, William, 292, 297
Hawes, Harriet Boyd, 76
Hayden, Sophia G., 30
Hayes, Ellen, 157
Hayes, Mrs Rutherford B., 24-5
Hays, Elinor Rice, 96

Hazlitt, William, 47, 52
head, women's alleged lack of, Ch. 6
  (47-62), 312-13, 332, 342
Healey, Regina, 275
Heath-Proctor, Dr Alice, 85
Heffernan, Cathleen, 79
Helmholtz-Phelan, Anna, 166
Helmholz, R. H., 311
Hemingway, Ernest, *see under* Gellhorn
Henry B. Blackwell League, 213
Henry, Josephine K., 155-6
Hephaestus, 290
Hermann, Nancy, 274
hermaphrodite, women cf., 26, 82, 349
Hewett, Kathleen, 274
Hierta-Retzius, Anna, 86n.
Higginson, Thomas W., 71, 98-9, 157
Hill, Elsie, 195, 200, 217, 229, 231, 233,
  334
Hinkle, Beatrice, 220, 224
Hippocrates, 297
Hirsch [Reben] Susan, 281, 284
Hiscock, Helen, 65
Hobbes, John Oliver, 42
Hobbs, Lucy, 60, 76
  see also Taylor, L. H.
Hoffman, Caspar Friedrich, 297
Hogarth, William, 320
Hoke, Calm Morrison, 214, 233, 236
holding office or job in own name, 162,
  186-7, 200, 201-4, 211, 217-18, 229,
  230, 236-7, 239-40, 241, 246, 247,
  249-50, 252, 253, 258, 259, 261
Holdsworth, Jane, 273
Holm, Saxe, 42
Holmes, Dr Oliver Wendell, 298
Holmes, Oliver Wendell, 131
Holt, Hamilton, 195-6
Home, Henry, Lord Kames, 2
Hone, Philip, 63
Hooker, John, 344
Hopkins, Ann, 53-4
Hopkins, Priscilla, *see* Brereton
Horney, Karen, 325
Horton, Dr Mildred McAfee, 229
hostessing, 24-6
hotel registration in own name, 103,
  137, 170, 182, 191, 196, 197-8, 215,
  217, 233, 338

housework, 24, 60, 66, 184, 212-13, 220,
  223-4, 227, 238, 307, 312, 340-1, 345
  see also child rearing
Howard, Caroline, 55
Howard [Hauptly] Elizabeth, 269,
  273, 281, 285
Howard-Maxwell, Claudia, 86n.
Howe, Marie Jenney, 166
Howells, William Dean, 2, 347
Hoyt, Margaret E., 266
Hoxie, Richard, *see* Ream, Vinnie
Hudnut, Ruth Allison, 210-11, 214
Hughes, Charles Evans, 190-1
Hughes, Marija A., 275
Hunt, Mrs, *see* Mossop
Hurd-Mead, Dr Kate, 88, 130
Hurst, Fannie, 178, 192, 197, 204-5, 209,
  211, 229, 233
husband
  as head of wife, 7-8, Ch. 6 (47-62)
    passim, 313-14, 318-19
  as sovereign of wife, 309-11
husband's jealousy of famous wife,
  67-71, 222-3, 227
husband's name, wife's use of, *see*
  surname
Huston, Olive, 215
Hutchinson, Abigail, 64
Hutton, Aimee Kennedy Semple
  McPherson, 75
Hutton, Barbara, *see* Mdivani
Huxley, Aldous, 304, 325
Hyde, Virginia Douglas, 211
hyphenated surname, *see* surname,
  double
hysteria, male, *see* male logic

Ickes, Anna Wilmarth Thompson, 75
identity, loss of professional, 35-9,
  43-5, 73-9, 80-92, 156-7, 160, 165,
  172, 228-30, 351
  see also sexual identity
illegitimate children, *see* bastards
Imlay, Gilbert, *see* Wollstonecraft
impregnation, supernatural, 291-2,
  294, 295, 300, 303
  see also Christianity
Inchbald, Elizabeth, 47
incomplete beings, men, as 313-14
infant care, 320-1
infanticide, father's right, 299, 303
infant mortality rate, 320

inferior sex
  men as, 291-3, 313-14, 317
  women as, 303-5, 317, 320-1, 329-30,
    331, 349-50
Ingen, George Van, 242
initiation ceremonies, 290-1, 293
inner space, 323, 324, 329
Innocent III, 320
Internal Revenue Service and women's
  names, 274
intuition, female, 303
Isaacs-Savage, Bessie J., 86n.

Jackson, Laura (Riding), 228
Jackson, Theresa, 195
Jackson-Houk, Mrs, 85
Jacobi, Dr Mary Putnam, 85, 87, 91, 183
Jacobs, Dr Aletta, 137
James, E. O., 292
James, Henry, 2, 22, 350
Jarvis, Dr Marjorie M., 202, 203, 204
Jay, Phillis, 322
Jeritza, Maria, 212, 245
Jerome, Jennie, 10, 24
  see also Churchill, Lady Randolph
Jewett, Eleanor, 195
Johnson, Mariana, 94
Johnson, Samuel, 52, 283
Joiner, Carol, 270
Joliot-Curie, Marie and Frédéric, 215
Jones, Rosalie G., 214, 231
Jonson, Ben, 53
Joy, Sally, 63
Jumel Madam, see Burr, Mrs Aaron
June, Jennie, 41

Kabis, Dorothy Andrews Elston, 261
Kael, Pauline, 266-7
Kahler-Evans, Blanche, 86n.
Kanowitz, Leo, 260, 267, 275, 278
Karstensen, Berthe-Louise, 215
Kate [*Taming of the Shrew*], 370
Kate Field's Washington, 160, 164
Kay, Herma Hill, 270
Kayaloff, Anna, 245-6, 247, 265
Kean, Mrs Charles, 36, 64
Keller, Helen, 75
Kelley, Florence, 87-8, 148
Kellogg, Frank, 206, 208
Kemble, Adelaide, 63
Kemble, Fanny, 63
  see also Butler
Kemble, Mrs, 35

Kemp, Harry, see Pyne, Mary
Kendig, Isabella, 206
Keys, Martha, 345
Kayberry, Phyllis, 291
King Arthur, 300
Kirchwey, Freda, 192, 209
Klumpke, Anna, 80
Klumpke's paralysis, see Déjerine
Knigge, Baron von, 47
Knowles, Gov. Warren P., 276, 282, 286
Koues, Helen, 196
Kramer, Dale, 188, 215
Kraus-Boelté, Marie, 85
Kristensen-Randers, Nanna, 86n.
Kronold, Selma, 87
Krupansky, Blanche, 258-9, 265
Krylenko, Eliena, 231

Lacy, Olive, 202, 206
Lachmann, Thérèse, 23
Ladd-Franklin, Christine, 86n.
Laddy, Paula, 189
La Follette, Fola, 170, 176, 177, 180,
  181, 182, 197, 209, 233, 287, 336-7
Laise, Caroline, 266
Lake, Leonora Barry, 87
Laks, Nancy Eliot, 335
Lamaze, Fernand, 322
Lamb, Charles, 40, 47, 49
Land, Agnes, see Perry
Landon, Letitia Elizabeth, 41, 47
Lane, Louisa, see Hunt, Mrs
Lane, Lucia, 335
Lao-Tze, 292, 313
Laurie, Annie, 41, 163
  see also Black, W.
law and married women's names, 94,
  97-8, 102, 106-9, Ch. 11 (111-131),
  162, 164, 178-9, 186-7, Ch. 15 (188-
  218) passim, 238, Ch. 17 (239-61),
  264-5, 271-88
  England, 9, 112-13, 115, 131, 186-7,
    250-1, 278
  United States
    Alabama, 253-4, 269, 272, 276-7,
      282, 286
    Arizona, 335
    Arkansas, 279
    California, 127-8, 276, 279, 282, 285
    Colorado, 162
    Connecticut, 119, 217, 253, 273, 280,
      286
    Delaware, 279

Florida, 253-4, 274, 280, 281, 287
Georgia, 281
Hawaii, 121, 260-1, 280, 283
Idaho, 253
Illinois, 120, 247-8, 251-2, 253, 275, 276, 279
Indiana, 269, 281, 285
Iowa, 253, 280
Kansas, 115, 120, 139, 280
Kentucky, 119, 124, 253, 280, 282
Louisiana, 202, 254-6, 257
Maine, 252, 274, 279, 281, 284, 286, 287
Maryland, 200, 252, 272-3, 277-80
Massachusetts, 111, 116-17, 118, 120, 124, 127, 212, 217-18, 243-5, 253, 276, 279
Michigan, 200, 249, 253
Minnesota, 210, 241, 253-4, 269
Missouri, 274, 281
Montana, 279
Nebraska, 126-7, 253-4
Nevada, 120, 252
New Jersey, 126, 274, 281, 287-8
New York, 111, 113-14, 114-15, 119, 124-6, 127, 128, 129-30, 174, 199, 215, 242-3, 245-6, 274, 280, 281
North Carolina, 281
Ohio, 242, 257-9, 278
Oregon, 178, 211, 250, 252
Pennsylvania, 214, 246, 279
South Carolina, 115, 119, 279
South Dakota, 252
Tennessee, 380
Texas, 120, 127, 128, 129, 242, 279
Vermont, 115, 120, 124, 125, 253, 279
Virginia, 273, 274, 275, 279, 281, 288
Washington, 215, 249, 269, 275, 276
Wisconsin, 128, 200, 241, 242, 269, 273-4, 275, 276, 281, 282, 287
see also automobile registration, Blackstone, change of name laws, changing name by court order, civil law and names, common law and names, holding office in own name, legal name (redefined), passports, prenuptial contracts, record keeping, watchdog laws
see also case index
Lawes Resolutions of Womens Rights, 8, 130, 308
Lawrence, Gertrude, *see under* Aldrich, R. S.

Lawrence, Harding, 346, 351
Lazarre, Jane, 341
learned women
female ridicule of, 48-9
male fear of, 49-50, 311
Lease, Mary Elizabeth, 158
Leblanc, Léonide, 23
Leboyer, Frederick, 322, 329
Lee, Ann, 139-40
Leeuwenhoek, Antony van, 296
legal guardian of children, father as, 298-9
legal name of married woman redefined, 245-8, 259-60
legs, 13, 57, 58, 312, 332-3
see also trousers
Leonardo da Vinci, 297
Leslie, Eliza, 5
Leslie, Frank, 27, 28-32
Leussen, Francia, 269, 275
Lévi-Strauss, Claude, 324
Lewald-Stohr, Fanny, 85
Lewis, Grace Hegger, 226
Lewis, Ida, 135
Lewis, Sinclair, 180, 219, 221, 225-6, 227
Libbey, Laura Jean, 198, 228
Library of Congress catalog, 88
Lillie, Judge Mildred, 266
Lincoln, Almira Hart, *see* Phelps, A. H. L.
Lind, Jenny, 37, 70, 88, 161
Linton, Eliza Lynn, 55, 56
Lippmann, Walter, 184
Littleton-Taylors, 269
Livingstone, Beulah, 192, 193, 209
Lockwood, Belva Ann Bennett McNall, 74, 75, 90, 351
Logan, Celia, 91
Logan, Olive, 142
London, Joan, 209
Long, Harry, 152-3
Longshore-Potts, Dr Anna, 85
Loos, Anita, 192, 209, 266
Lord Chamberlain, Charles II's, *see* pimp, royal
Loring, Ellis G., 98
Lothrop, Alice Higgins, 75
love and women, *see* self-abnegation, sexual stereotypes, sexual identity
Lowry, Dr Edith B., 171
Lozier, Dr Clemence, 82
Luce, Clare Boothe Brokaw, 229-30
Lucy Stone League, 187, Ch. 15 (188-218), 219, 220, 222, 224, 232, 238, 239, 262-5, 268, 271

Lucy Stoner, phrase gets into dictionary, 193
Lucy Stoners recant, 212-13, 222, 224, 228, 231, 232
Luther, Martin, 54, 292, 312, 313, 326-7
Lyell, Sir Charles, wife of, 12
Lyle, Robey, 265
Lynahan, Gertrude, 215

McAllister, Ward, 20
Macarthur, Mary, 171, 186-7
McCarl, Comptroller General, 202-4, 208, 211, 212, 236, 239-40, 245, 247, 249, 251, 285
McCarthy, Dr Charlotte, 233, 235
McCarthy, Mary, 217, 228, 351
McCord, Louisa, 20
McCormack, Ellen, 347
McCulloch, Catharine Waugh, 145
MacDougall, Priscilla, 282
McLean, Betty, *see* Guiberson
McMein, Neysa, 192, 198
Macpherson, Aimee Semple, *see* Hutton, A. K. S. M.
Macy, Anne Sullivan, 75
Madonna and Child, *see* Spock, Dr Benjamin
Mailer, Norman, *see* penis, as pen
Maimonides, 52
make up, 56, 185
male appropriating credit for women's work, 189, 220-2, 316-17
male compassion, 319-20, 321-2
male as God, 228, 293-5, 298, 303-4, 325
male logic, 284-8
male milk, 290, 294
male mothers, 289-98, 300, 313-14
  see also couvade, sole progenitor (male)
Malet, Lucas, 42, 56
Mannes, Marya, 270
Manning, Anne, 41
March, Mehitabel, 105
Maréchal, Sylvain, 54
Marines and women's names, 262-3
Markham, Violet, 186-7
Marlowe, Julia, 37, 70, 174
marriage
  church control of, 300, 311-12
  as homosexuality, 315
  new forms of, 338-9, 340
  trial, 306, 311, 338
  woman's career ended by, 63-7
  woman's only vocation, 311-13

Marryat, Florence, 44
Martin, Daisy, *see* title mania
Martineau, Harriet, 12, 49
Marvin, Michelle, 338
Marx, Eleanor, 175
Mary, 294, 312
Masaryk, Charlotte and Thomas Garrigue, 144
Masters, Sybilla, 316
Mastroianni, Marcello, 330
maternal impression, 296-7, 298
maternal instinct
  man's, 319-30
  primate's, 322-3
  woman's alleged, 184, 223-4, 225, 319-22, 322-3, 341
Mathews, Charles James, *see* Vestris
Matthews, Burnita Shelton, 203, 206, 207, 210-11, 217, 240
Matthews, Kim, 284
Maugham, Somerset, 219-20
Maupertuis, P. L. M. De, 297
May, Rev. Samuel J., 3, 57, 132-3
Mdivani, Barbara, *see* Reventlow
Mead, Margaret, 199, 231, 233
Mellon, Harriet, 64
Memmi, Albert, 350
Mendel, Gregor, 298
Mendelssohn, Fanny, 49
Mendham, Alice, 233
Menken, Adah Isaacs, 65, 89, 91
menstruation, 51-2, 59, 290, 295-6
mental creation
  and babies, 51-2, 303, 313, 327-8, 348
  and beauty, 52, 56
  as a male capacity, 15, 50-3, 303, 327-8
  as masculinizing women, 54-6, 348
  and semen, 50-1, 303
  women also capable of, 13-14, 59-61, 332
Merriam, Eve, 267
Merry, Mrs, *see* Wignell
Meyer, Arthur E., 292
Middleton, George, 170, 176, 185-6
Milholland-Boissevain, Inez, 179
Milinaire, Caterine, 341
Mill, John Stuart, 10, 67, 96, 117, 144
Millay, Edna St Vincent, 197-8, 233, 235
Miller, Alice Chapman, 179
Miller, Dorothy, 216
millionaires, 22
Millionaire, Mrs Richman, 22-6
Mills, Cotton Mather, 42

Milton, John, 303, 311
Mitchell, Mattie, *see* title mania
Montagu, Lady Mary Wortley, 6, 19, 54
Montez, Lola, 31
Montgomery, Dr Edmund, *see* Ney, Elisabeth
Moore, George, 51
Moran, Mary Nimmo, 81
Morgan, Geraldine, 163
Morgan, Lady, *see* Owenson
Morgan, Marabel, 347, 348
Morgan, Mary, 345-6
More, Hannah, 48
Morisot, Berthe, 80
Morrison-Fuller, Bernice, 145
Mossop, Mrs, *see* Drew, Mrs John
mother goddesses, 292-3, 294-5, 300, 302, 304-5, 306, 329
mother's first name as surname, 336
mothers, men as, *see* male mothers
mothers, women as incompetent, 319-21
Mott, Lucretia, 3, 94
Moulton, Dr Barbara, 266
Mountfort, Mrs, *see* Verbruggen
Mount Mary Vaux, *see* Walcott
mourning, significance of women's, 314-15
movies, men in, 310, 330, 349
Mowatt, Anna Cora, 44, 64
Mugglebee, Ruth, 215
Mulock, Dinah, 41, 42
multiple names of married women, 73-9, 80-8, 155, 228-30, 351
Murphy, Delia, 76, 183
Murray, Judith Sargent, 13, 40
Mussolini, Benito, 225
Myers, Margaret Good, 195, 201, 235

Name-Change, Massachusetts, 271
Name Choice Center, San Francisco, 271
nameless children, *see* bastards
names, wife taking husband's, *see under* surname
Napoleon, Prince, *see under* courtesans
Nation, Carry Moore Gloyd, 75, 166
National Organization for Women (NOW), 263, 268, 334
National Woman's Party, 195, 203, 204, 206, 207, 210, 211-12, 214, 218, 240
Needham, John T., 297
Nesbit, Edith, 45
Neuenfelt, Judge Lila, 249
Newman, Edwin, 317
Ney, Elisabet, 55, 133-4

Neyman, Olga, 65
Nicholls, Rev. Arthur, *see under* Brontë
Nichols, Mary S. Gove, 74
Nietzsche, Friedrich, W., 52
non-hereditary names, 137, 138, 171-2, 334-7
Normanton, Helena, 200, 205, 206, 207, 209, 210-11, 233
Notes and Queries, 86, 151-2
nuns, 306, 308, 311-12
Nuttall, Zelia, 148

Oakes Smith, Elizabeth, 91, 137
Oakley, Ann, 341
Oakley, Grace C., 192, 209
Oberlin College, 14, 57, 94
obstetricians, 328
O'Keefe, Georgia, 198
Olympia Brown League, 271
-one (suffix), 349
One, Varda, 336
O'Neill, Eugene, 317
O'Neill, Nena and George, 270
Onians, Richard, 50
Open Door International, 267
Opie, Amelia, 13
Origen, 293
O'Sullivan, Mary Kenney, 76
Ovid, 301
ovum, discovery of, 14, 297-8, 331-2
Owen, Robert Dale, 96
Owen, Ruth Bryan, 229
Owens-Adair, Dr Bethenia, 86n.
Owenson, Sydney, 43, 54

Page, Ruth, 209
Palmer, Alice Freeman, 65, 83
Palmer, Mrs Potter, 27-8, 29, 30-1, 32, 33
Pamela [Richardson's], 346
Pankhurst, Sylvia, 185
Papias, 293
Parker, Amos, *see* Smith, Julia
Parker, Deonne, 269
Parker, Dorothy, 181
Parsons, Elsie Clews, 167, 182, 184
Parsons, May, 23
passports in own name, 188, 190-1, 204-8, 210-11, 224, 234, 245, 256, 262, 266, 274, 282
paternal impression, 291-2, 297
Paul, Alice, 204, 209

Paul, St, 8, 50, 53, 57, 94, 294, 313, 314
Peabody, Josephine Preston, 165
Peale, Anna, 80
Pearl, Cora, 23
Pechey-Phipson, Dr Edith, 86n.
Peck, Ellen, 341
pediatrics, rise of, 321
Pegler, Westbrook, *see under* Harpman, Julie
penis
    male pride in, 59, 325-6
    as pen, 50
    see also womb envy
Percival, Mrs, *see* Mountfort
Perkins, Frances, 176, 180, 182, 187, 188, 189, 204, 218, 229, 231, 233, 235, 236, 261
Perkins-Ripley, Lucy, 179
Perry, Agnes, *see* Booth A.
Pethick-Lawrence, Emmeline, 163-4
Pethick-Lawrence, Frederick, 164, 231
Petruchio [*Taming of the Shrew*], *see* Kate
Peyrol-Bonheur, Juliette, 86n.
Phelps, Almira Hart Lincoln, 43, 70
Phelps, Elizabeth Stuart, 45
Philleo, Prudence Crandall, 76
Phillips, Wendell, 4, 158
Phipps, Betty, *see* Reeves
phrenology, 59-60
physicians, women as, 62, 71, 307, 308
Pickering, Ruth, 193, 209, 210, 224
Pickford, Mary, *see* Fairbanks, Mrs Douglas
Pilagá of South America, 295, 296
Pillsbury, Parker, 145
pimp, royal, 34
Pius, Pope, 225
Plato, 51, 317-18
Poe, Edgar Allan, 74, 137
Pollitzer, Anita, 218, 233
Poseidon, 305
Post, Emily, 239
Post, Marjorie Merriweather, 351
Potter, Grace, 176, 193
Powell, Mrs, *see* Renaud
pregnancy
    artificial, 325
    ridicule of, 321
    symptoms in men, 324-5, 326, 330
prenuptial contract to keep name, 146, 259, 269
Press, Aida K., 271

Preston, Margaret Junkin, 41
Pride, Ann, 336
Priest, Ivy Baker, 264, 266
Priestley, Joseph, 321
primitive mind and names, 10-11, 91, 301-2
Pritchard, Hannah, 35
Proctor, Mary, 345
professions, women entering, 2, 14, 25, 32-3, 34-5, 39, 42, 46, 61, 71, 76, 162
profundity, lack of, 52
Prometheus, 290
prostitution, 34-5, 36, 38-9, 46, 72
    see also courtesans
Pruette, Lorine, 224, 233, 236
pseudonyms, *see* authors
public speaking, women barred from, 57-8, 61
Pussycat League, 346, 347, 349
Putnam, George, *see* Smith, Emily
Putnam, George Palmer, *see* Earhart
Pyne, Mary, 176

Quaker marriage certificate, 131
Quimby, Harriet, 174

Raacke, Dr I. Dorothea, 266
Radcliffe College, 110, 271, 344, 345
Radegund, 306
Rago, Antonia E., 247-8, 251, 260, 265, 278
Rand, Ayn, 215
Rand, Ellen Emmet, 75
Rand, Gertrude, 179
Randolph, Martha Jefferson, 83
Rauh, Ida, 168-9, 192
Rawalt, Marguerite, 265
Read, Grantly Dick, 322
Ream, Vinnie, 64-5, 81
record keeping and names, 121, 127, 286
Redgrave, Vanessa, 338
Reed, John, 176
Reed, Myrtle, 165
Reese-Pugh, Fannie, 86
Reeves, Betty, *see* McLean
Reid, Charlotte, 332
Reid, Christian, 42
Reid, Thomas, 32
Reid-Slusser, Fannie, 86n.
Renaissance
    men's, 310-11
    women's, 332-4
Renaud, Mrs, 35

Reventlow, Barbara, *see* Grant
Revolution, The, 58, 145, 155
Richards, Louisa Green, 318
Rimmer, Robert H., 339
Rinehart, Mary Roberts, 201
Rivé-King, Julie, 84
Rivers, Pearl, 41, 43
Robb, Isabel Hampton, 75
Roberts, Dr Dorothea Klumpke, 163
Robinson, Henry Crabb, 48
Robinson, Mary, 96
Roche, Arthur S., 195
Rochester, Lord [John Wilmot], 314
Rodman, Henrietta, 175-6
Roerher, Millie, 206
Rohde, Ruth Bryan Owen, *see* Owen
Roland, 300
Root, Esther Sayles, 207-8
see also Adams, Mrs F. P.
Rose Jr, Cornelia B., 233, 236-7, 238
Ross, Betsy, 6, 73, 351
Ross, Harold (husband of Jane Grant),
181, 188, 199, 231
Ross, Mrs Harold (Nos. 1 and 2), 231
Ross, Ishbel, 63
Ross, Susan C., 271
Rothenberg, Rose, 209
Rousseau, 19, 321
Roys-Gavitt, Dr E. M., 86n.
Rubirosa, Barbara, *see* Cramm
Ruskin, John, 47
Russell Sage Foundation, *see* Sage,
Margaret S.

Sage, Margaret Slocum, 90
St Denis, Ruth, 178
Samuel, Dr E. Jeffrey, 209
Sand, George, 14, 55
Sander, Frank, 284
Sanger, Margaret, 197
Sarachild, Kathie, 336
Sarton, George, 184
Sarton, May 184
Saunders, Hortense, 215
Sawyer, Helen, 209
Schaller, George, 322
Scharnagel, Dr Isabel, 266
Scheff, Fritzi, 163
Schiff, Dorothy, 230
Schlafly, Phyllis, 347-8
Schoeffel, Mrs, *see* Booth, Agnes
Schopenhauer, Arthur, 55
Schouler, James, 124, 129, 240
Schreiner, Olive, 142-3

Schumann, Clara, 68, 70, 84
see also Wieck
Schumann, Robert, 51, 68, 70, 71
Schumann-Heink, Ernestine Roessler,
84, 88
Scott, Kathryn P., 273
Scott, Sir Walter, 42
Seabury, Florence Guy, 213
Sebastian, Ann and Arnelle, 336
Sedgwick, Anne Douglas, 165
self-abnegation, 63-7, 68, 69, 70, 71,
183-4, 212-13, 216, Ch. 16 (219-277)
passim, 346-51
self-identity and names, 350-1
Seligson, Marcia, 270
servants, women as, 304-5, 306, 311, 317,
346-7, 348-50
see also womb, woman as
Sewall, May Wright Thompson, 74, 83
Sewell, Samuel E., 98, 111
sex and reproduction, 291-2, 295-8, 304-5
sexual intercourse, male attitude towards,
see autoeroticism
sexual identity, 10-15, 16-18, 20, 26, 29,
42, 51-2, 54-6, 61-2, 66-7, 81-2, 184,
217, 266, 348-9, 351
sexual stereotypes, 15, 16-17, 185, 186,
318-19, 347-8
Shakespeare, William
Taming of the Shrew, 310
"What's in a name?" 149
Shaw, G. B.
Mrs Warren's Profession, 22, 22-3, 72,
167, 175
Sheley, Kathy, 274
Shelley, Mary, 48, 298
Shelley, Percy B., 14
Sheridan, Emma, 64
Sheriff, Dr Hilla, 266
Sherwood, Dr Mary, 55
shitwork, *see* housework
Siefert-Hoyt, Anne, 269
Siddons, Sarah, husband of, 70-1
Sigourney, Lydia Huntley, 56, 64, 69,
70, 91
silence and women, 53-4, 61
Silverman, Anna and Arnold, 341
Simone, Karla, 274
slavery and loss of name, 4, 95, 98, 135-6,
139, 140, 158, 160, 172, 194
Slesinger, Tess, 225
Slick, Grace, 336
Smith, Elsdon, 232, 350-1
Smith, Emily, 65

Smith, Evelyn, 209
Smith, Florence Kate, 23
Smith, Julia, 148-9
Smith, Margaret Bayard, 5
Smith, Rosa, 3
Smith-Eaton, Dr Cora, 86n.
society ladies, Ch. 3 (19-33)
  and courtesans, 22-4
  excesses, 21
  as hostesses, 24-6
Sojourner, Susan and Henry, 336
Solano, Solita, 193
sole progenitor
  female as, 291-2, 299, 302
  god as (same as male)
  male as, 50, 288, 289-90, 293-8, 298-305, 329, 331
Somerville, Mary, 54
sons, desire for, 302-3, 315, 323
Sowder, Leta, 266
spermatozoa, 296, 303, 304
  head as source of, 50-1
Spock, Dr Benjamin, 321, 322, 323,324, 342, 345
sports, women and, 312, 332-3
Spurzheim, Johann, 60
stage names, 36, 39
Stannard, Una, 267, 271, 336, 341
Stanton, Elizabeth Cady, 3-4, 15, 26, 83, 86, 89-90, 94-5, 98, 99, 126, 145, 149, 153, 155, 157, 158, 159, 166, 329
Stanton-Blatch, Harriot, 86
  see also Blatch
Star is Born, A, 227
Stearns, Rev. Jonathan F., 16, 57-8
Steffens, Lincoln, 175, 198
Steinem, Gloria, 343
Stetson, Charlotte Perkins, 45, 160-1
  see also Gilman
Stevens, Doris, 195, 209, 233, 263
Stokes, Rose Pastor, 214
Stone, Lucy, 92, Ch. 10 (93-110), 111, 115-16, 117-18, 122-3, 124, 131, 132, 135, 138, 141-2, 146, 153-4, 155-6, 160, 168, 172, 267, 346
Stopes, Dr Marie, 170-1, 179, 235-6, 334
Stowe, Harriet Beecher, 82, 83, 151
Stowe-Gullen, Dr Augusta, 86n.
Strange, Michael, 192-3
Stratton-Porter, Gene, 85
strength, women's, 312-13, 318-19, 332-3
Strickland, Martha, 136
Struggle, Dair, 336

Stuart, Mary E., 269, 272-3, 277-9
subincision, *see* initiation ceremonies
Summerskill, Dr Edith, 209, 231, 233, 234, 236, 334
surname
  double (and hyphenated), 37, 38, 84-8, 132, 135, 136, 142-4, 145, 146, 179, 214, 215, 267, 269
  husband changing to wife's, 142-3
  husband and wife combining, 142, 143, 144, 145, 215, 269
  husband's, wife's use of
    origin of custom, 1-2, 112-14, 151-2, 260-1, 306, 315
    custom in England, 112-13, 119, 131, 137, 144, 170-1, 205, 283
    France, 164, 215, 340
    Germany, 84-5, 132, 197, 214
    Holland, 137
    Russia, 197
    Scotland, 114, 121
    Spain, 114, 151, 152
    other countries, 114, 151-2
  husband's surname, and first name, wife's use of (Mrs John Jones style)
    and confusion of identity, 89-92, 213, 339-40
    feminist objection to, 3-4, 105, 149, 157-60, 165, 178, 271
    and the law, 4-5, 126-7, 129, 240, 242, 248, 253-4, 340
    origin of custom, 4-7
    prevalence of, 158-9, 183, 271
    significance of, Ch. 2 (3-18)
  as middle name
    father's name as, 83, 151, 152, 157, 166
    mother's maiden name as, 137, 157, 200
    previous husband's as, 83-4
  mother's
    given to children, 148, 154, 155, 171, 179-80, 209, 302, 334-6
    and matriarchy, 147, 155, 302
    see also mother's first name as surname
  origin of, 1, 112
  wife keeping surname as feminist cause, 3-4, Ch. 10 (93-110), Ch. 12 (132-50), 153-62, 165, 171-2, 173, 175-87, Ch. 15 (188-218), 219-20, 232-8, 337-46
suttee, 314
Swain, Doris Dean, 266

Swain, Reba, 209
Swedenborg, Emanuel, 9
Swift, Jonathan, 52
Swing, Betty Gram, 179, 231
Swing, Raymond Gram, 179, 231

Taft, Mrs William Howard, 17
Taylor, Harriet, 96
Taylor, Jane, 40
Taylor, Lucy Hobbs, 76, 82
Teasdale, Sara, *see* Filsinger
Tepper, Terri, 270, 275
Terry, Ellen, 30, 38, 334, 338
Tertullian, 294
Thomas, Dorothy Swaine, 266
Thompson, Dorothy, 225-7
Thompson, William, 14
Tiburtius-Hirschfelt, Dr Henriette, 86n.
Till, Irene, 265
Tingley, Katherine Westcott Cook
  Parent, 75
title mania, 23-4
titles
  Dr, not used for women physicians, 92
  Doctress, 105
  husband's title, use by wives, 17-18, 87,
    159
  Miss, 6-7, 38, 46, 133, 141, 172
  Miss or Mrs?, 133, 141-2, 200, 214
  Mrs, 6-7, 133, 136, 137, 141-2, 172,
    200
  Ms, 342-4
  no title to reveal marital status of
    women, 133, 157, 172, 175
Toffler, Alvin, 339
Toksvig, Signe, 178, 192, 193-4
tombstones, women on, 1, 19, 73, 91,
  95, 134, 149, 198, 228, 237
Total Women, 347, 349
Trafford, F. G., 42
Train, George Francis, 58
Treason Act, 308-9
Tree, Ellen, *see* Kean, Mrs Charles
Trethowan, Dr W. H., 324-5
Trollope, Anthony, 56, 67, 315-16
Troubetzkoy, Barbara, *see* Rubirosa
trousers, women wearing, 14, 55, 57, 95,
  104, 133, 134, 331, 332, 346
Truth, Sojourner, 336
Tucker, Charlotte Marie, 41
Tuthill, Louisa, 41
Twiggs, Sarah Lowe, 147
Tyler, Mrs John 17

Umstead, Lillie Devereux, 40, 46, 74
  see also Blake
Una, The, 58
unity of husband and wife, 1, 7-18, 117,
  120, 130, 139, 141, 219-24, 287,
  313-19
Utopian communities and names, 139-40

Valverde, 331
Vanderbilt, Amy, 266
Vanderbilt, Consuelo, *see* title mania
Vanderbilt Jr, Cornelius, 21
Vanderbilt, Mrs Cornelius, 21, 25, 26
Vassar College, 60-1, 217
Vénard, Elisabeth-Céleste, 23
Verbruggen, Mrs, 35
Vestris, Madame, 36-7, 64
virginity, 38, 300, 301, 312, 337-8
voices, soft, and women, 61, 217
  see also brank, silence
Voltaire, 55
vote, woman's right to, 14, 31, 66, 104-5,
  109-10, 144-5, 146, 147, 148, 153, 157,
  173, 174-5, 181-2, 186, 187, 219, 305,
  316, 333, 347, 348
voting, for single women, 316
voting in woman's own name, 108-110,
  187, 188, 199, 211, 235, 239, 247-8,
  251-2, 255, 257-9, 266, 272-3, 274-5,
  278-80

Walcott, Mary Vaux, 76
Walker, Alexander, 52
Walker, Dr Mary, 104, 132-3
Walker, Timothy, 94, 154
Walpole, Horace, 7
Walter, Cornelia, 64
Walters, Barbara, 349
war, women waging, 307
Ward, Mrs Humphrey, 90
Warren, Mrs, 35
Washburn, Marie, 178
Washington, George, 6
Washington, Martha, 32
watchdog laws, 252, 255, 272-3, 274
wedding ceremonies, and keeping name,
  270
Weed, Zerviah Porter, 76
Weiman, Rita, 198, 233
Weld, Theodore, 96
Wells, Mary, *see under* Lawrence,
  Harding
Wells-Barnett, Ida, 85

Wessels, Marie, 214
West, Jessamyn, 351
Westminster Abbey, 35
Wharton, Edith, 30
Wheeler, Anna, 14
Whipple, Dr Dorothy V., 198-9
whiskey, 58
White, Helen Magill, 76
White, Jessie Meriton, 11
Whitlow, Sylvia Scott, 282
Whitman, Dr Winifred, 214
Whittemore, Margaret, 206, 207
Wickersham, George, 201
Widman-Wallace, Anna, 86n.
Wieck, Clara, 68, 84
    see also Schumann, C.
Wiegand, Charmion von, 215
wife of, role label of wives, 1-2, 19, 36,
    39, 121, 149-50, 162, 208, 212-13,
    287, 337, 340, 342, 344, 345
Wiggin, Kate Douglas, 45
Wignell, Mrs, *see* Warren, Mrs
Wilde, Oscar, 52
Willard, Emma, 13, 60, 119, 147, 351
Willard, Frances, 81, 87, 166
William the Bastard, 300
Williams, Faith, 196
Willis-Berg, Portia, 215
Wilson, Belle, *see* title mania
Wilson, Margaret, 190
Wilson, Dr May, 179-80, 334
Wilson, Paul, 176
Wilson, Woodrow, 138, 190, 196
Wilty, Jr, Mrs Vernon J., 255, 257, 340
Winter, Ella, 198
Winthrop, John, 53
Woffington, Peg, 6
Wolfson, Theresa, 233
Woljeska-Tindolph, Helen, 86n.

Wollstonecraft, Mary, 13, 175
Wolstenholme-Elmy, Elizabeth, 86n.
Woman (Eve), 304-5, 313-14
Woman Pays Club, 190, 192
woman's fall
    in history, 305-13, 314
    myths of, 304-5
Woman's Journal, The, 105-6, 109, 111,
    124, 127, 137, 145, 146, 149, 156-60,
    164
womb envy, Ch. 19 (289-330) passim,
    325, 328, 330
womb, husband's, 295-8, 299, 300, 302,
    304-5, 312-13, 313-14, 333-4, 337
womb, woman's reduction to, 305-13,
    314, 318-19, 328, 332, 347
Women Lawyers' Journal, The, 187, 189,
    209
Wood, Henry Wise, 196
Wood, Mrs Henry, 90
Woodbury, Helen Sumner, 75, 91
Woodhull, Victoria, 91-2, 134-5
Woollcott, Alexander, 180, 227
Wright, Frances, 14, 57, 81
Wright, Lucy, 140
Wu, Chien-Shiung, 266

X, Laura, 336

yin-yang, 318
Yonge, Charlotte, 317
Young, Brigham, wives of, 140
Young, Fanny Kekelaokalani, 261

Zakrzewska, Dr Marie, 156-7
Zenger, Anna, 263, 316
Zeus, 290, 313
Zoretskie, Mary, 215